Agricultural Production in Communist China

1949–1965

Kang Chao

Agricultural Production in Communist China 1949-1965

The University
of Wisconsin
Press
Madison,
Milwaukee,
and London
1970

Published 1970
The University of Wisconsin Press
Box 1379, Madison, Wisconsin 53701
The University of Wisconsin Press, Ltd.
27-29 Whitfield Street, London, W. 1

First printing

Printed in the United States of America
George Banta Company, Inc., Menasha, Wisconsin

ISBN 0-299-05770-4; LC 70-121766

To Jessica,

Tonia, and

Constance

Contents

List of Maps

List of Tables

In Text

In Appendix

Acknowledgments

I am grateful to the Committee on the Economy of China and to the Center of Chinese Studies, University of Michigan, for providing me with financial support at various stages of the research embodied in this volume. In Chapter 8 I have made extensive use of Chinese provincial farm statistics to determine that nation's grain output. This body of data was first compiled by Professor C. M. Li, then at the University of California at Berkeley, and his research team. Later it was supplemented by additional data collected by my research assistants, Messrs David King and Wei-chien Chang, and myself. To all of them I wish to express my thanks. For their valuable comments, I am indebted to Professors Anthony Tang of Vanderbilt, Alexander Eckstein and Robert Dernberger of the University of Michigan, Dwight Perkins of Harvard, and Jung-chao Liu of McGill University.

Agricultural Production in Communist China

1949–1965

Chinese Units

Measurement

Mou (shih mou)	0.1647 acre 0.0667 hectare 667 square meters
Catty (shih chin)	1.1 pounds 0.5 kilograms
Tan (shih tan)	0.05 metric ton 50 kilograms 110 pounds 100 catties

Currency

Yuan US $0.382 (Feb. 1965 official exchange rate)

Governmental administration

Chinese	*US approximate*
Province	State
Hsien	County
Shih	Municipality
Chu	Ward
Hsiang	Township
Tsun	Village

Introduction

The ultimate economic goal of the Communist government in China is, no doubt, the modernization of the economy in the shortest possible time. This desire is rather common to virtually all growth-conscious governments in backward countries. What is unique in China, however, is that the Chinese Communist government has chosen to accomplish this goal by a different route than that followed by other developing nations. Therefore, it is of great value and interest to observe whether the so-called Chinese model has been successful, and why.

The economic conditions inherited by the Chinese Communist regime in 1949 were similar to those in many other underdeveloped areas at the beginning of their modernization drives. The economy of China was predominantly agrarian, with a backward farming technology. Thus, as in many other countries, industrialization was visualized as the most effective way to alter the status quo, to convert abackward agricultural country into a modern, industrialized nation. In fact, this emphasis on industrialization has been so strong that for many years industrialization was considered by Chinese Communist leaders and planners to be synonymous with economic modernization.

If economic growth is taken as the chief objective, the selective development policy could, theoretically, maximize the overall growth rate of the economy only when all economic sectors are independent of each other so that the slow-growing sectors in no way constrain the fast-growing sectors. Since in this case the overall growth rate would be no more than a weighted average of the growth of individual sectors, to concentrate on the sector that has the highest growth potential would yield the maximum overall growth rate.

Yet there exists an inextricable relationship between industry and agriculture, when both are broadly defined. The former depends on the latter for supplies of certain raw materials and wage goods (food). Industry also relies heavily on the rural population as buyers of manufactured goods. Furthermore, the agricultural sector is a source of the additional labor force needed for a rapid expansion of industrial production after the initial unemployment in the urban area has been absorbed. Generally, the constraints set by agriculture on industry are more rigid in a backward country than in an advanced economy. It is easier in an advanced country to solve most of the problems of interdependency through international trade.

The agricultural problem in China was especially acute when the Communist government began its industrialization drive. Although China's economy was preponderantly agrarian, the nation's agricultural resources were rather poor. Even now only 11 percent of China's total territory is under cultivation. The amount of reclaimable land has been variously estimated, and it ranges from 10 to slightly over 20 percent of the total area. However, it should be noted that whatever estimate of reclaimable land is used, it measures only the area where it is physically possible to convert land into farmland of one type or another. But the exceedingly high costs of reclamation often have prevented such conversion. The small proportion of cultivated land, when compared with China's huge population, gave the unfavorable man-land ratio of 2.5 mou, or about 0.4 acre, per person.[1] More than 80 percent of the total population lived in the farm sector. Given these unfavorable conditions, the Chinese had developed a system of highly intensive farming and land utilization long before the Communist take-over. This fact, on the one hand, meant that crop production in China, which in this respect was unlike many developing nations, had already advanced about as far as traditional practices and methods would permit. There was only limited room for further agricultural development that would not entail investment to bring in modern farm inputs or to introduce new technology. On the other hand, in spite of the fairly high yield per unit of cultivated land which resulted from intensive use and from other traditional inputs, the farm output per person was quite low. Chinese peasants lived barely above the subsistence level. Their low income made it impossible for them to accumulate enough capital to transform the sector technologically. Without an effective policy to promote agricultural production, the thin margin of farm surplus would soon form serious constraints on any ambitious program of industrialization that the government might wish to undertake.[2]

One salient feature of the Chinese Communists' attempt to achieve modernization lies in their special ways of dealing with agricultural production. Their special prescriptions for agricultural policy have been shaped by their ideological commitment and their visualization of the nature of China's agrarian problems.

Before 1949 the rural sector was regarded by the Chinese Communist leaders mainly as a political asset and as a source of military strength. Mao Tse-tung once explicitly stated, "Whoever wins the support of the peasants will win China; and whoever solves the land question will win the peasants."[3] But a positive, economically oriented policy for the agricultural sector could hardly be formulated until the end of the civil war.

After the Communist Party had consolidated its power on the mainland, agricultural policy was carried out along two lines. The primary line has been an institutional reform, or what in Communist terms is called the socialist transformation of agriculture. The secondary line, at least in the order of priorities in the 1950s, was the technological transformation of agriculture. But since there was no consensus among the Chinese Communist leaders, both transformations have been attempted at uneven speeds and with unsteady steps.

Were those policies successful in raising farm output? The answer from Peking is, of course, affirmative. According to the Chinese Communist official statistics, if 1949 is taken as 100, the gross value of agricultural output reached 148.5 by 1952 and 231.4 by 1958. For grain crops alone, with 1949 as the base year, the output index was 142.8 in 1952 and 231.3 in 1958. The average growth rate for the entire period of 1949–58 was 9.8 percent, and in a single year, 1958, the grain output jumped 35 percent.[4] The Chinese Communist authorities admitted that there was a setback in farm production in 1960–61, but they attributed the crisis wholly to natural factors, that is, to natural calamities of unprecedented severity in three consecutive years. After 1961 the Peking government again claimed advances in agricultural production, but did not give concrete quantities.

However, we do not have complete confidence in the Chinese Communist claims and wish to reassess the success or failure of China's agriculture in feeding one quarter of mankind. The three parts of this study are arranged so as to serve this purpose, and they appear in accordance with our analytical sequence. Part I is devoted to an examination of the so-called socialist transformation. The background against which various institutional changes were designed and the impacts of those changes on incentives and on the mobilization and utilization of various farm inputs are analyzed. Although these farm institutions in Communist China have been the subject of many previous studies by outstanding scholars,[5] to omit this background would make our analysis incomplete. However, we hope to minimize duplication by making this part of the study as brief as possible and by considering only the points which have direct bearing upon our output analysis.

Technological transformation is studied in detail in Part II. The supply of major farm inputs, especially the modern ones, and the degree of their utilization during the whole period are investigated. Although we examine in Part II the merits and deficiencies of each technological measure, a more important goal is to determine the quantities of effective inputs which will then be integrated into the input-output analysis.

The study of output is made in Part III, because one can hardly examine output figures without clear knowledge of organizational features, input supplies, and crop systems during that period. Our output analysis will concentrate on the production of grains which, according to the Chinese official classification, include rice, wheat, potatoes and various coarse grains, but not soybeans. Because of insufficient data, the production of nongrain crops is discussed only peripherally in Chapter 11, and not to our satisfaction.

The most annoying problem in undertaking this study was the shortage of information, especially of quantitative data, since we could work only with data made available outside China by the Peking government. The flow of economic information from Communist China diminished rapidly after 1959 and has virtually ceased since the outbreak of the Great Proletarian Cultural Revolution in mid-1966. As a result, the reader will notice that our treatments and analyses for the period 1949–57 and the period 1958–65 are not of comparable degrees of sophistication. After 1965, our knowledge of Communist China's economic situation virtually has been reduced to a blank except for a few personal speculations made by Western observers.

Although data are relatively abundant for the first decade of the regime, the data are not always of satisfactory quality. Consequently, considerable textual space is devoted to scrutinizing and adjusting basic data. This is especially so in Chapter 8. From our experience, there are two reader reactions toward this type of discussion. Some feel that such discussions should be relegated to appendixes, whereas others think that their paramount importance fully justifies the use of text space. There is no easy compromise. We can only advise those who are not interested in such discussions to treat Chapter 8 as an appendix and to skip it. All they have to know is in Table 8.15.

Some information gaps are filled with our own estimates based on certain assumptions which, although considered reasonable by us, are nevertheless arbitrary. Other gaps may appear as blanks in some of the tables. Needless to say, given the nature of the basic data used, our findings in this study cannot have a high degree of certainty. They are subject to revision when more information turns up.

The Chinese Communist statistics of land acreages and farm output are usually given in such Chinese measurement units as mou and catties (shih-chin). In view of the tremendous computational work involved in the study and to avoid possible errors, we have decided not to convert the Chinese units to metric units in processing official data. However, conversion information is given on page 2.

This study is based on the information drawn from an exceedingly large number of Chinese publications, and the passages quoted from official documents are taken from Chinese sources in Chinese. The translations, however, are mine.

Part I

Policy and Institutional Changes

Chapter 1

The Policy of Socialist Transformation

Two outstanding features are observable in the agricultural policies of Communist China. First, agricultural policies up to 1960 revolved around the institutional transformation of the rural sector, with agricultural investment relegated to secondary importance. Second, instead of a once-for-all reform, there have been frequent changes in the agricultural organization—so frequent that one can hardly find a single year since 1949 in which there was no reorganization of one kind or another going on somewhere in the rural sector. However, until recently, the precise backgrounds against which those policies were formulated were not too clear to the outside. In this chapter we shall trace, with the help of new information, the evolution of the Chinese policies of socialist transformation of agriculture. Discussions of organizational details of various rural institutions that existed in the Communist period and their economic implications and impacts will be dealt with in Chapter 2.

Some Western observers are inclined to believe that the frequent institutional changes in Communist China, at least up to 1960, were deliberately planned by the decision-makers to minimize the possible resistance of peasants to agricultural socialization. This theory postulates that the Chinese Communist hierarchy, acting as a monolithic decision-making body with consensus prevailing most of the time, decided to segment the whole process of the socialist transformation of agriculture into small steps to be implemented in succession so that drastic changes could be avoided between two successive steps.

However, this theory is not entirely valid. It is true that Chinese Communist leaders were aware of the violent experience in Soviet collectivization in the early 1930s and intended to make the transformation in China as smooth as possible from the outset. But not all of the frequent institutional changes in the rural sector were carefully designed for that purpose. Even before 1960, some of the changes were quite abrupt, or the same program was executed with a widely varying intensity in different years. Instead of appearing as the smooth steps of a well-conceived scheme, these changes looked rather like the results of some sharp variations in the guiding policy. The question is then: why were there so many policy variations?

Before the "Great Proletarian Cultural Revolution," students of Communist China were not fully aware of any serious disagreement or factionalism among the Chinese Communist hierarchies. The Chinese Communists were generally so well disciplined that dissenters did not openly criticize an official policy if it had been adopted by the Party's Central Committee. In published speeches and writings of high-ranking Party members or government officials, any shift in policy was always defended as a logical development of previous policies or events with the full support of all the top leaders in the Party. Occasionally, some deviating opinions were disclosed in official documents. But, without identifying the dissenters, these documents left the reader with an impression that the disputes were isolated, local cases.

It was from the recent Cultural Revolution that we learned more of the inside stories concerning policy disputes within the Chinese Communist Party in the past, disputes which heretofore had been carefully kept secrets. First, serious disagreements over important economic issues had existed among top Party leaders all along. The Chinese decision-making body was not a monolithic group acting from consensus, as we used to think. Second, disputes occurred more often in the area of agricultural policies than in other areas. Third, disputes over agricultural policies had never been completely resolved. The frequent variations in the announced policies represent either the alternate ascendancy of one of the contending groups or the breakdown of conciliatory resolutions reached by them. Lastly, as time went on, the differences in opinion between the contending groups widened steadily, and the possibility of reaching stable compromises gradually vanished until a bloody power struggle ensued.

In the course of that power struggle, called a cultural revolution, a great many defiant statements made in the past by Liu Shao-chi and his supporters were brought into the open for the first time by Mao Tse-tung's partisans as ammunition to attack his adversaries. Of course, some of the accusations made by the Maoists against their political enemies are distorted stories, and many quotations were taken out of context. Nevertheless, insofar as disputes on agricultural policies are concerned, many points in the accusations can be confirmed, and the sources of some quoted statements can be identified if one goes back to earlier documents and re-studies them carefully. In other words, in these published Chinese Communist documents, many of the ambiguous statements and references, which we have either overlooked or have not understood, now become clear.

One of the two contending groups is, of course, the Maoist group. The rival camp, on the other hand, is rather heterogeneous in composition and consists of the high-ranking Party members who have disagreed with Mao Tse-tung on various individual issues since 1949. Until 1961–62, they usually expressed their opposition individually; that is, there is no evidence that they had acted in concert. Sometimes the disapproving votes in the Central Committee of the Party were numerous enough to bar Mao's proposals; at other times, the dissenters yielded to his demand or pressure, again on an individual basis. Beginning in 1961–62, those dissenters became more inclined to take concerted actions under the tacitly agreed leadership of Liu Shao-chi. Judging from the information available so far, even then they had not organized themselves as an opposition clique aiming at the ouster of Mao, though Mao asserts that he was treated by them as a "dead parent." One common characteristic of these dissidents is that they, among the top leaders of the Party, had relatively more formal education and better international knowledge, especially of the experience of the Soviet Union. Because of their educational background, most of them had been put in charge of the departments of economic affairs in the central government in the 1950s. Like the "technocrats" in other Communist countries, they often held relatively balanced views and pragmatic attitudes towards economic and technical matters. To the Maoists, those views sounded too conservative. Thus, the technocrats were first repudiated as being right deviationists and finally accused of having taken the capitalist road.

Thanks to the information disclosed during the Great Cultural Revolution, when both new and old documents are assembled, a more telling picture looms. We are now in a better position to understand the formulation of important agricultural policies in Communist China and to see why they were altered subsequently. For the sake of clarity, in tracing this development we shall divide the whole Communist period into several segments according to discernible turning points.

Land Reform and Early Cooperativization in 1949–55

From all available data, it seems quite safe to say that disputes among Chinese Communist leaders over agricultural policies have centered around the problem of collectivizing the agricultural sector. In the beginning, there was a consensus among the leaders of the regime concerning land redistribution. Such a program was deemed necessary, because it could help the Communists destroy thoroughly the social foundation of the Nationalist government and rally those who would obtain land under the program to support the causes of the new regime. The great attention paid by the Chinese Communist Party to the rural society clearly indicates a fundamental difference in the general orientation between it and the Russian Communist Party. The Chinese visualized the rural sector as their chief source of strength.

By mid-1950, although land redistribution had been completed in varying degrees in the so-called old liberated areas, no such program was carried out in new liberated areas. What actually was enforced in the latter areas was a policy of "rent reduction and interest rate reduction." This cautious policy was chosen because the Communist victory in 1949 had come as a landslide, with the whole mainland becoming new liberated areas in a matter of a few months, so that the Party was unable to send enough cadres into such a vast territory to carry out land reform.

The law of land reform designed for a nationwide application was published in June 1950. One important feature of the Chinese Communist land reform was the fact that the whole program was launched from the top. The Party sent specially trained cadres to each village; under their supervision "land reform committees" and "peasant associations" were organized to foment class struggle. The landholdings of landlords and rich peasants were confiscated by these ad hoc committees or peasant associations and then distributed to peasants with no compensation payments. Clearly, and as intended, an impression was created among the peasants that their land acquisition was a benefit granted by the Communist government. If his land was not to be taken back by landlords in the future, a peasant must support the Communist Party in destroying the possibility that the Nationalist government might regain power.

Land reform was concluded in 1952, and the power of the Chinese Communist government was consolidated. The Party was now confronted with a problem: Where should they go from there? Divergent opinions among the Party leaders may have existed earlier, but now a definite answer must be reached. In an article published in November 1955 in praise of Mao Tse-tung's report "The Question of Agricultural Cooperation," Chen Yi stated, "Comrade Mao Tse-tung's report has resolved the disputes within the Party in the past three years over the problem of agricultural cooperativization."[1] This statement explicitly indicates that the disputes had begun in late 1952 or early 1953. However, the information revealed in the Cultural Revolution and the republication in November 1968[2] of the report made by Mao in the second plenary session of the Seventh Central Committee of the Chinese Communist Party, held in March 5, 1949, seem to suggest that the divergence of opinion on this issue may be traceable to 1949.

The arguments centered on the question of how much time should be allowed to elapse between the land reform and the beginning of socialization of agriculture and the question of how long a period would be needed to complete the whole process of socialist transformation of that sector. The opinion of Mao Tse-tung has been consistently clear. In his view, land reform was necessary only on political grounds; as soon as it had served this purpose, the peasant economy should be immediately replaced by socialized agriculture; the socialist transformation should be completed in the shortest period permitted by relevant conditions.

The republication of Mao's report to the Seventh Central Committee was intended to call the attention of Chinese Communists to his stress on this point as earily as 1949. In this report Mao said:

> The economy of individual peasants and individual handicraftsmen, who produce 90% of the total gross value of the national economy, can and must be guided, cautiously, gradually, and yet positively, to develop toward the direction of modernization and collectivization; the viewpoint of letting them drift along is erroneous. . . . With the state economy standing alone but no cooperative economy, we can never lead the economy of individual toiling masses to move gradually toward collectivization; we can never develop our new democratic society into a socialist society in the future; and we can never consolidate the leadership of proletarians in the political power of the state. Whoever overlooks or belittles this issue is making the gravest blunder.[3]

It is not clear from this speech, however, whether Mao visualized collectivization of agriculture as a developmental policy, in addition to his ideological reasoning that a socialized industrial sector could hardly survive if the agricultural sector remained private.

According to disclosed materials, Liu Shao-chi's opposition to a rapid agricultural collectivization in China was based on two considerations. First, he seemed to appreciate the strong initiative of peasants under the private ownership system. To him, therefore, even after land reform had served its political function, the peasant economy could still be maintained as an intermediate-term economic goal.[4] The government should make full use of the strong initiative of peasants under the private farming system before the introduction of collectivized farming. He postulated that when 70 to 80 percent of the peasants had attained the income level of "rich farmer," the time would be ripe for collectivization.[5] The rising capitalistic attitudes of peasants after the land reform was deemed by Liu as a healthy thing which should be encouraged. Liu is reported to have criticized those Communist cadres who tried to stop this tendency by forming mutual-aid teams and cooperatives; he denounced the attempt as the action of erroneous, dangerous, and utopian rural socialism.[6] Apparently, in the Chinese Communist Party there were others who shared Liu's theory at that time.[7]

Secondly, Liu Shao-chi was inclined to relate the time schedule of collectivization to the schedule of agricultural mechanization. To him, collectivization in China would be beneficial and feasible only after agricultural mechanization. Therefore, the government must let agriculture remain on the peasant basis for some years to come and in the meantime should concentrate state investment in industry. Agricultural collectivization should begin only after industry has been so well developed that it would be able to equip the agricultural sector with a sufficient number of tractors and other modern farm machines. Liu's policy of "collectivization after mechanization" represents a full application of the Soviet experience to the Chinese case. In their beginning, Soviet collective farms had suffered tremendously from the lost incentives of farmers, but the collectives were consolidated later by bringing in tractors. Liu believed that farmers must join collective farms voluntarily if the disincentive effect of the new system was to be avoided. The question then would arise: how can peasants be made to join collective farms voluntarily? The inescapable answer was that the government must first show the peasants some substantial advantages of collective farming over private farming. Unlike Mao and his followers, who believed in the all-around superiority of collective farms, the only economic advantage that Liu could see was the use of tractors and other farm machines on large collective farms. Based on this reasoning Liu concluded, "The consideration of when we should enter the socialized system in the rural sector . . . is contingent on the achievement of industry."[8] To state his reasoning conversely, there would be no point in launching a premature collectivization before China's industry had developed enough to supply tractors and other farm machines in large quantities. On the one hand there would be no economic benefits from this institutional change, and, on the other hand, without tractors to lure the peasants, the government would have to force peasants onto collective farms, thus generating a serious problem of disincentive.

There were other high-ranking members who were at that time opposed to Mao's recommendation of an immediate socialization of China's agriculture on somewhat different grounds. One was Teng Tzu-hui, who was in charge of agrarian affairs in the Party's Central Committee. While agreeing that collective farming was desirable and should be instituted as soon as possible, Teng emphasized the necessity for a roundabout and gradual process in bringing about collectivization. He repeated this view in 1956 when the great acceleration of collectivization was already underway:

> However, peasants are not determined in the very outset to struggle for their own basic benefits; we must . . . gradually promote their class awakening and confidence in victory. By doing so we can lead peasants, step by step, to walk toward a higher level of struggle. . . .[9]

Those who had a more prudent attitude and advocated a slow movement toward agricultural collectivization had at least one thing in common. They were apparently mindful of the bitter experience of Soviet collectivization in the early 1930s.[10]

The earliest decision on the socialist transformation of China's agriculture was embodied in the December 1951 "Resolution on the Mutual Assistance and Cooperation in Agricultural Production."[11] The resolution was a reconciliation of divergent views within the Party. The compromise was easily reached because none of the contending members was too sure about his judgment in this issue. The resolution was first distributed as an internal document circulating only among Party cadres at regional and local levels for experimentation. It suggested four types of cooperative arrangements: (1) the temporary mutual-aid team. (2)

the permanent mutual-aid team, (3) the elementary, semi-socialist cooperative, and (4) the advanced cooperative, or what is sometimes referred to as the collective. While setting no rigid timetable for transferring from one form to another, this document placed emphasis on mutual-aid teams for the time being and discouraged the premature organization of cooperatives. After about one year's trial, the resolution was formally announced in February 1953 as an established policy of the Party.

Shortly after the publication of this resolution, many cooperatives emerged in the country. The office responsible for agrarian work considered the total number of new cooperatives to be much larger than the plan had stipulated, and they were dissolved. This action greatly annoyed Mao Tse-tung who, in a top-level meeting of the Party held in late 1953, threatened the comrades responsible for this action with possible purge. The episode may be said to be the first direct clash between the two contending groups in the Party on this issue.[12]

It was perhaps in that meeting that Mao Tse-tung, in advocating an immediate and quicker cooperativization, made the famous statement, "With regard to the battle position in the rural areas, if socialism does not take it, capitalism will definitely occupy it."[13] As another writer explained on a later occasion, Mao was of the opinion that a backward peasant economy based on small farms could hardly survive; the small farms would eventually be transformed into either large socialist farms or large capitalist farms. The same article also applauded Mao's foresight by presenting statistical evidence that in 1953–54 there had been a rapidly rising trend of land reconcentration and a reappearance of usurers in villages.[14]

Another official source cites an important reason for Mao's upholding his collectivization theory as being that, if collectivization was to be instituted, it would be easier to do it when the influence of the old rich peasants had been greatly reduced by the land reform and new rich and middle farmers had not yet emerged.[15] Mao thought that the sooner collectivization was carried out, the less resistance it would encounter.

Under Mao's urging, a new resolution was formed in the Party's Central Committee and was promulgated on December 16, 1953.[16] The new resolution, basically still conciliatory in nature, raised the scheduled pace of collectivization moderately but reiterated the same policy of gradualism. In implementing the cooperativization policy, the resolution stressed the principle of voluntary participation and denounced "blind impetuous adventurism." The method to be employed was "persuasion"—the setting up of one or more model cooperatives in each locality to demonstrate to peasants the superiority of cooperative farming.

The compromising nature of the December 1953 resolution was fully embodied in the First Five Year Plan whose finalized draft was passed in July 1955.[17] Collectivization was then viewed explicitly as a developmental policy, one capable of raising farm productivity without state investment. According to the First Five Year Plan, the whole process of collectivization was scheduled to be completed in fifteen years. One third of farm households were to be brought into elementary cooperatives by 1957. By the summer of 1955, when the Plan was published, about 15 percent of all farm households had formed 650,000 cooperatives.[18]

A turning point came in that summer, about three weeks after the publication of the First Five Year Plan. Mao suppressed rival opinions and made a decisive move to accelerate collectivization. So far as the socialist transformation of agriculture is concerned, Mao's action invalidated the First Five Year Plan just after it was formally enacted by the People's Congress.

The Acceleration of Collectivization in 1955–57

Mao Tse-tung's speech "The Question of Agricultural Cooperation," delivered at a meeting of secretaries of provincial, municipal, and autonomous region committees of the Chinese Communist Party on July 31, 1955, was epoch-making in the history of Chinese agriculture. There began the escalation of socialist transformation. During 1953–54, in spite of the compromise policy, the basic conflict in the Party had not really been removed and the debate went on. The smooth transition in that period was interpreted differently by the two groups. The conservative group ascribed the smoothness to the cautious policy and insisted that the same gradualism should be maintained in the near future. When Mao came to examine the situation, he was convinced that Chinese farmers had a strong, inherent inclination toward socialism.[19] To him, all the precaution was unnecessary and represented an underestimation of the socialist tendency of the rural masses. Mao did not see why it would be unsafe to go further and faster.

Mao's determination to upset the planned schedule of collectivization was triggered by the decision of responsible officials in the central government to dissolve more than 200,000 unstable cooperatives. According to reports, during the first half of 1955, Liu Shao-chi, Teng Tzu-hui, and many other high-ranking officials thought that cooperativization had proceeded faster than the planned speed in some parts of the country. This pace was considered as going beyond "the practical possibilities, the consciousness of the masses, and the abilities of existing cadres." Consequently, an order of "drastic compression" was issued, and 200,000 newly formed cooperatives were dissolved in the two months of May and June 1955.[20] The fact that the action was taken while Mao was traveling and was out of Peking especially enraged him.[21] He angrily stated:

> With the adoption of a policy of what was called drastic compression in Chekiang Province—not by decision of the Chekiang Provincial Party Committee—15,000 cooperatives, consisting of 400,000 households, of 53,000 cooperatives were dissolved at one fell swoop. This caused great dissatisfaction among the masses and the cadres. . . . It was not right either to take such a major step without the consent of the leadership of the Party. As early as April 1955, the leadership gave this warning: Do not commit the 1953 mistake of mass dissolution of cooperatives again, otherwise self-critical examination will again be called for. Yet, certain comrades preferred not to listen.[22]

Mao took this opportunity to reopen the issue which was resolved in the Party's Central Committee in 1953. Mao's speech, "The Question of Agricultural Cooperation," was the first full manifestation of his theory on collective farming that had been revealed to the public. In this report he assembled all the arguments he had made before in support of agricultural collectivization. He then went further to castigate, very pointedly, all the objections raised by other Party leaders. In repudiating the so-called empiricism, he declared, "We should not allow some of our comrades to cover up their dilatoriness by citing the experience of the Soviet Union." Those comrades were believed to be wrong because they had underestimated the socialist tendency of the Chinese farmers and the capability of the Chinese Communist Party in leading them. Mao also assailed the argument that farm mechanization must precede collectivization. Since tractors and other farm machinery "can be found useful or can be used in large quantities only on the basis of large-scale, cooperative farming," collectivization must precede, not be preceded by, farm mechanization.

He accused those in favor of a slow and cautious transformation of losing sight of the "new upsurge in the socialist mass movement," and of guiding the movement by "grumbling unnecessarily, worrying continuously, and putting up countless taboos." He described them as "tottering along like a woman with bound feet, always complaining that others are going too fast."

One new element in the speech was Mao's concern about the disparity of growth rates between industry and agriculture as displayed in the past two or three years. He carefully pointed out the interdependence of the two sectors of the economy and the fact that a stagnating agriculture could eventually retard the development of industry. Thus, he remarked:

> Some comrades . . . consider that the prescribed rate of development for industrialization is all right, but there is no need for agricultural cooperation to keep in step with industrialization, that it should develop very, very slowly. . . . These comrades do not understand that socialist industrialization is not something that can be carried out in isolation, separate from agricultural cooperation. . . . If we cannot jump from small-scale farming with animal-drawn farm implements to large-scale farming with machines, . . . we shall fail to resolve the contradiction between the ever-increasing demand for marketable grain and industrial raw materials and the present generally poor yield of staple crops. In that case our socialist industrialization will run into formidable difficulties. We shall not be able to complete socialist industrialization.[23]

Here he explicitly identified agricultural collectivization as a developmental policy with an effect of raising productivity in the farm sector.[24]

The contradiction described by Mao between the ever-increasing demand for marketable grain and farm output had been felt by many other Party leaders who later supported Mao's acceleration of collectivization. This contradiction was reflected in the mounting difficulty in the work of grain procurement. Actually, the contradiction was attributable to two factors. It was partly a result of the disparity of growth rates between the industrial and agricultural sectors, as Mao had diagnosed, and partly an outcome of the land reform which raised the grain consumption in the rural sector. The latter factor was the basic reason that the Peking government had to initiate in 1953 the system of "uniform purchase and uniform sales" of grain, a program combining compulsory procurement and food rationing, when the country had just witnessed a bumper crop. In explaining the need for such a system, Chen Yun, one of the vice-premiers, said:

> Production of food was increased after the land reform. But, since the living

standard of peasants has improved, their food consumption has increased accordingly. They have no urgent need to sell their surplus grains. Consequently, the rate of marketed grains has declined instead of risen.[25]

Nevertheless, the worsening food shortage in the urban areas rendered an additional incentive to the collectivization movement. The cooperative manager controlled farm produce, and he would try to meet the obligation of compulsory delivery before distributing grains to member households. Besides, it was much easier for the government to deal with a small number of cooperatives than with some 100 million individual households. This was clearly indicated by Li Hsien-nien:

In the spring of this year [1955], the supply of grain was tight and the procurement work encountered difficulties . . . hence some comrades hoped to speed up agricultural cooperativization.[26]

Chen Yun was typical; he was always of the opinion that collective farming had no superiority in production, yet he supported the acceleration of collectivization in 1955 on the ground of grain procurement.[27]

It is interesting to note the strategy used by Mao Tse-tung to turn the tide on this occasion. Obviously, the strong resistance that Mao confronted came from the highest level decision-making body in the Party so that he was compelled to resort to unusual tactics to carry through his agricultural policy. On one occasion in 1956, when referring to his struggle in the preceding year, Mao remarked:

In China, 1955 was a decisive year for the battle between socialism and capitalism. This decisive battle was first shown in the three conferences called by the leadership of the Communist Party in May, July, and October of that year.[28]

About the May meeting we have heard nothing. It is evident, however, that Mao was defeated in that conference, because after May the "drastic compression" policy was carried out without his consent. The July conference was the one in which he delivered the report "The Question of Agricultural Cooperation." It is important to note that the July conference was a special meeting called by him with provincial and municipal secretaries as the only participants. It was to them that Mao hoped to appeal, and he succeeded. Once he had gained the support of the regional Party leaders, he could exert pressures on his opponents in the Central Committee. Thus, two months later in the early part of October 1955, an "enlarged meeting" of the Central Committee was held to discuss specifically the problem of agricultural cooperativization. In that meeting the 38 Central Committee members and 25 alternate members were outnumbered by 388 regional Party secretaries. As Mao had carefully calculated, the "Decision on Agricultural Cooperation," which was precisely based on his July report, was adopted at this meeting.[29]

In fact, Mao's strategy became increasingly clear in the next few years. All the important decisions that resulted in drastic accelerations in agricultural collectivization were reached in special meetings under Mao's personal auspices. New policies were then announced directly by the Party headquarters. On those occasions the State Council, the normal organ for decision-making in the central government, was not only bypassed, but its instructions and orders were also directly contradicted by the new directives issued by the Party headquarters.

At any rate, Mao's July report aroused a "high tide" which soon led to successively bigger steps in the socialist transformation. According to the decision of the enlarged meeting of the Central Committee in October 1955, the immediate targets for collectivization were raised, but only moderately. Elementary cooperatives were to be established in a majority of localities by the spring of 1958,[30] and 70 to 80 percent of the peasants should be placed in elementary cooperatives by 1960. In order not to disrupt farming operations, the work of reorganization, it was advised, should take place in winter, the idle season in agricultural production.[31] However, all these principles were soon discarded as a result of the interaction of the following forces. Many local and regional authorities, anxious to escape the accusation of having executed the previous "compression policy," tended to carry out the collectivization movement at a speed higher than that envisaged in the new decision. This acceleration soon generated competitive pressures among the local Party leaders themselves. Mao and his supporters at the central level in turn interpreted the overfulfillments of the targets by local and regional authorities as signs that the spontaneous momentum of socialization in the rural sector was still being underestimated; hence a further acceleration was necessary. From time to time, the conservative members in the central government attempted to apply the brake by urging a careful review of the current situation before going further; but they were less and less heeded.

Mao published two more works, in December 1955 and January 1956, which further speeded up the tempo of agricultural collectivization. The first document was the Preface to his book *The Socialist Upsurge in China's Countryside,*[32] in which he estimated that the formation of elementary cooperatives could be basically accomplished in a single year,

1956, instead of the earlier estimate of three or four years, with completion in 1960. The second document was Mao's "National Program for Agricultural Development, 1956–1967," published January 26, 1956. One official source explained how the program was formulated:

> In November 1955, Chairman Mao consulted with, respectively, 14 provincial secretaries and the secretary of the Inner Mongolia Autonomous Region and exchanged opinions concerning a national program for developing agricultural; they decided on 17 items. In January 1956, after further consulting with various regional responsible comrades, Chairman Mao expanded the 17 items to 40 items which formed the draft of the present Program.[33]

It is interesting to observe that even for such an extremely important economic program, Mao again deliberately bypassed the planning offices of the central government. His reasoning was that, with the high tide of socialist revolution, it was no longer the government that led the masses; the enthusiastic masses were driving the government toward a more rapid socialization. On January 25, 1956, Mao personally called a high-level meeting in the central government, in which he demanded the passage of his draft. The program, as adopted, formally set the following new targets for the collectivization movement:[34]

1. In some areas with favorable conditions, all peasants should be brought into the advanced type cooperatives (collectives) by 1957.
2. In the rest of the country, each district should organize one or more advanced cooperatives as models.
3. The conversion of the whole countryside into advanced cooperatives should be accomplished by 1958.

In other words, the country was now asked to carry out in two years the program originally scheduled for completion in fifteen years. The plan to organize collectives particularly was in complete contradiction to the directives issued by the central government only a few weeks earlier. In December 1955 there was a report that one elementary cooperative in Heilunkiang Province had decided to convert to a collective. Learning this, the central government issued a specific instruction on December 13, 1955, to forbid such a conversion for the following reason:

> The majority of cadres in the countryside not only have no experience whatsoever about managing advanced cooperatives, but also lack the experience of guiding a large number of elementary cooperatives. They do not understand or are not familiar with the technical knowledge of agricultural science. . . . In many localities the programs have been decided by a handful of cadres and activists without the support of masses.[35]

Actually, the officials in the central government then responsible for agricultural work were no longer able to bar Mao's escalation of the collectivization movement. All they could do was adjust themselves to the continuously raised targets and urge local activists not to proceed beyond that. Afraid that the work of organizing cooperatives in the countryside might disrupt the spring farming operation, the central government made another plea on March 4, 1956, to local cadres:

The pace of collectivization set in the National Program for Agricultural Development, 1956–67, cannot be considered too low. Do not race for advancement without due regard to reality. Do not continue to pursue one-sidedly the quantitative achievement in cooperativization so as to ignore the duties of organizing production works when those works are near and urgent.[36]

By mid-April 1956, 90 percent of farm households had joined cooperatives. Virtually all the advanced cooperatives were organized in a short period of about three months. The movement began to slow down after April, under the advice of the central government.[37] However, some serious defects of collective farming had become quite visible by then, including the soaring mortality rates of livestocks, especially hogs, frequent work accidents of female and juvenile workers in the fields, mismanagement, and confusions in the calculation of work points.[38]

At about the same time, the draft of the Second Five Year Plan was formulated by the planning agency of the central government. When it was published on September 16, 1956, the Plan still reflected to a considerable degree the cautious attitude of the planners. In the Second Five Year Plan, agricultural collectivization was scheduled to be completed by 1962, in contrast to the deadline of 1958 set by Mao in his National Program of Agricultural Development. The Second Five Year Plan also made it clear that blind conversion of elementary cooperatives into collectives should be prevented in an effort to avoid difficulties in management and production.[39]

Efforts made by the conservative elements in the central government to slow down the collectivization movement were momentarily successful in late 1956 and early 1957.[40] The Second Five Year Plan was passed in the National Congress of the Chinese Communist Party held on September 27, 1956. Attention was called to the serious defects of collective farms. And, finally, there came in early 1957 the reopening of free markets on a limited scale. However, even during the short period of ascendancy of the conservative group, Mao Tse-tung never gave up his own drive. He called a high-level conference on February 27, 1957, in which he repudiated those who were skeptical about the superiority of collective farming. A few months later he managed to launch two rectification campaigns all over the country—the Anti-Rightists Movement and the Movement of Socialist Education in the Countryside. The former was primarily aimed at non-Communist intellectuals, but the denunciation of "rightist deviation" could easily be applied to Mao's opponents within the Party. The latter campaign was an effort to combat the serious disincentive effects of collective farming through political indoctrination. Again, the same pressure could be exerted on anyone who was outside the rural sector but did not agree with Mao on agricultural collectivization. The two rectification campaigns immediately renewed the "high tide" of socialist agricultural transformation. In the meantime the revised version of the National Program of Agricultural Development was promulgated on October 25, 1957.[41] According to the new version, collectivization was to be completed by the end of 1957, one year earlier than stated in the first draft of the program.

It was claimed that a great debate concerning the choice between the "two roads"—capitalism and socialism—took place in the whole countryside in the fall of 1957. Most critics in the Party were silenced by the two rectification campaigns. However, a few dissenters remained unyielding and insisted on waiting to see the concrete results after the 1958 fall harvest.[42]

The Decision to Organize Communes and Its Aftermath

The emergence of communes in Communist China was rather accidental. The term *commune*, as a remote goal for agricultural transformation, had not appeared in any planning documents or Party resolutions before 1958. Before June 1958, the idea of forming such organizations in rural China had perhaps not even occurred to Mao Tse-tung himself. All the Party's directives in May and June of that year concerning agriculture mentioned that the task for the Second Five Year Plan period was to consolidate collectives which by 1958 had engulfed almost 99 percent of farm households. The few early communes were formed purely by local cadres to solve labor shortages in early 1958.

In April 1958, twenty-seven collectives in Suiping Hsien, Honan Province, merged into a new organization. It was named Weihsing (Sputnik) People's Commune and was the first of its kind. In June two other organizations of a similar nature were founded in Hsusui Hsien, Hopei Province, and Hsinhsing Hsien, Honan Province. In July a number of collectives in Hunan, Hupeh, and Fuchien organized mess halls without merging into communes. It was the Chinese Communist newspapers that, with the obsessive reporting of new heroic moves initiated by the masses in the direction of socialization, greatly publicized those new occurrences with premature judgments and undue praises.[43]

Since these organizations appeared unexpectedly and there was little experience even in other Communist countries that could be borrowed, policy-makers in China, including Mao himself, were not sure what attitude the government should take toward them. Thus, Mao made a special trip in August to Hopei and Honan to investigate the newly founded communes. He was deeply impressed by them. Mao's favorable comments served as a signal to encourage the mushrooming of this institution.[44]

The issue was then brought for the first time to the top leaders of the Party for a formal decision. The Politburo held an enlarged meeting in Peitaiho, lasting from August 17 to August 30, in which the problem of communes, among other issues, was discussed. The conference concluded that the people's communes were the "logical result of the march of events" and were based on the "ever-rising political consciousness of a half billion peasants."[45] However, as can be seen in this passage from the resolution reached in the conference, many members in the hierarchy were dubious about the merits of communes:

> When a people's commune is established, it is not necessary to deal with the question of private plots, scattered fruit trees, share funds, and so on, in a great hurry. . . . There is no need to transform collective ownership immediately into ownership by the people as a whole. It is better at the present to maintain collective ownership to avoid unnecessary complications arising in the course of the transformation of ownership. . . . The transition from collective ownership to ownership by the people as a whole is a process requiring three or four years in some places and five or six years or even longer elsewhere. Even with the completion of this transition, people's communes are still socialist in character, where the principle of "from each according to his ability and to each according to his work" prevails. . . . After the establishment of people's communes, it is not necessary to hurry the change from the original system of distribution, in order to avoid any unfavorable effect on production.[46]

Unfortunately, all these warnings had not been heeded by local authorities. In practically all communes the ownership system and the distribution system had been altered and private plots eliminated. By the end of September, about one month after the Peitaiho conference, 90.4 percent of Chinese peasants had been brought into communes; by December the whole countryside had been completely communized.[47]

The Great Leap Forward movement disarmed the binding power of any economic plan drawn by the central government. The decentralization further deprived the central government of many other levers to control or regulate the conduct of local and regional authorities. At the top level of the Party-government structure, Mao's personal influence was dominant, and the power of the more prudent members had reached its lowest point. Mao felt that any attempt to check a development spontaneously initiated from the bottom would be inconsistent with the position he had been holding all along.

It was not long before the Party had to evaluate the whole situation anew. The Central Committee met on December 10, 1958, to discuss the excesses and "individual biases" of local cadres. Up to this time the full adverse impacts of the commune movement on agricultural production remained to be felt. First of all, the main portion of the campaign occurred after August, hence the summer harvest and the planting of fall crops in most parts of the country were not hindered by the disincentive effects of the commune system. A definite test would come in the next year. Secondly, the fact that 1958 happened to be a year with favorable weather conditions prevailing in most regions and the fact that the flow of statistical information between the central government and local authorities or production units had seriously deteriorated, because of the rampant exaggeration in the production reports of the latter, made it nearly impossible for the policy-makers at the central level to assess the net result of the commune movement.

When the real test of the new system finally came in 1959, criticisms among the Communist hierarchies against communes began to mount rapidly until a climax was reached in the famous Lushan Conference held in June that year. In that conference Marshall Peng Teh-huai was ousted from his position as Defense Minister. Peng's critical statement, in the form of a letter addressed to Chairman Mao but distributed to all participants of the conference, had been kept secret for many years until it was unofficially disclosed by a Red Guard newspaper in October 1967.[48] Though pointedly criticizing the "three red flags" policy,[49] Peng's letter was moderate and quite polite in tone. According to subsequent reports, many Party members supported Peng's opinion before he submitted his statement to the conference. Some even had prepared similar statements but withheld them after seeing the ouster of Peng.[50] The fact that Mao was able to control this conference and purge Peng Teh-huai implies that even by this time Mao's rivals still had not formed a united front. They disagreed with Mao on certain economic issues but had no intention of removing him as Party leader. It is also possible that the ouster of Peng involved certain disputes over China's military policy,[51] so that those who were opposed to Mao on economic grounds might not have wanted to take sides.

The outcome of the Lushan Conference was only a partial triumph for Mao. Although he once again subdued the opposition in the Party, purged a number of high-ranking officials, and retained his leadership, he was nevertheless forced to yield on the economic front. This resulted in a succession of readjustment measures. In fact, the Lushan Conference marked the point after which Mao's prestige and influence in the Party began to subside precipitously.

Immediately following the dismissal of Peng Teh-huai, there was another full-scale rectification campaign within the Party. In the meantime, the economic crisis deepened. In 1960–61, the rival camp rallying under Liu Shao-chi took shape and began to act in concert. Even then their intention was probably not an outright removal of Mao as the Party leader;[52] their concern was to reduce Mao's hindrance to the reforms they were about to carry out.

The meager information available does not permit us to trace all the details of the reforms and their effective dates during this period, nor can we ascertain the extent to which the new policies had been actually implemented. But we do know that the Chinese Communist Party had proclaimed in 1959–61 the following three important directives in connection with agricultural production:

1. The Resolution of the Eighth Session of the Eighth Central Committee held in August 1959,
2. The Twelve Articles of Emergency Directives for Agricultural Work, issued in November 1960, and
3. The Sixty Articles Concerning the People's Communes, announced in May 1961.

The three directives led to a series of revisions and reorganizations of the commune system. By 1961, communes existed almost in name only.

Evidently, these modifications and policy reversals were made in defiance of Mao's wish. For instance, the "Sixty Articles," according to a Chinese source, were drafted by a number of the Central Committee members in early 1961 without the consent of Mao. The draft was then brought up for discussion in a special high-level meeting held in May in Canton, with Mao himself presiding. Despite his strong opposition, the draft was passed.[53]

However, the retrenchment measures still failed to arrest the extremely severe agricultural crisis as it entered the third year in 1961. Having now a fuller authority in determining economic policies, the Liu Shao-chi group was contemplating further liberalizing measures in order to stimulate farm production. To use Liu's phrase, they felt that they "had not retreated far enough." The new slogan in the second half of 1961 concerning agricultural work was "three private and one guarantee."[54] While the "three private" simply reiterated the gist of the previous directives—private plots, private markets, and private responsibility for losses and profits in rural handicrafts production—the one guarantee was a proposed new system close to individual farming. Under the new system, all communal land was to be distributed to individual households as "responsibility land"; each household must guarantee to produce a given amount, or quota, on his responsibility land.

In mid-1961, Liu Shao-chi and many other leaders made field trips to various provinces, partly to collect more facts and receive complaints and partly to make sure that the announced reforms had been faithfully implemented by local cadres.[55]

In December 1961, Peng Chen, then the Mayor of Peking, led a special task force to examine secretly the documents and instructions issued by the Party leaders to regional and local cadres since 1958. Peng Chen is reported to have said, "Many of the documents had never been discussed in the Central Committee but were issued by a single individual. . . . Those documents may contain some erroneous and problematic points." Finally, a total of more than 110 "problematic points" was collected from those documents, practically all pertaining to Mao's economic policies.[56] A top-level conference was then called in January 1962, in which Liu Shao-chi assembled all the findings and made an "extremely pessimistic conclusion" about the economic situation in China. He said, allegedly, "Our economy is now on the brink of a complete collapse." He added, "The economy can hardly recover in seven or eight years." He further contended that the economic crisis was 30 percent attributable to natural calamities and 70 percent to man-made disasters.[57]

Another important meeting was held by the dissenting members in early 1962 and is sometimes referred to by the Maoists as the "West Pavilion Conference."[58] After an exchange of the participants' critical views of the policies of the Great Leap Forward and of the communes, the conference decided to set up a five-man ad hoc investigation team to review the whole financial and economic situation. The five-man team prepared in May a report with a dismal conclusion. The report was approved by Liu Shao-chi and was later submitted to the Party's Central Committee in September 1962.[59]

According to the available information, in the September 1962 Committee meeting one of the key issues was the further liberalization of the agricultural organization, probably along the line of making the responsibility land system a nationwide institution. This was where Mao Tse-tung unfolded his counterattack. Mao's argument was that the failure of collective farming did not result from its inherent shortcomings but from a lack of adequate political education on the part of farmers. Therefore, instead of a complete abandonment of collective farming as a corrective measure, China needed to intensify socialist education in the countryside. Once more Mao attempted to shift the attention of the Central Committee from economic pragmatism to Communist ideology. To appeal to the Communist consciousness, Mao coined another famous battle cry in this meeting—"Let us not forget the class struggle."

To some Party members Liu's proposal probably represented too drastic a retreat from the ideological vantage point. Moreover, the summer crop of 1962 showed considerable improvement so that so sharp an institutional change was regarded as no longer warranted. Therefore, Liu's proposal was not accepted. The meeting has been acclaimed by the Maoists thereafter as a crucial victory for Mao Tse-tung, because he stopped the "black wind of capitalism" in the country.

This meeting was, indeed, another turning point in the history of the collectivization movement in Communist China. From then on Mao Tse-tung managed to regain his influence in the Party's decision-making, whereas Liu's group was forced to take a defensive position. Mao made another attacking move in March 1963 by drafting "A Resolution on Some Problems in the Current Rural Work." The proposal was aimed at initiating a new socialist education campaign in the rural sector, sometimes referred to as the "four-clearance movement." He brought the

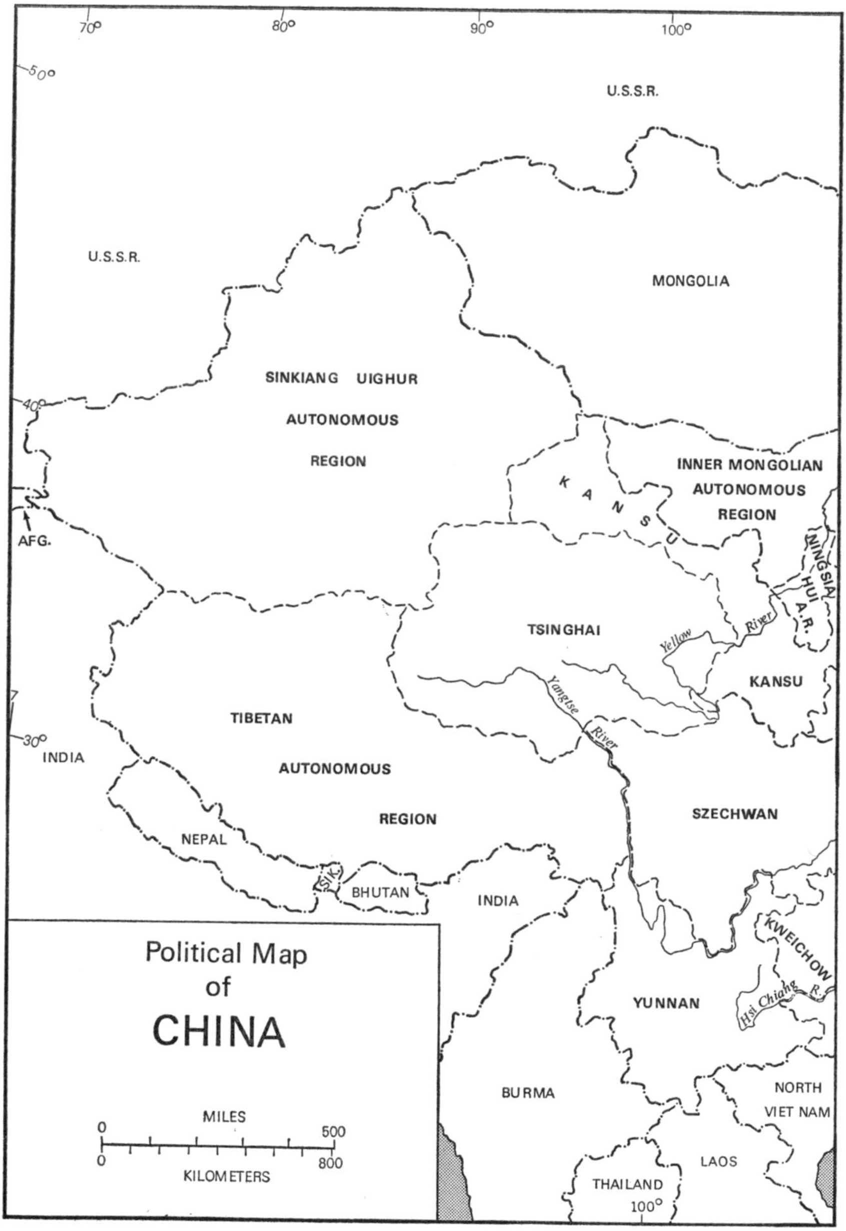

Map by the University of Wisconsin Cartographic Laboratory

100°
110°
120°
130°
50°
U.S.S.R.
U.S.S.R.
U.S.S.R.
MONGOLIA
HEILUNGKIANG
KIRIN
LIAONING
INNER MONGOLIAN AUTONOMOUS REGION
NORTH KOREA
SOUTH KOREA
Peking
HOPEI
SHANSI
SHANTUNG
Yellow Sea
KANSU
NINGSIA HUI A.R.
TSINGHAI
Yellow River
SHENSI
HONAN
KIANGSU
Shanghai
ANHWEI
HUPEH
Wu-han
SZECHWAN
Yangtse River
East China Sea
CHEKIANG
HUNAN
KIANGSI
FUKIEN
KWEICHOW
Taiwan
YUNNAN
KWANGSI CHUANG AUTONOMOUS REGION
Hsi Chiang River
KWANGTUNG
Canton
PACIFIC OCEAN
NORTH VIET NAM
South China Sea
LAOS
Hainan
20°
30°
40°

draft to the Eleventh Session of the Eighth Central Committee, which was convened on May 11, 1963.[60]

While the details of the struggle between the two groups in the meeting were not documented we have learned of them from revealed information about the general development of this case. Mao's original draft was passed in the Committee meeting, but it was not executed by the government which was still controlled by Liu and his followers. Under Liu's sponsorship, the draft was revised so that its revolutionary spirit was greatly watered down. The new version was published in September 1963, about four months after the Committee meeting.[61] Consequently, what actually had been carried out in the ensuing year was a diluted program of political indoctrination in the rural sector.

Frustrated and indignant with the diluted movement, Mao Tse-tung renewed his effort by introducing in January 1965 another draft entitled "Several Resolutions Concerning the Policy of the Socialist Education Movement in the Rural Areas," in which he demanded a full-strength indoctrination campaign along a hard line. The new draft was presented to and passed by the Politburo; but, for some reasons still unknown to us, it has not been brought to the Central Committee for sanction.[62]

It is necessary to point out that, based on disclosed data, Mao Tse-tung did not attempt to restore the commune system in its original form. All the reforms made in 1959–61 remained effective, at least until the outbreak of the Great Cultural Revolution. Mao's efforts were confined to his demand for a new rectification movement in the countryside.

In conclusion, the whole course of development in the policy of socializing China's agriculture can be summarized as follows. The initial debate in the Party led to a compromised policy which lasted until the summer of 1955. On the whole, up to this time conservative opinions prevailed, with Mao Tse-tung resisting them with only marginal effects. The first turning point came in July 1955, and Mao began to dominate the scene thereafter. The conservative elements were then relegated to the background and were barely able to apply braking power from time to time; they succeeded in doing so momentarily in early 1957. In the period from 1955 to 1959, Mao manifested a strong repugnance to the pragmatic attitude of the planners and technocrats in the government, not only in agricultural policy but in other economic fields as well. The First Five Year Plan was upset by Mao shortly after it was adopted by the Party and the People's Congress. Even the Second Five Year Plan was completely discarded by him after its publication. The "high tide of production" in 1956, the "Great Leap Forward" in 1958, "catching up with Britain in fifteen years," and "the general line of constructing a socialist economy" were all his personal decisions imposed on the Party and the government.[63]

The Lushan Conference in July 1959 marked another turning point after which Mao's influence subsided rapidly. All the retrenchment and readjustment policies during the crisis years were engineered by Liu Shao-chi and other conservative members in the Party. Perhaps Liu's recommendations for policy reversals were carried too far, so that they created a serious conflict with the basic ideological commitment of the Party. This provided a good opportunity for Mao to regain power in 1962. In the following three years, the two contending groups may be said to be more or less equal in strength, at least at the high level of the Party's power structure. In a sense the situation was an unstable equilibrium, because neither group was strong enough to carry out, unchallenged, what it wanted; yet each side was too hostile to the other to reach any stable compromise. Such a stalemate eventually must resort to a bloody power struggle for solution, as was witnessed in the Great Proletarian Cultural Revolution.

Chapter 2

Organizational Features and Economic Evaluation of Various Farm Institutions Since 1949

Land Reform

In pre-Communist China, as in many other countries, the tenancy system was widespread in the agricultural sector. According to the statistics of China's National Agricultural Research Bureau (NARB), 46 percent of the Chinese farmers in the 1930s were owners, 24 percent partial owners, and 30 percent were tenants.[1] Using sample surveys, Professor J. L. Buck attempted to measure the extent of tenancy both in terms of the land rented out by owners as a proportion of total private farmland and in terms of the proportions of farmers in various categories. His findings show that 71.3 percent of farmland was owned by farmers themselves and 28.7 percent was rented; 54 percent of farmers were owners, 29 percent partial owners, and 17 percent tenants.[2]

The whole problem of farm tenancy was a highly controversial issue, politically as well as economically, in prewar China, and it aroused heated debate for many years. Dr. Sun Yat-sen, founder of the Nationalist Party of China, cited the principle of "land to the tillers" as one of his key economic policies. However, except for a vague egalitarian notion, he did not offer any economic justification for the program. On the other hand, Professor Buck, his Chinese colleagues, and many Chinese economists who were educated in the West questioned the usefulness of land reform as a solution of the economic problems in agricultural production of China. As Buck has concluded on the basis of his sample surveys of Chinese farms, the extent of farm tenancy was no greater than that in many other countries. The basic problems, as he saw and others agreed, were the extremely unfavorable man-land ratio and the lack of modern farm inputs. He maintained that "a change in the system of tenure cannot be expected to affect the amount of land available for cultivation, as is sometimes stated by those interested in the reform of land tenure; also, according to previous studies, such a change cannot be expected to increase crop production, for it was found that tenants were better farmers than owners."[3] The "best future solution" recommended by Buck was "some method of population control," whereas the "best immediate solutions" were "measures to raise yields per unit of land."[4] However, Buck did feel that the rent level was too high in some localities, and he supported the efforts made by the Nationalist government to reduce rent.[5]

The attitude of the Chinese Communists towards the tenancy system was complex. On the theoretical level, all of them firmly believed that this system represented an exploitation relation, but many of them had no faith in land reform, even as a short-run solution to agricultural problems. In practice, the land policy of the Chinese Communist Party before 1949 had swung widely from one extreme of confiscating land from all owners to the other extreme of a moderate rent-reduction movement. These changes by no means reflected revisions or moderations of the basic belief of the Party in this connection; they were merely tactical maneuvers or political expedients.[6]

It is both imperative and interesting to make an objective analysis of the economic functions of the land reform in China as carried out by the Chinese Communists before 1953. One eloquent argument for agrarian reform has been advanced by Georgescu-Roegen.[7] He emphasizes the employment effect and output effect of the peasant economy in an overpopulated country. Overpopulation is defined as a situation where the marginal productivity of population falls below the minimum subsistence income. In such an overpopulated country, Georgescu-Roegen contends, the family farming system is the most desirable rural institution, for it maximizes employment and total output. On a capitalist farm, with hired hands to carry out production, the owner tends to employ workers up to the point that the marginal productivity of workers equals the subsistence wage, because that is the point at which profits are maximized. If the capitalist farm is the prevalent institution in an overpopulated country, there must be sizable unemployment. In other words, under the capitalist farming system it is not total output that is maximized but total profits of farm owners, for no one wants to hire a worker who costs more than he contributes to production. But for society as a whole, the unemployed must be cared for, in one way or another, regardless of their contributions to production. Thus, from the standpoint of the whole economy, it would be better to put the unemployed to work, even though their productivity falls below the cost of feeding them. The goal should be, therefore, the maximization of total output, which can be achieved only when people are employed until the marginal productivity equals zero. The solution is provided by the family farming system. Under such a system, the family using its members as workers tends to employ labor until the marginal productivity reaches zero. The family farm is not governed by the capitalist rule of profit maximization. It rather pursues the maximization of total output, given resources at its disposal. Consequently, from a welfare point of view, the family farming system is superior to the capitalist farming system, and "disguised unemployment" is better than "outright unemployment" in an overpopulated country.

While Georgescu-Roegen's theory is completely valid, it does not speak for land reform in China. True, China was definitely an overpopulated country by his standard. But the effects of land reform on the expansion of employment and total output as described by him did not appear in China. In this connection, what could be achieved by land reform had largely been obtained without it. The Chinese landlord was fundamentally different from the latifundia landlords in South European countries and Latin America. The Chinese landlord leased out his land in small units to tenant cultivators. To a smaller extent he hired workers to farm on a wage basis. The guiding principle of using labor in a tenancy system was the same as that in a peasant economy, namely the maximization of total output rather than profits.

Therefore, Chinese land reform has to be assessed from other angles. The whole analysis may be divided into two major aspects: (1) the relation between the Chinese tenancy system and the economy of scale in farm production, and (2) the consideration of incentives.

So far as the economy of scale is concerned, the tenancy system is not necessarily bad. In fact, historically it had made positive contributions in China as well as in other countries where it once existed. Its chief function was to enable farm production to be conducted at the best operational scale compatible with the existing farming techniques. In the preindustrialization period, the fact that land was the major object of investment resulted in land concentration in the absence of any public or social restrictions on the maximum size of landholdings. This tendency was especially strong in China where farmers were traditionally granted a higher social status than merchants and craftsmen. However, given the backward state of technology in the old days, farming could hardly be done efficiently in large units. In view of these conditions, a tenancy system was desirable or even imperative. In other words, the tenancy system has an important historical function similar to, but working in the opposite direction from, that of the modern corporation in the non-agricultural sector, namely to enable the production units to select an optimal scale of operation independent of the ownership system. The institution of modern corporations allows the pooling of small owners to form a much larger operational unit if such a scale of operation is called for. On the contrary, the tenancy system made it possible to break a large landholding into smaller operational units when a small scale of operation was considered optimal.

After the tenancy system had served its historical role, there arose a new problem. That is, the average size of operation units in agriculture gradually became too small to be optimal. However, the basic cause of the new problem was not the existence of a tenancy system. The new scale problem came from either one or both of the following two sources: (1) the agricultural population had overgrown the total size of farmland, and (2) farming techniques had progressed so that larger operational units were required from the viewpoint of efficiency.

In the 1930s the average size of farms in China was exceedingly small—4.2 acres.[8] But there was no discernible distinction in the size of farms held by owners, partial owners, and tenants.[9] Buck was certainly right in asserting that land reform would not solve the scale problem of China's agriculture, since removing the tenancy system would neither enlarge the average size of farms nor affect the total amount of land available for cultivation.

However, land reform may have some effect on the incentives of peasants, which, in turn, may influence output and utilization of farm inputs. Here one has to make a distinction between the incentive to produce and the incentive to invest.

So far as the incentive to produce is concerned, the potential advantage of land reform is still far from clear. In prewar China, Buck found that tenants were generally better farmers than owners. The relatively high efficiency of tenant farmers was partly a matter of allocating various farm inputs at the disposal of the household and partly a question of production incentives. Comparing two rural families with about the same low initial capital, the farmer who decided to buy land may have exhausted his entire capital, leaving very little for acquiring farm implements and current inputs. On the contrary, the tenant farmer could spend his capital on other inputs. In other words, with little capital to begin with, a tenant could afford a better combination of inputs. As Buck discovered, this was one of the reasons that most small owner-farmers were less efficient in operation, with resultant lower earnings, than tenant farmers.[10]

Buck also observed that "there are plenty of instances where the tenant works harder and farms better than the owner farmer."[11] This generally resulted from the lack of security felt by the tenants who did not own land. Their strong incentives to work may have been offset, to some extent, by the unfavorable factor stemming from the high rents that tenants had to pay from their income. Theoretically, the degree of the disincentive effect of rent payments depended on the nature of the arrangement under which the rent was paid. The whole analysis is quite analogous to that of the effects of taxes on work incentives. One may simply treat rent payments as private taxes. Therefore, the system of share rent (crop-sharing between the tenant and the landlord), which is equivalent to a proportional income tax, would have certain disincentive effects, whereas the system of fixed rent (in cash or kind), which is analogous to a lump sum tax, would have no disincentive effect at all. Fortunately, an absolute majority of tenant farmers in prewar China were under the fixed rent system.[12]

Under the tenancy system, the factors favoring work incentives hurt farm investment. This is the serious drawback of the tenancy system when viewed from an economic standpoint. The tenancy system may retard farm investment in two possible ways. First, when rent payments are excessively high because of strong demographic pressure and the monopolistic power of landlords, tenants are deprived of investable funds. Second, because of the uncertainty of tenure, tenants usually take a short-run position. They not only have no interest in making long-range investments to improve land but also have a tendency to maximize current output at the expense of future output by unduly depleting the fertility of land.

While these tendencies of tenants are detrimental to farm investment, the net results depend on the attitude of landlords and the normal length of tenure prevailing in the country. So far as the availability of funds is concerned, what tenants have lost are gains for the landlords, hence there is no net reduction for the agricultural sector as a whole. It boils down to whether landlords are willing to invest for the purpose of maintaining or improving the quality of their land. Therefore, the tenancy system would have the most harmful impact on agricultural investment when there is a large number of absentee landlords. From the viewpoint of individual landlords, there are two possible outlets for farm investment. One is to purchase more land; the other is to improve the quality of existing landholding or irrigation facilities. The first, clearly a legitimate investment for individuals, should not be classified as investment in the real sense when the economy is taken as a whole, because it does not result in any increase in the aggregate productive capacity of a society whose total supply of farmland is more or less fixed. Only the second type of investment leads to real increases in aggregate productive capacity. Unfortunately, since they are ignorant about the actual situation of farm production, absentee landlords would tend to use funds to purchase more land if they chose to invest.

Regarding the length of tenure in prewar China, farmers were fully aware of the undesirability of an unstable tenancy. There was a proverb, "Every time a tenant moves, three are hurt—the landlord, the tenant, and the land."[13] In some parts of China, there developed the so-called permanent tenancy system where tenants were granted the right to till the land on a permanent basis or with a long tenure. Under such a system the tenants usually acted as if they were owners.[14] In some localities of Kiangsu Province, there existed another variety of the permanent tenancy system: the ownership of land was separated from the right to use the land. The latter belonged not to the landlord but to the man who was tilling. Unfortunately, the permanent tenancy system declined during the 1920s and 1930s, and the average period of tenure became shorter and shorter. This deterioration was accompanied by a rising number of absentee landlords who had shifted their interests from the countryside to undertakings in the urban areas.

Before 1949, in spite of the "land to the tiller" policy set by Dr. Sun Yat-sen, only limited efforts had been made by the Nationalist government on certain small-scale, tenant land-purchase projects and a rent-reductions movement.[15] The farm tenancy system in mainland China was replaced by the land reform of the Communist government. On the completion of the reform in 1952, 43 percent of the total farmland had been redistributed.[16] As was pointed out in the preceding chapter, the chief purpose of the Communist regime in introducing land reform was political—to gain the support of poor peasants. This is quite clear from the following facts. Landlords were not allowed to reduce their landholdings by selling them or by bequeathing them to their relatives or friends. Land redistribution in each village had to be conducted under the auspices of the local Communist authorities so that an impression was created among those who received land that their gains were the gift of the Communist government. Second, although the Chinese Communists were ostensibly against the "exploitation relation" between landlords and tenants, in the process of land reform peasants were not stratified into those who rented out land and those who were tenants. Instead, using the exploitation criterion, the government classified peasants according to their income and wealth. It is a well-known fact that not all tenants in China were poor; many of them were well-to-do farmers. On the other hand, a great number of owner-farmers were even poorer than most tenants. It was not tenants but poor farmers who constituted a majority in the rural population and whose support the Party was anxious to obtain. Third, the regulations governing the land reform did not forbid the resale or renting of land after the redistribution.[17]

While the Communist land reform was a great political asset, its economic gains were rather limited. As was noted earlier, such an institutional change could not be expected to solve the scale problem of agricultural production in China. In fact, it divided the entire agricultural sector into production units of the same suboptimum size. As a result, a strong tendency toward land reconcentration emerged after the land reform. Land transactions rapidly increased in number, and in some regions the price level of land more than doubled in a year.[18]

There is no clear evidence of any substantial rise in peasants' incentives to produce after the land reform. The greatest merit of land reform is supposed to be its effect on farm investment. Yet, this investment effect did not materialize in China because of the Party's decision to collectivize the agrarian sector soon after the land reform.

The land reform, designed as a political measure, had two important features which are usually not found in land reforms in noncommunist countries. First, strictly speaking, it was not a program of "land to the tillers" but an egalitarian redistribution of land among the rual population, except for those who were destined to be eliminated. Secondly, no compensation payments from the land recipients were required. These two features had a number of results which were quite undesirable from an economic point of view.

When land is sold to a farmer, he tends to buy the amount of land that he can till with the labor power he possesses. On the contrary, when land is reallocated in a purely egalitarian way, it may be distributed with little respect to the labor force. Thus, in Communist China a middle-aged farmer with three robust sons received the same amount of land as did a widow with three small children.

The Communist land reform also led to a misallocation of land regarding farm implements and draft animals. In prewar times, the average size of Chinese farms had been reduced to such a small acreage that even backward farm implements and draft animals could not be fully and efficiently utilized if each farm had its own animals and all the necessary implements. Therefore, the landlord-tenant relationship went beyond the leasing of land; the landlord usually supplied draft animals and implements to his tenants or other farmers on a rental basis. This arrangement was more economical because it was equivalent to the pooling of animals and implements for better utilization. Using draft animals as an example, the population of oxen and buffaloes in 1952 was less than half the number of existing farm households.[19] This ratio was probably close to an equilibrium, given the total cultivated land in the country. It was too costly for each household to own an ox to cultivate a small piece of land. After the egalitarian redistribution, many households had draft animals but not enough implements, whereas other households had implements but no draft animals. Yet the previous pooling system no longer existed.

Another problem caused by the special features of the Chinese land reform was the curtailment of grain supplies to the urban areas. This compelled the Peking government to adopt the measure of unified purchase and unified sales of grains in 1953; in addition, it later added weight to the case for accelerating agricultural collectivization.

It is interesting to note that there was no sharp reduction in the commercialization of grain in noncommunist countries, such as Japan and Taiwan, which carried out land reforms. Before land reform, the tenancy system was instrumental to the commercialization of grain in the sense that landlords extracted surplus grain from tenants as rent payments, and then sold the grain in the urban market. This extraction mechanism naturally was destroyed by land reform. However, in a noncommunist country the land reform program usually imposed on those who obtained land the obligation to make compensation payments, over a number of years, either to the original landowners or to the government which had advanced loans to buy the land. Under such an arrangement, peasants must sell enough grain to meet the compensation payments. In a sense the compensation payments have replaced the lost mechanism of extracting surplus grain from the countryside. In Communist China, however, since no compensation payments were required after land was redistributed, the rural sector immediately fell back to a subsistence economy. Peasants naturally felt less need to sell grain in the market and tended to increase their home consumption.[20] It is essentially the same factor that created the problem of grain procurement in both the Soviet Union and Communist China at the beginning of their collectivization campaigns, except that the situation in the Soviet Union was made even worse by the "scissors crisis."

Mutual-Aid Teams and Agricultural Cooperatives

Probably most Chinese Communists realized by 1953, if no earlier, that land reform alone, except as a means to gain political assets, could not solve the problem of agricultural production in China. But opinions differed as to whether collectivization was a really promising way out. In the preceding chapter we discussed how a decision was reached by the Party in 1953 to socialize the agricultural sector and how the gradual process of transformation as originally formulated was subsequently revised and accelerated. According to the December 1953 resolution, the whole process should go through the following transitional steps, one by one: seasonal mutual-aid teams, year-round mutual-aid teams, elementary agricultural cooperatives, and advanced agricultural cooperatives (collectives).[21]

Actually, a small number of agricultural cooperatives and mutual-aid teams appeared long before 1953. Furthermore, in the years 1952–55, the four types of organizations existed side by side. The timing of the transition from one stage to another varied greatly in individual cases. Table 2.1 gives the official count of households under the four types of farming organizations, at year-ends, in the period 1950–56.

The arrangements of mutual-aid teams were relatively simple, though not uniform in details everywhere. The seasonal mutual-aid team, usually consisting of less than ten households, was nothing but a formalization

Table 2.1 Cooperativization of Agriculture by Farm Households, 1950–56 (1,000 households)

Type of organization	1950	1951	1952	1953	1954	1955	1956
National total of farm households	*105,536*		*113,683*	*116,325*	*117,331*	*119,201*	*120,000*
Seasonal mutual-aid team	11,313		33,916	32,308	37,765	27,546	0
Year-round mutual-aid team			11,448	13,329	30,713	32,843	0
Elementary cooperative	0.2	1.6	57	273	2,285	16,881	10,407
Advanced cooperative	0.03	0.03	1.8	2.1	12	40	107,422

Source: Nai-Ruenn Chen, *Chinese Economic Statistics: A Handbook for Mainland China* (Chicago, 1967), p. 370.

of the traditional practice of Chinese farmers to pool their labor or to exchange implements or draft animals during busy seasons. It was an informal organization which would be dissolved after the peak season. Compensations for labor, implements, and draft animals borrowed from other member households would be settled either on the spot or at the end of the busy season. There was no change whatever in ownership; each household controlled the disposal of its own produce.

When a seasonal mutual-aid team was transformed into a year-round mutual-aid team, the cooperation among member households extended beyond the busy season. They could pool their labor for certain sideline activities during the idle season. They might wish to acquire some capital goods to be collectively owned, but this was not required.

Generally, organizing mutual-aid teams could remove some minor difficulties stemming from the smallness of farm units, though this type of benefits was not new under the Communist regime. These teams were simple enough for Chinese peasants to handle. Consequently, there appeared to be considerable enthusiasm among peasants for organizing such teams.

The shift from the mutual-aid team to the so-called semisocialist elementary agricultural cooperative was a much bigger stride institutionally. In the beginning, organizational details of elementary cooperatives were far from uniform. The publication of the "Model Regulation for the Agricultural Producers' Cooperative," on November 9, 1955, represented an effort of the government to set standard norms for the operation of cooperatives. But as soon as the Model Regulations were adopted, most cooperatives had already begun their process of conversion to collectives.

Here we can mention only briefly the three major features which are relevant to our evaluation of the system: the average size, the system of ownership and income distribution, and the management. On an average the elementary cooperative embraced thirty to forty households and was several times as large as the mutual-aid team. One important change was the pooling of land under the unified management of cooperative authorities. The peasant, however, still retained the title or ownership of his land which was regarded as his share of capital contribution to the cooperative. A certain amount of land was left to each member for his own use and was often referred to as the "retained plot" or "private plot." The Model Regulations stated that no member in the cooperative should retain land exceeding "5 percent of the average individual landholding in the village in question," but before the publication of those regulations, the size of the retained plot was determined rather flexibly. The treatment of capital assets other than land, such as farm implements, farm transport, and draft animals, varied widely from case to case. Concerning draft animals, for example, there existed the following arrangements: (1) individual peasants kept and fed the animals but the cooperative used them on a rental basis; (2) peasants owned them but the cooperative fed them and paid certain fees for using them; or (3) the cooperative bought draft animals as common properties either from its members or from outside. It is important to point out that under the system of elementary cooperatives the peasant was to join voluntarily, and once he had joined a cooperative he still was free to withdraw if he chose. Before mid-1955, the freedom to withdraw did not merely exist on paper; people did exercise it.[22]

At the end of each harvest, the cooperative management first delivered a part of its produce to the state to meet tax obligations and the procurement quota. Costs of production, such as depreciation charges and obligatory payments to other units or persons outside the cooperative, were then deducted. Certain funds were usually set aside for purchases of common properties, for welfare purposes, or as a sinking fund. The percentage of gross income that was set aside for investment, called accumulation, varied considerably until the Model Regulations laid down a standard range. The residual was then distributed to the members in two forms: as dividends to the land shares and the contribution of other capital assets, and as remuneration for work performed by members. There was no uniform ratio between the two components of income distribution among cooperatives,[23] nor were there well-established standards of rating and recording labor contributions by members.

The evaluation of cooperative farming still revolves around the same two aspects: the scale problem and the incentive consideration. However, these two problems are not entirely independent of each other. Furthermore, there are ramifications for each of the two problems.

One type of scale economy may be found in the better utilization of land and other capital goods on farms even before agricultural production was mechanized. After fragmentary plots were consolidated under a single management, many boundary lines dividing private holdings could be removed, resulting in extra acreage for cultivation. There was also the advantage that instead of each farm household striving for self-sufficiency, the centralized management could allocate each crop to the field best suited to it. Other capital goods could be utilized more fully, too.

Another economy was the easier mobilization and better utilization of the labor force. The Georgescu-Roegen benefits were not lost in the Chinese agricultural cooperatives. The cooperative manager in China did not behave in the same manner as the owner of a capitalist farm or the manager in the Ward-Domar "pure model" of cooperative.[24] To maximize the unit value of work points earned by the members in the cooperative, as the manager of the Ward-Domar "pure model" cooperative is assumed to do, labor must be used to the point that the marginal productivity equals the unit value of work points. What the Chinese cooperative manager was concerned about, however, was not the maximization of the unit value of work points but the utilization of a maximum amount of labor. An important difference between the two organizations is that the Ward-Domar "pure model" cooperative has the freedom to hire and discharge workers, whereas the Chinese agricultural cooperative has no such freedom. The Chinese agricultural cooperative had the right to reject a man who applied to join the cooperative, but once he had joined he became a lifetime member and could be expelled from the cooperative only if he committed a "serious crime" and was "deprived of political rights." As long as he remained a member, he had the "right" to work, hence the right to receive the income that was his due.[25]

The Chinese rural sector was overpopulated before cooperativization. Since the institutional change did not alter the man-land ratio, cooperatives inherited this population pressure from the very beginning. Furthermore, when a child of a member family in the cooperative reached the working age, he automatically became a new member and acquired the "right" to work. Therefore, in the overpopulated cooperatives the managers did not hesitate to use as much labor as possible until its marginal productivity became zero. In other words, the Chinese cooperatives followed the same rule of employment as did family farms. In fact, cooperatives could do even better than family farms in this connection, for cooperatives could employ labor not only for current production but also for large-scale capital construction and sideline activities in which individual families were unable to engage. However, there was one possible drawback in the deployment of farm labor to such a wide range of activities. That is, with current production remaining more or less unchanged, a great number of work points was added by capital construction activities so that the unit value of work points was considerably diluted. The sharp reduction in the unit value of work points might hurt farmers' incentives.

Theoretically, there is another type of scale economy, as stressed by a few Western observers.[26] That is, an enlarged farm organization can hire specialized technicians and agricultural experts. Unfortunately, these benefits did not materialize in Chinese agricultural cooperatives or even in the subsequent collectives because of the shortage of trained personnel. There were not even enough bookkeepers for cooperatives, and still fewer agricultural technicians.

On the credit side of collective farming, one should not forget to include the extraction of surplus farm products. The nature of this problem was discussed earlier.

To increase the size of farm units is, however, not without disadvantages. There is at least one undesirable point, namely management. Or one may call this a diseconomy of scale of collectivized farming. Unlike peasant farming or even mutual-aid teams, in a collectivized organization there is a great deal of planning, administrative, and bookkeeping work. For a number of reasons the administrative work in an agricultural organization is far more difficult than in an industrial enterprise with a comparable number of employees. First, since many farming activities are sequential, it is impossible to adopt a strict scheme of division of labor and specialization among the workers, as is ordinarily done in modern industry. Moreover, farming operations are highly diversified and nonstandardized. There are numerous types of work; for one type, the required effort may vary substantially according to such factors as the quality of soil, the distances involved, weather conditions, and so on. Consequently, it is difficult for the manager of a large farm organization to make perfect job classifications, to arrange work forces, and to evaluate performances. Second, the timing for various farm operations has a crucial effect on output. Yet a good time schedule can hardly be made in advance by a central office. By its very nature, agricultural production entails decentralized, on-the-spot decision-making. Only those who know the growth situation of plants in each field and get up every morning to look at the sky can tell what today's work should be. People who do not directly participate in local production can hardly reach realistic day-to-day decisions. Third, workers in a large farm organization are spread out so that discipline is difficult to enforce.

The degree of managerial difficulty in collectivized farming is conditioned by two crucial factors. First, the diseconomy is a function of the size of the organization—the larger the more serious. Second, the educational level of farmers matters decisively. Managerial problems appeared to be acute in China after the socialist transformation of agriculture, because an absolute majority of Chinese farmers were completely illiterate. They were incapable of handling even the simplest bookkeeping.

The managerial problems of collectivized farming were intimately related to the state of incentives of farmers. Poor management inevitably invites complaints and grievances, which in turn weaken workers' incentives.

As to the incentive consideration, collectivized farming is on the debit side, though the seriousness of the impact depends on the structure and characteristics of the prevailing institution. Under certain circumstances, the weakened investment incentives of individual households may have been offset by the strong desire of the collective authorities to acquire new capital goods as common properties. As a matter of fact, because of the zeal of cooperative managers to set aside large sums as sinking funds before incomes were distributed to members and because of the relative ease in mobilizing labor for capital construction, the average rate of investment of cooperatives was found to be substantially higher than that of individual rural families. However, in some cases, capital goods on farms suffered extraordinary depletion or deterioration from waste, careless use, or lack of maintenance.

So far as the work incentive is concerned, it depends on how close the relation is between rewards and the work one has performed. Undoubtedly, this relation tends to be much looser when the farm institution has shifted from a system of self-responsibility to one of shared responsibility.

There is another important aspect of collectivized farming that involves both the scale problem and the state of incentives, and hence is a mixed blessing from an economic standpoint. That is the effect of the new system on risk-taking of farming units, a vital element in the introduction and diffusion of new technology. Conceivably, when the operation unit is enlarged, it tends to be more able to absorb losses stemming from risky innovations. The peasant cannot afford to risk his whole livelihood by adopting new farming techniques or new varieties of seeds when he is uncertain about the results. But a large collectivized farm can afford to assign experimental plots. On the other hand, there exists among common people a certain degree of risk-aversion that acts as a built-in safety valve in the economy, since it helps avoid disastrous damages from the unscrupulous adoption of wrong or untested innovations or technological changes. Since risk-aversion is simply the opposite of a profit motive, it is also a function of the state of incentives. When incentives are weakened in a new system, farmers become both unwilling to work hard and less concerned about potential losses resulting from inappropriate technological changes. The protective function of risk-aversion is especially important when a government, like that of Communist China, has a strong tendency to implement uniform technical policies by fiat. As will be shown later, after 1955 the average size of farm organizations was getting larger and larger, resulting in an increased ability to absorb risk. But in the meantime, the drastically reduced incentives of farmers had reduced risk-aversion to such a low level that they became virtually indifferent to any technical change ordered by the government. The disastrous consequences resulting from such technological changes as the irrigation construction in 1958 and the practices of excessively deep-plowing and close-planting in 1959[27] are now clearly visible.

From all available evidence, up to mid-1955 the merits of elementary cooperatives probably offset the demerits. The scale economy in land utilization was substantial when compared with the extremely small and fragmentary fields that had existed previously. It is also true that more labor had been mobilized under the new institution. On the other hand, mismanagement in cooperatives had not developed to an alarming degree partly because the average size of the cooperative was still in the manageable range, and partly because, perhaps more importantly, the speed of cooperativization was slow enough to permit the government to supply accountants and other functionaries to cooperatives through short-term training courses.[28] Some responsible officials in the central government insisted that the speed of cooperativization must not exceed the supply of managers and accountants. This was one of the reasons that numerous new cooperatives were ordered to dissolve in the spring of 1955.

It is interesting to compare the experience of collectivization in Communist China and the Soviet Union. In China the collectivization movement before mid-1955 had little adverse effect on farm production. Even in 1956–57, when the shortcomings of collective farming increasingly outnumbered its advantages, there was virtually no violent, organized rebellion of peasants. Their resistance was essentially passive and formed a striking contrast to Soviet collectivization, which was far more bloody. In retrospect, we may find a number of factors in the favor of Communist China in this connection.

1. Prior to collectivization the average size of Russian farms was not too small for efficient farming, given the farming techniques and implements prevailing at the time. The Russian peasant had no urgent need for an institutional change to achieve some economy of scale. The situation in China was quite different. The average size of Chinese farms after the land reform was exceedingly small, with less than one-half acre of land per person, or slightly over two acres per farm household. The size was too small for efficient operation, even with the backward farming technology then existing in China. Many peasants desperately sought to improve their plight. If they were barred from taking the capitalist road to accomplish this, many of them were willing to try some socialist means as long as the proposed new system did not imply an immediate surrender of ownership. This is how Mao Tse-tung and his followers obtained the notion that Chinese farmers had a strong inclination towards socialism. Or, to use the interpretation of Chen Po-ta, Chinese peasants were more revolutionary simply because they were poorer than their counterparts in other countries.

Knowing the tendency among some peasants and hoping to make use of it, the Chinese Communist government laid down the principle of voluntary participation in organizing cooperatives in 1953. Up to 1955, this principle had been generally observed. Occasionally local cadres applied pressures indirectly to farmers instead of using coercion directly.[29] But the central government repeatedly warned against such practices.

One of the reasons that the conservative elements in the central government dissolved more than 200,000 cooperatives in the spring of 1955 was that the cooperativization movement was regarded as having "gone beyond the consciousness of the masses." Evidently, the conservative elements realized that many new cooperatives had been formed purely to satisfy the political zeal of local cadres and activists but against the willingness of the masses. Thus, those cooperatives had to be dissolved if the government was to adhere to the principle of voluntary participation. It is safe, therefore, to say that most of the farmers who joined mutual-aid teams and cooperatives before 1955 did so more or less voluntarily. This was not the case in the Soviet Union in the beginning of its collectivization.

2. In striking contrast to the gradualism in the Chinese collectivization before the summer of 1955, there was no continuity of policies of social transformation in the Soviet Union. No counterpart of the Chinese mutual-aid teams can be found in the history of Soviet agricultural collectivization. There were three types of collective organizations in the Soviet Union during the early period of collectivization: the *toz* where most livestock and draft animals remained in private hands, the artel in which land and most other principal means of production became collective properties, and the commune where all means of production were socialized. But, those three organizations were not designed as different transition phases with one replacing the other. Rather, they were three alternative experiments. In 1930 the Soviet Party decided to take the artel as the model for the kolkhoz.

The step-by-step transition in China did not generate a feeling of suddenness and shock among the peasants. Treating land as capital shares contributed by members of the elementary cooperative, distributing cooperative earnings as returns for their land contributions, and allowing members to retain their draft animals and implements were affirmations of the basic system of private ownership.

3. The way that the Chinese Communists carried out the land reform had a profound influence on the psychology of Chinese peasants and subsequently helped to reduce their potential resistance throughout the process of collectivization. The greatest contrast between the Chinese Communist land reform and the land redistribution in the Soviet Union in 1918–20 is that the former was initiated "from the top" whereas the latter came "from the bottom." In the Soviet Union, land redistribution was a movement inaugurated largely by poor or landless farmers them-

selves without much assistance from the Russian Communist Party which was at that time busy fighting the civil war and ironing out problems in the urban centers. The landless and poor farmers, using the peasant community (*mir*) as the apparatus, confiscated land from landowners and conducted the redistribution. They felt no reason to be grateful to the Bolsheviks. When collectivization came, the Russian peasants resented it because they themselves had struggled alone to seize the land, and the government had no right now to take it from them. Thus, they rose to protect the fruits of their own efforts. On the contrary, the Chinese peasants played only a passive role in the land reform. The whole operation of land redistribution was initiated, organized, and supervised by the Communist government. Psychologically, the peasants felt that they were the beneficiaries of government actions, as the recipients of land granted by the government. Consequently, there was no strong resistence when the government decided to "take back" the land.

The land redistributions in the two countries differ in still another important respect. Land was redistributed in China after a violent "class struggle." The Chinese Communist government was determined to eliminate all landlords and most rich peasants as a rural class and to destroy thoroughly their social prestige and influence in the villages. The job was so successfully done that the landlords and rich peasants, if still alive, had no chance to regain influence in the countryside. Contrary to the Chinese case, land redistribution in Russia was conducted in a less violent manner. Kulaks, instead of being totally destroyed, merely sank below the surface of the agrarian society. They managed, however, to survive and many even rose again in later years. By the time collectivization came, many of them had become powerful and influential enough in the villages to challenge the Party. They were the ones who agitated, organized, and led the peasants to rebel against the Soviet government in many places.

4. Apparently the timing of collectivization has proved to be an element in favor of Communist China. As we mentioned earlier, many in the Chinese Communist Party disagreed with Mao in considering collectivization a basic solution to the agricultural problem in that country. However, Mao turns out quite right in that, if agricultural collectivization was something that had to be done on whatever ground, it would be better to do it earlier than later. With the process of socialist transformation immediately following the land reform, there was no time for peasants to develop their "capitalist tendency" to a threatening degree.

As we have seen in the preceding chapter, Mao from the very beginning fully sensed the danger in the appearance of new rich peasants. In a sense, the good timing of a wrong policy has substantially reduced the destructive potential of the policy. This is clear from the fact that, even in 1956–57, there was in China only passive resistance but no organized uprising or armed confrontation in the countryside.

This may be compared with the Soviet case where more than ten years had lapsed between the land redistribution and the movement of agricultural collectivization. In this long time interval, there had emerged a great number of new kulaks who eventually joined forces with old kulaks to organize and wage bloody wars against the Soviet government. The kulaks did not exist merely in Stalin's imagination.

5. Finally, one should not overlook the impact of the structural differences between the Soviet and the Chinese Communist Parties in the relative performances in collectivizing the agricultural sectors of the two countries. The Russian Bolsheviks were an urban-based group who concentrated their attention and activities primarily in the urban areas immediately after the revolution. Rural affairs were somewhat neglected by the Party in the early years of the regime, partly as a chosen policy and partly because of their own weaknesses. The new government had a weak control machine in the rural sector.

As is well known, the Chinese Communist Party rose to power through a rather unorthodox route, from a Communist point of view. For a long period before the founding of the government in Peking, the Party was contained largely in the countryside of certain regions in China. It was from those rural societies that the Party drew the majority of its members, and, in a real sense, the relative strength of the Party was in the countryside. That is why the Chinese Communists were able to bring about a land reform "from the top" on a nationwide scale soon after they defeated the Nationalists. Yet in the same time period they deemed it necessary to adopt pacifistic policies in the urban areas. So far as the Party's control over the rural sector is concerned, the land reform also had its important feedback effect. In the course of land reform the Party had absorbed a tremendous number of rural activists, either as new members or as workers for the Party without joining it.

In the Soviet Union, the highest estimate puts the total number of Communists working in the countryside at less than 100,000 on the eve of the collectivization campaign.[30] The number reached 343,947 by January 1930. A large portion of them consisted of the so-called workers' brigades—factory workers with very little experience in agricultural production—who were sent by the Party to villages for short periods to conduct political propaganda assignments and other organizational tasks.[31] On the other hand, as early as 1945 most of the 1.2 million members of the Chinese Communist Party were living and working in the rural areas.[32] There were about 4 million Party members stationed in villages in 1954;[33] the number reached 7.4 million in 1956 and constituted about 70 percent of the 10.73 million total membership in that year.[34] There was clearly no comparison of Party strength in the countryside between the two countries when they embarked on collectivization campaigns, even allowing for the difference in the size of their rural populations. With 7 million rural Communists, plus several million nonmember activists planted among the peasants, the Peking government naturally had far better control than the Russians for implementing institutional changes, whether through persuasion or by coercive means.

It is important to point out, however, that although the large number of rural cadres and activists was instrumental in a smooth transition in the early stages of socialization of China's agriculture, their existence eventually led the country into deeper problems than the Soviet Union had undergone. The enthusiastic local cadres and activists formed a formidable barrier to communication between the Party leadership and the rural public. After the rectification movement in late 1955, rural cadres began to substitute their political enthusiasm for the true feeling of common peasants, and they were prone to overdo rather than underdo the instructions of the central government. That is why Mao Tse-tung was so firmly convinced that "the mass movement is in advance of the leadership, which fails to keep pace with the movement."

In Soviet history the strong resistance of peasants at the outset of collectivization was a signal too clear to be ignored by the Soviet leadership. Accordingly, the Soviet government stopped at that point and never attempted to go beyond the stage of collective farms. In China, however, no such clear signal was transmitted to Peking. Consequently, Mao could easily silence the conservative voices in the Party, and, with the help of the local cadres and activists, he pushed the country from the collective system into the commune system in a short period of time. When the signal finally came, it was already too late. The country was on the brink of complete collapse.

At any rate, many of the disadvantages of the cooperative movement, which had been anticipated by the cautious members in the Party's

Central Committee, had not developed to any alarming degree by 1955; therefore Mao was confident that an acceleration was feasible. In a few months, from late 1955 to early 1956, more than 80 percent of the farm households which were outside cooperatives until this time were engulfed by the new cooperatives. In another few months, virtually the whole agricultural sector was converted from elementary to advanced cooperatives (collectives). In other words, in about eighteen months Communist China had reached a goal that took the Soviet Union more than seven years to achieve, in the percentage of farm households collectivized.[35] Undoubtedly, collectivization at such a high speed could be accomplished only by using force or other coercive means.[36] It was only then that a full manifestation of the shortcomings of collectivization could be seen.

The disincentive effects became noticeable in many new cooperatives in late 1955, but the most pressing problem still centered on management. The long existing shortage of accountants for cooperatives became more and more acute.[37] A system of work norms reasonably suitable to most cooperatives had yet to be devised. From revealed reports, the number of work norms actually in use in cooperatives varied from some two hundred to more than seven hundred.[38] Farmers kept on quarreling over how many work points should be awarded to each of the several hundred classifications of jobs. Sometimes the dispute became so heated that farmers refused to work until an acceptable solution was announced.[39] In other cases, a more democratic approach was taken, and the farmers evaluated each other's work to determine how many points each deserved for a day's work. Unfortunately, to carry out this democratic system farmers had to meet at the end of the working day to do the collective evaluation until midnight. In many cooperatives, the accountants could neither read nor write; the result was a complete mess in bookkeeping. To overcome the illiteracy problem some cooperatives adopted the stamp system: stamps were distributed to farmers at the end of each work day according to the points each had earned. But, oftentimes farmers complained that they had lost stamps or had them destroyed in washing clothes.[40] According to one survey made in early 1956, only one-third of the cooperatives investigated could finalize and close their annual accounts. Another report revealed that, in 520 out of 756 cooperatives surveyed, corruptions of one kind or another by the officials had taken place.[41]

The fact that the majority of Chinese peasants were illiterate and short-term training programs for cooperative accountants and managers fell far short of the rapidly increased needs, only partially explains the general deterioration of management in cooperatives. Another responsible factor was the method by which cooperative officials were selected. In the beginning, the government intended to set up a small number of cooperatives as models to demonstrate the superiority of collective farming. In view of the fact that middle peasants had relatively more implements and better managerial ability, they were especially welcome to join cooperatives and were usually selected as managers or other functionaries in the new organizations. Many cooperatives consisting of only poor peasants were dissolved in the spring of 1955 because these cooperatives had failed to give the demonstration effects. The favoritism towards middle peasants was severely denounced by Mao Tse-tung in 1955, since he thought that middle peasants were unreliable politically. From 1955 the guiding principle was to choose cooperative officers from the poor peasants who were also activists in the rural society. Unfortunately, those activists generally were not knowledgeable farmers. As a consequence, the selection of functionaries according to political reliability often led to the exclusion of potentially good managers.

During 1956 elementary cooperatives were converted into collectives. The collective was usually formed by merging a number of existing elementary cooperatives in the same locality, hence its size was much larger, varying from one to three hundred households. The collective differed also from its predecessors in the ownership system and the method of distributing income among members. The chief means of production previously owned by individual members were now transferred to the collective. This applied to land, draft animals, large farm implements, and so on. Private plots no more than "5 percent of the average landholding in the village in question" were allowed. As a result of the changed ownership system, dividends to land shares were abolished. The total income of the collective, after deducting taxes, reserve and welfare funds, and production costs, was to be distributed to members solely on the basis of work done. This method was called the principle of "from each according to his ability and to each according to his work."

Although the scale of operation in collectives was increased in comparison with that of elementary cooperatives, little improvement in land utilization could be gained. Without mechanization the economy of scale in this connection had almost reached its limit. Some gains were made in labor mobilization. This was reflected in the "leap" in water conservation construction in 1956, which, after a short lapse, was resumed in the winter of 1957 on an even larger scale. However, farmers' incentives sank to an even lower level in collectives.

One serious problem in this period was a decline in the number of farm animals. The number of hogs began to decline as early as in the second half of 1954. Chinese official sources, which attributed this decline mainly to the unreasonably low procurement prices set for hogs and the lack of fodder, nevertheless admitted that it had something to do with cooperativization.[42] Before organizing collectives, and as a preventive measure, the State Council had enacted a law forbidding individual farmers to sell or slaughter farm animals. All farm animals must be taken over by collectives at once.[43] The collective was to compensate owners according to "normal local prices" of the animals. But the actual compensations were usually much lower than that prescribed by the government regulations; sometimes no compensation was made at all.[44] The hog population continued to decline in 1956. In that year, for the first time, the number of large farm animals showed a reduction in official statistics. On the whole, the government's precautionary measures did prevent wholesale slaughtering by peasants before they were forced to join collectives, unlike the slaughtering of animals in the Soviet Union in the early 1930s, but those measures failed to arrest the rising death rate of animals after they were taken over by collectives. This problem was especially serious with draft animals, which were said to be getting weaker and weaker as they were overworked and underfed in the collectives.[45]

In a speech delivered before the People's Congress in June 1956, Party member Teng Tzu-hui, a critic of Mao's agricultural policy, summarized the shortcomings of collective farms. In addition to the animal-breeding problem, he pointed out the following defects:[46]

1. Wasteful and luxury spendings by collective authorities;
2. Domineering attitudes of manager toward members;
3. Chaotic management, planning, and bookkeeping; and
4. Blind adoption of new cropping systems and new varieties.

Other official reports disclosed the rising rate of deaths and injuries to women and children who had been forced to do heavy jobs.[47] The difficulty in managing large collectives was so formidable that many collectives in 1956–57 abandoned sideline production activities or even adopted an egalitarian distribution of income among members,[48] because doing so simplified the administration work. The reduction in subsidiary production in villages resulted in a drop in the average income of farmers.[49]

To sum up, when the socialist transformation of agriculture in China proceeded from cooperatives to collectives, the disincentive effects definitely worsened. On the other hand, there was almost no further economy of scale to gain. In fact the diseconomy of scale in the form of management difficulties became increasingly severe. So far as production is concerned, the net result of collectivization on the balance sheet must be negative.

Communes

The commune in its original form represented the most drastic institutional change that the Chinese rural society had ever undergone. The idea originated at the local level, but whether it should be adopted as a new rural organization for the whole nation soon became a policy decision to be made by the Party leaders. Since the issue arose so suddenly and the idea was so novel that even little Soviet experience could be borrowed, the whole Central Committee was caught in a state of bewilderment. Fascinated by the communistic features of the new organization and insisting on the principle that any spontaneous enthusiasm of the masses toward socialism should be encouraged by the Party, Mao Tse-tung made the go-ahead decision for the Central Committee. However, the Central Committee was unable to design any set of model regulations for the new organization. Consequently, there existed for some time a great deal of local variation in communes. In general terms, the following features may be found in communes in 1958–59.

The commune was an agglomeration of collectives, with the average size of about 5,000 households. Although a few early communes were set up as production units, soon most communes took over from local governments other functions such as social, educational, and military work. The commune became a basic economic, social, and political entity in the rural areas. In addition to agricultural and subsidiary production, it ran banks, schools, nurseries, factories, stores, and militia units. All production activities were organized, and all activities of all members were regulated by a centralized arrangement. Common mess halls were the uniform setup. In many cases, member households were required to reside in a few centralized living quarters in the commune.

In terms of ownership, the commune was the sole owner of all properties including dwellings and certain kinds of consumer durables. Private plots were confiscated. Thus, members were deprived of all means of personal earnings except by participating in the production activities under the commune authorities.

The system of income distribution also was drastically altered. All members were required to eat in public mess halls free of charge. In addition, the commune was obliged to assume certain types of expenses which previously were met by individual households—the so-called guarantees. Exactly what expenses were guaranteed varied greatly from commune to commune.[50] Free meals and guaranteed expenses fell into the so-called free supply system, which was applauded as a communistic distribution of income, because it fit the principle "to each according to his need." After deducting taxes, reserve and welfare funds, and the total cost under the free supply system, the residual income was to be distributed to members as "wages" according to their work.[51] It should be remembered that the average level of farm income in China was so low that very little was left for distribution after all the basic consumption items were met by the free supply system. Furthermore, under the new system, commune authorities had a strong tendency to set aside an unusually large amount as a reserve fund for future investment; per capita consumption of food in the public mess halls also exceeded the previous level when farmers ate at home. Consequently, the proportion of total income to be distributed as wages was small.

The reader may be curious to know whether the local cadres and rural activists in China were really so progressive ideologically as to wish to enter a communistic society when the economy was still so backward. The answer is no. They might have been fanatical and devoted politically, but they were certainly not so imaginative as to design a blueprint for a communist society for China. In reading the reports about how the early communes were established at the local level without any hint or guidance from the fancy theoreticians in the Party, one finds that the organizers were actually driven by a rather simple and practical motive. During the winter of 1957–58, a campaign of water conservation construction was launched by the government on an unpredecentedly large scale. In view of the declining subsidiary production in the countryside during 1956–57, the Party now urged collectives to restore or even to expand these activities. This was soon reinforced by the "Great Leap Forward" movement and the "walking on two legs" movement, under which collectives were charged to embark on many new tasks of industrial production. As a result, the labor-surplus rural sector of China felt for the first time an acute labor shortage. Local cadres, under a formidable pressure to fulfill the production and construction targets, desperately sought ways to secure extra labor.

Two kinds of attempts to recruit additional labor were then made in those places where the work of water conservation construction was especially pressing; the two measures led to the subsequent development of communes. One attempted to combine a number of collectives so that a "big army of farm workers" could be organized and deployed by the new management.[52] The other measure set up public mess halls where people could eat together. To explain the organization of public mess halls, the cadres of the early communes gave the following reasons:[53] First, when people previously had eaten at home, the meal time varied. Hence a longer time had to be allowed for a work team to assemble its members. Now with everyone eating in the mess halls and mealtime synchronized for all members, both the dining and the waiting time could be shortened. Second, by getting rid of cooking duties, women could be mobilized to work in the fields. The same applied to bachelors who used to cook for themselves.

Other features of the commune system were mostly the natural by-products or the extension of the same principle—to squeeze out more labor. Thus, there came communal nurseries, tailor teams, public laundries, and the like, all intended to save female labor for field work. Eventually the system developed into a complete regimentation of the private lives of the rural population, because only by doing so could a maximum amount of labor be extracted. In other words, under the commune system there was not only collectivized production but also collectivized living.

Until pointed out by some reporters and Communist theoreticians, the organizers of early communes did not appreciate, or even did not realize, the communistic nature of the new organization. To them instituting a free supply system was merely an expedient for solving the old, but now much aggraved, problem of administrative difficulties. With regimented living for a huge group of people, the simplest method of administration was to render all communal services free of charge. Otherwise, either a sophisticated payroll deduction system or a somewhat simpler pay-as-you-use arrangement would have to be established for each mess hall, tailor team, nursery, and the like. In either case, a tremendous amount of extra accounting work would be involved, while it was absolutely impossible to obtain the qualified persons to meet the needs. The organizers of the early communes fully realized this dilemma. Since everyone was compelled to use the communal services and everyone had to work for the commune, the organizers thought, why could we not provide all services free? The reasoning was obvious, but the long-run economic consequences were not foreseen. Nor was the ideological implication of the system realized by these organizers.

Easy mobilization of labor seems to have been the only achievement. Even here the economic gains depended on whether the extra labor so mobilized was fruitfully utilized. True, commune authorities were not responsible for the wasteful use of labor on water conservation projects. (These projects will be discussed in detail in Chapter 5.) However, even within communes labor was used in many undesirable ways. There was general tendency among managers to make their communes self-sufficient entities regardless of the availability of other resources. Thus, production activities were widely diversified, and the peasants were frequently transferred among different jobs regardless of their skills.

No other type of scale economy could be gained under the commune system. The commune in fact far exceeded the optimal size of operation, given the technological conditions that existed in China. With the commune's large size and its many extended functions, efficient administration was virtually impossible.

However, the most disastrous effect of the new system was on incentives. The free supply system means to distribute income completely independent of work performed. The principle "to each according to his need" is a utopian idea designed for a society in which the scarcity problem is assumed not to exist. But when it is applied to a poor country where the scarcity problem is most acute, it can be extremely destructive. If one can get everything without working, why should he work hard or even work at all? In the preceding chapter we discussed how various Communist leaders, after their inspection trips in 1961, commented on the universal lack of incentives in rural China. There is concrete evidence that, in the autumn harvest of 1958, the reaping and threshing were so poorly done in the whole countryside that a large-scale campaign had to be conducted to recover grain left in the fields or on the threshing grounds.[54] Even more serious were the widespread weed calamities in 1960. According to news reports from six northern provinces, the areas affected by weed calamities in 1960 ranged from 10 to 82 percent of the sown acreages. (Additional details can be found in Chapter 10.)

These weed calamities were unknown in Chinese history, because weeding was always routine work for Chinese farmers during the entire growing season.

No matter how appealing the communistic features of the new institution might sound to Mao Tse-tung and his followers, the destructive outcome soon became intolerable. The Peking government was compelled to introduce a series of decrees modifying and revising the commune system. In the beginning, the Communist leaders considered the disincentive effect and the chaotic management of communes as two separate issues to be dealt with separately. The December 1958 resolution of the Party's Central Committee, concentrating on the issue of income distribution, advised commune managers to abolish or deemphasize the free supply system. The Central Committee apparently failed to see the intimate relation between the egalitarian distribution system and the cumbersome size and the all-embracing functions of the commune. Later the Party leadership realized this dilemma, and the decrees issued in 1959–61 were aimed both at restoring incentives by changing the ownership and distribution systems and at reorganizing the administrative structure of the commune. Inasmuch as those new decrees have not been fully documented, many organizational details and effective dates of the reforms are still unknown to us. There are indications also that the reforms were flexible in binding power, with a wide range of local variations.

As administrative units, some exceedingly large communes were broken up into smaller ones. As a result, the total number of communes in China rose from about 24,000 in 1958 to 74,000 after 1962.[55] Within each commune the administrative power had been gradually decentralized. The history of socialist transformation of Chinese farms made this decentralization relatively easy. The commune evolved from the merging of collectives, which in turn were brought about by combining elementary cooperatives. In most communes the same three tiers were still being maintained with new designations. The production brigades in the commune closely coincided with the former collectives. Under each brigade there was a number of production teams which were comparable to the former elementary cooperatives. In some cases the production team was further divided into groups whose origin may be traced to the mutual-aid teams. The decentralization process simply reactivated all the lower layers of the commune.

The December 1958 resolution suggested that the administrative functions could be divided into three levels—the commune, the brigade, and the production team.[56] However, the resolution insisted that the commune was to be "responsible for losses and gains in a centralized manner," implying an economic equalization among all brigades and teams in the commune. A new rule was made in November 1960 that the brigade was to be an "independent accounting unit responsible for its own losses and gains." One year later the Central Committee issued another directive which firmly established the production team as the independent accounting unit.

However, the actual decentralization of the commune administration did not begin at the same time in all localities. In a few places, the last step of decentralization was postponed until 1965.[57] In still other cases, the brigade was retained as the basic accounting unit throughout.[58]

The exact division of work among the three levels of authorities in the restructured commune after 1961 is not yet clear to us. Indications are that the commune in function had been reduced to something slightly stronger than the ordinary local government. It also had the responsibility of transmitting the state economic plans to brigades and teams, collecting taxes and compulsory grain deliveries, and controlling relatively large communal industries and irrigation facilities. The brigade served as an organizational link between the commune and production teams.

The ownership system in communes had undergone a series of moderations parallel to the changes in the administration system. The December 1958 resolution decreed that properties in a commune were to be classified into three groups according to their nature and functions and were to be owned, respectively, by the commune, brigades, and teams. In August 1959, the new resolution set the brigade as the basic unit to own most of the common properties. Beginning in November 1961, the team was designated as the basic unit to own properties.

Actually, changes in the ownership system went much further than was required by the Party's decrees. In accordance with the "Twelve Emergency Measures in Agricultural Work" proclaimed by the Party in November 1960, private plots were formally reinstated and rural free markets reopened. However, with the connivance or encouragement of Liu Shao-chi and other leaders in the Party who sided with him, agricultural organizations in many localities retreated almost all the way to individual farming during the latter part of 1961 and 1962.[59] This was done through a variety of changes.

In some areas the limitation on the size of private plots was either relaxed or ignored. Communal land was reallocated to individual households under various pretexts or designations, such as plots for cultivation, plots for breeding animals, plots for private construction, and so on.[60] According to a report from a commune in Shantung, there were eight types of private plots. Consequently, most of the public land in that commune had been converted into private lands. Such plots were now really private in the sense that they not only were subject to private uses but also could be sold or rented by the owners to other people. In other localities, while only a small portion of communal land was redistributed as private plots, the farmers were allowed to expand their private plots through reclamation. In one known case the entire communal property was redistributed to individual households. Farmers there sent for their sons and daughters, who had left the village, to help them identify the lands, houses, or other properties that previously had belonged to them. A more common practice was the so-called responsibility land system which represented a reconciliation between the collective ownership of land and individual farming. Under this system a piece of land was assigned to each farmer or household; at the same time a production quota was attached to the land.[61] The farmer worked on the land independently, as if it were his own property. After the harvest, while the produce within the quota had to be submitted to the team for collective distribution, any excess amount went to the farmer.

Judging from published documents, the various methods of individual farming mentioned above were practiced in 1961–62 without the official sanction of the Party. Liu Shao-chi and his followers made trips to several provinces during this period to collect evidence and evaluate the unofficial arrangements. Apparently, the responsibility land system was proposed to the Central Committee meeting, in September 1962, for adoption as an official institution in the agricultural sector, but the proposal was defeated under the strong opposition of Mao Tse-tung.[62] The decision of that meeting was to reaffirm the production teams, not individual households, as the basic units of ownership.

During the experimental period of individual farming, farm animals also were distributed to households for breeding.[63] Farm instruments, too, were distributed, and their redistribution was perhaps more thorough than that of land. One official report has cited the ownership situation of farm implements in a production team in early 1965. There were 34 households and 826 pieces of farm implements in this team; 8.1 percent of the implements were collectively owned, whereas 91.9 percent belonged to individual households.[64] It is unlikely that this is an exceptional case.

With the reforms in administration and ownership in communes came the alteration in income distribution. The government's efforts were intended to reduce the free supply system. Since mid-1959, eating in mess halls was no longer compulsory. The summer harvest of that year was distributed to individual households instead of being delivered to mess halls. Recently, almost no mention of communal mess halls can be found in Chinese newspapers and other publications, implying that this institution has probably been discarded in most communes. Except for the earnings from private plots, the profits from business activities in the free market, and the rewards for above-quota production under responsibility land system, collective income was distributed to members by the authorities of the production team primarily according to work points.

In sum, the agricultural organization in 1964–65 was a heterogeneous mixture embracing features of both original communes and individual farms. There was no standardized model. This flexible system, as pointed out by Joan Robinson, had the advantage of permitting the selection of different operational scales suitable to different functions.[65] More important was the restoration of incentives under the restructured system, and it is to this restoration that much of the agricultural recovery in 1963–65 should be credited. During the period of Great Cultural Revolution, numerous local reports were divulged, with the intention of condemning the evil capitalist tendency induced by the revisionist policy of the Liu Shao-chi group in the early 1960s. Actually, what has been demonstrated by those reports is a vivid depiction of the revitalized incentives of farmers under material stimulus, for farmers were notably more eager to work under the new system. Private plots and free rural markets provided great incentives to them. One farmer was said to have reclaimed more than ten mou of land as his private plot. Another farmer earned more than one thousand yuan in a single year in rewards for above-quota production on his responsibility land.[66]

However, there are some disadvantages in the new system, either from an economic viewpoint or on the Communist ideological grounds. It is often reported that since the reorganization of communes there has been a widening differential in unit yield between private plots and communal land. While this yield differential undoubtedly signifies the importance of incentives in agricultural production, it represents a serious degree of misallocation of available farm resources when private and collective lands coexist. The tendency of farmers to devote excessive amounts of inputs to private plots results in the failure to maximize the combined output of public and private lands. This problem occurred as early as 1956–57 when collectives prevailed. Conspicuous in that period was the fact that farmers were inclined to apply to their private plots most of the natural fertilizers they could collect. Misallocation of farm resources became more acute in 1962–65, since the individual farmer then had both a larger proportion of land as private plots and greater freedom in allocating the resources at his disposal. It is reported that some people worked on the communal land as little as thirty work days per year and devoted most of their time to private cultivation or free market transactions. All natural fertilizers were saved for private plots. The intensity of cultivation on the private plots reached the extreme. But such practice is uneconomical in the sense that the overall farm output could have been raised somewhat if the resources had been more evenly allocated between collective and private lands. Still worse are the cases where farmers stole tools owned collectively or cut trees that belonged to the commune.[67]

From an ideological viewpoint, the new system was defective since it led to a renewed income differentiation among peasants. The establishment of communes in 1958 was acclaimed as having eliminated, for all time, classes in the rural society. A few years later rural classes reappeared, as a natural outcome of the reinstatement of private plots and free rural markets. Human beings are far from homogeneous. Some farmers are stronger, more diligent, and more enterprising than others. Even when they begin with more or less equal shares of private land and farm implements, they soon demonstrate their differences in productivity. With Chinese farmers the income differential tended to widen year after year as the better farmers accumulated more funds to buy more implements and fertilizers, which in turn made them more prosperous.

The income and wealth differentials among farmers reached such an alarming degree in 1964[68] that the Party decided to launch another class struggle in the rural areas. Farmers were classified this time into only three classes: the poor, the lower-middle, and the upper-middle. The struggle was supposed to be carried out between the first two classes on the one side and the well-to-do middle class on the other.[69]

However, in waging the 1964 class struggle the Party was confronted with a serious dilemma. The new differentiation of income was in no way a result of the exploitation of classes but was due to the unequal productivity of farmers. To suppress prosperous farmers would in effect be an antigrowth measure. Therefore, the Party did not eliminate the well-to-do middle farmers, but it did exert pressures on them in the hope that they would divert more of their energy and time to work on public land.

Actually, the new dilemma is just another phase of the same old conflict confronted by the Chinese Communist Party since 1952—a conflict between the ideological commitment of the Party and economic reality. Mao Tse-tung firmly believes that the right solution to the conflict lies in the "education of thought." If persistently and effectively indoctrinated, a selfish "economic man" can be converted into a selfless "Communist man." To Mao, the cost of conducting intensive and recurrent indoctrination campaigns is just a special type, to be sure the most important type, of investment in human resources.

State Farms

Our discussion of agricultural organizations in China would be incomplete unless we mention the state farms which have formed a small subsector immune to the frequent institutional changes. The state farm is defined as a socialist agricultural enterprise. It differs from agricultural cooperatives and collectives in the following respects. All assets of a state farm, including land, belong to the government, called "ownership by all the people" in the Chinese Communist terminology. Its manager and staff are appointed by the government, and all workers are hired wage earners. The wage system on the state farm differs from the work points system in that the remuneration for each working day under the wage system is fixed in advance, whereas the cash value of each work point is not known until the harvest is made and production costs, taxes, and so on, are deducted from the gross income. In a cooperative or collective, farmers shoulder the entire risk, whereas in a state farm the government is the residual claimant, absorbing losses or profits, whichever appear.

State farms in China have been established primarily to reclaim virgin land. Consequently, instead of being evenly distributed in all provinces, they are heavily concentrated in Manchuria, Northwest, and South China, the regions where reclaimable land exists. Originally, state farms were established by different government authorities—some by local or regional governments, others by the Ministry of Agriculture of the central government, and still others by military authorities either to settle demobilized servicemen or to obtain a self-sufficient food supply for garrison troops. In 1956 all state farms belonging to the central government were placed under the administration of the newly formed Ministry of Reclamation. As state enterprises, state farms have received subsidies from the government and are directly governed by the state production plans with regard to the product mix and farming techniques.

Table 2.2 shows that the state farms directly subordinate to the central government grew rapidly until 1960, both in numbers and in total cultivated acreage. On the other hand, local state farms have made relatively rapid expansion since 1958, that is, after the decentralization of administration in the whole governmental structure in China. After 1960 many central state farms were transferred to local authorities, as is reflected in the declined number of central state farms. On the whole, expansion of the state farm system was considerably slowed in the 1960s mainly because financial difficulties in the crisis years prevented the government from undertaking costly reclamation activities on a large scale.

In the absence of information, it is difficult to compare the unit yield and labor productivity between state farms and collective farms. Since the newly reclaimed land is of inferior quality and is located in areas with less favorable climatic conditions, the yield per unit of sown area in state farms is probably lower than the national average.[70] However, labor productivity on state farms may be higher than that of ordinary peasants, because state farms are better equipped with tractors and other farm machines. (For a more detailed discussion of this point, see Chapter 4.) The average annual income of workers in 1958 was about 480 yuan per person in state agricultural farms and about 360 yuan in state husbandry farms.[71] Yet the average annual income of peasants in the 228 collectives surveyed in 1957 was only 248 yuan per household, or 50 yuan per capita.[72] Even allowing for their higher productivity, the wage rates for workers in state farms were still considered to be excessively high. This fact is in part responsible for the chronic financial losses of many state farms.

In the Soviet Union, the share of state farms in total agricultural output was less than 10 percent during the whole Stalin era, but this percentage has risen rapidly since 1954 and is now over 25 percent. Since 1954 the general opinion in the Soviet Union about collectives has changed considerably. Collectives in their original form are increas-

Table 2.2 State Farms in Communist China, 1949–65

	Central			Local		Total	
Year	Number (1)	Cultivated area (1,000 mou) (2)	Grain output (1,000 tons) (3)	Number (4)	Cultivated area (1,000 mou) (5)	Number (1)+(4) (6)	Cultivated area (1,000 mou) (2)+(5) (7)
1949	18	460					
1950							720
1951							963
1952	404	3,820	193				
1953			169				
1954			225				
1955		13,360	329				
1956	454	13,620	525	86	1,380	540	15,000
1957	710	15,380	595	1,890	15,620	2,600	31,000
1958	1,442	34,080	2,350		12,920		47,000
1959	1,419			2,284		3,703	48,000
1960	1,490		2,500				
1961	2,500						
1962			1,400				
1963		31,000	1,785				
1964						6,400	62,000
1965	2,000						

Sources:

Col. (1): 1949, 1952, 1957, and 1958: *TGY*, p. 134.
1956: *JMJP*, Dec. 28, 1956.
1959: *CKNK*, 1959, no. 20, p. 1.
1960: *HC*, 1961, no. 7, p. 1.
1961: *PR*, July 28, 1961, p. 4.
1965: *NCNA*, Sept. 29, 1965.

Col. (2): 1949, 1952, 1957, and 1958: *TGY*, p. 134.
1955: *HHPYK*, 1959, no. 12, p. 71.
1956: *JMJP*, Dec. 28, 1956.
1963: *JMJP*, Mar. 14, 1964.

Col. (3): 1952–56: *CKNK*, 1957, no. 4, p. 25.
1957 and 1958: *CKNK*, 1959, no. 1, p. 12.
1960: *HC*, 1961, no. 7, p. 1.
1962 and 1963: *JMJP*, Mar. 14, 1964.

Col. (4): Col. (6) − Col. (1)

Col. (5): Col. (7) − Col. (2)

Col. (6): 1956: *JMJP*, Oct. 7, 1956.
1957: *CHCC*, 1958, no. 2, p. 17.
1959: *CKNK*, 1959, no. 20, p. 1.
1964: *NCNA*, Sept. 15, 1964.

Col. (7): 1950: *HKTKP*, Sept. 2, 1954.
1951: *EB*, Feb. 5, 1952.
1956: *JMJP*, Oct. 7, 1956.
1957: *CKNK*, 1959, no. 20, p. 1.
1958: *CKNK*, 1959, no. 14, p. 3.
1959: *CKNK*, 1959, no. 20, p. 1.
1964: *NCNA*, Sept. 15, 1964.

ingly regarded as an inferior type of farm organization. Two trends have been observable in that country, especially in the 1960s. First, a substantial number of collectives have been converted into state farms. Second, those collectives not converted have undergone a series of reforms toward more privately oriented organizations.

Interestingly, the position of state farms in the Chinese Communist economy is different. In spite of their rapid expansion in the 1950s, they have never played any important role in China's agricultural production. Even in 1964, state farms occupied only 4 percent of the country's total cultivated land. Their share in total farm output was even smaller because of the relatively low unit yield on state farms. Although the Chinese Communists continue to hold the theory that state farms are the more advanced form of agricultural organization, they have never really considered state farms a good substitute for collective farms.

This fact cannot be explained by the high investment requirement for establishing state farms, since converting existing collectives to state farms would entail little, if any, state investment. Yet even during 1958–59, when private ownership in the countryside was entirely abolished and many communes had already adopted a system of fixed wage rates for workers, the Chinese Communist government did not advocate a conversion of communes to state farms.

Part of the explanation may be found in the fact that a large proportion of state farms in China has been unprofitable. According to the Ministry of Reclamation, 71 of 220 state farms surveyed in 1956 sustained losses of various degrees.[73] Specifically, 149 state farms had total profits of 12.83 million yuan and 71 farms suffered total losses of 9.73 million yuan, for a net gain of only 3.1 million yaun to the government.[74] The situation in 1956 was described as a remarkable improvement over the previous years. Since it has no confidence in the workability of state farms, the government does not dare to assume the risk of converting communes or collectives to state farms, even if the conversion itself is costless.

What is more important is that the Chinese Communist government apparently realizes the different effects between state farms and collectives on employment and total output. A state farm is an enterprise. No matter how poorly it is managed, it is not likely to hire workers whose productivity approaches zero. But in a collective the manager has no freedom to reduce the membership. Therefore, he chooses to maximize output by using as much labor as he can until the marginal productivity reaches zero. To put it in another way, one big difference between Communist China and the Soviet Union is that the former is an overpopulated country whereas the latter is not. Probably the marginal productivity of the rural population in the Soviet Union is considerably above the level of subsistence income. The state farm may then be a good substitute for the collective farm, because the shift from the latter to the former may not cause a substantial sacrifice in total employment and total farm output, while such a shift may create gains in terms of management efficiency and in some other aspects. However, the state farm cannot be a good substitute for the collective farm in China, because such a substitution would inevitably lead to tremendous rural unemployment and a sizable reduction in total farm output. State farms in China appear to be a relatively good system only in a few regions with sparse local populations, that is, in the places where the Georgescu-Roegen type of benefits does not exist. This is why the Chinese state farms have been established mainly for reclamation in the border regions.

Part II

Inputs Utilization and Technological Changes

Chapter 3

Some General Aspects of Technological Transformation

There have been two principal types of agricultural policy under the Communist regime in China: socialist transformation and technological transformation. The former was dealt with in Part 1; we shall now turn to the latter, which is aimed at modernizing Chinese agriculture with new inputs and new farming techniques. While specific issues such as mechanization, irrigation, electrification, fertilization, and seed-breeding will be examined in detail in subsequent chapters, this chapter will be devoted to some general aspects which had across-the-board effects on specific technological measures.

Policy Choice and Implementation

As was true in the case of socialist transformation, members of the Chinese Communist hierarchy differed in opinion concerning technological transformation, but the disagreements were of a less serious nature. First of all, there was a difference of opinion as to the timing of technological transformation in relation to socialist transformation. Mao's group considered socialist transformation not only a prerequisite to technological reforms but also a developmental policy itself in the sense that institutional changes could promote farm production even in the absence of technological advances. The opponents of Mao, on the other hand, contended that socialist transformation should follow, not precede, technological transformation.

To some extent Mao's assertion that institutional changes may be instrumental in the introduction of new technology in farming is borne out by the Chinese experience. The large size of collective farms makes the use of farm machines feasible. It is also easier to diffuse new knowledge to a smaller number of collectivized production units than to a larger number of farmers in a peasant economy. Furthermore, the risk involved in adopting an innovation, which is usually too high to be borne by individual families, can be absorbed easily by large collective farms. These facts in part explain why the Chinese Communist government could implement so many technological changes in the form of crash programs after 1955. However, what was not foreseen was that, with farmers' reduced risk aversion resulting from weakened incentives under collectivization, many dubious technological policies were carried out widely, with incalculable damage to the economy. Therefore, the net contribution of the Communist institutions in the rural sector to technological advancement is not always positive. The ease of enforcing a wrong policy is actually extremely harmful. As a matter of fact, risk aversion is a natural protection that prevents the economy from sustaining serious losses stemming from any problematic innovation. In view of the risk involved, a new policy will not be widely employed by production units until it has clearly proven workable. The risk-sharing system under Communist institutions weakened the protection mechanism. Events of this sort will be studied in detail in Chapters 4–7.

Disputes also occurred as to the specific technological measures to be adopted. Four major issues, or as the Chinese Communists call them, "four hwa," were proposed: mechanization, electrification, irrigation, and chemicalization, the last item indicating the use of chemical fertilizers and insecticides. In addition, there was a miscellaneous category which included such measures as improving cropping systems, breeding, and seed selection. However, there was no agreement among the top leaders as to which measure should be given the highest priority. The selection of an appropriate policy had to be based on the comparative effectiveness of those measures on agricultural output and the constraints existing in the Chinese economy.

For many years, at the beginning of the regime, the Communist Chinese leaders had no clear notion of the comparative effectiveness of various farm inputs and techniques. It was only after 1955 that the planners concluded that, in view of the limited amount of arable land and the surplus of rural labor, the best way to raise the agricultural output was to increase unit yields. However, this was not the consensus of the party leadership; Mao Tse-tung and many others continued to stress mechanization even though its immediate contribution was to improve the productivity of labor, not land.

The two constraints faced by China in transforming agriculture technologically—the limitation of investable funds and the shortage of scientific personnel—are well known. Yet, the party leaders visualized different ways to cope with those constraints. Given the autarkic orientation in developing the economy, all the leaders seemed to agree that it would be undesirable to divert resources and funds for agricultural investment at this early stage. Since most modern farm inputs come directly or indirectly from the industrial sector, a diversion of funds to agriculture would slow down the rate of industrialization, eventually retarding the technological transformation of agriculture. The question on which Chinese leaders failed to agree, however, was: What should be done about agricultural production before industry became able to supply large quantities of modern farm inputs? To the planners and conservative members in the government the answer in the early stage was simply to select the technical improvement which would entail the smallest state investment. Measures of this sort included the selection of better seed varieties and the adoption of more profitable cropping systems.

Being both unwilling to divert industrial investment to the agricultural sector and impatient with the slow tempo of progress in agricultural production, Mao came up with a more complicated prescription, that of taking an indigenous approach. First of all, Mao firmly believed that indigenous inputs could be substituted perfectly for modern inputs over a wide range. As a matter of fact, Mao has applied this notion not only to economic problems but also to many other matters. For instance, his famous guerilla warfare is based, among other things, on the conviction that some indigenous elements can substitute for modern weapons and fire power. Therefore, a major task in developing agriculture before modern farm inputs became available was a fuller mobilization of indigenous inputs, a process that would not entail state investment.

Secondly, Mao also insisted that most modern agricultural inputs could be produced by indigenous units with indigenous methods, which again would not require state investment. Here, in the attitude toward scientific matters, one sees another fundamental difference in attitude between Mao and the technocrats in the government. The technocrats generally regarded technical and scientific work as delicate tasks requiring a high degree of expertise, to be handled carefully by those who had professional training. Accordingly, they respected scientists and engineers and heeded their professional opinions and recommendations. In determining and implementing policy, they have been quite cautious. On the contrary, while Mao appreciated the importance of technical work and scientific knowledge, he tended to minimize their complex nature. Mao's favorite "mass line" is the translation of this notion into practice. Thus China has witnessed the mass lines of designing and constructing water works and of manufacturing farm machines and chemical fertilizers, all with the ultimate purpose of carrying out technological transformation in the agricultural sector with as little state investment as possible.

Similar thinking of Mao is also reflected in the way he has chosen to cope with the shortage of personnel in agricultural sciences. Ordinarily, a new agricultural innovation is carefully tested in research organizations and then disseminated through agricultural extension services or similar institutions. But the ordinary process of diffusion would have taken too long to complete in China, because there were so few agricultural technicians available. Therefore, technical changes have often been implemented in Communist China as crash programs. That is, the government has resorted to fiat to enforce the implementation of an innovation throughout the whole country within a very short period of time. Sometimes the innovation has not been adequately tested through experimentation in a large area; its universal applicability was simply assumed.

An extreme case of uniform technological policy was Mao's "National Agricultural Development Program for 1956–67," first promulgated in 1956. In this program he listed eight important measures to improve agricultural production. They were subsequently condensed into eight Chinese words, or what is known as the "eight-word charter," so that farmers could easily memorize them. The eight words, in translation, are water, fertilizer, soil (soil conservation), seeds (seed selection), closeness (close planting), protection (plant protection), implements, and management (field management), and they are merely eight general principles for agricultural production. Yet, all farm units were ordered to obey the eight words strictly without being given detailed instructions as to how and to what extent these measures should be practiced.

Just as in the case of socialist transformation, the alternate ascendancy of contending opinions in the Party power structure has resulted in abrupt changes in technological policy in the past years. The period of 1952–55 was characterized by a compromise between the two groups. They agreed to mobilize traditional farm inputs to a reasonable extent and to focus on the technological measures that demanded the least investment. In the meantime careful studies and experiments were undertaken to prepare the ground for the future large-scale employment of modern farm inputs.

Another phase of technological transformation of Chinese agriculture was chosen during 1956–60, with Mao dominating the selection of policy. According to the planners' recommendations, the priority order for various technological measures was set: first, irrigation; second, fertilization; and third, mechanization and electrification.[1] Irrigation and fertilizer application have the effects of raising crop yields per unit of land, whereas both mechanization and electrification are essentially devices to save human and animal labor in agricultural production. Between the first two measures, irrigation received greater attention than fertilization, because the former could be accomplished by using surplus rural labor.

Unfortunately, 1956 saw the beginning of the reckless uniform technological policy based on Mao's personal judgment. His "National Program for Agricultural Development" not only specified what should be done by farmers technologically, but also it set many unrealistic targets not in accord with the economic plans formulated by the government planning agency. Technological changes were enforced by mandate. Crash programs were launched in the form of fanatical drives, regardless of the physical limitations of the country. Technological transformation generally followed this pattern until it reached its worst state in 1958–59.

It is not surprising that there was a large number of technological changes and crash programs which Chinese farmers were compelled to carry out in the short period between 1956 and 1959, thus proving that regimented rural organizations and mandatory technological policy were indeed effective instruments to overcome deficiencies of scientific personnel in diffusing new technology. Given the low education level of Chinese farmers, the inadequate agricultural extension services in the rural sector, and the vast territory, it would have taken much longer to promote an innovation through the normal process of diffusion. However, the Chinese experience also eloquently testifies that the normal process of diffusion of agricultural innovations is a much safer, if slower, way. As is convincingly illustrated by Professor Theodore W. Schultz,[2] uniform technological policy and its mandatory implementation might be workable in the industrial sector, but it is undesirable in agricultural production, because biological subtleties and the sensitivity of certain plants to local environment may make absentee arrangements and decision-making very hazardous. We shall show in subsequent chapters the disaster and various degrees of waste caused by such practices in Communist China.

The complete collapse of Mao's policy by 1960 put Liu Shao-chi and his supporters in the leading position in the decision-making body. Previous technological policies were carefully reviewed[3] and appropriate remedies were sought. The reckless construction of irrigation systems came to a halt. Although the mechanization program was continued, it was intended mainly to meet the needs for draft power after the severe loss of draft animals during the Great Leap Forward period. Great emphasis was placed on the production and application of chemical fertilizers as the chief means to increase farm output.[4]

Another important change after 1960 was that the readjustment policy had not been introduced as a crash program; the government acted more cautiously also in technical matters. Instead of enforcing uniform technological policy throughout the whole country, the government relied on demonstration farms to disseminate agricultural innovations, thus showing a revived recognition that technicians and experts in agricultural sciences were indispensable and of the complementarity of various modern inputs.

Investment in Agriculture

In the present section we shall examine the situation of capital investment in agriculture—one of the constraints in the technological transformation of that sector. However, because the data are incomplete, our discussions must be confined largely to the 1952–57 period.

During the First Five Year Plan period, as well as during the Great Leap Forward years, the desire of the Communist leadership to industrialize the country as rapidly as possible denied investment funds to the agricultural sector. This is true insofar as the state investment plans in those periods are concerned. According to official statistics, a total of 7.4 billion yuan, or 8.6 percent of the total basic construction investment within and outside state plans, had been allocated to agriculture, forestry, water conservation, and meteorology in 1952–58, in contrast to 44 billion yuan, or 51.1 percent, for industry.[5] However, if the investment made by farmers and agricultural cooperatives is taken into account, the percentage of agricultural investment in the total gross fixed investment would be much higher.

In another study, I have attempted to reestimate fixed capital formation in Communist China.[6] In the process of doing so, various items of rural investment in 1952–57 have been computed. The estimated totals of fixed investment in the farm and nonfarm sectors in 1952–57 are compared in Table 3.1. The share of fixed investment in the farm

Table 3.1 Farm and Nonfarm Investment in Fixed Capital, 1952–57 (million 1952 yuan)

	Farm		Nonfarm		
Year	Value	Percentage of total	Value	Percentage of total	Total fixed investment
1952	4,170	51.1	3,983	48.9	8,153
1953	4,253	36.8	7,292	63.2	11,545
1954	4,495	32.4	9,385	67.6	13,880
1955	5,656	36.7	9,777	63.3	15,433
1956	8,556	37.6	14,224	62.4	22,780
1957	7,548	36.2	13,296	63.8	20,844

Source: Kang Chao, *Capital Formation in Communist China* (forthcoming monograph), Table 31.

sector was above 50 percent in 1952 but decreased to 32.8 percent in 1954, clearly attesting the "industry first" policy of the government. In absolute terms, fixed investment, gross of depreciation, in the farm sector remained at a level slightly above 4 billion yuan in 1952–54. This is probably quite close to the minimum level of gross fixed investment needed in that sector to prevent farm output from falling. In other words, the bulk of the fixed investment in this sector in those years was used to replace worn-out assets such as houses and farming tools. Professor T. C. Liu has estimated the total stock of fixed reproducible capital in the agricultural sector in 1952 at 94.57 billion yuan.[7] If an average life span of twenty-five years is assumed for those capital goods, the annual depreciation would amount to about 4 billion yuan.

Farm fixed investment in 1955–57 not only rose substantially in magnitude but also increased slightly in share. This came as a result of Mao's new policy which mobilized farm investment from the traditional sources without draining the state funds intended for the nonfarm sectors.

In Table 3.2 we narrow our comparison to the investment shares between agriculture and industry, both excluding residential housing investment. The share of industrial investment was smaller than that of agricultural investment in 1952 and 1953, but it overtook the latter thereafter. The share of agricultural investment, never falling below 20 percent except for 1954, was still far from being as insignificant as some observers have believed. Actually, this finding should not be surprising.

Table 3.2 Comparison of Gross Fixed Investment in Agriculture and Industry, Excluding Housing, 1952–57

	Agriculture		Industry	
Year	Value (million yuan)	Percentage of total fixed investment	Value (million yuan)	Percentage of total fixed investment
1952	2,595	31.8	1,792	22.0
1953	2,966	25.7	2,858	24.8
1954	2,659	19.2	4,158	30.0
1955	3,487	22.6	4,840	31.4
1956	4,974	21.8	7,125	31.3
1957	4,902	23.5	7,605	36.5

Source: Chao, *Capital Formation*, Table 33.

In spite of China's energetic industrialization drive and the heavy concentration of state investment funds in industry, gross fixed investment in agriculture maintained an important position in total fixed investment, because agriculture in China has historical weight. This pattern can hardly be changed in the course of a few years. While agricultural investment had a predominant share historically, the industrialization drive has allotted a large proportion of "marginal investment" for industry. This is fully reflected in the rapid rise in the share of industrial investment.

In Table 3.3, gross fixed investment in the farm sector for each year is broken down into specific items. Those items are self-explanatory except for "other imputed investment" and "state investment in agriculture, forestry, and meteorology." Other imputed investment represents the imputed value of labor contributed by farmers in such activities as land improvement and the manufacture of simple farm tools. Anyone who is familiar with agrarian life in China is aware of the significant contribution of these activities to rural capital formation. State investment

Table 3.3 Gross Fixed Investment in Agriculture, Forestry, Water Conservation, and Meteorology, 1952–57 (million yuan)

Type of investment	1952	1953	1954	1955	1956	1957
Rural housing construction	1,575	1,287	1,836	2,169	3,582	2,646
Modern farm implements	0	8	27	116	448	394
Old-type implements, carts, and livestock	842	1,146	1,098	1,139	1,317	1,161
Water conservation	560	540	362	702	1,332	1,266
Other imputed investment	835	848	864	1,053	1,066	1,080
Reclamation	169	140	152	267	331	541
State investment in agriculture, forestry, and meteorology	189	284	156	210	480	460
Total	4,170	4,253	4,495	5,656	8,556	7,548

Source: Chao, *Capital Formation*, Table 20.

refers to the fixed investment in agriculture, forestry, and meteorology made under the state plan and financed by government appropriations. It presumably includes the construction of office buildings, warehouses, and other structures; the purchase of equipment, tractors, and other farm machines in agricultural research institutes; extension service stations; and other government organizations in these three fields.

To visualize the relative significance of individual items of investment, we may convert the data in Table 3.3 to annual per capita figures as follows:[9]

	Percentage distribution	*Annual per capita investment (yuan)*
Housing	37.8	4.15
Implements, carts, and livestock	22.2	2.44
Water conservation	13.7	1.51
Other imputed investment	16.6	1.83
Reclamation	4.6	0.51
State investment in agriculture, forestry, and meteorology	5.1	0.56
Total	100.0	11.00

Among the six items listed above, three—water conservation, reclamation, and state investment in agriculture, forestry, and meteorology—are expenditures of the government; they do not create a direct financial burden on farmers. For the remaining three items, the combined cash value is 8.42 yuan per person per year. Of this amount, investment in implements, carts, and livestock and in rural housing construction take the two largest shares. Even for these two items, the bulk of the investment represents annual depreciation, leaving little net capital formation. The housing item includes investments in rural residential construction and in office buildings, warehouses, and other structures collectively owned by agricultural cooperatives.[9] Using prewar data concerning the average value of residential housing per rural household and the price index between 1933 and 1952, Professor T. C. Liu has derived an average value of 750 yuan per household, or 150 yuan per person, for rural housing in 1952.[10] If an average life span of fifty years for housing is assumed, the annual depreciation of rural residential housing would be fifteen yuan per household or three yuan per person. The annual depreciation would be higher if the average life span of rural housing was actually shorter than fifty years.

Therefore, it is statistically evident that net capital formation was rather small in 1952–57, in spite of the magnitude of gross investment in fixed capital in the farm sector. Still smaller was the investment in modern farm equipment.

Since we lack quantitative information, the situation of fixed investment in the farm sector since 1958 is not too clear to us. During the Great Leap Forward years (1958–60), both total investment and investment in the farm sector are reported to have been augmented tremendously. However, as will be discussed in greater detail in the next few chapters, investment activities in the farm sector, such as water conservation construction, were largely fruitless. As an aftermath of the Great Leap Forward movement, the death rate of draft animals soared in 1960–63. All these factors should be considered as disinvestment in agriculture.

Beginning in 1961, Communist China entered a period of "economic readjustment, consolidation, filling out, and raising standards." The keynote of economic policy in that period was the assignment of the highest priority to agricultural production, with the primary emphasis on the supply of chemical fertilizers. Investment in fixed capital was not stressed, however. In all likelihood, fixed investment in the farm sector in 1961–65 was no larger than that of the First Five Year Plan period.

Every year agricultural production units need working capital to buy current inputs, but it is difficult to estimate the size of working capital and its annual increments. Prior to the cooperativization movement, working capital in the rural sector was in the hands of individual peasants; most of it was handled thereafter by cooperatives or communes. One 1954 Communist survey of more than 16,000 individual farm households in twenty-five provinces disclosed that each rural household spent an average of 62.6 yuan to purchase "means and materials of production."[11] It is not clear, however, what proportion of the 62.6 yuan was for the acquisition of fixed assets. According to another sample survey of 228 agricultural cooperatives, consisting of 76,749 households in twenty-four provinces, each household had 75 yuan of working capital at the end of 1956, and the amount had increased to 93 yuan by the end of 1957.[12] To state the figures on a per capita basis, they are 15 yuan for 1956 and 18.6 yuan for 1957. Apparently, there had been a considerable increase in rural working capital during those years.

There were four major sources from which the farmer or agricultural cooperative could obtain working capital: (1) funds supplied by peasants themselves and later on by cooperatives or communes, (2) credits extended by private concerns or rural credit cooperatives, (3) prepayments by the state to agricultural production units for the grains to be procured by the government, and (4) farm credits provided by the state.

Since an extensive credit system in rural China was not available, the preponderance of working capital was self-financed. However, the total amount probably did not rise appreciably until the farm sector was collectivized. Since 1956, a sizable investment in working capital has been made annually by cooperatives and communes from their own accumulated funds.

In prewar China, landlords and rural moneylenders supplied certain portions of the working capital needed by peasants. Credits of this type were curtailed during the land reform period; but they did not disappear completely until 1955–56.[13] To replace private lenders, the Communist government encouraged the organization of credit cooperatives in villages, and about 110,000 rural credit cooperatives had been formed by 1956.[14]

Another source of rural working capital in the Communist period has been the prepayments made by the procurement agencies to peasants or collective farms. The payments are usually made in the spring, and they are automatically settled when peasants or collective farms turn in grain or crash crops after the harvest. If the factor of procurement prices is ignored, these payments are equivalent to interest-free loans to agricultural producers. It is reported that a total of 2 billion yuan had been received by peasants and collective farms in the form of procurement prepayments from 1953 to 1957,[15] or about 0.76 yuan per year per capita. The total size of prepayments has not risen much year after year, because it is related to the procurement plan of the government.

Farm credits extended by the government to agricultural producers increased rapidly in the first decade of the Communist regime (see Table 3.4). But, they probably decreased in 1959–63 as a consequence of the deteriorated financial situation of the government during those crisis years. The total amount was restored to about 2 billion yuan in 1965, but this figure was still far below the level of 1956 and 1958.

Table 3.4 Farm Credits Made by the Government, 1950–65 (1,000 yuan)

Year	Total loans made in year (1)	Total loans outstanding, end of year (2)	Annual increase of (2) (3)
1950	212,410	94,900	
1951	401,470	204,820	109,920
1952	1,076,270	481,550	276,730
1953	1,263,980	666,180	184,630
1954	840,590	782,670	116,490
1955	1,004,130	1,000,670	218,000
1956	3,387,070	3,029,470	2,028,800
1957	1,504,200	3,580,990	551,520
1958	3,189,850		
1964	1,540,000		
1965	2,000,000		

Sources:
1950–57: *NTCY*, 1957, no. 19, p. 10; and *HHPYK*, 1958, no. 9, p. 81.
1958: *CKNP*, 1959, no. 19, p. 32.
1964 and 1965: *NCNA*, May 15, 1965.

In addition to being used as working capital, farm credits also went into other uses. One official source has provided a breakdown of those credits by use from 1953 to 1957.[16]

	Percentage distribution	*Amount (million yuan)*
Fixed assets	21.8	1,744
Working capital	43.1	3,448
Consumption	16.0	1,280
Relief	8.0	640
Others	11.1	888
Total	100.0	8,000

The credits for working capital were mostly used by the borrowers to finance purchases of chemical fertilizers. In view of the tremendous increase in the supply of chemical fertilizers in recent years, the proportion of such loans must be much larger now. When farm credits were used for fixed assets such as farm implements, draft animals, and so on, they were likely to be long-term loans. In 1956 in particular, the government furnished about 700 million yuan in credits to 40 million poor households to pay their capital shares when they joined cooperatives.[17] Farm credits for consumption and relief purposes were relatively small during the First Five Year Plan period, but such loans are believed to have constituted a more significant portion of total farm credits during the crisis years.

Research Organizations and Technical Personnel

As we mentioned in the first section of this chapter, the limited supply of qualified scientific personnel influenced the manner in which the Chinese Communist government chose to promote new farming technology. Following is a brief review of the situation in this aspect.

The number of agricultural research institutes and extension service stations has grown rapidly during the Communist era. However, because of their generally poor quality, the contribution and services of these organizations have not increased in proportion to their number. According to official counts, there were in 1957 the following numbers of institutions related to agricultural research in one way or another.[18]

Husbandry research organizations	821
Veterinary service stations	2,930
Animal breeding stations	1,300
Seed breeding stations	1,700
Demonstration farms	2,053
Plant protection organizations	360
Agricultural experiment stations	180
Agricultural middle schools	159

In addition, the number of large-scale agricultural research institutions rose from 5 in 1950 to 460 in 1958.[19] The total number of persons engaged in agricultural research, excluding the so-called research personnel in communes, was said to be about 10,000 in 1959,[20] and the number reached "several tens of thousands" by 1964.[21] It should be noted, however, that universities and colleges under the Chinese Communist education system have become more or less purely pedagogical in nature, and many of the new research organizations are actually those formerly attached to agricultural colleges.

During the period 1950–57, agricultural research institutions were regional organizations with localized interests. They did not specialize along one or two lines of research work. The Chinese Academy of Agricultural Sciences was founded in 1957 as the central organ to coordinate research work in various places. Established under this organization were many specialized research institutes to pursue such specific research work as breeding, soil studies, fertilizer experiments, and farm mechanization.[22]

The year 1958 witnessed a "great leap" in this field, too. Not only were numerous branches of the Chinese Academy of Agricultural Sciences founded, but also countless small research units were established under local authorities or in communes.[23] As one would expect, 1958 was also the year during which the quality of agricultural research in the country deteriorated seriously. Unrealistic and incredible research "findings" were fabricated and disseminated, thus confusing both the public and the government as to what was feasible and what was not.

We should point out here that agriculture is perhaps the only area in which China did not benefit from any Soviet technical assistance in the 1950s. Unlike its industrial production, the Soviet Union is a backward country agriculturally, and there is little that China could learn from the USSR. In fact, the Soviet Union has generally received technical aid from China. Since the Sino-Soviet technical cooperation agreement in the field of agriculture was signed in 1954, agricultural experts from the two nations have held nine conferences. China has supplied the Soviet Union with 62 items of agricultural materials (presumably research findings) and more than 2,500 varieties of seeds and seedlings. On the other hand, very little has been mentioned or documented in Chinese publications about adopting superior varieties from the Soviet Union except for one type of sunflower and one kind of winter wheat. Lysenko and another noted Soviet biologist visited China and gave a few lectures in 1952–53. However, it does not seem that their theories have gained wide reception among Chinese biologists and agricultural scientists, most of whom were educated in the West. The only traceable effects of Lysenko's theories on the Chinese farming techniques are "deep-plowing" and "close-planting."[24] These practices were strongly advocated, not by Chinese agriculturists but by Mao Tse-tung. However, these practices caused trouble in 1958 and were soon abandoned.

Extension service stations were not engaged in agricultural research work but were supposed to be responsible for the dissemination of new farming techniques. The numbers of stations and staff workers are officially given as follows:[25]

	Number of stations	*Number of staff*
1950	10	(not given)
1953	(not given)	28,000
1954	4,400	36,000
1957	13,669	95,000

The number of staff workers in extension service stations in 1964 is given as "more than 100,000."[26] The fact that 1964's number was only slightly larger than 1957's is believed to result from the changed attitude of the Chinese government in the early 1960s, when quantitative expansion was replaced by the promotion of the quality of existing units.

The most pressing problem in the development of agricultural research organizations and extension service stations has been the recruitment of qualified personnel. According to one estimate, 92,000 students graduated in China from institutions of higher learning in agriculture or forestry during 1949–63.[27] The total enrollment of agricultural middle schools in 1957 is given as 99,000, implying that approximately 20,000 students could be graduated annually thereafter.[28] However, most graduates of agricultural colleges and middle schools have been absorbed by agricultural administration offices at various levels in the government. Employment in the government agencies dealing with agricultural affairs reached 1 million in 1957; half of this number was completely detached from agricultural production or research.[29] On the other hand, extension service stations could hardly get qualified agriculturists to serve as staff. It was openly admitted that, to meet their staffing needs, agricultural extension service stations hired large numbers of persons who had been "laid off by other organizations but had no knowledge about agriculture" or who "were under fourteen or fifteen and did not have adequate common sense." People working in the stations "had no confidence in themselves," "did not know what to do," and "had no sense of security." In many cases they "forced the masses to adopt erroneous measures and techniques," which caused losses and public discontent.[30] One survey made in 1957 showed that only 5 percent of extension service station employees were college graduates, 31.7 percent were graduates of agricultural middle schools, and 63.3 percent had only an elementary school education or were from ordinary middle schools.[31] This article concluded:

In view of the low quality of cadres, those stations could make little contribution to the improvement of farm technology in our country. As a matter of fact, those cadres spent most of their time assisting local governments in administrative work.[32]

In the early 1960s, after the quality of their staff had improved and the policy of mandatory implementation of innovations had been abandoned, extension service stations began to play a more important role in the promotion of new farm technology. Members of those stations worked with farmers more closely and actively. In 1963, a number of farms were designated as demonstration plots in each locality, and about half the personnel of extension service stations was dispatched to those demonstration farms.[33] Each model farm served as a show window where farmers in the neighboring area might see and accept the usefulness of scientific knowledge concerning agricultural production. In addition to the demonstration farms, in recent years many farm technique promotion centers have been formed, and mobile teams consisting of agricultural specialists have been organized to help farmers solve technical problems on the spot. In sum, it was during the early 1960s that the technological policy for agricultural production was more or less normalized.

Chapter 4

Agricultural Mechanization and Improvement of Farm Implements

Agricultural Mechanization as A Policy Issue

The collectivization and mechanization of agriculture have been two controversial issues in Communist China, and they have aroused widely divergent opinions among top Party leaders. The two issues are closely related to each other. In the beginning, the focal point of the debate was whether the production of farm tractors should precede collectivization in the socialist transformation of agriculture or vice versa. Liu Shao-chi held the former view, while Mao Tse-tung and his supporters maintained the latter opinion.[1]

Many Communists in China, as well as in other countries, who have observed that agriculture in the Soviet Union was collectivized and "tractorized" simultaneously in the early 1930s, tend either to make tractors a symbol of socialist farming or to consider collectivization and the use of tractors as two indispensable elements in a socialist transformation of agriculture. However, Liu Shao-chi's contention seemed to be more sophisticated than the rather naive interpretation of the relationship between collectivization and mechanization. Although Liu's theory has never been disclosed in full detail, its essence can be deduced from statements of his critics. For instance, Wang Ssu-hua, one of the important decision-makers in Communist Chinese economic affairs, made the following comment in an article published in January 1956.

> But some people do not understand the correct relationship between agricultural mechanization and cooperativization. They think that cooperativization cannot be carried out without tractors. Only after industrialization is accomplished, they think, will it be possible to reequip our agricultural

production with farm machinery; and only then will it be possible to carry out complete collectivization of agriculture on a voluntary basis. That is to say, a socialist transformation of agriculture is impossible otherwise.[2]

Apparently, Liu tried to equate the availability of tractors and the voluntary participation of peasants in collective farms. In other words, his reasoning seemed to be: Collective farms which are not organized on a voluntary basis can hardly survive or are impossible, presumably because collective members will lack incentives. To organize collective farms on a voluntary basis, the government must demonstrate tangible advantages to entice peasants. The tractor is the only item that will serve this purpose satisfactorily. Logically, there cannot be a viable collective farming system before the government can supply farm tractors in large quantities.

In Mao's analysis, collectivization, with its large farms, should precede mechanization, because the former provides preconditions for the latter, not the other way round.[3] As for voluntary participation, in his view it was purely a matter of educating the peasants politically. Furthermore, Mao believed that there would be enough other substantial advantages besides the use of tractors in a collective farming system so that China could benefit from an early socialist transformation of agriculture without waiting for the mass production of tractors.

The whole debate in the early 1950s reflects some deep-rooted conceptual confusions among Chinese Communist leaders. These confusions can be traced back to the peculiar theory of production advanced by Marx and Engels, and the inconsistency therein. There are two misconceptions. The first involves the conditions of agricultural mechanization. The second is the belief that tractors and other farm machines can increase farm output, because these machines tend to increase labor productivity.

Having observed the enclosures in England and the advantages of large factories in industry, Marx had mixed feelings about the future trend of agriculture. On the one hand he vaguely visualized a certain superiority in large-scale agricultural production over the small peasant economy, and on the other hand he rejected the system of capitalist farms which existed at the expense of small landowners.[4] However, his reasoning in this connection was rather confusing. His assertion about the superiority of large-scale agricultural production does not necessarily indicate that he recognized "returns to scale." Theoretically, if Marx's one-factor theory of production, that is, the labor theory of value, is strictly and consistently followed, no increasing returns to scale should be admitted, just as Communists deny the law of diminishing returns. Therefore, when Engels came to examine the problem of farming efficiency, the emphasis shifted from the size of farms to the ownership system of land. A socialized farm is superior, as Engels put it in his *Anti-Duhring*, not because it is larger but because it is an institution "of a far higher and more developed form of possession which, far from being a hindrance to production, on the contrary for the first time frees production from all fetters and gives it the possibility of making full use of modern chemical discoveries and mechanical inventions."[5] The foundation of Engels's argument is a theory of the relationship between ownership systems and the "organic composition of capital," which is in fact a distorted way of presenting the problem of factor proportions in production. In other words, it is not the small size of peasant farms that is not conducive to the use of farm machines but the private ownership of land that makes landowners unwilling to adopt mechanized farming. As Engels saw it, the important difference between a peasant economy and socialized agriculture, or the true factor making the latter distinctly superior, is not a difference of degree (size) but a difference of kind (ownership).[6] After collective farms had been instituted in the Soviet Union, farms both large in size and using big tractors and other farm machines, the distinctions among the three concepts—the size of farms, the collective ownership system, and the superiority of mechanized farming—which are closely related but by no means identical, became blurred in the eyes of the Chinese Communists. Large tractors were taken as a symbol for them all. However, we find that some Chinese Communist economists still occasionally use Engels's interpretation in this connection. For instance, Wang Si-hua said:

> Socialist industry can supply agriculture with tractors and other modern farm machinery, which can greatly promote labor productivity. . . . Under the system of capitalism, private ownership of land prevents a wide employment of machines in agriculture, keeping a constantly low degree in the organic composition of capital in farm production.[7]

More important is the confusion between the rise in labor productivity and the increase in total output. Actually, it is natural for a loyal Communist to confuse these two concepts, because the labor theory of value recognizes only one productive factor. If labor were indeed the sole productive factor, a rise in labor productivity would be almost synonymous with an increase in total output. Yet the difference between the two concepts is a crucial point in the determination of technological policy for China's agriculture. One must ask first of all: Can mechanization really raise total farm output in China?

Although we do not know the details of Liu Shao-chi's theory in this connection, he must have had the same confusion when he asserted that the use of tractors could attract peasants to join collective farms voluntarily. Mao's position on this matter is unmistakably clear. He said in his famous article "The Question of Agricultural Cooperation" in 1955:

> In the first place, as everyone knows, the level of production of marketable grain and industrial raw materials in our country today is very low, whereas the state's demand for these items grows year by year. Therein lies a sharp contradiction. If, in a period of roughly three five-year plans, we cannot fundamentally solve the problem of agricultural cooperation, if we cannot jump from small-scale farming with animal-drawn farm implements to large-scale farming with machinery, . . . we shall fail to resolve the contradiction between the ever-increasing demand for marketable grain and industrial raw materials and the present generally poor yield of staple crops.[8]

Obviously Mao envisaged the mechanization of large-scale farming as having the important effect of increasing crop yields, and collectivization was to pave the road for mechanization which would eventually solve the problem of agricultural production in China.

A new theory then came to challenge this viewpoint of Mao, and the whole debate shifted to a new angle. The new argument, held by a number of people who are both pragmatic and familiar with modern economics based on multiple production factors, revolved around the following facts: Modern farming technology has different impacts on the productivity of various inputs. In carrying out the technological transformation of its traditional agriculture, a country must select the appropriate measures according to its factor endowment. The guiding principle is that a country should choose measures capable of raising the productivity of inputs that are in limited supply, not the productivity of inputs whose supplies are fairly elastic. Mechanization is believed to have the primary function of saving labor. Mechanization is a correct measure in a country where labor is the limiting factor in agriculture, because, after farm labor productivity is increased, the superfluous farm labor can then be used to reclaim more land or be transferred to industrial production. On the contrary, in a country like China, where the limiting factor in agriculture is the amount of arable land and there is a surplus of labor, increasing labor productivity through mechanization only creates more unused labor and has little effect on total farm output. A better approach under these circumstances should be to raise the productivity of land, that is, to increase the yield per unit of land.

The argument against agricultural mechanization, based on the factor proportion, was reinforced by the fact that China in the 1950s had a serious natural deficiency in petroleum reserves. The high price of petroleum products made the large-scale employment of tractors and other farm machines using fuel oil uneconomical.

Po I-po was later identified as the chief advocate of this contention. He is reported to have prepared, sometime in the mid-1950s, a long document to be circulated within the Party and the government. In that document he demonstrated that mechanizing agriculture in a labor surplus country would be completely senseless.[9] This negative attitude challenged the opinions of both Liu and Mao. There are indications that Liu, a relatively flexible technocrat, was soon convinced by Po's advocating an indefinite postponement of agricultural mechanization. Mao, however, was unyielding. The opposition to agricultural mechanization, right or wrong, was based on certain real factors and technical considerations, hence could hardly be refuted on purely ideological grounds. Thus, in 1956 surveys were ordered by the Party's "central responsible comrades" to find answers to the following questions:[10]

1. Can mechanization increase crop yields per unit of land?
2. Can farm machines be used in an intensive farming system?
3. Is the system of tractor stations the appropriate way to mechanize Chinese agriculture?
4. To the extent that mechanization can raise crop yields, will the increase in output offset the higher cost of using machinery? That is, can mechanization raise both output and the net income of farms?

Conclusions derived from the surveys reconciled the views held by both sides. The whole situation was summarized in an article by Huang Ching, then the director of the State Technology Commission, who was responsible for important technical policies in Communist China:

> The chief avenue of promoting agriculture production in our country is to raise yields per unit of farmland. Therefore, reclamation is of secondary importance. The methods of raising yields are: fertilization, irrigation, intensive farming, double-cropping, seed selection, shifting from low-yield to high-yield crops, and preventing damages of pests and natural calamities. Their contributions have been affirmatively recognized. However, with regard

to the problems of mechanizing farm implements and the utilization of mechanical power in our agriculture, our understanding has changed back and forth twice. Prior to 1956, we had only a general understanding that technological transformation of agriculture in China must be conducted on the foundation of a social reform. We learned superficially from the situation of agricultural mechanization in the USSR and the USA, and sweepingly thought that mechanization could raise labor productivity as well as crop yields, hence it should be one of the main directions of the technological transformation of our agriculture. . . .

During the high tide of economic construction in 1956, we began to ponder the fact that our agriculture is basically characterized by having too many people but not enough land. In the USSR and the USA, both sparsely populated, there is a shortage of labor in agriculture, consequently, the substitution of machinery for human labor has raised labor productivity, enabled the expansion of cultivated areas, and resulted in substantial increases in output and faster accumulation of capital. Our country is different. Although the territory is large, both cultivated land and reclaimable land are extremely limited. Moreover, there is a large population. Under these circumstances, the necessary approaches to raise agricultural production would be intensified farming and some other complex measures. Furthermore, most foreign farm machines are only suitable for cultivation in dry land and in large fields on plains; and those machines use petroleum as fuel. Yet, the natural resource features in our country, such as the dominance of paddy fields, small plots, and hilly lands, and the inadequacy of petroleum, would require new types of farm machines. . . . All these tell us that, to carry out a technological transformation of our agriculture, we should absorb the advanced experience of other countries as well as pay attention to the special features of our own country. In other words, we should seek our own road . . . with the emphasis on the increase of crop yields. However, there has occurred a new biased view in this period concerning the speed and scope of agricultural mechanization: taking mechanization and the principle of raising unit yields as two contradictory things. Those people hold that if the chief function of agricultural mechanization is to increase labor productivity, there cannot be any significantly favorable effect on unit yields. . . . The results would be more labor surpluses and more waste of investment.

Recently, we have organized a group of cadres and technicians and sent them to villages for field surveys. We have also talked with people in the agricultural and water conservation departments. We begin to understand the true conditions in the countryside, which are quite different from what we used to think. Chairman Mao's instructions concerning agricultural mechanization have enabled us to understand this problem more clearly and to realize that our previous thought was erroneous.[11]

According to those survey reports, farm machines did have a positive effect on output; however, the favorable effect was not reflected in higher yields per unit but came rather indirectly. As a result of the rapid rise in the double-cropping index, demands for labor and draft animals per unit of farmland had risen sharply, and shortages of manpower and draft animals occurred during the busy seasons. The conversion from a one-crop system to a double-crop system in the northern plains had created two peak-load periods per year for agricultural labor during about twenty days between the harvesting of wheat and the sowing of fall crops and about forty days between the harvesting of fall crops and the sowing of winter wheat. The peak-load demands for labor were even more serious in the double-cropping rice areas where a great portion of yearly farm activities was concentrated in a short period of ten to twenty days. This meant that while China was still a labor-surplus country in a general sense, there existed seasonal agricultural labor shortages. This bottleneck limited the further promotion of double or multiple cropping practice. The use of machinery might solve this problem, thus making it possible to extend the double or multiple cropping system to a wider area. In other words, mechanization in China might increase farm output not through higher yields per unit but through a higher double-cropping index.

Certain direct contributions of farm machines to higher crop yields have been cited, too, in some survey reports.[12] Tractors can plow deeper than manual operations, and sowing machines sow more evenly. These factors would make closer planting possible, which in turn might lead to higher unit yields.

These survey reports came too late for the Chinese planners to incorporate an agricultural mechanization program into the First Five Year Plan. Even in the draft of the National Program for Agricultural Development, 1956–67, which was formulated in January 1956, little mention was made of agricultural mechanization. Except in state farms where imported tractors were employed for land reclamation, the policy was to "reform and improve" traditional farm implements as a transitional step toward mechanization.[13] However, attempts were made in this period to set up experimental tractor stations in selected localities in North China.[14]

The survey results were utilized by the State Technology Commission to determine the direction of future agricultural mechanization, and the following specific points were included:[15]

1. Requirements of farm machines in various areas were to be de-

termined according to population densities. In North and East China, the urgent need was to mechanize irrigation systems. Cultivating machinery was required in the areas with intensive multiple cropping.

2. Requirements were to be determined also according to local climatic conditions. For instance, while North China needed drilling equipment to dig more wells, the southern regions needed equipment for drainage.

3. Farm machinery should meet local soil conditions. Ordinary tractors could not work in paddy fields because they sank or skidded in the mud. Efficient transplanters for rice culture were urgently needed.

4. New machinery should be developed to fit some special cropping systems in China.

5. Special attention should be given to the utilization of local energy resources such as water and wind power and solid fuel.

Generally speaking, in 1956–57 and the early part of 1958, the State Technology Commission merely attempted to temporize with Mao. Basically it still regarded agricultural mechanization as a target for the remote future but with a low priority at the present moment.[16] The improvement of implements was considered more important.

A turning point came in 1958. In that year Mao's personal influence reached its peak. In addition, there emerged a new element in favor of an acceleration of mechanization. China suddenly suffered acute labor shortages over the whole country, as a result of the Great Leap Forward movement which employed a tremendous labor force in the mass construction of water conservation projects and backyard furnaces to produce steel.[17] It was estimated that the nine northern provinces were short of labor by 50 percent generally and by as much as two-thirds in some localities in that year.[18] Although the production of new farm implements was greatly speeded up, the labor shortage in the rural sector was not substantially relieved. To achieve the even more ambitious goals set for agricultural production in 1959, a total of 65 billion man-days would be required, with the anticipated availability of only 33 billion man-days.[19]

In seeking a solution to the problem, Mao reiterated more emphatically the importance of complete mechanization. Obsessed by the "leap forward" psychology, he insisted that China could and must accomplish this goal ahead of schedule. After all, the process of collectivization had been greatly accelerated in 1956–57, and it had jumped once more by an even bigger stride into the commune stage in 1958.

Consequently, a special conference was held in December 1958 to plan for "agricultural mechanization and electrification over the whole country";[20] and an entirely new and ambitious program, drafted in 1959, called for thorough mechanization in the next ten years.[21] It was anticipated that by the end of the ten-year period China would have 1.5 to 2 million tractors which would release 60 percent of the rural labor force for use in nonagricultural production. To implement the new plan, the Ministry of Agricultural Machinery was established in August 1959.

Mao's leadership diminished after the Great Leap collapsed in 1960. Many of his policies were reversed by the group of technocrats who gained control in the government. The program of agricultural mechanization was reexamined also. Many articles appearing in the period 1961–65 expressed more or less skeptical views of making mechanization the chief means to develop China's agriculture. However, the production of tractors continued at a fairly high level for an entirely different reason. As a result of the Great Leap and the formation of communes, large numbers of draft animals had died from overwork, lack of care, or malnutrition. Like the Soviet Union immediately after its collectivization in the early 1930s, China urgently needed tractors to replace the lost draft animals, at least as a short-run measure.

When economic recovery was under way and the number of draft animals was gradually augmented, tractor production began to slow down, thus reflecting the reserved attitude of the Chinese technocrats.[22] Later in 1964–65, the focus of farm machine production was shifted to small garden tractors and other machinery for paddy fields.

However, there are indications that Mao's mechanization policy formulated in 1959 may have been reinstated after he gained the upper hand in the 1966–68 power struggle.[23]

As for research work on agricultural machines, in 1957 there were thirty research organizations, with a staff of about three hundred, devoted to studying farm machines.[24] These institutions belonged either to the central government or to various provincial authorities. In 1959 Mao Tse-tung applied his favorite "mass line" to this field and urged each hsien government to establish its own farm machine research bureau. As a result, a total of 600 to 700 research bureaus mushroomed over the country. However, just as the failure of Mao's "walking with two legs" policy applied to other fields, these small research units proved to be unsuccessful. Most of them were either abolished or were merged later into larger units in the economic retrenchment period.[25]

In the following sections we shall study the actual performance of Communist China in improving farm implements and using tractors, the two major aspects in modernizing China's agriculture.

Improvement of Farm Implements

The policy of improving traditional farm tools has been less disputed in China than has outright mechanization. Up to 1959 most planners accepted it as a realistic and promising approach and envisioned it as a necessary step toward thorough mechanization in the rural sector. As a matter of fact, in the draft of the First Five Year Plan, finalized and published in 1955, it was popularization of improved or new implements rather than mechanization that was recorded as a part of the agricultural plan. However, there are few quantitative data available to us, even for the mid-1950s, for an analysis or assessment of the achievements of Communist China in this aspect. The scarcity of statistics has in part stemmed from the difficulty of classification for statistical purposes. There is an exceedingly wide variety of farming implements, tools for processing farm products, and rural transportation means that have been or could be improved in a number of ways. The designations of published statistics in this category were often vague and confusing, and the Chinese official sources usually did not give precise definitions of the terms used. Table 4.1 shows the progress in improving farm implements, on the basis of the quantitative information we have gathered.

The task of improving farm implements included: (1) the improvement of implements, manual and animal-drawn, traditionally used by Chinese peasants; (2) the introduction of foreign designs of farm tools that have been proven more efficient than Chinese traditional ones; and (3) the production of implements complementary to farm machines, such as machine-drawn plows. Of course, the various aspects have not been given equal weight, and the emphasis has shifted from time to time.

At the outset of the regime, the attention of the government was focused on supplying traditional implements to peasants to replace those lost during wartime. A total of 59 million pieces is reported to have been added in the period 1950–53. At the same time, experimental work was conducted and stations were established to demonstrate and popularize new or improved tools.[26] Since most of the new implements introduced at that time were designed for farming operations in dry and level fields, these experimental stations were located only in the northern provinces.

Table 4.1 Improved Farm Implements in Use, 1953–64 (1,000 units)

Type of implement	1953	1954	1956	1957	1958	1959	1960	1964
All improved implements	*690*			*4,680*	*350,000*			
Semimechanized implements							10,000	30,000
Improved animal-drawn implements	690			4,680				
Two-wheeled share plows	510	40	1,547	1,622		1,700		
Other types of improved plows			1,930	1,973				
Rakes			63	76				
Seeders			48	56				
Rollers	30		28	36				
Intertiller weeders			130	319				
Harvesters				20				
Threshers				318				
Processing implements	150			258				

Sources:
1953: *HHYP*, 1955, no. 4, p. 134.
1954: *CKNP*, 1958, no. 3, p. 8.
1956: *CCYC*, 1958, no. 2, p. 3.
1957: *CKNP*, 1958, no. 3, p. 8.
1958: *CCYC*, 1959, no. 3, p. 42.
1959: *CKNP*, 1960, no. 1, p. 2.
1960: *CKNP*, 1965, no. 2, p. 2.
1964: *JMJP*, Oct. 15, 1964.

The central task during this stage was the improvement of animal-drawn implements or the introduction of new ones, especially those for plowing. For this reason, the chief item selected for popularization was the Soviet two-wheeled share plow. This term was used by Chinese Communists to describe both two-wheeled two-share plows and two-wheeled one-share plows.[27] Their merit, when compared with the Chinese traditional plows, had been confirmed by field tests.[28] However, they also displayed certain defects when used under the peculiar conditions then existing on Chinese farms. The two-wheeled share plow was too heavy to be drawn by one ox or buffalo. To draw it, a team of two oxen or buffaloes must be used, side by side, to supply enough draft power. Unfortunately, Chinese draft animals had not been trained to work as a team. Because of its heavy weight, this plow could hardly be employed in paddy fields with soft bottoms or on hilly land with steep slopes. The passages between fields usually were not wide enough for moving such bulky instruments. Finally, the price of two-wheeled share plows was still beyond the financial means of most Chinese peasants. But these drawbacks were not too serious when the new plows were used in the plains in North China. Therefore, about 40,000 had been sold to farmers by 1954.

Realizing that large-scale mechanization at that time was still a remote possibility in China and that a feasible alternative to raise agricultural labor productivity and farm output would be the use of the new plows on a large scale, and in view of the fact that Chinese peasants were gradually being organized into mutual-aid teams and cooperatives to provide better conditions for the use of these new plows, the Party Central Committee resolved in 1954 to promote two-wheeled share plows in a much wider area. A "Conference on the Work of New Animal-Drawn Farm Implements" was held in July of that year, with participating representatives from the Ministry of Agriculture, the First Ministry of Machine-Building, and the network of rural commerce. A plan was made for the mass production of these plows. Their price was to be reduced 40 percent by setting lower railway freight rates, by exempting them from certain sales taxes, by and limiting the sellers' profit margin to 1 percent.[29] This promotion plan did not encounter any serious resistance in the beginning. As shown in Table 4.2, both output and sales of two-wheeled share plows sharply increased during 1954 and 1955.

A turning point came during the latter part of 1955 when Mao Tse-tung silenced dissentient voices in the Party and forcefully raised the acceleration rate of the cooperativization movement. This institutional

Table 4.2 Production and Sales of Two-Wheeled Share Plows, 1952–58 (1,000 units)

Year	Production	Sales
1952	5	1
1953	3	15
1954	60	23
1955	524	426
1956	1793	1086
1957	1800	95
1958	0	628

Sources:
Production: Kang Chao, *The Rate and Pattern of Industrial Growth in Communist China* (Ann Arbor, Michigan, 1965), pp. 122, 128.
Sales: *TGY*, p. 171.

change in the rural sector made some planners overoptimistic about the possibilities for the use of the new plows. They tended to believe that the crucial barrier was financial, that is, the inability of individual peasants to pay for them, and once the peasants were organized into larger production units, this barrier would no longer exist. Consequently, the "National Agricultural Development Program for 1956–67," as promulgated in January 1956, set a production target of 6 million plows in the next three to five years.[30] The annual goal for 1956 was 2.36 million.[31] However, because of bottlenecks in production, only 1,793,000 plows were actually produced in that year. Of this number only 60 percent, or 1,086,000, were sold to agricultural cooperatives; the remainder simply stockpiled. Yet Chinese planners, who were under the pressure of Mao's imperative demand and were influenced by their own overoptimism, did not heed the warning. Despite the enormous stockpile, the Peking government set an even higher target for 1957—4 million.[32] Soon stark reality compelled the government to scale down the production target, and by the end of 1957 only 1.8 million plows had actually been produced. Tragically, only 95,000 units, or slightly over 5 percent of that year's output, were sold. Many of the plows sold to peasants or cooperatives were returned later to the selling agencies because they were unsuited to local conditions.[33]

The production of two-wheeled share plows was discontinued in 1958, and new efforts were made to dispose of the huge stockpiles. All possible means were mobilized to convince Chinese peasants and cooperative managers of the advantages of the plows and to teach them how to avoid or remedy the drawbacks. As Liao Lu-yen, then Minister of Agriculture, put it, one of the central tasks of his ministry in 1958 was to restore the reputation of the two-wheeled share plow.[34]

In 1958 the tragic episode of two-wheeled share plows was terminated, and a new phase was opened in the process of modernizing farm tools in China. In 1958 and 1959, the whole of China was suddenly plagued by an unprecedentedly acute labor shortage resulting from the "great leap forward" movement. In spite of the bitter experience with new plows, modernization of farm tools was the only feasible solution to shortage of rural labor until China could produce farm machines in large quantities. The new approach adopted at this time was the installation of ball bearings in traditional farm tools. The central government issued a directive, in August 1958, instructing that "all districts in the country must reform farm implements before the end of the year" by installing ball bearings in all turning joints.[35] Such farm tools were called "semimechanized" implements.[36]

Another aspect of the program was the introduction and popularization of new implements for farm operations in paddy fields, because they were an area absorbing too much labor. A new cable-drawn plow was designed especially for use in paddy land. In field tests it was reportedly quite successful. Consequently, the Party Central Committee ordered that these plows be put in use in every single agricultural cooperative or production brigade within one month.[37] The government was less certain in the beginning about the value of the newly invented transplanters. Large-scale production and application of transplanters was finally decided upon by the government in early 1960, after seven national conferences had been held for the specific purpose of examining and evaluating this new tool.

It is reported that by 1960 there were 10 million units of semi-mechanized farm implements in the whole rural sector, and another 20 million units had been produced in the period 1960–64, bringing the total stock of implements in this category to 30 million units in 1964.[38] Production of machine-drawn implements has also been accelerated since 1959 to cope with the enlarged scale of mechanization. The total quantity of machine-drawn implements existing in 1965 was said to be 4.3 times that of 1956.[39]

Another sign of progress was the great variety of implements that were improved. In 1957 there were only thirteen major items of improved implements,[40] whereas the number rose to sixty in 1964.[41] There are indications that since 1960 attention has gradually shifted from implements for field operations to the improvement of native means of transportation and to tools for processing farm products. For example, millions of small wheelbarrows equipped with rubber tires are produced and sold each year.[42]

With the scanty information available, it is difficult for us to assess the economic gains accomplished by the Chinese Communist government in the past years through their drives to modernize farm implements. It is probably true that all the so-called improved implements do have labor-saving effects of varying degrees. But it is difficult to know how much of the labor saved had contributed to increased output in other production lines. In discussing the new and improved farm implements, official sources have never failed to cite their advantages in directly raising unit yields, the primary concern of the Chinese farmers. The validity of those reports is, however, doubtful. Favorable effects on yields could result from other inputs which were simultaneously increased at the time of adopting new implements.

Among all new and improved implements introduced by the government, the new plows were least successful. A total of 180 million mou of farmland were cultivated by the new plows in 1956. The amount rose to 200 million mou in 1957 and to 240 million mou in 1960.[43] The last figure accounts for about 15 percent of the farmland in mainland China.

After 1959, the program of modernizing farm implements was somewhat overshadowed by mechanization. However, any objective analysis would undoubtedly show that, in the short run, improving farm implements remains preferrable to large-scale, outright mechanization. It entails a smaller investment and less technological know-how to produce simple implements. And the wider variety of them can better meet the diversified needs stemming from China's complex farming system. It is probably because of this realistic consideration that Chinese planners changed their priority order once more in 1964. In that year, a "National Conference on the Work of Semimechanized Farm Implements" was held,[44] and the higher priority of "farm implement reform" over mechanization in the near future was reestablished.

Tractors

Production

In this section we shall review the use and production of farm tractors in China—an important item in the program of mechanizing agriculture in that country. Production of tractors in China did not begin until 1958. There were 401 tractor units when the Communists came to power in 1949,[45] and the number rose to 24,629 standard units by the end of 1957. All tractors added in this period were imported. In the First Five Year Plan period (1953–57), fifty-four types of tractors had been brought in from twelve countries. The most popular types were the Stalin-80 (93 hp), the DT-54 (54 hp), and the DT-35 (37 hp), all Soviet-built.

Construction of the first Chinese tractor factory began in September 1955 in Loyang, Honan Province. It was completed in 1958 and went into full operation in November of the following year. This factory was one of the 156 Soviet-aided major projects under construction in the First Five Year Plan period, and it has a designed production capacity of 54,000 standard units. In 1958 China started building several smaller plants in other cities to manufacture tractors, and a few other machine workshops were converted for this purpose. The total number of tractor plants was twelve in that year, and it rose rapidly to more than two hundred by the end of 1962. The Ministry of Agricultural Machinery was formed in 1959, and it was in charge of large tractor factories and other agricultural machine manufacturers. Small plants were placed under the jurisdiction of provincial and local governments.[46]

The numbers of tractors produced in China in various years are given in Table 4.3, in standard units. In 1958 the Loyang First Tractor Factory began trial production, and the output of tractors quickly jumped to the peak level of 24,800 units in 1960.[47] But it declined by about 40 percent during the next year. To a large extent the precipitous reduction was attributable to the curtailed imports of quality steel and petroleum fuels from the Soviet Union, after the rift between the two countries was brought into the open in the summer of 1960.

The output of tractors resumed an upward trend after 1961–62, but at a slower rate, reflecting in part the continued existence of the aforementioned problems and in part the changed attitude of the government. The persons responsible for the "economic adjustment" policy deemed that, after the urgent need for tractors to replace the lost animal power had been met, further expansion of tractor production should be slowed down.

After 1961 an increasing portion of the current output of tractors was used to replace worn-out units.[48] As can be seen in Table 4.3, the stock of tractors in China rose by only 27,100 units from 1962 to 1965, far short of the cumulative total output in the three years.[49] The output in 1966 is estimated to be over 25,000 units.[50]

Up to 1964, tractor production in China was proceeding uncertainly along the line of selecting models to fit the needs of Chinese agriculture. What actually was produced in those years was a few copies of foreign models. They were primarily heavy types ranging from 24 to 93 hp. By the end of 1962, about 120 new models of tractors had been produced in various plants; but most of them had to be tested before mass production could be ordered. Finally, eight production models were selected by the Ministry of Agricultural Machinery in 1964:[51]

1. Tung-fang-hung 54: A model imitating the Soviet DT-54, a two-caterpillar model.
2. Tung-fang-hung 75: A caterpillar type, adapted from the Tung-

Table 4.3 Farm Tractors in Communist China, 1952–65 (standard units)

Year	Tractors produced	Tractors in use
1952	0	2,006
1953	0	2,719
1954	0	5,061
1955	0	8,094
1956	0	19,367
1957	0	24,629
1958	957	45,330
1959	5,598	59,000
1960	24,800	79,000
1961	15,200	90,000
1962	14,800	103,400
1963	17,800	115,000
1964	21,900	123,000
1965		130,500

Sources:

Tractors produced:

1952–58: *TGY*, p. 98.

1959: *JMJP*, Apr. 11, 1960.

1960: *KTTH*, 1961, no. 16, p. 20. It is confirmed by *CKCNP* (Mar. 12, 1961) which says that the output of tractors in 1960 was 4.25 times that of 1959.

1961: In 1960–61, 40,000 tractors were produced (*KJJP*, Jan. 18, 1962). From this number we subtract the 1960 figure to derive the output for 1961.

1962: In 1961–62, 30,000 units were produced (*CKHW*, Sept. 13, 1963). From this quantity we subtract the 1961 figure to obtain the 1962 output.

1963: The output of tractors increased 20 percent in 1963. See *PR*, Mar. 13, 1964, p. 9; and *CKHW*, Aug. 14, 1964.

1964: In the first eight months of 1964, the output of tractors increased 23 percent from the corresponding figure for 1963. We assume the rate of increase for the year 1964 was about the same (*NCNA*, Sept. 26, 1964).

Tractors in use:

1952–58: *TGY*, p. 135.

1959: *JMJP*, Feb. 16, 1960.

1960: *JMJP*, Jan. 14, 1961.

1961: *China Monthly*, no. 579 (1964), p. 8.

1962: *CCTP*, Oct. 1, 1963.

1963: *CKHW*, Sept. 23, 1964; and *HKWHP*, Jan. 6, 1964.

1964: *JMJP*, Dec. 31, 1964.

1965: *JMJP*, Apr. 13, 1966.

fang-hung 54 model, with greater power and higher speed, capable of plowing fourteen mou an hour.

3. Tung-fang-hung 28: A wheeled model specially designed for use in cotton and corn fields, with a maximum speed of 25 kilometers per hour.
4. Hung-chi 100: The largest model designed by the Chinese, mainly for reclamation and other earth work, caterpillar type, adapted from the Soviet model Stalin-80.
5. Tieh-niu 40
6. Hung-ho 37
7. Feng-shou 35: Specially designed for paddy fields in South China, weighing one and a half tons, with excellent maneuverability and able to plow a field as small as three to five mous.
8. Kung-nung 7: A hand-drawn garden type for vegetable fields, orchards, and terraced land.

The number stated in each model indicates its maximum horsepower. The last is a small garden cultivator, whereas the other seven models are large- and medium-sized caterpillar tractors or medium-sized wheeled tractors. Some of them are designed to be multipurpose. However, for some technical reasons, only six of the eight chosen models were actually put into production in 1965 on a regular basis.[52] Among the six models, the garden type, 7 hp, hand-pushed tractor has attracted special attention, because it can be easily and efficiently used in small plots as well as in paddy fields. The technique of manufacture is simple enough for small tractor factories. After the trial production of this model, a special team of experts was assigned by the central government to examine its quality and usability, and a large number were distributed to various localities for field tests. Mass production began in 1964. In the first eight months of 1965, its output increased five and a half times the 1964 production figures.[53] Another three-fold increase was reported in 1966.[54]

Ownership and Management

There have been three types of tractor ownership in China—by state farms, by agricultural machine stations, and by agricultural cooperatives or communes and research institutions. Table 4.4 shows the distribution of tractors under the three ownership systems.

State farms were the most important users of tractors in the early years. Those farms, especially the large ones directly subordinate to the central government, were organized as new settlements in sparsely

Table 4.4 Distribution of Farm Tractors by Ownership, 1949–65
(standard units, 15 hp each)

Year	Total number in use	Owned by state farms	Owned by agricultural machine stations	Owned by agricultural cooperatives or communes, and research institutions
1949	401	401	0	0
1950	1,286	1,160	30	96
1951	1,410		30	
1952	2,006	1,745	30	231
1953	2,719	1,801	68	850
1954	5,061	2,766	778	1,517
1955	8,094	4,036	2,363	1,695
1956	19,367	7,243	9,862	2,262
1957	24,629	10,177	12,036	2,416
1958	45,330	16,955	10,995	17,380
1959	59,000	21,000	17,300	20,700
1960	79,000			
1961	90,000			
1962	103,400			
1963	115,000	34,000	68,040	12,960
1964	123,000	39,400	71,500	12,100
1965	130,500	40,000	79,300	11,200

Note: Most figures here refer to year-end numbers.

Sources:

Total number of tractors in use: From Table 4.3.

Tractors owned by state farms:

1949, 1957, and 1958: *TGY*, p. 134.

1950: *SSB Communique, 1955.*

1952–56: *CKNK*, 1957, no. 4, p. 24.

1959: *CKNK*, 1959, no. 14, p. 3.

1963: *JMJP*, Sept. 19, 1964.

1964: *SCMM*, 1964, no. 451.

1965: According to *JMJP* (Apr. 13, 1966), the total number of tractors owned by state farms and agricultural machine stations in 1965 was 6.96 times that in 1956. This gives a quantity of 119,300 units. Since there was a considerable increase in the number of agricultural machine stations in 1965 (from 1488 to 2263), whereas the number of state farms did not increase, we assume that virtually all the increase in the number of tractors in 1965 took place in agricultural machine stations. In other words, it is assumed that state farms only replaced their worn-out tractors, with the number of tractors in use approximately unchanged in 1965.

Tractors owned by agricultural machine stations:

1950: *JMJP*, May 10, 1950.

1951–53: There was no increase until 1953. See *HHYP*, 1954, no. 11, p. 6.

Continued following page

Sources for Table 4.4, continued

1954: *SSB Communique, 1954.*
1955: *CKNP*, 1956, no. 8, p. 10.
1956: *SSB Communique, 1956.*
1957: *CKNP*, 1958, no. 3, p. 10.
1958: *NYCH*, 1959, no. 1, p. 5.
1959: There were 383 AMS in 1957 (*CKNK*, 1958, no. 2, p. 1), and the number rose to 553 in 1959 (*CKNP*, 1959, no. 19, p. 32). We use the average number of tractors in those stations in 1957 (31.4 units) to estimate the total number of tractors owned by AMS in 1959.
1963: *NCNA*, Jan. 5, 1964.
1964: Obtained by subtracting from the total number of tractors in use the number of tractors owned by state farms, communes, and research institutions.
1965: As explained in no. 2, 1965, above.

Tractors owned by agricultural cooperatives, communes, and research institutions.

1949–57, 1959, and 1965: The difference between the total number of tractors in use and the number of tractors owned by state farms and AMS.
1958: Derived in the same manner. Many AMS sold their tractors to communes in 1958, and some communes also bought tractors directly from the manufacturers. According to *NYCH*, 1959, no. 1, p. 5, communes had bought altogether 15,102 standard tractor units in 1958. This suggests that about 2,280 tractor units belonged to research organizations or other government agencies in 1958.
1963 and 1964: Estimated from the 1965 figure and the annual scrapping of about 900 units.

populated frontier areas. They needed relatively heavy caterpillar tractors for large-scale land reclamation, contouring, or cultivating operations on dry land. Since only small quantities of tractors were imported each year in the early 1950s, their use was concentrated in a handful of so-called state mechanized farms. (See Tables 4.5 and 4.6.) The use of tractors was gradually extended to other state farms after 1955. In terms of cultivated area, state farms expanded rapidly until 1958, and they began to decline thereafter as the government halted reclamation activities during the years of economic crisis. But the government continued to supply, until 1963, new tractors to those farms which did not possess enough units. In a relative sense, the importance of state farms as users of tractors has declined. Prior to 1953 they owned almost 90 percent of the tractors, but the percentage declined to less than 30 percent after 1964. Tractors on state farms are managed by and used on those farms. Occasionally, the tractors may serve cooperatives or communes in neighboring areas on a contract basis.

Table 4.5 shows that the agricultural machine stations (hereafter called AMS) enjoyed a steady expansion except in 1958–59. The AMS were originally called tractor stations; they changed to the present name some

Table 4.5 Development of Agricultural Machine Stations, 1950–65

Year	Number of stations	Tractors owned (standard units)
1950	1	30
1951	1	30
1952	1	30
1953	11	68
1954	89	778
1955	138	2,363
1956	326	9,862
1957	383	12,036
1958		10,995
1959	553	17,300
1963	1,482	68,040
1964	1,488	71,500
1965	2,263	79,300

Sources:
Number of stations:
1950: *JMJP*, May 10, 1950.
1951–53: *HHYP*, 1954, no. 62, p. 152.
1954: *HHYP*, 1955, no. 8, p. 24.
1955: *CKNP*, 1957, no. 14, p. 8.
1956: *SSB Communique, 1956.*
1957: *CKNK*, 1958, no. 2, p. 1.
1959: *CKNP*, 1959, no. 19, p. 32.
1963: *NCNA*, Jan. 5, 1964.
1964: *JMJP*, Aug. 31, 1965.
1965: *JMJP*, Apr. 13, 1966.
Tractors owned: From Table 4.4.

time after 1959, presumably because of a widening of functions. Patterned after the Soviet tractor machine stations, the first of the Chinese AMS was formed in 1950 in the suburb of Shenyang, Liaoning Province, mainly to serve the farms run by various government offices in that area.[55] The early AMS were no more than an experiment. Their rapid development came only after the Party's Central Committee decided in 1955 to accelerate agricultural cooperativization. A conference was held in early 1956 to draw up plans for the expansion of the AMS system,[56] and as a result, their number rose from 138 in 1955 to 325 in 1956, and the number of tractors owned increased from 2,363 to 9,350 standard units. In 1965 there were 2,263 AMS in 1,300 hsien,[57] that is, in about 70 percent of the hsien in China.

The AMS have no farmland of their own and only sell services to

Table 4.6 Development of State Mechanized Farms

Year	Number of farms	Tractors in use (standard units)	Cultivated area (1,000 mou)
1950	36	1,160	1,340
1952	50	1,532	2,036
1953	59	1,627	2,120
1954	97	2,235	2,782
1955	106	2,839	4,040
1956	166	4,422	

Note: Statistics include mechanized farms operated by central and local governments.

Sources:
1950–55: *SSB Communique, 1955.*
1956: *SSB Communique*, 1956.

collective farms or communes on a fee basis. The functions of the AMS were formerly confined to plowing and raking. But later on, when equipped with additional types of farm machines, the AMS began to undertake other field operations and processing jobs. In measuring work volume and setting customer fees, the AMS converts all operations to a standard unit of work volume which is equivalent to plowing a unit of ordinary farmland.[58]

In the beginning of the AMS system, management responsibility was in the jurisdiction of provincial governments. Some of the stations were later transferred to hsien or city governments.[59] In 1957, when the USSR abolished her tractor machine stations and sold the tractors to collective farms, the Chinese reviewed the administrative system of the AMS. Most opinion favored the transfer of the AMS to agricultural cooperatives.[60] The most important reason advanced was that the proposed new ownership system could remove conflicts between the AMS and the cooperatives requiring tractor services. Under the old AMS system, agricultural producers and owners of tractors were separate units. The AMS signed contracts with a number of farm cooperatives for the services of tractors, and a time schedule was arranged in advance for the actual operations of tractors in various fields. However, the proper time for plowing could hardly be predicted with a high degree of accuracy by any cooperative. Yet under a contract system, with so many customers involved, the time schedule prepared by the AMS did not provide enough flexibility to meet this special need of agricultural production.

The relationship between the AMS and the cooperatives it served was also hampered by the fact that both sides were pursuing different interests according to their own vantage points. The AMS was primarily interested in how to achieve its annual quota, stated in quantitative terms, and tended to ignore the quality of its work, which might subsequently affect crop growth. The transfer of tractors from the AMS to cooperatives was viewed as an ideal solution to these problems. It had also been observed that both tractors and their operators in the AMS system had a strong seasonality in their work; that is, they were idle in the off-season. Under the proposed new system, tractor operators would become regular members of agricultural cooperatives and would have other tasks to do in the off-season, hence, a better utilization of manpower could be achieved. Moreover, the new system would shift the burden of financial investment from the state to individual cooperatives. As an experiment, a small-scale decentralization of the AMS was carried out toward the end of 1957.[61]

However, certain shortcomings became immediately obvious in the trial management. Since the size of a farm cooperative was usually not large enough to warrant the efficient use of more than one or two tractors, the dispersion of tractors created serious inconvenience regarding facilities and mechanics for maintenance and repairs. Agricultural cooperatives also were too small to pool enough funds to purchase tractors from the AMS. These drawbacks were partially alleviated in 1958 after the establishment of communes which were much larger in size.[62]

A policy reversal occurred in 1961 after the decentralized system failed. The AMS regained control over some of the tractors and other farm machines bought by communes.[63] A large number of new AMS were formed in 1961–65, absorbing practically all the new tractors added in those years, and by 1965 the AMS owned about 60 percent of the tractors in China. The following paragraph describes the present system of AMS management in most of China.[64]

There are three levels of administration. The lowest unit is the tractor team which owns somewhere from four to ten units. This unit signs contracts with, and provides services to, agricultural producers. At the intermediate level is the AMS which controls five or six tractor teams. The AMS is an independent accounting unit in the sense that it has its own balance sheets and profit-loss statements. Then, in each hsien government there is a general station which serves as an administrative office in charge of all AMS within the hsien. The general station equalizes the profits and losses of all the AMS under it and integrates the net earnings into the hsien budget each year. To avoid conflicts between the AMS and agricultural producers over such problems as the timing of tractor operations and other working relations, each tractor team is assigned to deal with one commune exclusively on a more or less permanent basis. Consequently, the commune is not a temporary customer of the tractor team but is empowered to supervise constantly the whole operation of the team.

As can be seen from Table 4.4, for each year the numbers of tractors owned by state farms and by the AMS do not add up to the total number of tractors in the whole country. The small residual represents the tractors owned by former cooperatives, and subsequently by communes, plus those in agricultural extension stations and research institutions.

In 1957 two farm cooperatives in Heilungkiang Province for the first time bought a few tractors with their own funds.[65] This practice did not spread widely until late 1958, when 1770 of the newly established communes purchased a total of 15,102 tractor units, either from the AMS or directly from manufacturers.[66]

The new system of commune ownership was not the success originally anticipated. First of all, with the serious scarcity of qualified operators and mechanics for maintenance and repairs, there were great advantages in concentrating tractors and other modern farm machines in the AMS. Secondly, because of severe crop failures in most of China in 1959–61, communes simply were unable to accumulate capital to purchase expensive tractors.[67] The financial constraints became more prohibitive after communes were broken down into smaller units, and their administrative authorities were transferred to such lower level units as production brigades or teams.

However, the emphasis on the ownership of tractors by communes has revived recently.[68] This new policy coincided with the government's decision to shift the production emphasis to the small garden tractors. The fact that these small, hand-pushed tractors are much cheaper and easier to use and maintain makes a wider ownership by communes feasible.

Utilization of Tractors and Related Problems

Table 4.7 gives the acreage of farmland cultivated by tractors in various years. This acreage accounted for only 2.7 percent of total farmland in 1957[69] and 5 percent in 1959. In spite of the ambitious ten-year program of agricultural mechanization promulgated in 1959, the percentage of farmland cultivated by tractors was still as low as 10 percent in 1964.

Aside from technical and economic factors, there is a physical limitation that restricts a wider employment of tractors in farming. The usefulness of large tractors in reclamation is undisputed, and it is reported that state farms on the plains of North China were basically mechanized by 1964.[70] However, reclamation activities in China have been restricted by the small amount of land that it is economically feasible to reclaim under present conditions. Since 1961 there has been very little progress in land reclamation. In provinces other than the frontier areas, the fragmentation of farmland and the dominance of paddy fields are not conducive to a large-scale employment of tractors. Thus far, efficient machines for operations in paddy fields remain to be invented.

Table 4.7 Total Area Cultivated by Tractors

Year	Cultivated area (1,000 mou)
1954	1,225
1955	4,900
1956	28,720
1957	46,000
1959	81,000
1964	162,000

Sources:
1954 and 1955: *SSB Communique, 1955.*
1956: *SSB Communique, 1956.*
1957: *JMJP*, Mar. 13, 1958.
1959: *CKNP*, 1960, no. 4, p. 3.
1964: *China Monthly*, 1965, no. 7, p. 5.

For the same reasons, tractors in China have not been evenly distributed geographically. The eleven AMS established in 1953 as demonstration models were all in the area north of the Huai River.[71] In 1956, 66 percent of the 325 AMS and 80 percent of the tractors owned by them were in eight northern provinces.[72] Even in 1964 the 1,300 hsien that had one or more AMS are believed to have been concentrated in the northern regions. The following provinces appear to have a relatively high degree of mechanized farming:

1. Heilungkiang: This province has the highest degree of agricultural mechanization in China. There were 16,000 tractors, or 17.8 per-

cent of the national total, in 1961,[73] and 20,000 units, or 20 percent of the national total, in 1962.[74]

2. Liaoning: There were 400 AMS equipped with an estimated total of 16,000 tractors, or 16 percent of the national total, in 1962.[75]
3. Hopei: 74 AMS, or about 19 percent of the national total, were located in this province in 1957. It had 10,300 tractors, or 11.4 percent of the national total, in 1961.[76]
4. Sinkiang: It had 10,000 tractors, or 7.7 percent of the national total, in 1965.[77]
5. Shantung: It had 8,000 tractors in 1963.[78]

In terms of distribution by crop, cotton and wheat are the most favored items, presumably because the fields used for these crops are dry and relatively level.[79]

Even with this moderate scale of mechanization, there have been many serious problems. Some were extremely annoying in the early years, whereas others remain unsolved even today. One of the most pressing issues is the high cost of using tractors. Aware of the relative cheapness of labor in the countryside, the Chinese government avoided charging high fees to tractor users. In fact, all AMS in China have been operating on less than a full-cost basis, and they are responsible for operation costs with no depreciation allowance. Yet in 1955 virtually all AMS failed to collect enough users' fees to cover their operation costs. Even after their operation costs were reduced in 1956, only 25 percent of the AMS managed to balance current resources and current expenses. The percentage rose to 44 percent in 1957.[80] If depreciation allowances are taken into account, probably none of them made any profit in those years. There are indications that the operation costs of the AMS have not gone down substantially since 1957.[81]

Even with government subsidies to the AMS and the below-cost rates of users' fees, only a small number of agricultural production units have been convinced of the desirability of using tractors. For this reason, the AMS system in China has been unable to duplicate the role played by the Soviet machine tractor stations. First, since the Chinese government has constantly subsidized the AMS, they could not function as extractive agencies to transfer surpluses from the agricultural sector to the state. Second, since tractors are far from indispensable to the Chinese agricultural production units, the AMS cannot be used by the government as an instrument of political control over the rural sector.

The high operation costs in Chinese AMS are apparently not ascribed to low rates of utilization, because the average amount of land cultivated by each tractor, approximately 2,000 mou in most years, is no less than that of Western countries or of the Soviet Union.[82] The following factors have been officially identified as the causes of high operation costs in most Chinese AMS.

1. Prices of petroleum products in China were traditionally high. Until recently, domestic production of petroleum made up only a small percentage of its total consumption, whereas large amounts were imported from the USSR and Rumania. In addition, the average rate of fuel consumption of operating tractors in China had been comparatively higher than in other countries, because the average farm size was relatively small so that tractors had to make more turns per unit of land cultivated. According to Chinese reports in 1957–58, the average cost for cultivating one mou of land with a tractor was approximately 1.50 yuan, of which 0.90 yuan, or 60 percent of the cost, was for fuel consumed.[83] The high cost of fuel was further increased by poorly selected locations of the AMS, or because the few agricultural producers who were willing to use tractors were so widely scattered that the AMS had to undertake work assignments in points quite distant from the depots. As a result, tractors used a considerable amount of extra oil between the depots and the fields. Fuel consumption of this nature was sometimes as high as 30 percent of the total.[84]

2. Like other government agencies in Communist China, the AMS system also was plagued by excessive personnel, especially of managerial staff. In 1955, on an average, there were 4.5 persons attending each tractor.[85] The figure rose to 4.7 persons in 1957[86] and to 7 persons in 1960.[87] In the beginnings of the AMS system, the government suggested that, as a rule, two operators should be assigned to each tractor so that the tractor could operate day and night, if necessary.[88] Moreover, the work of the AMS had a seasonal pattern, with an active period of about 100 days per year for most of them, yet tractor operators were year round, full-time employees. During the off-season they simply remained idle.

3. The high frequency of repairs has been another important factor responsible for the high operation costs in the Chinese AMS. The high rate of machine breakdown largely resulted from the generally low technical standards of operators and maintenance personnel, most of whom had received only a short period of training. This problem was particularly acute during 1958 and 1959, after a large number of tractors had

been transferred to communes. The poor quality of domestically produced tractors and the necessity for some machines to operate in deep water have also been cited as causes for high damage rates.

In the early 1950s, tractors were imported from twelve different countries in fifty-four different models. None of the spare parts needed could be produced at home, and this created formidable difficulties in maintenance and repair work. Repair shops and a number of small plants to produce spare parts for tractors were established in 1956–57, but they were so few that they did not spread to all locations of the AMS. An AMS often had to send tractors to a distant city for major repairs. Needless to say, the repair shops were overloaded with work, hence the time required for repair was much prolonged.[89] What is worse, most of the spare-parts producers and repair shops were converted to tractor-producing plants in 1958 under the pressure of the Great Leap Forward campaign.

As more experience has been accumulated and improvements have been made, some of these problems have become less serious today. To increase the operational efficiency of tractors and to reduce fuel consumption rates, the Chinese government has instructed agricultural production units to combine small fragments of land into larger pieces suitable for modern farm machines. However, when the size of fields is enlarged, irrigation utilizing the force of gravity becomes more difficult. The problem, then, is to find the optimal size of field in different areas that will assure a minimal combined cost for irrigation and tractor cultivation.

Official reports indicate that the technique of linear programming has been employed to determine the best combination of different types of tractors needed by the AMS so that the needs of various farms in the locality can be met with minimum costs. Linear programming has also been used to select the best location for the AMS so that the total distance between the depot and working points will be minimal. The rule used is that each tractor team should serve an area with a radius no greater than three kilometers.[90] All these practices or rules are designed to reduce operation costs, especially fuel consumption. However, the domestic production of petroleum has increased rapidly since the discovery and development of a new oil field in Taching. Effective January 1, 1965, nationwide prices of fuel oils for civilian uses were cut on an average of 18.6 percent—the first substantial adjustment in the price of fuel oils in the history of the regime.[91]

Another important measure adopted by the AMS in recent years, and aimed at cost savings, is subsidiary production, such as the processing of farm products. Thus, tractor operators and certain other personnel can be kept occupied during the idle season.[92]

During 1961–64, a policy was initiated to strengthen the production of spare parts and accessories for tractors and other farm machines. More repair shops were established, and investment in this area was more than doubled during the period. By 1964 there were more than 800 large repair shops which formed a network to serve the AMS.[93]

While there are improvements in the general situation, many problems are still far from solution. The major barriers encountered in the process of mechanization were summarized by Teng Chieh, a high-ranking official in the Chinese Communist government, as follows:[94]

1. The industrial capacity is far from adequate to supply farm machines in large quantities.
2. At the present time, communes are based on the three-level ownership system, with production teams as the independent accounting unit. This unit can hardly raise enough funds to buy farm machines.
3. The average size of production teams is too small to permit the efficient application of large farm machines.
4. The technical manpower in the rural sector lags behind. The shortage of operators and mechanics is still formidable.
5. The supply of fuel, including electric power, coal and, gasoline, is inadequate.

He has concluded, therefore, that China should seek other means to develop agricultural production, without waiting for a full-scale mechanization. This is certainly a realistic assessment of the situation up to the present time.

Chapter 5

Irrigation and Rural Electrification

Irrigation and Water Conservation

The Chinese people learned to irrigate farmland long ago. Some regions in China have been under irrigation for over two thousand years, with the oldest irrigation aqueducts traceable to about 200 B.C. On the other hand, because of the special geological formation along some major rivers and the uneven distribution of precipitation, China has suffered frequent floods and droughts throughout history. According to documented records, between the years 206 B.C. and 1936 A.D., a period of over two thousand years, there were 1,031 relatively severe floods and 1,060 droughts, or about one natural calamity in each year. During the 267 years of the Ching Dynasty alone, there were 201 recorded serious droughts.[1] Therefore, it has been a constant task of responsible government throughout history to find ways and means to combat calamities caused by too much water or the lack of it.

China is rich in water resources. According to a 1955 survey of 1,598 rivers in China, the estimated total volume of surface water is 2,680 cubic km per year. The Yangtze River is the largest contributor, with an annual flow of about 1,000 cubic km.[2] However, surface water resources are not evenly distributed. Of the total volume of surface water, 75 percent is in the southern part of the country, while the northern plains receive only 7 percent. In a sense the uneven geographical distribution of water sources is rather desirable from the viewpoint of energy sources, because water represents potential hydroelectric power and compensates for the unevenly distributed coal reserves in various parts of China. But the uneven distribution of water resources is extremely unfortunate from the viewpoint of irrigation. The southern part of the country is endowed with 75 percent of the total water resources and only 38 percent of the nation's farmland; the northern plains, on the other hand, have 52 percent of the total farmland but only 7 percent of the total surface water.[3] This fact, which will be discussed later, has greatly, if not decisively, influenced the policy choice of the government in irrigation construction.

Table 5.1 gives the official data on total irrigated area and the percentage of irrigated land in the total cultivated area in various years.

Table 5.1 Total Irrigated Area, 1949–64 (million mou)

Year	*TGY* data	*SLFT* data	Sum of provincial data	Other sources	Irrigated percentage of total cultivated area
1949	240	303.9	222.1		16.3
1950	250	311.7	229.3		16.6
1951	280	326.4	253.5		18.0
1952	320	350.5	287.0		19.8
1953	330	360.4	309.1		20.3
1954	350	372.2	326.4		21.3
1955	370	391.6	350.9		22.4
1956	480	540.0	433.8		28.6
1957	520		535.0		31.0
1958	1,000				61.9
1959				1,070	
1960				700	
1963				550	
1964				480	
1965				500	

Sources:

TGY, p. 130.

SLFT data are given in *SLFT*, 1957, no. 7, reprinted in *TLCS*, 1957, no. 10, p. 474. The 1956 figure refers to the situation in June 1956.

Sum of provincial data is derived from provincial newspapers or official reports.

Other sources:

1959: *JMJP*, Oct. 29, 1959.

1960: *KTTH*, Apr. 19, 1961.

1963: *HKTKP*, Oct. 1, 1963.

1964: *EB*, no. 895 (1964), p. 20. The amount is given as "nearing 500 million mou."

1965: *FCYC*, 1966, no. 1, p. 11. It cites a communist source. "The total area of irrigated land in 1965 was 500 million mou, which was 20 million mou more than the 1964 figure." Therefore, the 1964 amount should be 480 million mou.

Irrigated land as percentage of total cultivated land is based on the data given in *TGY*, pp. 128, 130.

While the accuracy of the official data is questionable, the magnitude and the general direction of changes revealed by them are indisputable.

According to a survey made by Professor J. L. Buck, 15 percent of the cultivated land in the wheat region and 69 percent in the rice region were under irrigation in 1929–33. The total irrigated area was then estimated to be 46 percent of the cultivated land in China proper.[4] Statistics of the Chinese Communist government (*TGY* figures) give the total irrigated area in 1949 as 240 million mou, or 16.3 percent of the total cultivated land. The difference between the two estimates is astonishingly wide. A number of factors may account for the difference. First, as part of the general statistical defect in Buck's study, his ratio of irrigated land to total cultivated land is an unweighted average, and a sizable upward bias is embodied.[5] As a matter of fact, the *Statistical Monthly* published by the Nationalist government in the 1930s gave a lower ratio (29 percent) of farmland under irrigation.[6] Second, both Buck's estimate and the figure of the *Statistical Monthly* refer only to China proper, whereas the Chinese Communist statistics include Manchuria and Inner Mongolia. The inclusion of these two areas would significantly reduce the overall ratio of irrigated land to cultivated area. Third, wartime destruction and the disuse of irrigation facilities are, of course, another source of the discrepancy.

In fact, all the estimates of irrigated area are not strictly comparable even without the above-mentioned factors. The term irrigated land had never been clearly defined in China prior to 1956. Those dry lands served by irrigation facilities are called "watered fields" in China. As for paddy fields, some receive water from irrigation channels; others use stored rainfall only. Even for the truly irrigated land, a distinction may be made between fully irrigated and partially irrigated fields, according to the length of time that irrigation water is available.

A definitional confusion also exists in the official data published by the Peking government after 1949. The three series shown in Table 5.1 differ from each other substantially in almost every year before 1957. An effort was made by the State Statistical Bureau in 1956–57 to adopt a uniform definition of irrigated land and a synchronized reporting date of irrigation statistics. The *TGY* series represents the final official accounts.

The Peking government has paid special attention to water conservation construction from the outset. However, before 1957 a higher priority was given to flood control than to irrigation.[7] The preference for the "prevention or alleviation of flood disasters" over the "beneficial utilization of water" has a long tradition in China. In comparing the degrees of danger, the Chinese people used to think that droughts would at worst reduce crops in the affected area, whereas inundation would not only destroy entire crops but might also endanger human and animal life as well as property. Even in selecting inundation control measures, a higher priority was given to river floods than to the waterlogging caused by surface runoff water, again because the former was regarded as more fatal than the latter.[8] During the First Five Year Plan period (1953–57), 48.7 percent of the total state investment in water conservation was used for flood control projects, whereas 19.9 percent was used for the elimination of waterlogging.[9]

Along this traditional line the Communist government began to enlarge the discharge capacities and to reinforce the dikes of rivers, especially of the most troublesome rivers in the northern plains—the Yellow, Huai, and Hai rivers. Attention was paid primarily to large-scale projects on the river courses for flood detention or diversion.[10] As for the vast low areas in the plains, areas away from the rivers but frequently suffering waterlogging from surface runoff after heavy or localized rainfalls, the corrective method was the construction of additional channels to drain off the water.

Only a few reservoirs, other than those along the major rivers, had been built by the state in the plains region to impound surface water. One objection to such construction was the conviction that, if storage reservoirs were built in isolation in the plains, they might cause even more severe disasters in the time of extraordinarily heavy rainfall. Such projects were considered undesirable also on the grounds that they would occupy too much farmland and entail the high cost of removing and resettling inhabitants.[11]

Insofar as irrigation is concerned, large projects financed by the state did not make an appreciable contribution, since these projects had been built mainly for flood control. Even the large multipurpose reservoirs functioned only to detain floods and generate hydroelectricity, not to help irrigate a large area, because they were not connected with water distribution courses. Only a handful of long canals for irrigation purposes had been built before 1957.[12] As can be seen from Table 5.2, altogether only 8.3 percent of the total increase in irrigated area in 1949–56 was attributable to large irrigation works.

About 90 percent of the irrigated area added in 1949–56 was served by small-scale irrigation systems. One official source has admitted that

Table 5.2 Types of Irrigation, in Selected Years (million mou of land irrigated)

Type of irrigation	1949	1952	1956	1964
Gravity: large canals	23.5	31.9	43.2	278.0
Gravity: small ditches and aqueducts	261.6	289.2	182.0	
Farm ponds and weirs			216.5	82.0
Pumping, with mechanical and electrical power	4.2	5.0	11.9	86.0
Wells and other subterranean water sources	14.6	24.5	86.4	34.0
Total	303.9	350.6	540.0	480.0

Sources:

1949 and 1952: From *TLCS*, 1957, no. 10, p. 474.

1956: From *PC*, 1957, no. 20, pp. 20–28. Figures given in this source were originally stated in acres. It reports, "by 1956, there was 82,350,000 acres of irrigated land in China—32 percent of all land under cultivation" (p. 22). Judging from the above statement, this source has apparently adopted the *SLFT* figure of total irrigated area for 1956 (540 million mou) but has used a conversion rate of 6.56 mou to the acre. We use the same conversion rate to derive figures in mou. The resulting breakdown is quite close to that given in *TLCS*, 1957, no. 10, p. 474, with a few minor discrepancies.

1964: *EB*, no. 895 (1964), p. 20.

the bulk of this increment actually resulted from repairing and restoring old irrigation systems which were unused during wartime because of a lack of maintenance and the displacement of farmers.[13]

Traditionally, Chinese peasants and the local governments were so keenly concerned about the scarcity of agricultural land that irrigation systems normally had been built with a minimum use of land. In South China farm ponds were common. They served to conserve water as well as soil. In the terraced area, soil was washed away from higher land and deposited in the ponds; during the winter, farmers dredged out the pond mud and put it back onto the fields. Some ponds were isolated, whereas others were connected by a few short leading channels. Farmers used waterwheels or other instruments to convey water from ponds or channels into the fields. Cases of exclusive reliance on the force of gravity to distribute water were not common, because this type of irrigation used too much land. In the north, subterranean irrigation with either shallow or artesian wells was important. There was a strong aversion to reservoirs. The new irrigation systems built in 1949–56 did not depart too much from the traditional patterns.

Although the general tone of the water conservation policy in 1949–56 was relatively conservative, and the expansion of irrigated area was moderate when compared with that of 1957–58, the economic effects were nevertheless positive. Buck's survey has demonstrated that the introduction of irrigation into the wheat region increased the yield per unit of crop land, on the average, by 60 to 70 percent, but the increase in unit yield resulting from irrigation in the rice region was much less because of the greater rainfall in the south.[14] In other words, the benefit of irrigation in southern China is reflected not in the increased yields per unit of crop area but in the expansion of double-cropping. In some places in the south, even if the growing season is long enough for two crops, the concentration of rainfall in a few months makes double-cropping impractical unless there are irrigation facilities to supply water during the dry seasons. Table 5.3 presents some data on yield increases in the areas served by new irrigation canals built in 1949–56 in the northern provinces. The yield increases shown are higher than Buck's findings because they were the results of some "packaged programs." Along with the construction of new irrigation channels, other measures, such as improved seeds and greater fertilizer application, were also used in those areas.

However, all the traditional lines that shaped the early policies of water conservation construction were discarded toward the end of 1957.[15] The major policy changes were the following: (1) a shift from

Table 5.3 Effects of Irrigation on Crop Yields (catties per mou)

Province	Name of canal	Crop	Average yield in irrigated fields (1)	Average yield in non-irrigated fields (2)	Percentage increase
Shantung	Yehynan	wheat	260	120	217
Shensi	Chinghui	cotton	95	65	146
Shensi	Weihui	corn	417	220	190
Szechwan	Kuansungpengnien	rice	585	360	163
Hopei	Yungchen	millet	200	90	222
Kiangsu	Erhling	rice	418	297	141
Shantung	Hsiuhwei	wheat	186	93	200
Honan	People's Victory	cotton	40	14	286
Hopei	Shihchiachuang	cotton	93	34	274

Sources:
JMJP, Dec. 22, 1957; and *PC*, 1957, no. 20, p. 27.

the prevention of floods to the full utilization of water resources, (2) a shift from draining water to storing it, and (3) a shift from large projects financed by appropriations of the central government to small projects undertaken by local authorities and individual agricultural cooperatives, or what was known as the mass line.

Cost consideration was, no doubt, an important factor in the favor of small projects. They could be constructed by mobilizing peasants and local resources with little or no subsidy from the state budget, and the planning period for small projects is much shorter. More important was the new emphasis on "full utilization of water for irrigation purposes." Local needs in a vast area could be met only by a large number of local facilities.

The policy change was also greatly influenced by the survey of China's water resources conducted in 1955. This survey confirmed that the whole northern plains area was seriously short of water sources if irrigation was to be further expanded there. One way to solve this problem was a fuller utilization of underground water.[16] This was attempted in 1956, when the principal method of irrigation was drilled wells in the northern plains. Unfortunately, the campaign was unsuccessful because of insufficient knowledge about the distribution of underground water resources in those areas. The majority of the wells failed to provide adequate water, and some, no water at all. The problem was further aggravated by the fact that both well-drilling and water-lifting required machines or other equipment which China's industry could not supply in sufficient quantities.

Consequently, the policy was reoriented in 1957 to the economizing of surface water for expanded irrigation. This was clearly pointed out by Tan Chen-lin, a member in the Party's Central Committee in charge of agriculture and water conservation affairs, during the Water Conservation Conference held in October 1957:

> The principle of water conservation in our country should be the storage of water. Since the whole area north of the Huai River has an adequate water supply, including the entire flow of the Yellow River, we should not discharge water as we have been doing up to now.[17]

Beginning in the latter part of 1957, not only was the emphasis of water conservation policy entirely changed, but also the scale of construction in the whole country was stepped up. The annual target for irrigation construction in 1958 was rapidly escalated to a fantastically high level;[18]

1. In August 1957, the target for 1958 was set to increase the irrigated area by 44,080,000 mou.
2. In October 1957, the target was raised to 61,840,000 mou.
3. In December 1957, the target was further raised to 92,210,000 mou.

As soon as the last target was set, it was abandoned; and a "high tide" of water conservation construction swept the whole country with no specified target. By the end of 1958, the Chinese government declared that 480 million mou of irrigated area had been added during the year, almost eleven times the original target. The total irrigated area was said to have been increased from 520 million mou in 1957 to 1 billion mou, and the percentage of irrigated land in total cultivated area was increased from 31 percent to 61.9 percent. An equally ambitious plan for 1959 was immediately drawn up by the Central Committee in August 1958, calling for another half billion mou of irrigated land, with the percentage of cultivated land under irrigation reaching 89 percent by the end of 1959. In the meantime, the government embarked on a gigantic plan to transfer water from the rivers in the south to the north where water resources would soon be exhausted.[19]

Although the 1958 statistics for water conservation construction are far from accurate, the immensity of the scale is evident from the progress reports of various local and provincial governments published in that year. Mass line construction was going on everywhere. The following patterns of water conservation work were typical; they were widely publicized and imitated.

1. One pattern of construction was called "the starry-sky reservoirs." They were numerous small, isolated reservoirs and ponds in a large plains area, resembling the many stars in the sky. This type of construction appeared mainly in the Hopei plains to impound surface runoff water from rain.[20]

2. Another popular pattern was called "strings [or clusters] of grapes" (pu-tao-chuan). As the term indicates, it involved the digging of many latitudinal canals in a large plains area to receive runoff water; each canal was connected with a large number of off-channel reservoirs.[21] Or many reservoirs were built adjacent to the banks of a natural stream but were connected with it by short leading aqueducts as water intakes.

3. There was also the pattern called "a white horse's mane"[22] which described the diversion of water from a natural stream by many new channels or ditches. Temporary or permanent diversion weirs were built

every few miles along the river. The new diverting channels radiating from both sides of the river were like the mane hanging on a horse's neck.

4. Another plan, perhaps the most ambitious, was made by the Anhwei provincial government. It consisted of a network of water courses to serve the plains north of the Huai River. The network was to contain: 9 new large canals; 2,600 large channels (30–50 meters wide, 6 meters deep); 15,000 medium channels (20 meters wide, 5 meters deep); and 110,000 small aqueducts (10 meters wide, 4 meters deep). The canals and channels, when completed, would have a total length of 125,000 kilometers, spanning a total area of 26,700 square kilometers (40 million mou). By June 1958, the following construction projects were already underway: 1,062 large channels; 8,067 medium channels; and 90,690 small aqueducts.[23]

5. In the mountainous areas of the south and northwest, new diverting channels were dug upstream, connecting to major rivers. In some cases the new channel extended far more than a thousand kilometers so that it virtually became a new river, winding among the mountain tops. A good example is the 1,400 kilometer diversion canal from the Tao River in Kansu.[24]

The scale of construction was indeed enormous. By the end of 1957 there were 1.76 million projects of canals and ditches and 8.31 million water-storage projects under construction in the whole country.[25] In Honan Province alone, 30,000 reservoirs and 1.1 million individual projects—canals, weirs, and ponds—were constructed in the winter and spring of 1957/58.[26] The number of projects underway in the country must have been greatly increased in the latter half of 1958.

Practically all the new construction was carried out by provincial and local governments with draft labor. In the first few months of 1958, it was reported that there were more than a hundred million peasants working every day on water conservation projects.[27] Evidently, this enormous manpower could be mobilized only after the whole rural sector had been collectivized.[28]

What then are the economic effects of such grandiose plans? Unfortunately the results have been negative and have created, in fact, one of the greatest tragedies in Chinese history. The basic idea was not necessarily unsound; but the overenthusiastic implementation was destructive. So far as can be ascertained, the movement of water conservation construction led to many immediate disasters and to two long-term, large-scale damages on the economy.

The immediate disasters were floods over the whole country for three consecutive years beginning in 1959. Agricultural experts have observed that, prior to 1958, changes in aggregate agricultural output in China were almost completely determined by inputs and productivity changes but were only peripherally influenced by harvest conditions.[29] The great size of China and the diversity of agricultural and climatic regions are responsible for the relative stability of overall yields. In almost every year there were natural calamities of varying severity in some areas, but the effects were often partially offset by unusually favorable harvest conditions in other areas. But since 1959 natural calamities have not only become increasingly serious in extent, but also they have occurred in a rather uniform pattern over the whole country. The total area of farmland affected by floods in 1959 was officially reported to be 330 million mou. For 1960, although the area damaged by floods has not been revealed, the total area suffering from natural calamities is said to have increased from 650 million mou of the previous year to 900 million mou, or 56 percent of the total existing agricultural land. Of this total, 300 to 400 million mou were classified as the area with the most severe losses.[30] Official sources stopped citing statistics of the calamity-affected area in 1961 and merely indicated that general harvest conditions were no better than those of the preceding year.[31]

Many students of Chinese economy are inclined to think that the government's attributing the great production shortage in 1959–61 to natural calamities is unwarranted,[32] because this would be a serious contradiction to the history of Chinese agriculture. According to historical records, the occurrence of natural disasters over the whole country in a single year was extremely rare, and the occurrence of them in this pattern for three consecutive years was even rarer. Therefore, some observers suspect that the official reports of natural calamities during 1959–61 have been greatly exaggerated to cover up human errors made in the commune system and the Great Leap movement. Yet if one studies carefully the nature and conditions of the water conservation work done in 1958, he will accept the official reports. The intention of the authorities to cover up their human failures and erroneous policies is undeniable, since they have never admitted either, but human factors undoubtedly brought about the post-Leap crisis. In any event, it is nevertheless true that unprecedentedly severe calamities did occur in the three consecutive years of 1959–61.

However, it is questionable to call the calamities in that period natural.

To a large extent they were man-made, or at least man-induced, calamities, because there would not have been so many nationwide disasters, and lasting for three years, if the government had not carried out wholesale water conservation construction. In other words, human action created a new pattern of calamities unseen in Chinese history. What the Chinese Communists did in 1958 had not only destroyed most of the flood-control facilities but also had made the areas previously flood-free now vulnerable to heavy rainfall.

In their long history of fighting floods, the Chinese people had built, over many, many generations, extensive flood-control dikes along the more troublesome rivers. The dikes might not have measured up to modern standards, but they nevertheless functioned well except in the case of extraordinarily severe floods. In reading the reports published in 1958 concerning the progress of water conservation work in various localities, one gets the impression that many river embankments and dikes had been cut so that water-diverting channels or water intakes could be built. These projects were constructed in haste and were too poor in quality to resist even moderate floods. What is more, along each river numerous weirs had been erected to change the level of the river for water diversion, but most of the detention weirs had no regulating gates. These factors offer a plausible explanation for the "greatest flood in a thousand years" that occurred along the Huai River in 1959.

Ordinary flood-control measures in China were weakened in still other ways. As the Peking government proudly declared, the "laboring mass" had completely metamorphosed the "fatherland's mountains and rivers." The statement, though somewhat figurative, does depict what was taking place in China as a result of extensive water conservation construction. Unfortunately, the topographical changes were so drastic and took place so quickly that the agencies in charge of flood prevention were suddenly deprived of hydrological knowledge concerning Chinese rivers. All the hydrological records, accumulated over many years, became virtually inapplicable to the new situation. These agencies were left with no idea as to what the new rhythms, speeds, and intensities of floods would be if they should come. In fact, worries of this sort had been expressed by the Chinese experts on water conservation before the mass construction of water works was actually launched.[33] A similar comment was made by Korniev, the chief Soviet water conservation expert, at the National Conference on Water Conservation and Hydroelectric Power in 1959:

In the rural areas vast changes have taken place in conditions of direct flow as a result of the energetic construction of mass water conservation projects . . . therefore major amendments have to be made in respect to hydrological calculations.[34]

The large-scale construction had also relaxed the alertness of some flood-control personnel who had faith in the quality of the new work. If these projects could successfully detain and divert a large amount of water, as was claimed, floods should no longer be a threat.

Furthermore, the mass line imposed additional difficulties in the work of flood control. Under the mass line, construction work was carried out chiefly by local governments, individual cooperatives, or communes. In some cases there was a master plan for the area as a whole. Efforts were then made to synchronize construction tasks, and eventually the entire system would be connected to form a network. However, at least in 1958, no government unit was a permanent organ responsible for coordinating the administrative duties of various segments of the new network. The administration duties also were performed in the mass line manner and rested in the hands of individual cooperatives or communes. This fact has drawn sharp criticism from Korniev, the Soviet expert, who commented:

Because the problem of management was underestimated, many projects did not play their economic role in irrigation and flood prevention. Because of improper management, many projects met with accidents, damaging the materials of the people and the state.[35]

Some floods were created by the new policy of storing water. The idea of storing water for irrigation was basically justifiable, but it had been implemented with dangerous biases. With the slogan of "not letting a single drop of water go unused," a great number of reservoirs had been built with no flood-escape courses.[36] Those reservoirs later caused localized floods.

Another important change in policy in 1958 was the reliance on the force of gravity for irrigation, because this type would not require the water-lifting instruments which China's industry could not supply in sufficient quantity to cope with the scale of new irrigation construction. Although the construction costs of gravity irrigation were relatively high, the subsequent operational costs would be substantially lower. Typically, a canal was dug at an upstream point on a natural flow, some distance from the field to be watered. A gradient was chosen that would allow a flow of water through an aqueduct to the field. To utilize the force of gravity, the water level of the natural stream was raised artificially by dams or weirs, and water in the aqueduct was maintained at a level higher than the field to be irrigated. Yet many irrigation works of this type built in 1958 had no provision to regulate the water level during flood periods. Moreover, in order to use water for irrigation as soon as possible, water was diverted into many channels or ditches before their construction had been completed.[37] Even toward the end of 1958, numerous channels and ditches were dead ends. They received water but had no way to discharge it. In sum, the overstoring of water and the overreliance on the gravity type of irrigation in 1958 became major flood causes in subsequent years in many localities, especially in the northern plains.

In many cases disasters have resulted from the inferior construction of water conservation works. Quality problems were not confined to those constructed under the mass line; they occurred with large water conservation projects as well, including the Soviet-designed ones. Disasters caused by poor engineering, inadequate geological surveys, and erroneous design took place on large projects such as the hydroelectric generating stations in Huang-Tan-Kou, I-Li-Ho, Tzu-Ping-Pu, and Hsin-An-Chiang. Another bitter lesson was learned at the giant Kuanting Reservoir near Peking, the construction plan of which had been greatly publicized. Shortly after the completion of the dam, it was discovered that the depositional delta that had formed between the mouths of the Sang-Chien and the Yang rivers, the waterways connecting the Kuanting Reservoir and the Yellow Sea, had shifted back and forth and that the roadbeds of railways in the general area of the reservoir had sunk.[38] More interesting is the case of the San-Men Gorge Dam, a Soviet-designed, multipurpose project at the midreach of the Yellow River, with a rated generating capacity of 1.1 million kw and the largest in China. The dam, which is 350 feet high and 2,800 feet long, was completed in the summer of 1960. However, there was apparently one important miscalculation made by the Soviet experts who designed the project. The silt deposit at the reservoir bottom is building up more rapidly than originally was expected, so that the gigantic reservoir (120 miles long with a total surface area of 900 square miles) will become useless within twenty to thirty years.[39] Another serious engineering (or management) defect of the project was manifested immediately after the dam blocked the river in the summer of 1960: the lower stream of the Yellow River near Tsinan, Shantung Province was so dry that for forty days people could walk on the river bed.[40]

Constructional defects were more common in local projects. The quality problem was already serious enough to cause considerable alarm and concern among the experts after the first wave of construction for water conservation in 1956. The experts warned the authorities and urged that greater care be given to the design of water conservation works.[41] An editorial appeared in the *People's Daily*, June 1956, and was entitled "Immediately Examine and Improve the Quality of Water Conservation Projects."[42] It was in effect an instruction issued by the central government, and it cited local surveys, one of which revealed that 22 percent of the 688 new reservoirs built in the three districts of Shouyang, Hsiangtan, and Hengyang, all in Hunan Province, had severe defects. The editorial emphatically warned that the defective projects, if not improved immediately, could easily collapse under torrential rains and result in the destruction of farmland and the loss of human and animal life.

The quality problem became ubiquitous in 1958, when water conservation construction was carried out at an unprecedented scale and speed. Most of the projects resulted from rush decisions with no careful planning and designing in advance. In fact, the number of qualified personnel in China to design such works was sufficient for only a very small fraction of the projects to be undertaken. In most cases the designing was done by the peasants themselves, as part of the mass line. On many occasions peasants had to produce their own survey instruments since these instruments were, of course, in short supply. On still other occasions no survey had been performed before construction; farmers simply dug the ditches and waited to see whether water would come into them.[43] Equally acute was the shortage of building materials. As a "remedy," bamboo was a commonly used substitute for structural steel, and mud or clay replaced cement.[44]

Experts were no doubt aware of the great danger from defective water conservation works, but they remained silent because they were afraid they would be accused of being rightists. Or their warnings were not heeded at all. The responsible departments in the government merely remarked, "We have noted the unsatisfactory quality on some projects, but are confident that the enthusiastic mass will quickly correct those defects."[45]

The year 1958 was one of unusually favorable weather conditions in most of China. The test of conservation construction came only in the ensuing years. When heavy rains came in 1959, with them came widespread, induced disasters. The situation persisted for three years. It is difficult, however, for outside observers to determine how many dams, canals, and reservoirs collapsed or were out of commission after 1958. One official report indicated that 40 to 60 percent of the large irrigation systems were leaking.[46] Another source admitted that about 40 percent of giant and intermediate projects and about 30 percent of drainage and irrigation systems could not be put to normal use.[47] There were also local reports to that effect.[48] More revealing are the official statistics of the total irrigated area in China. As Table 5.1 shows, the total area of irrigated land in 1959 was 1,070 million mou, or 430 million mou short of the planned target.[49] After 1959 the amount of irrigated land began to decline dramatically. It dropped to 480 million mou in 1964, even less than the figure for 1957. In other words, the prodigious efforts made by the country in 1958 had been tragically wasted.

In addition to the disasters immediately caused by new water conservation projects, there are two other effects on the economy that have lasted much longer. The first is the sizable reduction in available farmland because of the extensive scale of water conservation construction. The loss of agricultural land per unit of irrigated field was much larger in 1958 than before, because of the heavy reliance on irrigation by gravity. This is a sharp departure from the pattern in 1949–57. In the area north of the Huai River in Anhwei Province, about 10 percent of the cultivated land had been occupied by new conservation works in 1958.[50] It has been calculated that, on the average, 250,000 cubic meters of earth work would have to be done in each square kilometer of area.[51] According to one study, to build small reservoirs in the northern plains would require five to eight mou per one hundred mou of land irrigated.[52] The actual land removed from cultivation in that area is believed to be larger than this estimate, because the small reservoirs actually built were much shallower than originally planned, most of them with a depth of one to two meters.[53] Therefore, they would occupy more land to store a given amount of water or to irrigate a given size of field. The heaviest reported loss of land occurred in the plains in Honan Province, where new irrigation canals reduced the cultivated area by about one-fifth to one-third.[54]

For the country as a whole, the total cultivated area was reduced by 60.7 millon mou from July 1957 to July 1958. It should be noted that this is the net reduction in cultivated area, that is, the total reduction minus the land added in that period by reclamation. The amount of land reclaimed is officially given as 18 million mou.[55] Therefore, the gross land reduction was 78.7 million mou. Of this amount, 90 percent is believed to be attributable to water conservation projects. If construction was carried out at the same speed and scale in the period from July 1958 to June 1959, at least a comparable amount of farmland must have been used up. In other words, we estimate that the total reduction of farmland due to water conservation works could be as much as 140 million mou, or 8.7 percent of the total cultivated land, in the period of two years. If these projects eventually did not bring any benefit to China's agriculture, the reduction in farmland would mean a pure loss to the economy.

In fact, land-conscious Chinese farmers would traditionally have had doubts about the net benefits of gravity irrigation, even if the systems were not defective in other ways. Chinese peasants favored a combination of gravity water distribution systems and of certain water-lifting devices because of the smaller area of land used. The traditional resistance to extensive storage reservoirs and to the pure gravity type of irrigation was considerably weakened after agricultural collectivization.

The other lasting effect of the irrigation systems carelessly built in 1958 is the salinization of the land. In any irrigation system, drainage is of the first importance. All natural surface water contains a certain amount of dissolved salts which become injurious to plant life if they are concentrated. Yet numerous irrigation systems built in China in 1958 made no provision for draining irrigated fields, so that the soil gradually became saturated with salts and less productive agriculturally.

Another important factor responsible for salinization, especially in low land in the northern plains, was the "starry-sky" reservoirs which raised the water table of the neighboring land above the critical level.[56]

A soil survey, which investigates textural and structural conditions of the soil profile, infiltration and hydraulic conductivity, water retention characteristics, nutrient status, salinity, and so on, is indispensable to any successfully designed irrigation system. Only with such investigation can soil behavior under irrigation be predicted and a proper design made for the proposed project. Yet if one searches the agricultural journals and other relevant publications in Communist China during 1957 and 1958, he can find hardly any evidence indicating that soil surveys had ever been conducted in any locality before irrigation projects were conceived.

In some instances salinization was caused by improper irrigation practices of the farmers. New irrigation systems were built in the areas where such facilities had never before existed, and farmers had no knowledge of appropriate irrigation methods or optimal water consumption for various crops. In other instances the irrigation system was extended so fast that farmers had no time to prepare furrows in their fields or to level their lands. The farmers simply irrigated by a general flooding of the whole plot and held water in the field for a prolonged time, or irrigated with unnecessary frequency. As a consequence, the land became salinized and packed.[57]

All these practices had been warned against by experts, but the warnings were not heeded.[58] Even after 1958 no immediate concern was aroused. Unlike the induced floods whose destructive effects are immediately visible, the process of salinization usually takes many years to complete. According to one Chinese study, if the water table before irrigation was eight to ten meters below the surface, then the use of an irrigation system without drainage outlets would completely salinize the soil in six or seven years.[59] The total area of salinized land in China in 1959 was estimated to be about 100 million mou, and about 60 percent was in the irrigated area.[60] The same source also estimated that the salinization process was progressing in another 200 million mou of irrigated land. Salinization in the newly irrigated area became so severe by 1961 and 1962 that one agriculturist urged that irrigation be stopped temporarily until irrigation systems could be provided with better drainage provisions.[61] A later publication indicated that the Chinese government did stop using the new irrigation facilities in North China in an attempt to prevent salinization in that area from worsening.[62] Reports may be occasionally found of reduced unit yields because of land salinization. Taking Tahsing Hsien near Peking as an example, it is reported that more than 500 new water channels with a total length exceeding 900 kilometers were constructed there in 1958. These channels only irrigated land and did not discharge water, thus causing increasingly serious salinization. As a result, in 1961–62 the unit yield of rice dropped from the 1956 level of 300 catties to 200, and the unit yield of wheat, from 150–200 catties to 40.[63]

The slow recovery of China's agricultural production after the crisis years may be attributable, no doubt, to a considerable extent to the slow process of soil salinization and the difficulty of removing it once it had formed.

Official reports show that large-scale construction of water conservation works continued in 1959 and 1960.[64] But there was no increase in the total area of irrigated land, since a great portion of construction done in the preceding year soon became inoperative. Stark reality eventually forced the Chinese Communist leadership to review and revise the whole policy for water conservation.

As part of the economic readjustment measures, water conservation construction was discontinued after 1960, except to repair or improve existing irrigation facilities.[65] The total yearly volume of earth and stone work in water conservation construction from 1963 to 1965 is officially given as follows: 1963, 191 million cubic meters;[66] 1964, 287 million cubic meters; [67] and 1965, 600 million cubic meters. The amount of construction in 1963 and 1964 is smaller than that in any year prior to 1961. Even the 600 million cubic meters for 1965 is only comparable to the level of 1950, and this work was done primarily to improve existing irrigation structures.[68]

An important corrective measure was taken in 1961–65 to add, where possible, drainage outlets to the existing irrigation structures. Even by the end of 1964, about 30 to 40 percent of large and intermediate irrigation systems still needed some provision for drainage.[69] The bulk of the small projects was beyond salvation either because they had been constructed from utterly wrong designs or because they had been completely destroyed by floods. Table 5.1 shows that the total area of irrigated land dropped from the 1.07 billion mou in 1959 to less than 500 million mou in 1964.

The excessive reliance on the force of gravity for irrigation has been criticized and rectified. Many irrigation systems have been reconstructed and pumping installations added.[70]

Table 5.2 shows the distribution of various types of irrigation systems (in terms of area irrigated) in selected years. Irrigation by gravity flow increased by 53 million mou, or 23 percent, from 1956 to 1964, suggesting that most of this type of irrigation facility constructed after 1956 had fallen into disuse by 1964. The 23 percent increase is believed to result from large canals built with better standards of quality. The area irrigated by small farm ponds and weirs fell drastically from 216.5 million to 82 million mou between 1956 and 1964. Obviously, small water conservation constructions did not last long. This is also evidenced in the case of irrigation by wells. Well irrigation has a long history in the middle and lower reaches of the Yellow River, north Kiangsu, and the plateau in northwest China where annual precipitation is insufficient. There were about 2 million wells in China in 1949 which irrigated 14.6 million mou of farmland. The total number of wells rose to about 3.5

million in 1955.[71] A great increase occurred in 1956, and the total number of wells reached 8 million in that year. One Chinese Communist report mentions that a total of 4.5 million wells were drilled in a period of seven months—from October 1955 to May 1956.[72] In Shantung province alone, 2.7 million wells had been dug in the period 1949–56.[73] Yet a considerable portion of the new wells were not useful. For instance, an official survey disclosed that only 20 percent of the new wells in Liaoning province were functioning.[74] By 1963 there were altogether only 2 million wells left in the whole country,[75] a number equal to that in 1949, but only one quarter of the number for 1956. However, wells that survived in 1963 had a larger capacity, and on the average each irrigated 17 mou as compared to 7.3 mou in 1949.

The only successful case is that of pumped-water irrigation, which served about 86 million mou in 1964. This figure is slightly larger than the planned target for the Second Five Year Plan.[76] Such new types of irrigation as overhead sprinkler pipes and underground perforated pipes have been introduced,[77] but they probably have not played any significant role because of their high cost.

Rural Electrification

As Table 5.4 shows, the total electricity used by China's rural sector was negligible in the early 1950s, and rural electrification did not become a major concern of Chinese planners until 1958. The First National Conference on Rural Hydroelectric Generation was held by the Ministry of Agriculture in mid-1958. This conference set the following targets[78] to be accomplished by 1961:

1. A total generating capacity of 15–18 million kw was to be installed in the rural sector with an annual output of 37.5–45 billion kwh.
2. The consumption of electric power per rural household was to reach 100–150 watts.
3. From 60 to 80 percent of the water-lifting work in irrigation and the processing of agricultural products was to be powered by electricity.
4. Electricity was to be used as the principal power source in small industries below the hsien level.

No doubt this ambitious plan was a by-product of the Great Leap Forward in water conservation construction in 1958. Thermal generating units have proven uneconomical in rural China because of the small

Table 5.4 Electric Power Consumption in Rural Areas, 1952–65

Year	Power consumption (million kw)
1952	43
1953	40
1954	44
1955	50
1956	77
1957	108
1958	142
1961	1,000
1962	1,550
1963	2,100
1964	2,500
1965	3,200

Sources:
1952–56: *CH*, p. 72.
1957: *NCNA*, Dec. 22, 1961.
1958: *EB*, Oct. 1, 1963.
1961: *NCNA*, Oct. 17, 1962.
1962: *HKTKP*, Mar. 12, 1964.
1963: *HKTKP*, Mar. 12, 1964.
1964: *JMJP*, Dec. 31, 1964.
1965: *CKHW*, Dec. 25, 1965.

scale of operation. Technically, it is possible to use local fuels, such as wood, rice hulls, dung, straw, leaves, and so forth, for engine generators. However, some of these fuels are seasonal in supply and are too bulky to stockpile. Furthermore, most of them have more urgent alternative uses as agricultural mulch, fertilizers, building materials, or animal feed. Hydraulic power seems to be the only feasible solution to rural generating stations. Based on this consideration, a plan of rural electrification was charted in 1958 to take advantage of the growing number of local water conservation projects.

There were 139 rural hydroelectric stations by the end of 1956.[79] The number grew to 20,324 in 1957 and then jumped to 151,324 in 1958.[80] The average size of those stations was very small—about 10 to 14 kw each. The plan was to increase the total generating capacity of rural hydroelectric stations to 4 million kw in 1959.[81]

Since the mass construction of water conservation projects proved to be a fiasco, the ambitious plan for rural electrification failed also to materialize. By the end of 1959, the total capacity actually installed was

400,000 kw, only 10 percent of the planned target. The total capacity reached 520,000 kw by May 1960,[82] and there was no increase at all from 1960 to 1964. The total electricity consumption by the rural sector in 1964 was reported to be 2.5 billion kwh. Of this amount, about 60 percent was supplied by national power networks and only 40 percent, or 1 billion kwh, was generated by the rural hydroelectric stations.[83] The utilization rate of those hydroelectric plants was generally very low, about 2,000 to 2,500 hours a year.[84] Therefore, the total generating output of rural hydroelectric stations in 1964 was somewhere between 400,000 to 500,000 kw. To some extent, the stagnation in the construction of rural generating stations also reflects a change in policy. The planning authorities must have realized that it is more economical to transmit electricity from the national networks than to generate power in small rural stations with extremely low load capacities.[85] In 1965, as Table 5.5 shows, 3.2 billion kwh were consumed by the rural sector, only 7 percent of the target planned for 1961, or less than 6 percent of the nation's output of electric power in 1964. Of this 3.2 billion kwh, 2.2 billion are believed to have come from the national networks. About 80 percent of the electric power currently consumed by the rural sector is used for irrigation, and the remaining 20 percent is used for such activities as subsidiary production, grain processing, and lighting.[86]

As we mentioned in the preceding section, one of the policies of water conservation and irrigation in recent years has been the promotion of pumped water irrigation. The total area of land irrigated with power-driven pumps rose from 11 million mou in 1956 to 86 million mou in 1964 (see Table 5.2). Table 5.5 shows that the installed capacity of power-driven irrigation and drainage equipment rose from about .5 million hp in 1957 to more than 10 million hp in 1966.

The new power-driven pumping installations are concentrated in the major, high-yield, grain and cotton regions and in the lower reaches of rivers. In the northern plains, power pumps have been installed in many wells, especially deep wells, to replace man or animal power in lifting and conveying water.

However, the proportion of electrically powered irrigation and drainage equipment is still small. According to one official source, the total capacity of electric irrigation and drainage equipment was 2 million hp in 1963,[87] and it accounted for about one-third of the total capacity of irrigation and drainage equipment existing in that year. The proportion was estimated to be about 24 percent in 1964.[88] The low percentage of

Table 5.5 Existing Capacity and Annual Production of Power-Driven Irrigation and Drainage Equipment, 1950–66 (1,000 hp)

Year	Existing capacity	Annual production
1950	12	
1954	176	
1955	220	
1956	390	
1957	560	260
1958	1,610	700
1959	3,380	2,000
1960	5,900	2,700
1961	4,500	600
1962	4,000	640
1963	6,000	1,760
1964	7,300	1,400
1965	8,570	1,680
1966	10,400	2,240

Note: Statistics include both electricity-driven and other types of power-driven equipment.

Sources:

Existing capacity:

1950: *CKNP*, 1960, no. 1, p. 2.
1954: *SSB Communique, 1954.*
1955 and 1956: *SSB Communique, 1956.*
1957: *China Monthly*, 1964, no. 7, p. 8.
1958: *NYCH*, 1959, no. 18, p. 1.
1959: *HC*, 1960, no. 4, p. 4.
1960: *JMJP*, Jan. 14, 1961.
1961: *EB*, Jan. 1, 1964.
1962: *China Monthly*, 1964, no. 7, p. 8.
1963: *JMJP*, Jan. 1, 1964.
1964: *JMJP*, Dec. 31, 1964.
1965: *JMJP*, Apr. 13, 1966.
1966: Of the current output, about 400,000 hp is assumed to be for replacement, whereas 1,800,000 hp is assumed to be the net addition to the existing capacity.

Annual production:

1957: Chu-yuan Cheng, *A Study of Machine-Building Industry in Communist China* (forthcoming), Chapt. VII, Table 7.
1958: According to *JMJP*, Jan. 14, 1961, a total of 5.4 million hp had been produced in 1958–60. The 1958 output is derived by subtracting from this total amount the known output figures for 1959 and 1960.
1959: *PR*, Aug. 9, 1960, p. 17.
1960: *KTTH*, 1961, no. 16, p. 20.
1961: *KJJP*, Jan. 18, 1963, mentions that the total output of power-driven irrigation and drainage equipment in 1960 and 1961 combined was 3.3 million hp. Therefore, the 1961 output should be 600,000 hp. This amount appears consis-

Continued following page

Sources for Table 5.5, continued

tent with the well-known sharp decline in industrial production in Communist China in 1961.

1962 and 1963: These figures are derived from the following pieces of information:

1. The combined output in the period from 1961 to 1963 was 3 million hp (*CKHW*, Aug. 14, 1964). Thus, 2.4 million hp was produced in 1962 and 1963.
2. There was a notable upturn in production in 1963. Output in the first half of 1963 was reported to be 100 percent higher than that of the corresponding period in 1962 (*PR*, Aug. 2, 1963, p. 16). In the first eight months, the increase in output was 175 percent (*PR*, Oct. 4, 1963, p. 18). We take 175 percent as the rate of increase for the whole year of 1963.
3. The upturn in current output in 1963 is quite consistent with the change in the existing capacity in that year.

1964: Total current output is estimated as the increment of existing capacity in that year plus about 100,000 hp for replacement needs.

1965: Estimated by using a rate of increase of 20 percent which is slightly smaller than the rate of increase given in *PR*, Sept. 24, 1965, for the first half of 1965.

1966: *NCNA*, Jan. 8, 1967.

Note: Without significant imports and exports of irrigation and drainage equipment, the figures of domestic production and existing total capacities in various years are quite consistent. The 1956 capacity and the amounts produced in 1957–59 add up to 3.3 million hp, which is almost identical to the total capacity of 1959. The 1959 capacity and the 1960 output add up to the 1960 total capacity. The sharp decline in capacity from 1960 to 1962 represents obsolescence of the equipment produced with indigenous methods during the Great Leap Forward period, and in 1960–62 the Communist authorities conducted quite thorough inspections of the irrigation projects built during the movement. In this period the production of irrigation and drainage equipment was greatly curtailed. The total output of equipment during 1961–64 was 4.4 million hp. The bulk of this quantity was accounted for by the capacity increase of 2.3 million hp in 1963 and 1964. The remainder probably was used as to replace worn-out or defective equipment. The output in 1965 and 1966 was barely enough to meet replacement requirements.

electric irrigation systems implies either that their operation costs were still quite high compared with pumping by mechanical means, or that internal combustion engines were preferred because they are portable and can be used for a variety of other farming activities.

The most important areas where electric irrigation systems are employed are the Pearl River delta and the Yangtze River delta. In the Pearl River delta, well known as the "granary" of Kwangtung Province, an electric irrigation network was completed in 1963.[89] It consists of 2,600 pumping stations with a combined capacity of 246,000 hp and irrigates about 5 million mou of farmland in twenty-two hsien and shih. The Yangtze River delta includes the southwest part of Kiangsu and north Chikiang. It is reported that 80 percent of the pumped irrigation in that general area was power-driven in 1964, of which half was powered by electricity.[90]

Another important region of electricity-powered irrigation is the Shensi plateau, which is bypassed by the Wei River. A network made up of seventeen pumping stations and fifty-one sets of electric pumps has been constructed.[91] Water is elevated from the Wei River to the plateau, seventy-three meters of vertical lift.

Chapter 6

Fertilization

After centuries of intensive cultivation, most Chinese farmland is deficient in plant nutritive elements. In general, the soil also lacks organic matter, because farmers cut the stalks and leaves of crops for fuel and fodder.[1] In some places even the plant roots are pulled up for these purposes. The deficiency in soil fertility has been augmented in some regions by the serious loss of good topsoil because of erosion. Consequently, the application of fertilizers has long been imperative if Chinese farmers are to maintain soil fertility and yield levels.

The Communist government has paid special attention to the problem of soil fertilization. As a matter of fact, among all the technological policies adopted by the government to promote agricultural production, the policy on fertilization is the only one that has been persistently stressed, least disputed, and relatively successful. It is generally agreed that, given the man-land ratio in China, the application of fertilizers is an unquestionably appropriate measure because of its obvious effect of raising crop yields per unit of land.

Generally speaking, the government's policy emphasis in the 1950s was placed on mobilizing the resources of natural fertilizers traditionally used by Chinese peasants. The emphasis has shifted in recent years, however, to the application of chemical fertilizers. The first two sections of this chapter will examine the existing circumstances and the reasons for the shift in emphasis.

Natural Fertilizers

Table 6.1 lists the average plant nutrient content and the absorption rate of various natural fertilizers traditionally used by Chinese farmers.

Table 6.1 Nutrient Content and Absorption Rate of Various Traditional Fertilizers (percent)

Type of fertilizer	Nutrient content				Absorption rate
	N	P_2O_5	K_2O	Total	
Night soil	0.6	0.2	0.3	1.1	45
Pig manure	0.5	0.4	0.5	1.4	20
Draft animal manure	0.6	0.3	0.8	1.7	20
Compost plant residues	0.3	0.2	0.6	1.1	30
Oilseed cakes	7.0	1.3	2.1	10.4	65
Green manure	0.4	0.1	0.4	0.9	65
River and pond mud and others				0.2	10

Sources: The data are the averages directly taken, or computed from the data, in the following publications:
JMJP, Nov. 18, 1957.
CKNP, 1959, no. 17, p. 35.
HTNYKHTP, 1958, no. 4, pp. 202–8; no. 1, pp. 39–40; no. 6, pp. 303–10; and 1958, no. 2, pp. 67–72.
NYKHTH, 1958, no. 4, pp. 207–11.
KTNYTH, 1958, no. 6, pp. 19–22.

Among the seven types listed, the last item, river and pond mud and others, is a catch-all category lumping all minor sources of natural fertilizers. For any item, the actual nutrient content varies considerably from place to place and from time to time. Chinese Communist research organizations have made many chemical analyses of samples drawn from various localities. The findings presented in Table 6.1 are approximate averages; they are generally in agreement with the results of studies of this kind conducted in prewar China, Taiwan, and Japan.[2]

The absorption rate of fertilizers appears only in the Chinese Communist analyses; it has been ignored by similar studies made in Japan, Taiwan, or prewar China. In the Chinese Communist studies they are called utilization rates, a somewhat misleading term. For a given type of fertilizer, the utilization rate does not indicate the proportion of the existing supply that has been used or has become available to farmers. That proportion cannot be derived through chemical analyses. For instance, the average utilization rate of animal manure is 20 percent.[3] Yet anyone who is familiar with Chinese farming conditions knows that the proportion of animal manure actually used by Chinese farmers as fertilizer has always been much higher than that. The same source gives the utilization rates of various chemical fertilizers as 80 percent. This does not mean that 20 percent of chemical fertilizers has been discarded. What the term actually indicates is the percentage of the nutrient per unit of fertilizer which can actually or effectively be absorbed by plants. Therefore, the term absorption rate is used in Table 6.1.

The absorption rate is less than unity for a number of reasons. First, all natural fertilizers are organic, so that the nutritive elements have to decompose and become soluble before they can be absorbed by plant roots. Sometimes this process takes a long time or is never complete, hence only a fraction of the nutrient content can be eventually absorbed by plants. Second, plant roots can absorb only the nutritive elements within their reach. Therefore, in comparing various fertilizers, one finds that the absorption rate is correlated to the degree of nutrient concentration. The lower the percentage of nutrient content, the lower the absorption rate, because most of the nutrients cannot be reached by plant roots even though a large amount of the fertilizer is applied to the surface of a given unit of land. Third, some of the nutritive elements will be lost before the fertilizer is applied. For the last reason, the 45 percent absorption rate for night soil is suspected to be too high. Night soil is collected during the entire year and is stored until the time of application. According to one study, 77.17 to 78.42 percent of the nitrogen content is lost when night soil has been stored for seventy-five days.[4]

Among various traditional fertilizers used in China, animal manure and night soil are the two most important sources. They are not only relatively rich in plant nutrients but are also regarded as composite fertilizers in the sense that they contain practically all the plant nutritive elements needed in the Chinese soil. However, night soil is a carrier of various intestinal diseases, and some experts are of the opinion that, from a benefit-cost viewpoint, it would probably be more economical to discard night soil than to incur the diseases resulting from its use.[5]

The use of compost is also common almost everywhere in China. It consists mostly of barn compost, whereas outdoor compost is less important because plant residues are less available. While oilseed cakes have both a high nutrient content and a high absorption rate, their application is rather limited because their production directly competes with other crops for land. The same is true of green manure, which was a popular source of fertilizer in South China only, where the long growing season made it possible to raise one crop of green manure in addition to the main crop.

River and pond mud is a poor source of natural fertilizer, since it contains a low percentage of plant nutrients. Its use entails a great deal of labor in digging and transporting. Consequently, only the farms close to rivers and ponds can use it conveniently.

Among various natural fertilizers used by Chinese farmers, only oilseed cakes (and sometimes night soil) involve cash costs. Others require only the farmer's own labor. So far as human efforts are concerned, green manure is the least demanding, since it is grown and used on the same field.

According to Buck's survey, during the 1930s an average of about 3,024 kg of night soil and animal manure was applied per acre of cropland, or 498 kg per mou.[6] If a multiple cropping index of 130 is assumed, the average amount of night soil and animal manure applied to each mou of cultivated land would be 647 kg, or about 2.5 kg in terms of plant nutrients.[7] This amount, however, is too high to be considered a national average, since, in the regions excluded from Buck's sample, a much smaller amount of fertilizers was applied because of the lower density of human and pig population.

Of course, fertilizers were not applied in equal quantities to all land; they were rather concentrated on the land sown for major crops. It is also reported that the amount of manure applied was nearly 50 percent greater in the rice region than in other regions, because there was a denser animal population in the former.[8]

Chinese Communist sources have disclosed the average amounts of natural fertilizers applied in 1952–57.[9] It is claimed that in 1952 fertilizers were applied to 60 percent of cultivated land at the rate of 750 kg per mou, and the figures rose to 80 percent of cultivated land with 1,000 kg per mou by 1957.[10] Taking this report and using the official statistics of total cultivated area, one may derive a 78 percent increase in the total use of natural fertilizers over this period. Yet, when converted into plant nutrients, the increase was much less than the gross weights have implied, because the increments were mainly in the fertilizers that had extremely low nutrient contents and absorption rates.

As was explained earlier, the production of oilseed cakes, the most effective natural fertilizer, competed with other crops for land. Night soil and animal manure had been almost fully utilized by Chinese farmers. In response to the government's increasing pressure on rural communities to mobilize more natural fertilizers, farmers often complained that they had already exhausted all possible sources and no further increase would be possible. To satisfy the government's demands, farmers collected more of such inferior fertilizers as river and pond mud, regardless of their lower effectiveness. For instance, Kiangsu, a province relatively successful in collecting natural fertilizers in both the prewar time and 1952–57, reported the following composition of a total of 2,535 kg of fertilizer applied per mou of cultivated land in 1957: night soil and animal manure, 505 kg; green manure, 30 kg; and river and pond mud, 2,000 kg. There was no significant increase in terms of plant nutrients. Even inferior sources of fertilizers were nearly exhausted by 1957. The same article claims that virtually all rivers, ponds, and aqueducts in the province were "bottom up" by 1957.[11]

In an all-out, fanatic campaign launched by the Chinese Communists in 1958, and ignoring the above facts and other existing physical limitations, the central government ordered farmers and agricultural cooperatives to collect more natural fertilizers. Under strong pressure, provincial and local governments set incredibly high goals for peasants and cooperatives to achieve. What actually resulted was widespread fabrication of statistics concerning amounts of natural fertilizers collected and the piling up of useless "fertilizers" on the fields.

The extent of statistical exaggeration in 1958 was beyond the imagination of any sensible man. For example, the *Anhwei Daily*, provincial newspaper of Anhwei Province, reported in August 1958 the achievements attained in six localities.[12] The average amount of fertilizers applied per mou in 1958 ranged from 93,750 kg to 419,350 kg. Using the highest figure would mean that 628 kg of fertilizers were applied to each square meter of land surface. Whatever materials the so-called fertilizers might be, this amount would be more than enough to bury a small tree, let alone a rice plant. Another example of statistical exaggeration was the report that in Anhwei two million people were engaged in collecting fertilizers every day for two months. A total of 3.05 billion tons of fertilizers was reported as collected during this same period,[13] the equivalent of more than 50 million tons per day. This would mean that each person had collected more than twenty-five tons per day.

Although Chinese official newspapers in 1958 were full of this sort of report, and a tremendous fanfare was given to such glorious achievements, the planning agency perhaps did not take those statistics too seriously. An official bulletin published in October 1959, summarizing achievements in the area of agricultural fertilizers in past years, gave the average amount of natural fertilizers applied per mou for several years prior to 1958. However, it only mentioned that "the amount of fertilizer application per mou was greatly increased in 1958," without citing any concrete figure.[14]

No doubt, under strong governmental pressure, the amount of natural fertilizers actually collected in 1958 must have been larger than in 1957, but far less than the wildly exaggerated statistics. However, the increments were not all useful. It is reported that in some localities untreated industrial wastes and household rubbish were dumped on farmland as fertilizers. Even river and pond mud removed in that year was no better than ordinary dirt. Farmers were mobilized to tear down the dirt walls of rural houses and to use the dirt obtained as fertilizers.[15] The nutrient content of such materials was negligibly low. Moreover, their absorption rates would be reduced to zero when applied in excessive quantities. As one Chinese professor of agriculture points out, sometimes those materials were even injurious to crops.[16] In such southern provinces as Kiangsi and Kwangsi, farmers removed the top layer of grassland and put both soil and grass on farmland as fertilizers. This practice had gone on for several years so that many green hills and slopes had become bare. As a result, there was severe erosion.[17]

The amount of labor wasted in collecting these useless materials was even more serious. The Chinese Communist government was using rural sector labor literally as free goods with no opportunity cost. In 1958 and 1959, many localities reported that 30 to 40 percent of the total farm labor force had been used to collect natural fertilizers.[18]

During the period of "economic readjustment" (1961–64), there was a policy change in this area. The senseless campaign of fertilizer accumulation came to halt, and, aside from the increasing emphasis on chemical fertilizers, stress was placed on green manure,[19] which is higher in nutrient content than other natural fertilizers. Furthermore, it requires a minimal amount of labor, because it will be used on the field where it is grown.

The production of green manure expanded fairly rapidly in South China in 1952–57, since this area has a long growing season and abundant rainfall. In recent years there has been an attempt to extend the production of green manure to North China. It is quite possible to do so in an area where one crop is grown per year, or three crops every two years, since there is some time after the main crop is harvested and before the growing season ends. This interval is too short to raise another main crop but should be long enough to raise certain types of green manure. It has also proven more profitable to replace one regular crop with green manure, under the system of three crops every two years, because the yield of the two regular crops is much higher when green manure is used as fertilizer.[20] During 1961–65, among important tasks in agricultural work were the search for high-yield species of green manure plants and the attempt to overcome a shortage of seeds for those plants.

In order to analyze farm production in subsequent chapters, we need quantitative data on natural fertilizers applied in various years. However, as we have demonstrated, official statistics are not useful for this purpose. We must make independent estimates and convert gross weights to plant nutrients. The results are presented in Table 6.2.

The amount of plant nutrients from natural sources rose from 1.66 kg per mou in 1952 to 2.73 kg per mou in 1959, mainly as a result of

Table 6.2 Application of Natural Fertilizers, 1952–65

Year	Total gross weight (million tons)	Total plant nutrients (1,000 tons)	Nutrients per mou of cultivated area (kg)	Nutrients per mou of sown area (kg)
1952	729	2,759	1.66	1.24
1953	796	3,014	1.81	1.34
1954	867	3,289	1.98	1.43
1955	904	3,432	2.05	1.49
1956	940	3,594	2.13	1.50
1957	1,078	4,066	2.42	1.74
1958	1,121	4,212	2.61	1.80
1959	1,165	4,374	2.73	1.97
1960	950	3,764	2.38	1.71
1961	745	3,137	2.01	1.45
1962	797	3,267	2.11	1.51
1963	858	3,492	2.41	1.73
1964	925	3,740	2.44	1.74
1965	992	3,959	2.58	1.85

Source: Appendix Table 16.

rising densities of human and farm animal populations and the rising utilization rate. The reduction in the number of farm animals in the years immediately after the Great Leap Forward was responsible for the declining supply of natural fertilizers. The 1966 level was probably close to the previous peak; any substantial increase since 1966 would be unlikely.

Supply of Chemical Fertilizers

It is understandable that the production of chemical fertilizers has been visualized by the Chinese Communist authorities as a long-range solution to the problem of raising farm output. Collecting natural fertilizers is labor-consuming and unsanitary, and these fertilizers are ineffective and bulky. But, most important of all, they are in limited supply and can never keep pace with need if farm output is to be raised. The emphasis on natural fertilizers in 1952–59 was a makeshift policy to meet temporarily the need to maintain soil fertility until chemical fertilizers could be produced in large quantities.

Table 6.3 gives annual production, imports, and the total supply of chemical fertilizers in various years in the Communist period. Output

Table 6.3 Domestic Production and Imports of Chemical Fertilizers, 1949–66 (1,000 tons)

Year	Domestic production	Imports	Total supply
1949	27		
1950	70		
1951	134		
1952	188	130	318
1953	249	343	592
1954	326	476	802
1955	403	852	1,255
1956	703	905	1,608
1957	871	1,073	1,944
1958	1,462	1,246	2,708
1959	2,227	1,078	3,305
1960	2,550	865	3,415
1961	2,000	882	2,882
1962	3,000	991	3,991
1963	4,200	1,789	5,989
1964	5,900	1,134	7,034
1965	8,900	1,989	10,889
1966	11,600	2,305	13,905

Source: Appendix Table 17.

data for 1949–57 are fairly reliable. There was no serious quality problem either; the products were manufactured by newly built, modern factories and had standard nutrient content. At the beginning of the regime only ammonium sulfate could be produced, but production had been gradually extended to other types of fertilizers.

Official data on fertilizer output for 1958–60 are confusing. One cause for this confusion is the increasing variety of fertilizers that were being produced. Some published figures referred to ammonium sulfate only; some referred to the total output of all nitrogen fertilizers; still others included all types of chemical fertilizers. More bothersome to statistics users was the deterioration in the quality of fertilizers produced in small factories by "indigenous" methods during the Great Leap Forward period. For instance one Chinese official openly admitted,

> . . . According to the regulations of the State Statistical Bureau, granular fertilizer and bacterial fertilizer should not be included in the statistics of chemical fertilizers. . . . However, when the gross production value index is computed, these fertilizers . . . are all included. . . . A rough estimate shows that 46 percent of the total value of the fertilizer industry in 1958 was of nonchemical fertilizers.[21]

Although this statement refers to the exaggeration in computing the gross value of the fertilizer industry, the same underlying motive must also have affected the reliability of physical output figures reported by local fertilizer plants.

Not only might some nonchemical fertilizers have been included in the reported output data of chemical fertilizers, but also the quality of the latter had greatly deteriorated in some cases. For instance, some plants claimed in 1958 that they had produced sodium nitrate by a new method and that the product contained 4 to 10 percent nitrogen. However, a sample test by the Laboratory of the Ministry of Commerce showed that it actually contained less than .001 percent nitrogen.[22]

By 1961, most of the plants producing chemical fertilizers by indigenous methods had been scrapped.[23] For the country as a whole, only 2 percent of the total output of chemical fertilizers in 1961 was turned out by small plants in 1961,[24] and the small factories that had survived were those with modern facilities. In view of this situation, it would be safe to conclude that since 1961 the quality problem is no longer serious and the products are quite up to standard.

Unfortunately, however, less quantitative data concerning chemical fertilizer production have been released since 1961 under the policy of the Peking government to withhold economic information. Most of the time, the Chinese authorities have released percentage increases in output; absolute quantities have been given only occasionally. The output figures presented in Table 6.3 for 1961–66 are estimates derived by linking the percentage increases and a few known quantities.

The estimates given here for this period are considerably higher than all estimates made by other Western experts on the Chinese economy. Although we do not claim complete accuracy in these figures, we believe that they are more plausible than other estimates, because they demonstrate a higher degree of consistency with other relevant information. In Table 6.4 are compiled the official reports on the annual production of

Table 6.4 Check of Annual Production of Chemical Fertilizer Against Progress Reports, 1961–66 (1,000 tons)

Year	Entire year	January–April	January–June	January–August
1961	2,000			1,620
1962	3,000		1,480	1,950
1963	4,200	1,260	2,100	2,800
1964	5,900	2,270		4,280
1965	8,900		4,800	
1966	11,600		5,800	

Sources:

Output of the entire year: From Table 6.3.

Progress reports:

1961: January–August: *EB*, no. 788 (1962), p. 12.
1962: January–June: *CKHW*, Oct. 9, 1963.
January–August: *PR*, Oct. 4, 1963, p. 18.
1963: January–April: *CKHW*, May 27, 1964.
January–June: *CKHW*, Oct. 9, 1963.
January–August: *CKHW*, Sept. 26, 1963.
1964: January–April: *CKHW*, May 27, 1964.
January–August: *JMJP*, Sept. 26, 1964.
1965: January–June: *PR*, Sept. 24, 1965, p. 4.
1966: January–June: *NCNA*, July 28, 1966.

chemical fertilizers during various time intervals from 1961 to 1966. There is an almost perfect consistency between the official progress reports and our estimated annual outputs. In addition, the following information may serve as a consistency check on our output estimates. During the first eight months of 1964, 3.66 million tons of chemical fertilizers were reportedly supplied to the strategic areas of grain and cotton production in seventeen provinces; this amount accounted for about 80 percent of all fertilizers delivered to farmers in that period.[25] This implies that a total of 4.58 million tons of fertilizers was delivered to the agricultural sector in the period from January to August in 1964, that is, 65 percent of our estimated total supply for the entire year of 1964.

For the period 1949–66 as a whole, the increase in domestic production of chemical fertilizers in China is quite impressive. The total output rose from a trickle of 27,000 tons in 1949 to 11.6 million tons in 1966, representing an annual growth rate of 42.9 percent. This is perhaps one of the highest growth rates of chemical fertilizer production over a prolonged time period ever witnessed by the world. In fact, chemical fertilizer production is the only item, except military goods, that did not show any decline in production in the crisis years. The reported output did drop in 1961 by about .5 million tons; but this loss resulted from the scrapping of indigenous plants built in the Great Leap Forward period, whose products were so poor in quality that they should not have been included in the output data in the first place. To put it in another way, the reported outputs for 1958–60 should be discounted.

According to the plan made in 1956, the output of chemical fertilizers was to reach 3 to 3.2 million tons by 1962, the last year of the Second Five Year Plan.[26] This plan was formulated before the "walking with two legs" policy came into being, and the output target was calculated on the basis of a plan to construct regular fertilizer factories in the next few years. Apparently, the construction plan was carried out without delay and output did reach 3 million tons in 1962.

Under the new policy of "all industries to support agriculture" adopted in 1961, the construction plan for fertilizer factories was enlarged. The difficulty caused by the termination of equipment imports from the Soviet Union for fertilizer manufacturing was offset by increased purchases of equipment from Western countries. Some of these countries also provided technical assistance to install equipment.

In the meantime, China managed to expand its own capacity to produce equipment needed for fertilizer production. Since 1961, more than a hundred large-scale factories designed to make generators have been converted to produce equipment for the chemical fertilizer industry.[27] However, for technical reasons China is able to supply equipment for small and medium-size plants only. The largest plant ever reported to have only Chinese-made equipment has an annual capacity of 100,000 to 120,000 tons.[28]

Aside from the technical limitations, small plants are preferred also because they can be scattered throughout all farming regions so that transportation costs for distributing fertilizers can be reduced. The savings on transportation costs compensate for the higher production costs per unit of output in small plants. It should be noted, however, that the small plants constructed since 1961 are not like the indigenous units erected in 1958–59. The new small plants use modern equipment and produce a standard commodity.

Official statistics show that small plants turned out only 2 percent of the total output of chemical fertilizers in 1961.[29] The relative output of fertilizer plants of different sizes in 1964 was: large plants, 60 percent; medium plants, 10 percent; and small plants, 30 percent. The average capacity of small plants was about 12,000 tons per year in 1964.[30] More than two-thirds of the small plants in 1964 were those producing phosphorous fertilizers. A goal was set in that year to build 180 medium-size plants and 2,000 small ones in the near future.[31]

Regarding imports of chemical fertilizers, except for a few years, the general trend has been a rising one. Imports are supplementing domestic output to meet the rapidly increasing needs for chemical fertilizers in the country. Before the large-scale construction of the fertilizer industry at home was underway, imports provided the immediate solution to the fertilizer problem. Therefore, as one can see in Table 6.3, up to 1957 imports rose faster than domestic production, but the growth rate of the former began to fall short of the latter thereafer.

China's imports of chemical fertilizers were also complementary to domestic production in another sense. The output of different types of fertilizers did not grow at a comparable rate; thus, a changing variety of fertilizers was imported to maintain the balanced nutrient ratio most suited to China's agricultural need.[32]

Allocation of Fertilizers

The total amount of plant nutrients from both natural and chemical fertilizers applied per mou of cultivated land in each year is presented in Table 6.5. Until 1959, both categories of fertilizers increased steadily. But the reduction in natural fertilizers in 1960–63 was too severe to be offset by the rise in the supply of chemical fertilizers, with the result that smaller total amounts of fertilizers were used in those years. The peak application level achieved in 1959 had been restored by 1964. In spite of the rapid growth in the supply of chemical fertilizers, the bulk of plant nutrients came from natural sources throughout the period. The proportion of natural fertilizers in total usage was always more than 80 percent before 1962, and it was still as high as 64 percent in 1965.

As Table 6.6 shows, if we take chemical fertilizers alone, even the

Table 6.5 Fertilizer Application, 1952–65
(kg of plant nutrient per mou of cultivated land)

	Native fertilizers		Chemical fertilizers		
Year	Amount	Percentage of total	Amount	Percentage of total	Total
1952	1.66	98	0.03	2	1.69
1953	1.81	96	0.07	4	1.88
1954	1.98	96	0.09	4	2.07
1955	2.05	93	0.15	7	2.20
1956	2.13	92	0.19	8	2.32
1957	2.42	91	0.24	9	2.66
1958	2.61	88	0.35	12	2.96
1959	2.73	87	0.40	13	3.13
1960	2.38	86	0.40	14	2.78
1961	2.01	83	0.41	17	2.42
1962	2.11	79	0.55	21	2.66
1963	2.41	75	0.81	25	3.22
1964	2.44	72	0.94	28	3.38
1965	2.58	64	1.44	36	4.02

Sources of data and estimation procedures: Data on natural fertilizers are from Table 6.2. Data on chemical fertilizers are derived in the following way:

Basic data on domestic production of chemical fertilizers are given in Appendix Table 17. However, some adjustments have to be made for the figures for 1958–65. First, outputs in 1958–60 are not comparable in quality with those of other years. Since the increments in ammonium nitrate and phosphorous fertilizers in the three years are not too large, we assume that they maintained the standard quality. This amounts to assuming that the substandard fertilizer was in the category of ammonium sulfate. Therefore, an adjustment is made to scale down outputs of ammonium sulfate in the three years. Second, for 1962 and 1963, outputs of phosphorous fertilizers are derived through interpolation. Third, for each year of 1960–65, the output of nitrogenous fertilizers is broken down into ammonium sulfate and ammonium nitrate by assuming that the output of the latter remains 450,000 tons a year. After these adjustments, the 1958–65 data appear as follows (in 1,000 tons):

Year	*Ammonium sulfate*	*Ammonium nitrate*	*Phosphorous fertilizers*
1958	700	307	344
1959	900	444	450
1960	1,000	450	550
1961	900	450	570
1962	1,650	450	900
1963	2,450	450	1,300
1964	3,650	450	1,800
1965	6,450	450	2,000

The plant nutrients contained in the three types of fertilizers are as follows:

Ammonium sulfate	N = 20.5 percent
Ammonium nitrate	N = 34 percent
Phosphorous fertilizers	P_2O_5 = 17 percent

Sources of data and estimation procedures for Table 6.5, continued

Imports of chemical fertilizer in various years are given in Table 6.3 for 1953–64. They are distributed into two categories (nitrogenous and phosphorous fertilizers) according to the proportions calculated by Jung-chao Liu, *A Study of the Fertilizer Industry in Communist China* (forthcoming), Chap. 4, Table 4.5. The proportions between the two categories of imported fertilizers in 1952 and 1965 are assumed. Following are the proportions we have used in our computation (in percent):

Year	*Nitrogenous fertilizers*	*Phosphorous fertilizers*
1952	80	20
1953	80	20
1954	68	32
1955	86	14
1956	80	20
1957	88	12
1958	97	3
1959	99	1
1960	100	0
1961	100	0
1962	100	0
1963	94	6
1964	88	12
1965	85	15

The nutrient contents are:

Nitrogenous fertilizers $N=20.5$ percent
Phosphorous fertilizers $P_2O_5=17$ percent

The total amounts of plant nutrients of domestically produced and imported chemical fertilizers in various years are divided by the total cultivated acreages given in Table 8.5 and Appendix Table 15.

1965 level was still below the world average. However, the comparison would be less unfavorable to Communist China if natural fertilizers are included. The combined total fertilizer application in 1965 was 60 kg per hectare, which is slightly higher than in the United States.[33] It is true that many other countries also use natural fertilizers, but none to the high degree that Communist China does.[34]

Chemical and cake fertilizers are distributed by the central government, whereas other natural fertilizers are collected and used locally by peasants and agricultural production units. The distribution of chemical and cake fertilizers has been based on a discriminatory rationing system designed to accomplish a number of goals: (1) to compensate for the uneven distribution of natural fertilizers, (2) to instrument the government's procurement of farm products, and (3) to attain a maximum output increase by selecting crops and areas.

Beginning in 1955, when the Peking government launched the agri-

Table 6.6 Chemical Fertilizer Application in Selected Countries (kg per hectare)

Country	Fertilizer application
Communist China	22
Netherlands	562
Japan	302
U.S.A.	57
U.S.S.R.	19
India	4
World average, excluding Communist China and North Korea	30

Sources:
Communist China: 1965 figure, from Table 6.5. One hectare equals fifteen mou.
Other countries and the world average: From Liu, *Study of the Fertilizer Industry*, Chap. 6, Table 6.3. The data refer to 1964–65.

cultural cooperativization movement on a large scale, a special pattern of application of natural fertilizers was evident. Farmers tended to retain the bulk of natural fertilizers for use on their private plots. In a sense this signifies a kind of misallocation of fertilizer resources induced by institutional changes, and it has been criticized by some Communists in China. As a rule, private plots were used to grow minor crops, yet they received an unduly large proportion of fertilizers. This bias was removed in 1958–59 by the elimination of private plots, but it reappeared as soon as the private plot system was reinstated during the readjustment period.[35]

A policy was then set by the government to distribute chemical fertilizers almost exclusively to agricultural cooperatives or communes to compensate for the disproportional use of natural fertilizers. Although there has never been any regulation forbidding sales of chemical fertilizers to individual farmers to be used on private plots, the nearly exclusive allocation to cooperatives and communes has been achieved through the discriminatory policy of farm credits which provide most of the working capital in the rural areas for purchasing fertilizers.

The allocation of commercial fertilizers was also used by the government to induce agricultural production units to sell farm products to the procurement agencies. The intimate relation between fertilizer rations and procurement programs was particularly noticeable in the case of cotton. A cotton grower was entitled to buy commercial fertilizers only when he had sold a certain amount of cotton to the government.

To obtain a maximum output increase from the limited availability of commercial fertilizers, their distribution has been selective according to crop. Crops favored are cotton, rice, and wheat. Table 6.7 lists the estimated quantities of chemical fertilizers distributed to various crops in the period 1952–65.

In terms of fertilizers applied per unit of land, cotton has been the most favored crop. One official source indicated in early 1952 the following distribution percentages of chemical fertilizers: cotton, 38.5; rice, 33.5; wheat, 17.1; and other industrial crops, 10.9.[36] These percentages are believed to be based on the actual distribution figures for 1951, a year when the Communist government placed the highest priority on cotton in its program of agricultural production. The sown area of cotton jumped from 57 million mou to 82 million mou in that year in response to various policies of the government to encourage cotton production. Except in 1954, the amount of chemical fertilizers allocated to cotton land remained in the range of 100,000 to 133,000 tons a year until 1958. After 1958, the proportion of chemical fertilizer applied to cotton land sharply declined as the incremental supply of chemical fertilizers went to grainland, though the application per unit was still higher in cotton land than in grainland.[37] The ratio of chemical fertilizers distributed to cotton and grains rose slightly in 1958 when the absolute amount of fertilizers allotted to cotton was raised by 75,000 tons. The policy of gradually equalizing the distribution of chemical fertilizers between these crops was probably based on the consideration of obtaining a maximum total return by avoiding diminishing returns of fertilizer application to cotton fields only.

During the crisis years of 1959–61, the government, preoccupied with grain production, could at best maintain the same amount of chemical fertilizers per unit of cotton land and use all the increments of fertilizers for grain production. It was only after grain output had been restored to a more or less self-sufficient level that the attention of the government was shifted to industrial crops again, and cotton regained its prominence in fertilizer distribution. The rapid growth in unit yields of cotton land in 1963–65, it is believed, resulted from the increased application of fertilizers. In 1965, each mou of cotton land received about 14.3 kg of chemical fertilizer, whereas grainland received 5.7 kg per mou. This proportion is perhaps close to the optimum distribution that would maximize the total return of chemical fertilizers.

It should be noted, however, that even for such priority crops as cotton and rice, chemical fertilizers have not been distributed evenly to

Table 6.7 Distribution of Chemical Fertilizers to Various Crops, 1952–65 (1,000 tons of gross weight)

Year	Cotton: Quantity	Cotton: Percentage of total	Other industrial crops: Quantity	Other industrial crops: Percentage of total	Grain: Quantity	Grain: Percentage of total	Total
1952	100	31.4	35	11.0	183	57.6	318
1953	100	16.9	35	5.9	457	77.2	592
1954	66	8.2	23	2.9	713	88.9	802
1955	133	10.6	40	3.2	1,082	86.2	1,255
1956	125	7.8	40	2.5	1,443	89.7	1,608
1957	125	6.4	40	2.1	1,779	91.5	1,944
1958	200	7.4	70	2.6	2,438	90.0	2,708
1959	200	6.1	70	2.1	3,035	91.8	3,305
1960	190	5.6	66	1.9	3,159	92.5	3,415
1961	175	6.1	60	2.1	2,647	91.8	2,882
1962	326	8.2	80	2.0	3,585	89.8	3,991
1963	426	7.1	100	1.7	5,463	91.2	5,989
1964	779	11.1	150	2.1	6,105	86.8	7,034
1965	900	8.4	180	1.7	9,809	89.9	10,889

Sources of data and estimation procedures:

1. Total supplies of chemical fertilizers in various years are taken from Table 6.3.
2. Chemical fertilizers apportioned to cotton land in various years are estimated through the following procedures:
   a. 200,000 tons of chemical fertilizers were to be supplied to cotton-growers in 1958. See *CHCC*, 1958, no. 4, p. 12; and *HHPYK*, 1958, no. 11, p. 106. It is clearly stated in these two authorative sources that this amount was the total supply to cotton land. In fact, *CHCC*, 1958, no. 4, p. 14, has given other relevant information:
      (1) 150,000 tons were to be allotted to 15 million mou of "high-yield" cotton lands with a consumption of 10 kg per mou.
      (2) According to experiments, each kg of chemical fertilizer could raise cotton yields by 1 to 1.5 kg. Therefore, the increase of chemical fertilizers by 75,000 tons in 1958 was expected to result in an increase of cotton output in that year by 75,000–105,000 tons.
   b. The 1957 amount is derivable from the above information.
   c. 1954 and 1955: From the official data cited in *China Monthly*, 1965, no. 7, p. 19.
   d. 1956: The 1955 and 1957 amounts are almost the same. Thus it is assumed that a policy was set in 1955–57 to allocate roughly the same amount of chemical fertilizers to cotton-growers.
   e. 1953: The quantity in 1954 is said to have been 33 percent lower than that in 1953. See *HHYP*, 1955, no. 4, p. 127. This source also states that this decline was unfortunate and that the "normal" amount should have been one-eighth of the total supply of chemical fertilizers, which means 100,000 tons on the basis of the 1954 total supply.
   f. 1952: It is assumed that 100,000 tons was the actual allotment made in 1952 and 1953. That is why this amount was regarded as "normal." *CFJP*, Jan. 21, 1952, reported the following proportions for the distribution of chemical fertilizers:

Sources and estimation procedures for Table 6.7, continued

cotton, 38.5 percent; rice, 33.5 percent; wheat, 17.1 percent; other industrial crops, 10.9 percent. These distributional shares are believed to be those for 1951, which again gives approximately 100,000 tons for cotton land. Thus it is very likely that the Chinese government had decided in those few years to fix the quantity of chemical fertilizers for the cotton crop at the 100,000-ton level.

g. 1959–1962: From the information cited in par. a. above, we have learned the following distribution policy of the Chinese government: For the 15 million mou "high-yield" cotton land, each mou would receive 10 kg. For the "low-yield" cotton land, each mou would receive only 0.7 kg.

One Chinese publication has reported the result of an experiment conducted on a demonstration farm in Siyang, Kiangsu Province, in order to find out an "optimal" amount of chemical fertilizers to be applied to cotton land. This farm used 15.5 kg of chemical fertilizers per mou, and the result was a very high unit-yield of cotton (75 kg per mou). See *HTNYKHTP*, 1958, no. 4, p. 208. Obviously the ration of fertilizers for the high-yield cotton areas could not have approached 15 kg per mou, given the limited total supply in 1958.

Another report (*TKP*, July 27, 1962) indicates that in Hupeh Province, a high-yield cotton area, the per mou consumption of chemical fertilizers on cotton land was 15–20 kg, about twice that of 1961. This information not only confirms the distribution policy of chemical fertilizers set in 1958 but also tells that this rationing quota was maintained throughout the period 1958–61 and was raised only in 1962.

Using these rationing quotas, we may estimate the total chemical fertilizer consumption on cottonland in 1959–62 in the following way: The sown areas of cottonland in various years are given in Appendix Table 15. From the total cotton-sown area in each year during 1959–62, we subtract the 15 million mou that had been designated "high-yield" cotton fields to obtain the size of "low-yield" cotton land. The underlying assumption is that the country had converted some of the low-yield cottonland into grainland during the crisis years, but the high-yield cotton fields remained unchanged because of the substantial comparative advantages those fields had. Thus, we can apply the 1958 rationing quotas to the high- and low-yield cotton fields respectively for 1959–61, and use the new quota for 1962.

h. 1963–64: In the absence of information concerning the rationing quotas of chemical fertilizers distribution, we are forced to use the following indirect procedures to estimate consumption of chemical fertilizers on cotton fields. We assume that the remarkable yield increases of cottonland in 1963–65 were due solely to the augmentation of chemical fertilizer application. We also accept the lower end of the official estimates of yield response of cotton to chemical fertilizers, namely a 1:1 ratio (*CHCC*, 1958, no. 4, p. 12). Furthermore, from scattered sources we can derive the following relevant quantities as shown in Table 11.4:

Year	*Output of cotton (billion catties)*	*Sown area of cotton (million mou)*	*Unit yield (catties per mou)*	*Average consumption of chemical fertilizers (catties per mou)*
1962	2.06	53	39	12.3
1963	2.48	61	40	
1964	3.40	69	49	

Continued following page

Sources and estimation procedures for Table 6.7, continued

Therefore, the total consumption of chemical fertilizers on cotton fields in 1963 should be:

$[12.3\times61]+[2,480-39\times61]=851$ million catties or 425,500 tons.

And for 1964 it should be:

$[12.3\times69]+[3,400-39\times69]=1,558$ million catties or 779,000 tons.

i. 1965: A personal guess.

3. Consumption of chemical fertilizers for other industrial crops: We begin by accepting the officially given proportions of chemical fertilizer distribution in 1952, between cotton and other industrial crops, namely 38.5 to 10.9. We further assume that the rationing quotas for other industrial crops have moved more or less along the same line as for cotton.
4. Consumption of chemical fertilizers for grains: These figures are the results of subtracting the quantities for cotton and other industrial crops from the total supplies of chemical fertilizers.

all growers.[38] The policy has always been to concentrate on the areas where factors complementary to the application of chemical fertilizers are present and the yield responses are relatively high. For example, of the 200,000 tons of chemical fertilizers allotted to cotton land in 1958, 150,000 tons were distributed to 15 million mou of high-yield land, or 10 kg per mou, in contrast to the 50,000 tons for 70 million mou of low-yield land, or 0.71 kg per mou.[39] In 1964, the government designated the strategic areas of cotton and grain production in seventeen provinces.[40] The allocation of 4.58 million tons of chemical fertilizers between the strategic areas and the rest of the farmland in the period from January to August 1964 is given as 3.66 million tons for the former and .92 million tons for the latter. In the same eight-month period in 1963, before those hsien were designated as strategic areas, they received 2.07 million tons, or 55 percent of the total 3.75 million tons of fertilizers distributed.[41] The strategic areas comprise about one quarter of the total cultivated land in China.[42] Thereafter, the per mou application of chemical fertilizers in those areas in 1964 was about 3.2 times the national average, or 2.7 kg of plant nutrients. If the amount of natural fertilizers used in those areas was no less than the national average (2.3 kg per mou), the combined amount of plant nutrients would be 5 kg per mou, or 75 kg per hectare. The strategic areas were presumably the places that had shown more favorable yield responses to chemical fertilizers and had better irrigation facilities and other conditions complementary to fertilizer application. For grains, the selected areas for preferential distribution were likely to be those with high multiple cropping indexes.

Chapter 7

Cropping Systems and Breeding

Changes in Cropping Systems

Changes in cropping systems during the Communist period have taken place in two main directions: the extension of multiple cropping and the substitution of one crop for another in the hope of attaining greater economic gains. Of course, there have been various combinations of the two in many cases. For instance, the system of single cropping may have been converted to double-cropping with an alteration of the crops grown.

Professor Buck has classified China proper in 1930s into the following eight agricultural areas according to the cropping system.[1]

1. Spring wheat area, including the northern parts of Hopei, Shensi, Shansi, and Kansu, and the southern parts of Jehol, Chahar, Suiyuan, and Ningsia;
2. Winter wheat-millet area, embracing large portions of Shansi, Shensi, and Kansu, and small portions of Honan and Hopei;
3. Winter wheat-kaoliang area, including the whole province of Shamtung, a large part of Hopei and Honan, and northern parts of Kiangsu and Anhwei;
4. Yangtze rice-wheat area, including the valleys of the Yangtze River in Hupei, Anhwei, and Kiangsu;
5. Rice-tea area, including a large part of Hunan, Kiangsi, Chekiang, and Fukien;
6. Szechwan rice area, consisting of the whole province of Szechwan and a small part of Hupei, Shensi, and Kansu;
7. Double-cropping rice area, covering the whole province of Kwangtung, the eastern and central parts of Kwangsi, and the southern parts of Fukien and Kiangsi; and
8. Southwestern rice area, referring to the southwestern corner of the

country, that is, the whole province of Yunan, a large part of Kweichow, and the western portion of Kwangsi.

Buck has grouped the eight areas into two regions, the rice region and the wheat region. T. H. Shen later classified four agricultural areas outside the territory covered by Buck's study:[2]

1. Mongolian pastoral area: Inner Mongolia;
2. Soybean-kaoliang area: Manchuria;
3. The pasture lands of Tibet: Tibet; and
4. Oasis farming area: Sinkiang.

Each of the above agricultural areas had long since developed the cropping pattern best adapted to local conditions under the existing farm technology. According to Buck's survey, the average double-cropping index was 166 for the rice region but only 127 for the wheat region; when the two regions were combined, the index was 149.[3] The last figure is too high to be the average index of double cropping for the country as a whole in that period, because, aside from possible sampling biases, Buck's survey excluded the vast area of Manchuria and Sinkiang where only one crop was grown each year.

Because of the shortage of arable land, it has been a policy of the Chinese Communist government from the onset to extend double-cropping as a chief means of raising farm output. As shown in Table 7.1,

Table 7.1 Official Indexes of Double-Cropping in Communist China, 1952–58

Year	Index
1952	130.9
1953	132.7
1954	135.3
1955	137.2
1956	142.3
1957	140.6
1958	145.0

Source: TGY, p. 128.

the official index of double-cropping rose from 130.9 in 1952 to 145 in 1958. Its continuous increase was interrupted by only a temporary setback in 1957. The largest jump occurred in 1956, and the total area of land on which more than one crop was grown per year expanded by 209 million mou from 1952 to 1956; the increase in 1956 alone was 94.9 million mou.[4]

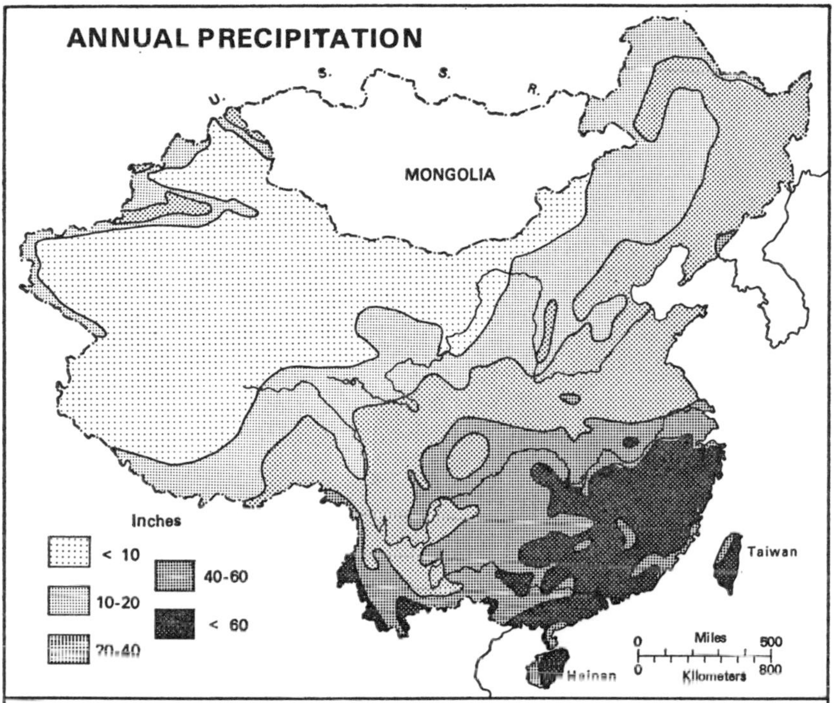

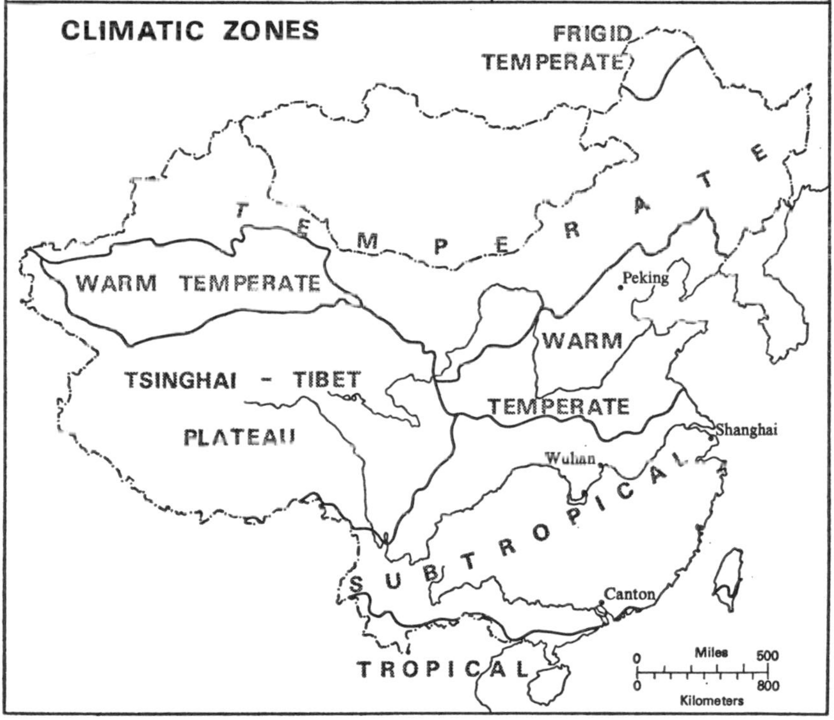

Map by the University of Wisconsin Cartographic Laboratory

However, the progress varied from region to region. The claimed achievements in 1952–57 and the planned targets for 1967 for individual regions, based on the Communist division, are presented in Table 7.2.

Table 7.2 Achievements and Planned Targets for Double-Cropping in Various Regions (in terms of double-cropping indexes)

	Achievements in 1952–57			Planned targets for 1967	
Region	1952	1957	Increase	Planned target	Increase over 1957
South China	167.2	186.8	19.6	230	43.2
The area north of the Wuling Mountains and south of the Yangtze River	147.2	171.1	23.9	200	28.9
The area north of the Yangtze River, and south of the Yellow River and the Chinling Mountains	149.4	154.2	4.8	160	5.8
The area north of the Yellow River and the Chinling Mountains, and south of the Great Wall	109.2	113.5	4.3	120	6.5

Source: CKNP, 1957, no. 24, p. 4.

One can see from this table that rapid increases in double-cropping took place mainly in the first two regions, that is, in the area south of the Yangtze River. The major changes were in rice planting—a conversion from single-cropping to double-cropping, from nonconsecutive rice crops to consecutive rice crops, from upland rice to paddy rice, and from the indica varieties to japonica varieties.

The changes were the most drastic in 1956. In that year the total area of double-cropping rice was suddenly expanded by 32.2 million mou. In Szechwan Province the area of double-cropping rice rose from 80,000 mou in 1955 to 6.8 million mou in 1956. Chekiang and southern Kiangsu, including the suburbs of Shanghai, were another important area where the double-cropping of rice was expanded by more than 7 million mou in 1956.[5]

Unfortunately, most of these changes in 1956 proved to be failures. Since the large-scale expansion of double-cropping rice was carried out under government order without paying attention to local conditions and complementary factors required for such a change, many adverse effects on agricultural production resulted.

Physiographically, the area south of the Yangtze River has an average annual precipitation exceeding 1,250 mm and a frost-free period longer than 250 days,[6] hence it is basically suited to the double-cropping of rice. However, such a cropping system would not be suitable unless the following requirements are met:

1. More fertilizer is needed for both the first and second crops.
2. Since rainfall usually comes in one season of the year, the land dependent on the storing of rainwater is good for only one crop of rice; the artificial irrigation system has to be improved if a second crop of rice is to be raised outside the rainy season.
3. In order to squeeze two rice crops into the growing season of one year, new varieties of early maturing rice have to be adopted. Early ripening varieties may be used for the first crop and varieties that are more cold resistant for the second crop, so that the plants will not suffer possible winterkill toward the end of the growing season.
4. There are tremendous peak demands for manpower and draft animals during the short time between the harvesting of the first crop and the transplanting of the second crop. These peak demands can be met only when there is a sufficient supply of manpower, draft animals, and farm implements.

Yet in many localities where farmers were forced to adopt rice double-cropping in 1956, these complementary factors were not present. Consequently, the total grain output actually fell in these localities after the conversion to double-cropping. Because of a lack of early maturing varieties of rice seed, the late rice in some areas suffered winterkill. In parts of Hunan, Kiangsi, and Chekiang, the yield of late rice was exceedingly poor because of insufficient water. In the Yangtze valley where the growing season is relatively brief, the peak load of farm work fell within the short period of seven to fifteen days. In these areas, even with everyone working at full capacity, labor was still not adequate to guarantee the timely planting of the second crop. The peak-load problem could have been alleviated somewhat if different rice varieties had been used in the same general area. By doing so, crops could be planted at different times and harvested at different times so that labor, draft animals, and implements could be shifted around among farms. However, this was not done when double-cropping was introduced in 1956; both planting and harvesting times were synchronous in the same general area.[7]

Let us take Szechwan as an example to assess the experience of changing cropping systems in 1956. Professor Yang Kai-chu, of the Szechwan Agricultural College, has emphatically pointed out that the lack of technical advice to farmers was one major cause for the failure. He states:

> Now, all of a sudden, we are ordered to move in this direction at a flying speed. Although conservatism should be avoided, the biological rules of plant growth, nevertheless, can be neither ignored nor "reformed" by sheer enthusiasm. Farmers in Szechwan have rich experience in growing single crops of rice, but double-cropping of rice is something totally new to them. Our agricultural cadres are also novices so far as the task of double-cropping of rice is concerned. They have not grasped the fundamental knowledge of the biological features of rice plants and have never accumulated any practical experience. In advising farmers on the new cropping system, the cadres resorted to the limited knowledge that they had just drawn from a few pamphlets about how to grow double-cropping rice, or from some newspaper editorials concerning this problem. This whole practice is very questionable.[8]

Extensive debates appeared in virtually every Chinese agricultural journal in 1957 about the expansion of rice double-cropping during the preceding year. Many writers thought that this change should not have been introduced in many areas, simply because it was not feasible there. The combined yield under the double-cropping system actually fell short of the single-crop yield in many localities. Even in the areas where the combined two-crop yield was higher than that of a single crop, the change was still considered inadvisable, for the cost increment exceeded the value of output increment. In other words, the net marginal gain was negative. Others thought that the new system should be continued, because they believed that all the causes for failure in 1956 could be easily removed. To support their argument they proposed measures to solve the labor shortage during the peak load time and to change the dates for planting early rice.

At any rate, the Communist authorities were forced to retreat in this connection. The area of rice double-cropping in 1957 was considerably reduced, as the decline in the double-cropping index for that year clearly reflects.

Another important change took place in the Taihu area in 1956. This area had a well-established system of one crop of rice and one crop of wheat in a single year, with the unit yield for both crops above the national average. In 1956 the Communist government, hoping to raise the combined yield of the two crops, ordered the farmers to grow an additional rice crop instead of wheat. Again the innovation turned out to be a complete failure. According to a sample study, the combined yield of two crops of rice fell short of the combined yield of rice and wheat by 136.2 catties per mou. The net output of two rice crops was eighteen yuan less than that of the single rice crop. The economic losses would have been much greater if the value of the wheat crop were counted in. The causes of the failure were similar to those discussed above. However, the situation was worse in the Taihu area, because the conversion to two rice crops had created an environment favorable for the breeding of Pyralididae, moths which attacked farm plants.[9]

Another unsuccessful attempt was made to add a third crop in some places in Kwangtung and Kwangasi, areas which were already under the rice double-cropping system. In Kwangsi the government policy was to add one crop of winter wheat to the double rice crops. The total area under this three-crop system increased as follows:[10]

1951	0.84 million mou
1952	1.00 million mou
1953	1.23 million mou
1954	3.33 million mou
1955	5.03 million mou

In spite of these increases in the area under multiple cropping, the output actually decreased. The whole problem was evaluated by a technician in the Agricultural Bureau of the Kwangsi provincial government.

In the past, especially the last two years, owing to the overeager, wishful thinking of the leadership on various levels to increase grain production, they ignored the reality and set excessively high targets. Not only was a high target decided on at the upper level of the government, but also the original target was raised higher and higher by the subordinate governments. Taking 1955 as an example, the provincial government decided to grow wheat on double-cropping rice land over an area of 4 million mou. Yet, a total of 5.03 million mou was finally reached. However, the technical guidance provided by the agricultural departments in the governments lagged far behind. Consequently, what cadres at the lower level had to implement the policy was their enthusiasm and desire to fulfill the assigned targets. They enforced the policy regardless of the local soil conditions, the availability of fertilizer, the length of the growing season, the existing amount of farm labor, and the willingness of farmers. All the cadres cared about was the obligation to fulfill or overfulfill the targets. . . . This is the origin of all troubles.[11]

In North China, a main direction of change in the cropping system during the period of 1952–57 was the conversion from three crops in two years to two crops each year in some places. That is, there was one crop of winter wheat every year, plus another crop of a coarse grain.[12] Another development was the introduction of paddy rice.

One study shows that although the total area sown in winter wheat rose by 13 million mou between 1952 and 1957 in Hopei, the total output of grain in that province actually decreased by 1.3 million tons, mainly because the expansion of the winter wheat area caused a reduction in such spring crops as kaoliang and corn, which had higher unit yields than winter wheat. The same result was reported for certain districts in Honan.[13]

There is a long historical record of rice production in the area north of the Huai River, for it can be traced back to 300 B.C.[14] However, rice had never become an important crop in North China because of a general shortage of water. Under the policy of the Communist regime, the total area of rice cultivation in the northern provinces and Manchuria had been enlarged from the 1952 level of 17.6 million mou to 30 million mou in 1957;[15] of the latter amount, 12 million mou were in Manchuria.[16] The line of rice production had been pushed northward to 50° north latitude, to the Heiho district of Heilungkiang Province.[17] Up to 1957 the promotion of rice production made positive contributions to grain output in the northern provinces, since the unit yield of paddy rice was higher than that of both wheat and coarse grain. A plan was drawn up to increase the rice area in the northern regions to 80 million mou by 1958 and to 300 million mou by 1962.[18] This plan was based on an optimistic expectation of large-scale construction of irrigation facilities. When the mass extension of irrigation works in 1958 proved a fiasco, the planned increase in the rice area failed to materialize. For instance, there was a plan to enlarge rice cultivation in the Tientsing district from 95,000 mou in 1957 to 200,000 mou in 1958, but the actual acreage was less than 70,000 mou in 1958.[19] For North China and Manchuria as a whole, the acreage sown to rice actually attained in 1958 was given as 30 million mou, no increase from the 1957 level. However, in some rice fields in North China the unit yield dropped as much as 30 percent from the 1956 level, because the new irrigation system had no drainage facilities and the land became salinized.[20]

The really successful program launched by the Communist government in changing cropping systems has been the promotion of potato planting. This has been carried out in practically all parts of China, and so far no report of any adverse effect has been heard.

Table 7.3 gives the official data on changes in acreages sown to various crops between 1952 and 1957. The rice area had the largest expansion

Table 7.3 Official Data on Changes in Sown Areas of Various Crops, 1952–57

Crop	Increase in sown area from 1952 to 1957 (in million mou)	Percentage increase 1952 = 100
Rice	57.9	13.6
Wheat	41.4	11.1
Coarse grains	2.4	0.3
Potatoes	27.1	20.8

Source: Computed from *TGY*, p. 129.

in absolute terms, resulting from double-cropping in the south and the introduction of rice cultivation in the north. The enlargement of the area sown to wheat in the north was offset to a small extent by the conversion from wheat to rice in other regions of the country, leaving a net wheat increase of 41.4 million mou. The sown area of coarse grain remained practically unchanged. Its losses in the north were fully compensated by the gains in Manchuria where the newly reclaimed land could be used to grow coarse grain only. The gain in acreage sown to potatoes was not so great as for rice and wheat in absolute terms but was more impressive in percentage, because the sown acreage of potatoes in 1952, as a comparison base, was small.

Official data also indicate that the sown area of rice increased by 7.6 million mou in 1958; but even so it was still 8.5 million mou short of the 1956 peak level. Both wheat and coarse grain substantially decreased in sown area in 1958; by 13.8 million mou and 74.3 million mou respectively.[21] The losses in wheat and coarse grain apparently were offset by the gain in potatoes, where the sown area was enlarged by 86.8 million mou in that year, nearly double the 1952 acreage.

Very little is known about developments after 1958, but the double-cropping index could hardly have increased during the crisis years. However, some land on which cash crops were previously grown had been switched to produce grain. It is also believed that the sown area of coarse grain must have risen in that period. Since coarse grain generally has better ability than rice and wheat to endure the rigorous conditions of too much or too little water and poor soil, Chinese farmers have always tended to replace main crops with coarse grain as soon as the early signs of crop failures appeared. As one Chinese source indicated, when the agricultural conditions in the country had more or less returned to normal after 1962–63, the sown acreage of coarse grain dropped again, whereas that of rice, wheat, and cotton gained gradually.[22]

Seed Selection and Breeding

With her long history of cultivation, vast territory, and great variation in local physiographical conditions, China has developed a great number of crops. For each crop there exists a large species variety. For example, there are more than ten thousand varieties of rice grown in China.[23] In the past, Chinese farmers, through natural and artificial selection, grew the varieties best adapted to local conditions. However, the use of scientific methods for seed selection and breeding is relatively new in the country.

Since the beginning of the Communist period, the work of scientific selection of seeds has been considerably accelerated. It was reported that by the end of 1957 about 630 improved grain varieties had been grown over a total area of 1,045 million mou, or 56.5 percent of total area sown in grains.[24] By 1959, it was claimed, a total of 1,200 new varieties had been selected and bred, 60 percent of them chosen by farmers from local species and 40 percent by agricultural research organizations.[25] Yet a report published in 1961 gave only 212 new species of rice, wheat, cotton, and corn selected by agricultural research organizations.[26] This numerical contradiction may represent in part definitional differences and in part reflect the general statistical exaggeration during the Great Leap Forward years. Furthermore, some new varieties which originally were considered superior proved not to be, when planted in large areas. In addition, the promotion of improved seeds became part of the economic planning of the state; that is, new varieties were introduced to a wide area by government fiat. While this measure has indeed quickened the process of dissemination, it has also produced certain adverse results which were quite disastrous.

As Table 7.4 shows, only 28 of 212 improved varieties bred in the period 1949–60 had been developed through hybridization; most new species had been developed by pure line selection. Furthermore, except

Table 7.4 Breeding Methods in Communist China (numbers of improved varieties)

Crop	Foreign varieties	Local varieties	Systematic selection	Hybridization	Other methods	Total
Rice						
South China	3	11	12	2	0	28
Central China	1	16	18	2	0	37
North and Northwest China	1	1	3	0	0	5
Northeast China	5	0	2	3	0	10
The southwest plateau	0	11	5	0	0	16
Total	10	39	40	7	0	96
Wheat						
Winter wheat in the north region	3	0	1	6	0	10
Winter wheat, north China plains	1	3	3	5	0	12
Winter wheat, south China	4	0	1	4	1	10
Spring wheat region	5	0	0	4	0	9
Total	13	3	5	19	1	41
Cotton, whole country	8	0	9	2	1	20
Corn, whole country	1	8	2	0	44	55

Source: CKNYKH, 1961, no. 8, p. 2.

for wheat, most of the improved varieties were those which already existed in China rather than those imported from other countries. In the Soviet Union, work on hybridization had been discouraged for some time because it was inconsistent with Lysenko's theories of heredity and biology.[27] This was probably not the case in Communist China, where the theories of Lysenko have not decisively influenced the thinking of Chinese agriculturists and biologists, most of whom have received their professional training in the West. Pure line breeding was preferred, because it required the minimum time to achieve.[28] Even in the prewar time, breeding work was carried out preponderantly through the pure line selection.[29]

New varieties of any crop are introduced for two main purposes. First, a new variety is needed to replace an existing type because a higher yield, better quality,[30] or a better ability to resist plant diseases and adverse natural conditions is desired.[31] Second, a new variety is needed because of changed cropping systems, such as the introduction of paddy rice in North China and the conversion from single to double rice cropping in Central China. Table 7.5 presents the official claims of the Peking government as to the achievement in promoting improved seeds in the period 1952–58.[32]

It is difficult to measure the economic gain brought about by the wider used of improved seed. According to one official analysis, of the 30.9-million-ton increase in grain output from 1952 to 1957, 11.6 million tons, or 37 percent, was attributed to the expansion of multiple cropping, whereas 9.8 million tons, or 32 percent, was attributed to the use of improved seeds. The remaining 31 percent of the increase presumably was accounted for by increases of other inputs such as labor, fertilizers, and irrigation facilities. Another Chinese publication reveals that, if other factors are constant, the new varieties adopted in the period 1952–57 would increase the average unit yield of corn by 10 to 15 percent, of wheat by 15 to 20 percent, and of coarse grain by 20 percent.[33] If one assumes that the percentage increase in the unit yield of potatoes resulting from the use of new varieties was about 10 percent, and if one accepts the lowest percentages given above and takes the official data of sown areas and unit yields of various grain crops in 1952 and the sown areas in 1957, plus the information furnished by Table 7.5, he can derive a total increase in grain output of 12.5 million tons in 1957 over 1952, resulting from the use of new seeds.

Yet either the 12.5 million tons or the 9.8 million tons can be regarded as an overstatement. There are reports that the adoption of new

Table 7.5 Percentages of Area Sown to Improved Seeds of Staple Crops, 1952–58 (total area sown = 100)

Year	Grain crops (including tubers)						
	Rice	Wheat	Coarse grains	Potatoes	All grain crops	Cotton	Oil-bearing crops
1952	5.4	5.1	5.0	0.4	4.7	50.2	1.9
1953	7.9	7.4	8.0	2.2	7.4	61.4	2.4
1954	12.0	23.5	12.9	9.9	14.9	67.7	2.9
1955	19.0	32.7	16.5	13.8	20.6	70.5	4.0
1956	41.3	58.7	21.4	38.3	36.4	89.5	31.5
1957	62.9	68.7	42.5	56.5	55.2	93.9	47.7
1958	81.9	86.1	67.9	81.5	77.5	97.0	61.6

Source: TGY, p. 131.

seeds in some cases has caused output reductions on a large scale. Following are the two most serious instances.

1. The first instance was Pima No. 1, a species of winter wheat hybridized from a foreign variety (Piyu) and a local species (Machia) from Shensi. The yield of this hybrid wheat proved to be 35 percent higher than the local variety of Machia wheat. Pima No. 1 was also noted for its stable yield, superior quality for flour-making, immunity to rusts, stiff straw, and strong cold-resistant ability. It was first bred by Professor Chao Hung-Chang at the Northwestern Agricultural College during World War II. It was considered an ideal type of wheat to be grown in China. The popularization of Pima No. 1 began in 1950 under a government program. The total area sown to this variety jumped from 7.5 million mou in 1953[34] to more than 20 million mou in 1955.[35] At least 10 percent of China's wheatland had adopted Pima No. 1 by 1956; in the northwestern provinces the percentage was as high as 80 to 90 percent.[36] For some reasons that are still unclear to agriculturists in China, this variety suddenly lost most of its original superior qualities, especially its immunity to rusts. This phenomenon was first noticed in the northwestern provinces where the Pima No. 1 wheat crop was uniformly plagued by serious rusts, so that the yields dropped to 50 or 60 percent lower than the yields of local, inferior varieties in some localities.[37] Thus, Pima No. 1 was called by farmers, "Pima the disaster." The same problem spread to Shansi Province in 1957 and to practically all areas in North China where Pima No. 1 was grown in 1958. By then this species had become the most susceptible to rusts of all the wheat varieties in China. Still worse, since Pima No. 1 had been adopted over so vast an area, the country was for many years unable to supply the seed of other types to replace it.[38] Pima No. 1 was not completely removed from cultivation until some time in 1961. The total losses incurred are described as "tremendous."

In tracing the origin of the disaster, aside from some biological factors which are suspected to be responsible for the degeneration of Pima No. 1, experts in China have pointed out two policy errors. First, Pima No. 1 was promoted by strong pressure of the government, and it was brought to areas where it could not be favorably adapted to local conditions. For instance, local governments in Kansu forced farmers to grow Pima No. 1 in spite of the warnings given by local experimental stations of its undesirability and unsuitability.[39] The second policy defect was the uniform application of a single variety over a large area. The chief consideration underlying this policy was that doing so would easily maintain the purity of the superior species; that is, undesirable crosses of the superior variety with local inferior varieties would be avoided. However, this practice led to the disappearance of all the original local varieties. This was why China suffered disaster from Pima No. 1 for many years without being able to replace it with other types of seed.[40]

2. The second instance involves the substitution of japonica rice varieties for indica varieties in areas south of the Huai River. The japonica varieties originally were imported from Japan and grown in North China and Manchuria, whereas the indica varieties were the common types of rice grown exclusively in the areas south of the Huai River. The japonica varieties generally demonstrated higher yields and better quality than the indica varieties. Furthermore, since japonica varieties were adapted to climatic conditions in the north, they manifested a better cold-resistant ability. The second feature was attractive to the Chinese Communist planners. It had been observed that in Central China, where two rice crops were traditionally grown, the late rice crop ordinarily had very low yields because the growing season in that area was not long enough to guarantee full maturity of the late rice. Therefore, the theory arose that if the japonica varieties were substituted for either the early or the late rice crop, the yields for both crops could be raised substantially because the growing season would be stretched by the cold-resistant characteristics of the japonica varieties.

Thus, an order was issued by the government in late 1955 to implement such a substitution in Central China and Szechwan in 1956. Two major japonica varieties, Chingsen No. 5 and Yinfang, were selected for this purpose. By the time the 1956 crops were harvested, both varieties had proved to be complete failures.

Chingsen No. 5, a japonica type of early rice originally planted in Manchuria after its importation from Japan, was now introduced to Hunan and Hupei. It replaced the local indica types of early rice over an area of 3.8 million mou in the two provinces in 1956. With few exceptions, there was a serious yield reduction in that vast area. The average yield of Chingsen No. 5 in the two provinces was not only much lower than its records in Manchuria, but it was also lower than some local indica varieties of early rice by 30 to 80 percent. On the average there was a 50 percent yield reduction as compared to the old local varieties. The total loss in the rice output of the two provinces was estimated to be more than 130,000 tons, not counting the cost of shipping 29,000 tons of seed from the north.[41] The grave news was reported in the *People's Daily* in Peking, and an ad hoc investigation team was dispatched by the central government to Hunan and Hupei.[42]

It is interesting to read some of the reports made by agricultural experts on the issue of Chingsen No. 5. The Central China Agricultural Scientific Research Institute, which was responsible for selecting Chingsen No. 5 for use in Hunan and Hupei, has confessed:

Our institute began in 1951 to breed Chingsen No. 5 and planted it in a small plot (200 square feet) for observation. It was not until 1955 that we began to calculate its yield. It was our first blunder that we introduced this species to the public without comparing it with other rice varieties, without testing it in a large area, and without demonstrating to the public the techniques of planting it. During that time, the high tide of agricultural cooperativization led to a high tide of reforming cropping systems and a high tide of converting from indica varieties to japonica varieties; both the government and the public urgently demanded us to introduce some japonica species. Although we had no confidence in Chingsen No. 5, we suggested its use for trial in the flood-detention areas on the grounds that there were no seeds of other types of japonica rice available at that moment and that Chingsen No. 5 had the feature of early maturity, and it could be harvested before the flood season. However, we committed another blunder in that, when the government wanted to adopt it in a larger area, we did not express our objection too strongly, though we did not approve of this.[43]

This report further concluded that while the general direction of substituting japonica varieties for indica varieties in Central China was basically correct, the conversion had to wait until all the necessary conditions were present. Since the japonica varieties generally require relatively large amounts of fertilizers, they should not be introduced into Central China until the application of chemical fertilizers there reached 15 to 20 catties per mou.[44]

The report submitted by Ting Chin-tsai, director of the Agricultural Research Institute of Kiangsi Province, was more critical and attributed a greater blame to the central government. Specifically, he accused the central government of falsifying information and misleading the public and local cadres to believe that adopting japonica varieties in Central China had merit. Ting Chin-tsai stated:

In the Central China Panel of the National Conference of Paddy Rice Production Technique held last year [1955], a few agriculturists brought up the problem of substituting japonica varieties for indica varieties in Central China as a possible direction for future research. This was a brand new subject. But the topic was not discussed or studied in the Conference. After the Conference, the Food Production Bureau of the Agriculture Ministry published a book entitled *Techniques of Planting Paddy Rice*. It is said on page 31 of that book that if japonica varieties are introduced to Central China, they can raise rice yields in that region because japonica varieties have the quality of early maturity. . . . This was the theoretical basis on which Chingsen No. 5 was vigorously popularized in Hunan and Hupei.[45]

Mr. Ting went on to point out that there had never been any experiment clearly indicating that a japonica variety of early rice planted in Central China had produced a higher yield than local varieties. In fact, this was a new subject which had not been studied heretofore. He also cited another article, published in *CKNP* (1956, no. 5), which mentioned the high yields of several japonica varieties in a few experiments made in Hupei. Although he considered the statements of that article interesting, Mr. Ting suspected that the basic information was falsified because the results were biologically impossible. Consequently, he contended that while the whole idea might be set as an objective for future research, it had no practical value at the present time.[46]

Yinfang was a variety of middle rice first brought into China by the Japanese in 1940, and it had become popular in the Tientsing district of Hopei Province. Its unit yield in that locality rose rapidly from 590 catties per mou in 1940 to 818 catties per mou in 1949. This species was introduced into Szechwan and certain parts of Kiangsu in 1956 to replace local varieties of middle rice.[47] It turned out to be a failure in both places. The average output reduction attributed to the introduction of the new species was estimated as 22 percent. However, reports of subsequent studies tended to agree that the output reduction was caused by farmers' lack of experience in the two areas. In a number of experiments conducted in Szechwan,[48] it was shown that although Yinfang was not the best japonica variety that could have been adopted in that province, it did raise yields somewhat as compared with the local indica varieties. According to the analysis, an inadequate supply of fertilizers was the chief cause of output reduction of Yinfang in 1956.

Again, very little is known about the work of seed selection and breeding in Communist China after 1957. There are indications, however, that a more cautious attitude has prevailed after these bitter lessons were learned. It has been realized that a new variety can be widely promoted only after many years of experimentation on large areas and that local physiographical conditions must also be heeded. Greater attention has been given to selecting better seed from local varieties than to bringing in new species from other places.

Not many improved varieties are reported to have been developed in recent years.[49] It would seem that attention has shifted recently to studying the degeneration of some superior species,[50] degeneration that came partly from crosses between superior and inferior varieties and partly from the deterioration of farming conditions during the crisis years. The two most notable cases of degeneration cited by Chinese Communist publications are Nanteh rice[51] and potatoes in general.[52]

Another important emphasis in breeding work in recent years has been the wide application of hybridization, especially for corn. It is reported that hybrid corn has been extended to millions of mou in China in the past few years.[53]

Part III

Output

Chapter 8

Estimation of Cultivated Acreage, Sown Area for Grain, and Grain Output, 1949-57

Introduction

Official farm statistics in the aggregate form are available for the period 1949–57, but their quality is considered unsatisfactory. Agricultural data released by the Peking government for the Great Leap Forward years (1958–59) are even more unreliable, so much so as to render them devoid of any economic significance. The Chinese government has published almost no economic statistics since 1960, presumably to cover up the economic crisis that it began to feel in that year.

The output of various crops and the aggregate production in the Chinese agricultural sector have been estimated by a number of Western scholars for different time periods between 1949 and 1959. These estimates, however, differ from each other considerably, and none of them has gained wide or unreserved acceptance. For the years after 1959, we have only several educated guesses, without the firm support of first-hand, quantitative information.

Since national totals are the sums of provincial data, an investigation of the claimed farm production development in individual provinces in the Communist period, combined with the information furnished by some scholarly studies of Chinese agriculture in the 1930s, may provide us with better knowledge about the quality of national totals.

In this chapter we will try a different approach to reestimate grain production in China in 1949–57. An important feature of this study is that, unlike previous works on this subject which used primarily aggre-

Agricultural Production Map

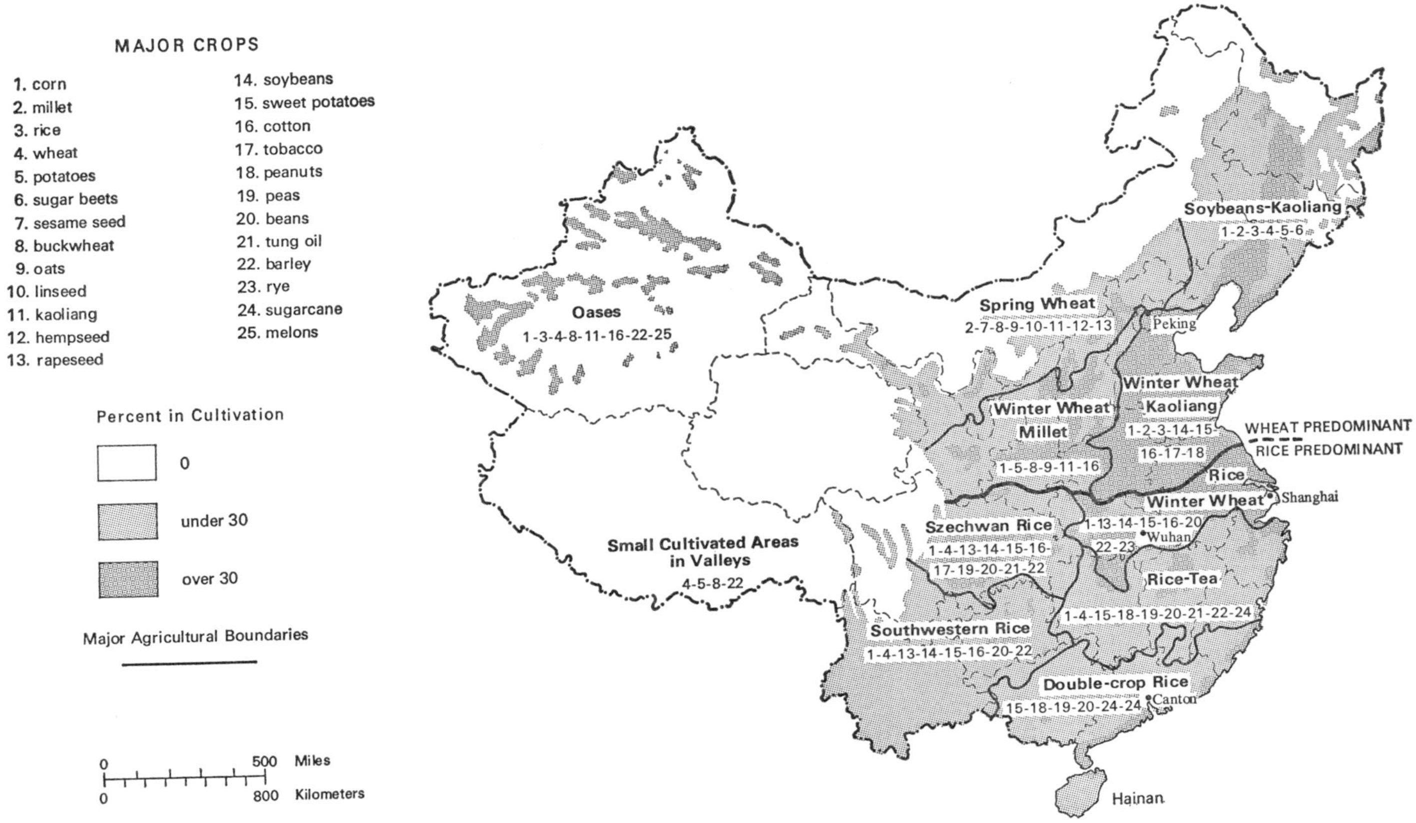

Map by the University of Wisconsin Cartographic Laboratory

gate data, we have begun with Chinese Communist provincial statistics. One reason to use provincial data is that they may throw light on the reliability or unreliability of official aggregate statistics.

Moreover, using provincial data instead of national totals may reduce the range of possible error in the new estimates. For instance, one factor affecting agricultural production in China was the changing amount of cultivated land. Some land had been withdrawn from cultivation every year because of construction activities, whereas new land had been added to cultivation as a result of reclamation. If one uses national totals, changes in the two opposite directions will offset each other, leaving only a net increase or reduction in the acreage of cultivated land. However, this cancellation will inevitably create serious errors in the estimates of farm output, because most construction activities during the period took place in those provinces where land was relatively fertile, whereas reclamation was carried out, as a rule, only in remote regions where the productivity of land was much lower.

The provincial agricultural data used frequently in this study, and which may be useful to other researchers, are presented in the Appendix. These data are taken from a larger compilation of Chinese provincial agricultural statistics and were collected first by the research staff in the Center for Chinese Studies, the University of California at Berkeley, under the directorship of Professor Choh-ming Li, and are supplemented by new data which my assistants and I have subsequently gathered.

The majority of the data in this compilation has been gleaned from a tremendous number of Chinese Communist provincial newspapers held at the University of California at Berkeley, the Library of Congress, and the Union Research Institute of Hong Kong.

There are many pitfalls and difficulties in dealing with these provincial data, and certain initial adjustments are necessary before the data can be used. The first problem is to determine the geographical coverage of each province. As is generally known, before 1957 the Peking government had made changes almost every year in the administrative divisions at the provincial level; the divisions have been stabilized only since 1956. We have decided to use the 1957 administrative divisions, namely twenty-five provinces or equivalents, plus two municipalities (Shanghai and Peking) directly under the central government. This selection was made partly because most of our data has been gathered from sources published after 1956, especially from the "Ten Great Years Reports" released by various provincial authorities in September and October

1959. For any province whose geographical coverage had been altered, the data referring to a coverage different from that of 1957 have been adjusted accordingly.

Another type of adjustment is entailed by the changes in official statistical definitions. For instance, until 1956 food grains were defined to include rice, wheat, sweet and Irish potatoes, various coarse grains, and soybeans. According to the new definition adopted in 1956, soybeans are excluded. In this study the new definition is employed, and all food grain statistics released before 1956 have been adjusted to coincide with the new definition.

Very often one finds several different figures under the same heading and for the same year. Thus a problem arises as to which one of the conflicting figures should be used. Examination shows that these discrepancies may have come from a variety of sources; hence, different treatments are required. Sometimes the discrepancy stems from the changed geographical coverage or statistical definition, as was mentioned above. Another typical case involving conflicting figures occurs when one figure refers to the planned quantity, another represents the preliminary result, and yet another the final accounting. Occasionally, dissimilar figures have been given by different government offices or by persons with different official positions. The rule of selection in those cases is that the final figures or the figures given by the most authoritative person are preferred. In still other cases two conflicting figures were published by the same government office several years apart, and we have failed to find any possible explanation for the discrepancy. It is suspected that in such situations the government deliberately revised its statistics released in earlier years. As a matter of fact, revisions of earlier statistics are numerous. Some are so indicated in the sources, whereas others are not. In these cases we decided to use the revised figures, that is, the data published at the latest dates.

Another important principle for selecting a figure from conflicting ones is consistency with other relevant data. For instance, the data on output, sown area, and yield of a given crop are all related, and the most consistent set of the three indicators has been chosen.

For many items we have failed to collect information for some years in the period so that those items are incomplete time series. Consequently, we have been forced to make our own estimates on the basis of relevant information in an effort to fill the gaps which are vital to our later computation and analysis. The estimation method varies from case to case.

In spite of our efforts, data obtained for the municipalities of Shanghai and Peking are too incomplete for us to make estimates for the missing data. For Tibet, no agricultural information whatsoever has been uncovered. Consequently, these three areas are omitted in our computation, and the coverage of our data compilation is incomplete in this sense. However, so far as Chinese agricultural production is concerned, Tibet is negligible. The combined amount of cultivated land in Shanghai and Peking, as of 1957, was given as 2.51 million mou,[1] but a considerable portion of this land was used to grow vegetables for the population of the two big cities. In any event, the omission of these three areas has only a negligible effect on our evaluation of the national output of grain. The sums of provincial quantities may be taken as national totals with only an insignificant downward bias resulting from this omission.

How the Official Agricultural Statistics Were Collected

The inferior quality of agricultural statistics for 1949–57 not only has been suspected by Western students of the Chinese economy but has also been openly admitted by several responsible officials in the Peking government. Premier Chou En-lai stated in 1956, "We are not yet completely clear as to what the actual amount of food production was in 1954."[2] Similar statements have been made by Hsueh Mu-chiao, then Director of the State Statistical Bureau, who once said, "The survey of agricultural output remains a very weak link in our statistical work."[3]

As will be explained later, the major biases of farm statistics for this period have led to a serious understatement of agricultural land and production for the early years. Consequently, the official growth rate of agricultural production over the whole period is an exaggerated one.

In order to remove or reduce the distortions in the official agricultural data, we have to know the methods used by the government in compiling the basic farm statistics. Since our immediate purpose is to estimate the total grain output in 1949–57, our attention will be concentrated on the factors that had, directly or indirectly, affected the accuracy of the official grain output statistics.

Throughout this period the annual output of a crop in a given locality was officially calculated by the following formula:

Total sown area × yield per unit of sown area = total output.[4]

Sown area refers to the area sown or transplanted with a given agricultural crop.[5] Stubble rice, tobacco, and kaoliang are those plants grown from the stubble of harvested crop without going through the process of resowing and transplanting; they are therefore not counted again as sown acreage. Seedbeds themselves are not included in sown area; but when the land is used for growing regular crops after the removal of seedlings, it is considered sown area. When the crop is sown one year and is harvested during the next year, the sown acreage is counted as that of the harvest year. When two or more kinds of crops are interplanted in the same field, prorated sown areas are computed for all the crops. For example, on a mou of mixed corn and beans, with corn occupying 70 percent of the land and beans 30 percent, the sown acreage of corn shall be 0.7 mou and the sown acreage of beans 0.3 mou.

Statistics on sown area and yield per unit of sown area were separately collected, and their product was taken as the estimated total output. The Communist term, "yield per unit of sown area," or "yield" for short, is the equivalent of the "harvest rate" in the West, except that the former refers to sown area rather than harvested area. During 1949–57, the yield of a crop was obtained by dividing the total harvest in a sample of farms by the total acreage of sown area in the same sample.[6] The reason for using sown area instead of harvested area as the computational basis was that the Chinese government intended to use yield as an indicator that would fully reflect the harvest reduction resulting from natural calamities.[7] Thus, a rate of yield per sown area would be lower than the harvest rate in a given locality if there was land that had been sown but did not produce any harvest because of some calamity. In that case, had the harvest rate been used, one might find that both the sown acreage and the harvest rate might not be lower than those of the preceding years, although there was a reduction in total output.

The measurement of sown area as defined by the State Statistical Bureau was complex and had been criticized by several agricultural statisticians.[8] The statistical problems stemmed mainly from the practice of interplanting and the existence of perennials. So far as can be determined from Chinese Communist publications, the same definition of sown area has been used consistently except for a minor change made in 1956 to refine the measurement. The 1956 revision in definition had little effect on the measured sown area of principal grains; hence, the revision may be ignored here.

Our concern here is not whether the official definitions of sown area and yield are perfect statistically. We are interested in finding out whether the techniques actually employed in China during this period to measure the two indicators had created distortions in what the government intended to measure.

Cultivated Area and Sown Area

The method of investigating sown area varied from period to period and from region to region. Generally speaking, the method prevailing in most of China had undergone the following important changes. During the years immediately after 1949 the method was simple, but it usually resulted in quite unreliable figures. The hsien or chu was used as the unit for estimation. The responsible personnel of a hsien or chu would discuss the matter in local production conferences. A figure of sown area would then be derived by the conferees on the basis of "available relevant information and materials." The so-called relevant materials included the farmland registration records of that locality. This unsatisfactory method was gradually replaced by model surveys in 1952 and 1953, except in remote regions. The new method was to stratify the subdivisions (usually hsiang or tsun) of the whole hsien according to cropping patterns and land fertility. A sample hsiang or tsun was then selected, and within it a number of representative farms were picked for actual investigation. Important statistical parameters were derived from these model surveys. Insofar as sown area was concerned, presumably the investigators would have to compute an average ratio of sown area to cultivated area from the sample farms and apply this ratio to the total cultivated acreage registered in the hsien in order to obtain total sown acreage in that hsien.[9]

There were serious shortcomings in the model surveys. For one thing, the sample was not a random one. Instead, it was chosen according to the subjective evaluation of the investigators as to the representativeness of the sample. Owing to the heterogeneity of individual farms, even within a hsien, in farming practice, terrain, and land quality, proper stratification for drawing a sample was extremely difficult to achieve. Furthermore, the subjective evaluation of investigators could be easily biased by many factors. The investigators might tend to choose farms less distant from their offices or the more cooperative households regardless of the representativeness of the resulting sample, or they might deliberately choose nonrepresentative farms in order to obtain higher or lower figures, as they wished. Another shortcoming was the size of a model sample, which was usually exceedingly small in relation to the universe. For instance, there were 640 tsun consisting of 81,953 farm households in Wulien hsien, Shantung, yet only three tsun were selected, and in each, only six to nine individual households and their farms were chosen as the sample.[10] In other words, the sample size was only .03 percent of the universe. The theoretical justification for using small samples was that if a sample were truly representative, it need not be large in size. The practical reason, however, was that local governments lacked sufficient statistical manpower to handle larger samples.

In view of these shortcomings, and to meet the need for more reliable data to carry out the unified purchase and unified sales policy, the State Statistical Bureau soon introduced a new system to acquire farm statistics. In both 1954 and 1955, the prevailing method was to issue investigation forms by the hsien government to the hsiang or tsun, which was requested to fill out the forms. The actual method used by the hsiang or tsun office to gather information varied among different types of farm organizations to be investigated. Both state farms and agricultural cooperatives were to submit periodical reports of farm statistics based on their own operation and assets records. As for private farms, the sown area was estimated by the hsiang or tsun office with the help of land registration records. The estimates were considered more accurate than those provided by the former production conferences at the hsien level, because the hsiang or tsun offices had more intimate knowledge of local farming conditions and could use the help of mutual aid teams, peasant leaders, local cadres, and other activists to gather information. In short, the new method was a combination of enumeration and estimation by the lowest level of government.

The success of the collectivization movement in 1956–57 gave the Chinese Communists a good opportunity to reform the agricultural statistical system. Beginning in 1956, all agricultural cooperatives were required to submit statistical returns on sown acreage by product.[11] The reports were to be based on the daily records of a cooperative's production teams and on the cooperative's final accounts after the sowing of each crop was completed. Only in the cases of new cooperatives, which were still unable to set up such a recording and reporting system, was the use of estimates based on cultivated acreage permissible. In the meantime, the State Statistical Bureau often conducted sample surveys to check the accuracy of the reports submitted by individual cooperatives.[12]

It was not until 1957, when virtually the whole rural sector had been collectivized, that the sown area data became close to what would have been obtained from a complete enumeration.[13]

Yield

The technique of gathering yield data had undergone similar changes in the period 1949–57. In the early years of the period, the average yield of various crops was estimated by the statistical personnel of each hsien government or was reported by its subdivisions. After 1952, or even later in some regions, model surveys became more widely used for this purpose. In 1956 two important improvements were made in the measurement of crop yields. The State Statistical Bureau began in that year to require all agricultural cooperatives to report yield data, among other things, in their periodical statistical schedules. In addition to the statistical reports submitted by cooperatives, hsien or hsiang governments continued to conduct model surveys to collect information on the remaining private farms or to check the reports of cooperatives. The random sample survey was discussed in the Chinese statistical literature during 1956–57, but it was seldom used because of its technical complexity in drawing samples.[14]

As another significant improvement, the Statistical Bureau urged both cooperatives and government survey teams to measure the actual harvest on the sample land during the time of cutting,[15] instead of reporting the observed biological yield as they did previously.

Adjustment of Official Data on Cultivated Area

It becomes quite clear that, prior to 1957, official data on sown area were only estimates, and the estimation methods were in one way or another related to the official farmland registration. Therefore any bias existing in the official cultivated land data must also exist in the official data on sown area. The question, then, is whether the Communist cultivated area data contained distortions.

To examine this issue, we must go back to the pre-1949 data on cultivated land, by province. There are three important sources of cultivated land statistics for the period of the Nationalist government.[16] One source is *Crop Reports*, published monthly for about five years (1933–37) by the National Agricultural Research Bureau (hereafter referred to as NARB).[17] This organization was established under the

Ministry of Industry in Nanking in 1932 and was charged with the compilation of agricultural information. Most of the NARB crop statistics were based on reports from field workers stationed in some 900 to 1,200 hsien among a total of 1,680 hsien then existing in the twenty-two provinces of China proper. The number of field reporters varied from 2,600 to 6,000 in different years.

However, the data on cultivated acreage for the twenty-two provinces as used by the NARB in its *Crop Reports* were not the result of its independent investigation; instead, they were taken by the NARB from the *Statistical Monthly*,[18] together with the figures for Kwangsi province from *Kwangsi Yearbook, 1933*. Although how those data were originally gathered has never been explained, their source is believed to be the farmland registration records of the Nationalist government. This set of cultivated acreage data had been used by the Chinese authorities for all official purposes throughout 1943. The total acres of cultivated land in the twenty-two provinces was given by this source as 65.8 million hectares, or 986 million mou (short for shih mou).

Another important source of farm statistics for China is Professor J. L. Buck's *Land Utilization in China*, which is the outgrowth of some carefully planned field surveys on a sample of 16,786 farms in 168 localities and 38,256 farm families in the same twenty-two provinces during the period 1929–33. From his surveys, Buck discovered that the official cultivated land data were unreliable because landowners had underreported their land holdings to evade taxes. Estimates of cultivated land not reported in the official records of various hsien were made by Buck's fieldworkers for 111 hsien. They varied from 0 to 80 percent of the cultivated area reported for different localities and averaged about one-third of the reported cultivated area. This high percentage of unreported land under cultivation was also confirmed by other local surveys.[19]

To arrive at a good estimate of total cultivated area and to determine its reliability, Buck used a number of methods to derive four different figures for the eight agricultural areas[20] (equivalent to the twenty-two provinces). Buck's estimates are presented in Table 8.1. A brief mention of Buck's estimates is in order, however.

Buck's estimate IV was obtained by correcting the official records of only those hsien which had been surveyed by his fieldworkers. No correction was made on the official data of other hsien. Detailed information was given in a table in the statistical volume of his study.[21] His estimate

Table 8.1 Prewar Estimates of Cultivated Acreage (million mou)

Estimate	Twenty-two provinces in China proper (1)	Entire mainland, excluding Tibet: Computation I (2)	Entire mainland, excluding Tibet: Computation II (3)
Buck I	1,408	1,662	1,747
Buck II	1,317	1,571	1,656
Buck III	1,244	1,498	1,583
Buck IV	1,144	1,398	1,483
NARB	986	1,240	1,325
DS–1946	1,143	1,397	1,482

Note: Buck estimate IV for the twenty-two provinces was originally given as 1,158 million mou because of a computational error. The correct figure is 1,144 million mou.

Sources:

Col. (1): All of Buck's estimates are from his *Land Utilization*, 1:165. The original figures in acres have been converted into mou by using a rate of 6.07 mou to the acre. The NARB figure is from Chinese Ministry of Information, *China Handbook, 1937–1943*, p. 547. The DS-1946 figure is computed from T. H. Shen, *Agricultural Resources of China* (Ithaca, N.Y.), p. 142.

Col. (2): Obtained by adding 254 million mou to the figures in Col. (1). 254 million is the pre-war official cultivated acreage of Sikang, Sinkiang, Jehol, and Manchuria, as given in Shen, *Agricultural Resources*, p. 142.

Col. (3): Obtained by adding 339 million mou to the figures in Col. (1). The figure of 339 million mou is the result of multiplying 254 million mou by a correction factor of 1.337, which is the correction factor used by Buck to derive his estimate II.

III was obtained by multiplying the average size of farms in his sample surveys by the official total number of farms in individual provinces. In deriving his estimate II, Buck computed a correction factor for each of the eight agricultural areas on the basis of his field surveys and applied these correction factors to the official cultivated land data. His estimate I was the result of combining the higher figure for individual agricultural areas from estimate II and estimate III. Although he thought that his estimate I was "probably the most accurate," he accepted estimate II for use in his text because it was "the better figure statistically."

In 1948 the Nationalist government released a new set of data on cultivated area, as of the end of 1946 (hereafter referred to as DS-1946 data).[22] This set of data included the twenty-two provinces in China proper and other parts of the Chinese mainland not covered by the NARB and Buck's studies. For the twenty-two provinces alone, the total area of cultivated land is given by this source as 76.2 million hectares, which is larger than the NARB's 65.8 million hectares but smaller than any of Buck's four estimates. Since the Directorate of Statistics had never explained how it compiled these data, such experts as Buck and Shen tended to believe that the data were the result of an independent estimation made by the Directorate of Statistics.[23] Yet a careful examination of Table 8.2 shows that the DS-1946 data for nineteen of the twenty-two

Table 8.2 Comparison of Pre-Communist Data on Cultivated Land, by Province (1,000 mou)

Province	Buck	NARB	DS–1946
Charhar	15,530	15,520	15,530
Kansu	26,170	21,670	26,170
Ninghsia	1,810	1,850	1,850
Suiyuan	17,090	17,180	17,090
Shansi	72,880	55,810	72,880
Shensi	45,630	30,870	45,630
Tsinghai	4,330	7,810	7,810
Honan	98,500	104,120	98,500
Hopei	109,130	95,320	109,130
Kiangsu	85,300	84,480	85,300
Anhwei	73,130	49,320	73,130
Shantung	100,450	101,990	100,450
Hupeh	64,500	56,230	64,500
Hunan	50,210	42,040	50,210
Chekiang	41,660	37,980	41,660
Kiangsi	43,340	38,370	43,340
Fukien	21,090	21,460	21,090
Kweichow	23,170	21,200	23,170
Kwangtung	40,990	39,120	40,990
Kwangsi	27,490	29,890	27,490
Szechwan	155,450	88,720	151,440
Yunnan	26,220	25,000	26,220
Total for 22 provinces	1,144,070	985,950	1,143,580

Sources:
Buck's data: Buck, *Land Utilization*, 3:21–29.
NARB data: Taken from Chinese Ministry of Information, *China Handbook, 1937–1943* (New York, 1943), p. 547.
DS–1946 data: Shen, *Agricultural Resources*, p. 142.

provinces were taken from Buck's estimate IV, as presented in *Land Utilization*, 3:21–29. The difference between the DS-1946 set and Buck's estimate IV stemmed from two sources. First, Buck made a computational error in deriving his estimate IV. The total cultivated land, as corrected, for the Rice-Tea Area was 95,709 square km, but he recorded incorrectly a figure of 104,711 square km. This error had been removed in the DS-1946 data. Second, the Directorate of Statistics had adjusted Buck's figures for Szechwan, Ninghsia, and Tsinghai, which it thought unsatisfactory.[24] However, the adjustments for these three provinces, coincidentally, almost cancelled each other out. For nineteen provinces the DS-1946 data are identical with those of Buck's estimate IV. Apparently the Directorate of Statistics was convinced that Buck's estimate IV was more accurate than that of the NARB, but it was either unwilling or unable to adopt any higher estimate made by Buck.[25]

Mention should be made of a wartime effort made by Nationalist government to correct local records of cultivated land. The Nationalist government began in 1940 to conduct a new cadastre. However, because of unfavorable circumstances, the coverage of the cadastre was not nationwide. By the time the program was terminated in 1942, only 400 hsien in thirteen provinces had undertaken it, with only 23 percent of China's farmland covered.[26] Although results of this partial cadastre had never been published, a study made by Ma Li-yuan had used them to estimate the total cultivated acreage in all provinces.[27] It has been revealed that the results of the partial cadastre showed larger cultivated acreages than the old land records in many localities by varying proportions.[28] The total of Ma Li-yuan's estimates for the twenty-two provinces in China proper is 1448.8 million mou.[29] As can be seen from Table 8.1, this estimate is the largest among all pre-Communist estimates of cultivated land for the twenty-two provinces, and it exceeded Buck's estimate I by 40.8 million mou.

However, the general opinion is that the results of this partial cadastre and the aggregate estimates derived therefrom have contained considerable upward biases. Since it was made during the war and the government was anxious to save both money and time, in virtually all localities where such surveys took place, land areas were "observed," not actually measured by surveyors, or "declared" by owners or pao-chia officials. A recheck was ordered by the government in 1942 for Szechwan province because of numerous complaints by landowners that their landholdings had been overstated. In Chekiang, the figure obtained from an actual measuring of cultivated land in three hsien proved to be smaller than the figure obtained by the original survey. One factor responsible for the upward biases in the survey results was the fact that the surveyors were remunerated according to the total area that they had surveyed, consequently they were strongly inclined to exaggerate their survey results.[30]

In any event, the wartime cadastre was both incomplete in coverage and inaccurate in measurement. The fact that the Nationalist government, instead of publishing the results of this cadastre, had adopted Buck's estimate IV as the official statistics, that is, the DS-1946 set, suggests that the government itself had no confidence in the results of the partial cadastre.

So far the following conclusions can be drawn concerning pre-Communist data on cultivated land. First, after Buck conducted his sample studies in 1929–33 and published the results in 1937, there was no new official estimate of cultivated area on a nationwide scale throughout 1949. Second, the Nationalist government adopted Buck's estimate IV as the official figures in an effort to adjust upward their farmland records. Third, since the set of Buck's figures accepted by the Nationalist government was the lowest one of his four alternative sets of estimates, it is doubtful that the new official records had completely eliminated the concealment of cultivated land.

Buck's estimates and two official figures for the twenty-two provinces are presented in Column (1) of Table 8.1. In order to facilitate a direct comparison between pre-Communist and Communist data, the geographical coverage of the pre-Communist data has been adjusted to include the regions outside the twenty-two provinces of China proper. According to the DS-1946 data, the total acreage of cultivated land in Sikang, Sinkiang, Jehol, and Manchuria was 254 million mou.[31] In Column (2) of Table 8.1, 254 million mou have been added to each of Buck's estimates and to the NARB figure. Since 254 million mou is the official figure before being adjusted for any possible underreporting, we may use the same correction factor (1.337) that Buck used to obtain his estimate II and increase the 254 million mou to 339 million mou. A new set of estimates has been computed and presented in Column (3) of the same table.

Now let us turn to the evaluation of Communist data on cultivated area. Specifically, we will attempt to answer the following three questions. First, what farmland records did the Communist governments at various levels have at the outset of the regime (1949–50)? Second, had changes or adjustments ever been made by the Communist government of those initial records in later years? Finally, what distortions can be detected in Communist statistics of cultivated acreage?

In Table 8.3 we compare pre-Communist data on cultivated acreage

Table 8.3 Comparison of Pre-Communist and Communist Data for 1949 on Cultivated Land in Selected Provinces (1,000 mou)

Province	Pre-Communist data: NARB	Pre-Communist data: DS–1946	Communist data for 1949
Anhwei	49,320	73,130	77,000
Fukien	21,460	21,090	21,000
Kiangsi	38,370	43,340	35,400
Kwangsi	29,890	27,490	24,600
Kwantung	39,120	40,990	35,020
Kweichow	21,200	23,170	23,800

Sources:
NARB data: *China Handbook, 1936–1943*, p. 547.
DS–1946 data: Shen, *Agricultural Resources*, p. 142.
Communist data for 1949: From *PAS*; figures used in this table were officially published some time in 1950.

with those for 1949 as published by Communist governments in 1950 for selected provinces. Only six provinces are included in this comparison because, for some provinces, the figures for farmland areas in 1949 were not published until 1955–56, and these figures might be revised figures instead of the original figures existing in 1949. Or since the provincial territories in 1949 were drastically different from their prewar divisions, direct comparisons of cultivated acreage are not meaningful. Furthermore, a few other provinces are excluded because they lack official data for 1949. While the small number of provinces in this comparison may not enable us to arrive at a firm conclusion, they will nevertheless throw some light on the Communist provincial data on cultivated land.

As is shown in Table 8.3, although the provincial farmland records used by the Communists in the beginning of the regime are different from the two pre-Communist sets, they are very close to either one. Moreover, except for Anhwei, the Communist data for 1949 are not larger than the higher of the two pre-Communist sets.

There was no report that a new cadastre had been conducted in 1949 or 1950 by which the Chinese Communists could determine independently the area of farmland in various provinces. The existing circumstances simply did not permit the Peking government to undertake such an endeavor. One official source has summarily described what the Communist government had done with regard to farm statistics before the establishment of the State Statistical Bureau in late 1952.

Before the formation of the State Statistical Bureau, regional or local governments and other interested government offices were requested by, and under the direction of, the Central Financial and Economic Committee to gather, rearrange, and check the data on agricultural production left by the old regime. Through land reform and the movement to investigate the land and to determine the assets, and in preparation for the coming general election, those governments and offices checked and verified the basic data such as argricultural population and acreage of cultivated land.[32]

It is most likely that the majority of hsien in the beginning of the Communist rule took over the land records held in the Nationalist hsien governments and used them as working bases. In a few localities, the Communist hsien governments had asked individual peasants to report their landholdings.[33] Other governments may have adjusted for what they deemed to be possible wartime reductions of farmland.

At any rate, the Communist data on cultivated land for 1949, as published in 1950, must have contained some degree of understatement, though they appear to be different from the NARB and the DS-1946 data. This is so because the basic biasing elements embodied in the hsien records of farmland had not been removed.

Efforts were made by the Communists in 1950–52 to measure independently the total farmland in various localities and provinces. It is quite certain that the landholdings which were redistributed during the land reform must have been measured by the Communist authorities. Sample studies were performed also by some hsien and provincial governments to determine the current amount of cultivated land in their jurisdictions.[34]

However, those new investigations did not necessarily lead to adjustments of the original figures for 1949. Among the known survey reports, there is only one case in which the hsien government explicitly treated the differences between the survey findings and the original land records as an underreporting by the peasants in earlier years, and it adjusted the earlier land records accordingly. The estimated underreporting rate in this hsien varied from 10.66 to 21.62 percent.[35] In all other cases where the survey results are revealed, the hsien or provincial governments simply treated the discrepancies between the survey findings and the original land records as "changes" in the size of cultivated land during the time interval. Thus, six survey reports claimed that cultivated land in 1950 had increased from the prewar level at a rate ranging from 1 to 163 percent, and another seven surveys found that cultivated land in 1950 or 1951 had increased by 33.1 to 167 percent as compared with previous years (1945, 1948, or 1949).[36] However, no reduction in cultivated land was reported.

Of course, the sizable increases in cultivated land as reported by the sample surveys could not be all real. The bulk merely represented the discovery of unregistered farmland. For the country as a whole, a great amount of land concealment had been brought to light in the process of land redistribution.[37] However, the land reform program did not eliminate all land concealment, because altogether only 43 percent of the farmland in the country had gone through redistribution.[38] Most of the remaining unregistered land was discovered later during the period of the rural collectivization movement.

What is important is the fact that in most hsien or provinces the discovery of unregistered farmland in any year was treated as a "current" increase. At best only the size of the preceding year's cultivated area was adjusted accordingly. There were only three known cases where the originally published provincial data on cultivated area in 1949 had been revised drastically upward. The 1949 farmland area for Kwangsi, given in 1950, was 24.6 million mou, but it had been revised to 33.1 million mou according to an official source published in 1959. When the revision actually took place is not known. The cultivated area of Kwangtung for 1949, reported in 1950, was 35 million mou. It was immediately changed, however, to 51.9 million mou. Publications before 1955 always cited the cultivated area in Sinkiang in 1949–50 as from 15.6 to 15.9 million mou, but local sources in 1959 raised the figure for 1949 to 18.1 million mou.

Upward revisions of farm statistics for the preceding year have also been made by the central government for the country as a whole. The State Statistical Bureau (SSB) announced in 1954 the revision of some 1952 figures released in 1953.[39] This was the first official revision of aggregate farm statistics. About one year later, when the final draft of the First Five Year Plan was published, some of the important agricultural indicators for 1952 were changed once again—a 6.8 percent raise in total sown area and a 2.4 percent raise in food grain production.[40]

Shortly after that, there came another revision by which the sown area and grain output in 1953 were adjusted upward by 5.2 and 1.1 percent respectively.[41]

The final data on cultivated acreages for the early years of the Communist period were first published by the SSB in its *Statistical Abstract 1949–1954*,[42] and the same figures were used in the *Ten Great Years* (*TGY*) published in 1960.[43] Obviously, no further revisions on earlier data had been made after 1955.

In Appendix Table 1 are assembled all provincial data on cultivated land in various years. Whenever possible the revised figures have been used, that is, the latest published data. Numbers in parentheses are our estimates, derived from relevant information, to fill in the gaps where no officially published data are available. As was mentioned earlier, Tibet, Shanghai, and Peking are omitted in our data compilation because of a lack of information. However, the amount of farmland in these three areas combined may be approximately estimated. For 1957, we have official data on cultivated area for all provinces except Tibet, Shanghai, and Peking. On the other hand, the national total cultivated area is given in *TGY* for that year. The difference between the sum of the provincial data and the *TGY* national total for that year must be the amount of farmland existing in 1957 in the three omitted places, which is 16.31 million mou. The combined amount of cultivated land in Shanghai and Peking, as of 1957, has been given as 2.51 million mou.[44] Thus, the size of farmland in Tibet was about 13.8 million mou in 1957, which was only 46 percent of that in Sinkiang but exceeded that in Tsinghai by 85 percent. In view of the comparative size of territories and farming conditions of Tibet, Sinkiang, and Tsinghai, this estimate sounds quite reasonable.

If we assume that the combined amount of farmland in Tibet, Shanghai, and Peking had remained more or less stable in the period 1949–57, the same 16.31 million mou may be added to the sum of provincial data on cultivated area in various years to obtain a full coverage for the whole mainland. The resulting amounts are then compared, in Table 8.4, with the national totals of cultivated area as given by *TGY*. The discrepancies between the two sets show an interesting pattern. Except for 1949, 1956, and 1957, where the two sets are about equal, the sums of provincial data, Column (3), fall short of the *TGY* data, Column (4). The discrepancy rises in magnitude after 1950, reaches its maximum in 1952, and then gradually tapers off.

Table 8.4 Comparison of Provincial and *TGY* Data on Cultivated Area, 1949–57 (million mou)

Year	Provincial data: Sum of provincial data, excluding Tibet, Shanghai, and Peking (1)	Provincial data: Estimate of cultivated acreage in Tibet, Shanghai, and Peking (2)	Total (3)	*TGY* data (4)	(4)−(3) (5)
1949	1452.85	16.31	1469.16	1468.22	−0.94
1950	1470.86	16.31	1487.17	1505.34	18.17
1951	1506.50	16.31	1522.81	1555.07	32.26
1952	1560.25	16.31	1576.56	1618.78	42.22
1953	1571.20	16.31	1587.51	1627.93	40.42
1954	1596.29	16.31	1612.60	1640.32	27.72
1955	1631.18	16.31	1647.49	1652.35	4.86
1956	1661.12	16.31	1677.43	1677.37	−0.06
1957	1661.14	16.31	1677.45	1677.45	0

Sources:
Col. (1): From Appendix Table 1.
Col. (2): Estimated; see text, p. 200.
Col. (3): Col. (1)+Col. (2)
Col. (4): From *TGY*, p. 128.

It is recognized that some error probably was introduced when we used estimates in the place of missing provincial data on farmland, but it is hardly conceivable that the net result of the error so embodied could take on such a peculiar pattern. It is more likely that this peculiar pattern of discrepancies resulted from the efforts of provincial governments to adjust upward their original cultivated land statistics, based on the amount of unregistered land that had been newly discovered. Most of these revised figures are not available to us.

In other words, a great portion of the discrepancies between the two sets of data, Column (5) in Table 8.4, represents the adjustments of farmland because of the discovery of land concealment in various years. The amount of discovered land concealment rose gradually after 1949, as the land redistribution program was extended to more provinces, and reached its maximum when this program covered the whole mainland in 1952. Thereafter, some land concealment was discovered annually but at a decreasing rate.

From Tables 8.1 and 8.4 one can see that the total acreage of cultivated land for 1949, as given by the Communist authorities, is still smaller than all but one of Buck's estimates—Columns (2) and (3) in Table 8.1.[45] This seems to suggest that, in spite of the upward revisions made by the Chinese Communist government in farmland records, the final figure for 1949 may still contain a considerable degree of understatement. As is shown in Table 8.4, the final official statistics show a total increase in cultivated land of more than 209 million mou between 1949 and 1957. Yet no possible explanation can be found as to the source of this tremendous amount of new farmland. As will be discussed in more detail later in this section, if one combines all the officially claimed reclamation achievements and other activities which could bring more land to cultivation, the total amount of new farmland added in this period falls short of 209 million mou by a large margin.

Moreover, official sources disclosed that farmland concealment had been consistently uncovered during the period of the collectivization movement. The Chinese statistical authorities openly admitted on one occasion that about 30 million mou of unregistered farmland had been uncovered in the period 1953–57, but this amount was treated as newly increased cultivated land in official statistics.[46]

There are indications that by 1956–57 the SSB had become fully aware that there were still serious understatements in the farm statistics for the earlier years. Therefore, one item on the agenda of a national conference on agricultural statistics, convened in Peking in October 1957, was to "adjust agricultural statistical materials for all the previous years."[47] However, no revision of farm statistics was revealed in the Communist press after the conference. The proposed thorough revision was not carried out, either because too much work would be required or because the proposal was killed on the grounds that such a revision would scale down so drastically the agricultural growth rate announced previously that the government's propaganda would be discredited.

At any rate, the cultivated land data in *TGY* can be regarded at best as partially adjusted for land concealment in the early years of the regime. The biases may have declined over time, however, as more and more unregistered farmland was discovered, and the official records came closer and closer to reality.

In the light of the above examination of official data on farmland and the identifiable biases in them, some adjustments are called for. In adjusting the official data on cultivated area, as well as the data on sown area and yield in later sections of this chapter, we have made one fundamental assumption: the official 1957 data are assumed to be relatively free of distortion. We have either taken the 1957 situation as a reference point or adopted that year's statistics as the basis on which we have worked out retroactively our adjustments for earlier years' data. This important assumption is made for the following reasons. Because it was aware of the inaccuracy of the earlier statistics on agricultural production, the SSB had endeavored, sometimes quite successfully, to improve its data-collecting mechanism in 1956 and 1957.

More important, the institutional change in the Chinese rural sector in 1956–57 was instrumental in promoting the quality of farm statistics. The completion of the collectivization movement by 1957 reduced the basic reporting units of agricultural production from 120 million individual households to 700,000 agricultural cooperatives.[48] To a large extent, this change compensated for the serious shortage of statistical staff in the government and reduced computational errors in compiling and aggregating agricultural data.[49]

Secondly, improvement in the quality of farm statistics came also from the urgent needs of the cooperatives themselves for more accurate information to carry out such operations as work assignments and income distribution among member peasants or teams.

Thirdly, the very nature of the new rural institution alleviated land concealment. Underreporting by a collective farm was not so easy as by a family farm because of the possible conflict of interest among different teams in a cooperative or between the ordinary member peasants and party cadres who had a strong desire to boast achievements.[50] The larger the size of a collective farm, the greater the difficulty in reaching a consensus for the concealment of land and output.[51] By 1957, not only had the whole rural sector of China been organized into cooperatives, but also their average size had become much larger.

Clear proof can be found in official data to support this assumption. As was shown in Table 8.4, the total cultivated area increased steadily throughout 1949–56, ceased to rise in 1957, and declined for the first time in 1958. Apparently, part of the increase before 1957 was only statistical and resulted from uncovering concealed holdings. This factor had virtually disappeared by 1957; and the reduction in cultivated land in 1958 was real, reflecting the large quantity of farmland occupied by the extensive construction activities in that year.[52]

For each province the 1957 cultivated acreage, as officially given, is taken as the starting point, and adjustments are made retroactively. The principle is to compute the amount of farmland withdrawn in each year for nonagricultural purposes and the amount of new farmland added in each year. Then, beginning with the 1957 cultivated area and working backward, we add what had been reduced and deduct what had been added in order to compute cultivated area in each of the years before 1957. Four items are involved in this adjustment.

1. Land reclaimed and actually put to agricultural uses in each year: to estimate the amounts of reclaimed land in various provinces during the period 1949–57, we have to begin with national totals. Communist sources frequently cited a total of about 70 to 80 million mou as the land reclaimed in the period 1953–57.[53] Interesting and more useful for our computation, however, is the breakdown provided by one of these sources. According to it, the total of 77.56 million mou, the so-called reclaimed land in the period 1953–57, consisted of the following four components,[54] in million mou: land reclaimed by state farms, 20.86;[55] land reclaimed under the resettlement program, 6.90; land reclaimed by agricultural cooperatives, 19.80; and unregistered farmland discovered in the period, 30. The last item should be excluded from our computation of the bona fide result of reclamation. The third item, which refers primarily to the cultivated land gained through the removal of farm boundaries and graves after the formation of agricultural cooperatives, will be discussed separately in the next section. Here we shall concentrate on the first two categories.

For the country as a whole, the total amount of cultivated land in state farms in each year has been given in the official press, and the data appear fairly consistent. Since state farms were under the direct control of the government and the total number of state farms was relatively small, the data may be regarded as reasonably reliable. From this body of information we can easily determine the amount of land reclaimed by state farms in each province in various years in the period under study (see Appendix Table 2). For some provinces the resulting figures may contain certain errors, but the errors offset each other, leaving the national totals unaffected.

The amount of reclamation under the resettlement program in various years remains to be determined. There were two approaches used by the Chinese government to resettle peasants.[56] One approach was to move the peasants to other established rural communities and integrate them into the cooperatives already existing there. The other method involved transporting farmers to remote and sparsely populated areas and requiring them to build new villages or resettlement communities on virgin land. The second method led to land reclamation. Movements of rural population under the resettlement program were mainly from Shantung to Heilungkiang, from Honan to Kansu, and from Shanghai to Kiangsi. Among the areas receiving immigrants, Heilungkiang was the most important. Evidence indicates that Heilungkiang not only had absorbed a preponderance of the new settlers, but also that it was the only area where resettlement led to the reclamation of new land. For example, it was reported that the total number of people resettled by the end of 1958 under this program was 1.49 million, yet about 660,000 families had been accepted by Heilungkiang alone for resettlement by the end of 1957.[57] Assuming an average size of two persons per family, the number of people moved to Heilungkiang by the end of 1957 would be 1.32 million. Evidently almost all the resettlers were sent to that province. Therefore it is reasonable to postulate that the 6.9 million mou of newly reclaimed land in 1953–57 under the resettlement program were located largely in Heilungkiang.

Using the relevant data from provincial sources in Heilungkiang to allocate the 6.9 million mou to various years in 1953–57, we have computed the estimates and presented them in Appendix Table 3.

2. Increases in cultivated area resulting from the removal of boundary lines, graves, and so on: this type of increase occurred exclusively in the years of the collectivization movement (1955–57), which integrated small private farms under the administration of cooperative authorities. Individual cases showed that these increases represented from 2 to 6 percent of the existing farmland.[58] For the country as a whole, the total amount of farmland so increased before 1957 was 19.8 million mou. We have distributed this total amount to individual provinces in three years (1955–57), according to the progress of collectivization in those years in each province.[59]

Specifically, we used the official total of cultivated land in the whole country in 1955 to divide 19.8 million mou and thus obtained the result of 1.21, which means that about 1.21 percent of cultivated land had been gained from this source. We then applied the same percentage to the official amount of cultivated land in each province to obtain an answer for the whole country.

Statistically, the above ratio is a weighted average of ratios of individual provinces. For a province which had a relatively high density of farm population per unit of cultivated land, the ratio would be higher than the national average because the average size of farms in that province before collectivization must be relatively smaller and more boundary lines could be removed after collectivization, and because more graves could be removed, too. Therefore, our estimated increment of cultivated land from this source in each province was adjusted by a correction factor which was the ratio of the farm population density of the province to the nation's farm population density.[60] The adjusted amount of farmland increase in each province was then allocated to the three years of 1955–57 according to the progress of collectivization in that province (see Appendix Table 4).

3. Farmland used for the construction of irrigation systems: virtually all the new irrigation systems built in Communist China in the period under study were the type that used surface water and gravity. According to one Chinese Communist study, an average of 3.6 mou had been used by water distribution courses to irrigate 100 mou of land.[61] This ratio and the official data on the increase in irrigated land in each province have been employed to compute the farmland reduced by this factor in that province in various years. The results are presented in Appendix Table 6.

4. Farmland occupied by new buildings, factories, railways, highways, and other construction projects: one official source indicated that 200 million mou were requisitioned by the state in the period 1949–57 for construction projects.[62] However, it is difficult to allocate this total land reduction to individual provinces and to various years. We have derived only rough estimates through the following steps. From provincial data of basic construction investments in various years, and from our own estimates where official data are absent, we have obtained an average rate of 578 mou bought by the state for every million yuan of basic construction investment. Using this rate, we have computed the farmland reduction in each province in each year. This unsatisfactory method undoubtedly leaves a considerable margin for errors in the estimates for individual provinces and years, but the errors are largely offset when the provincial estimates are aggregated. The results are given in Appendix Table 8.

With the preceding four sets of estimates, we have adjusted the official statistics on cultivated area. For each province, beginning with the 1957 official cultivated acreage, we have worked backward by adding what had been reduced and deducting what had been added in each of the previous years. The new estimates for individual provinces have then been aggregated to arrive at national totals.

Our new estimates of cultivated acreage in mainland China in 1949–57 are presented in Table 8.5, along with the Communist data for comparison. Since the four items which have been used to adjust the official data cover all the important factors affecting the size of cultivated land in China, our new estimates are believed to be close to the real situation in that period.

Table 8.5 Estimates of Cultivated Area in Mainland China, 1949–57 (million mou)

Year	Sum of original provincial data, excluding Tibet, Shanghai, and Peking (1)	Sum of adjusted provincial data, excluding Tibet, Shanghai, and Peking (2)	Cultivated area in Tibet, Shanghai, and Peking (3)	Total cultivated area in mainland China (4)	(2)−(1) (5)
1949	1,452.85	1,650.84	16.31	1,667.15	197.99
1950	1,470.86	1,650.43	16.31	1,666.74	179.57
1951	1,506.50	1,648.92	16.31	1,665.23	142.42
1952	1,560.25	1,647.33	16.31	1,663.64	87.08
1953	1,571.20	1,646.64	16.31	1,662.95	75.44
1954	1,596.29	1,645.89	16.31	1,662.20	49.60
1955	1,631.18	1,656.43	16.31	1,672.74	25.25
1956	1,661.12	1,670.24	16.31	1,686.55	9.12
1957	1,661.14	1,661.14	16.31	1,677.45	0

Sources:
Col. (1) and (3): From Table 8.4.
Col. (2): From Appendix Table 9.
Col. (4): Col. (2)+Col. (3).

If our new estimate of 1.651 million mou, Column (2) in Table 8.5, of total cultivated land in 1949 is compared with various prewar estimates as listed in Table 8.1, it is very close to Buck's "most accurate" estimate for the twenty-two provinces, plus the unadjusted official figure for the regions outside these provinces (total 1,662 million mou). It is almost identical with Buck's estimate II for the twenty-two provinces, plus the blown-up acreage for the regions outside these provinces (total 1,656 million mou). The consistency between our estimate for 1949 and Buck's estimates for the 1930s tends to reinforce the credibility of both.

To the best of our knowledge, there was very little change in the amount of farmland between the 1930s and 1940s. As a result of the efforts of the wartime Chinese government to expand the base of food supply, the reclamation of wasteland took place on a limited scale in the early 1940s in inland China. Yet the actual amount of land so gained was small,[63] and the small gains may have been offset by the reduction of cultivated land in the war zones.

Our new estimates support our contention that in spite of the attempts of the Communist government to adjust upward its statistics on cultivated land in the early years of the regime, the final official figures for those years are still too low. It is simply impossible to explain where the officially claimed increase of 209 million mou of cultivated land between 1949 and 1957 came from. The Peking government must have realized by 1957 the inaccuracy of its farmland data for the early years, but it was unwilling to make a further revision.

The differences between our new estimates and the sums of provincial data, Column (5) in Table 8.5, are supposed to represent, in a very crude way, the unregistered farmland in various years. The amount declined year after year in this period, but the largest reduction came in 1951–52, a time when the land redistribution program was vigorously carried out in the whole country. Another relatively large reduction occurred around 1955, a period when the collectivization movement began.

According to our new estimates, the total cultivated area in China remained fairly stable throughout this period because the land-reducing factors more or less offset the land-adding factors. The yearly decline was slight from 1949 to 1954; but it rose by about 24 million mou from 1954 to 1956 because of the enlarged scale of reclamation and the elimination of boundary lines of farms that had been integrated into agricultural cooperatives. The year 1956 seems to be the year when the total cultivated acreage in mainland China reached a peak level. The data show a reduction of 61 million mou from 1957 to 1958.[64] This reduction is likely to be real, and it reflects the farmland used by the fantastically extensive construction activities under the Great Leap Forward Movement.[65]

Adjustment of Official Data on the Area Sown in Grain

Now let us examine possible distortions in the Chinese Communist data on the area sown in grain. Again, we assemble all provincial data on grain-sown area in individual provinces for various years, as published at the latest dates. All gaps of missing data are filled in by estimates. The sums are presented in Column (1) of Table 8.6. These sums do not include grain-sown areas in Tibet, Shanghai, and Peking. The combined sown area for food grains in these three places is assumed to be approximately equal to the total cultivated area on the following grounds. First, nearly all the cultivated land in Tibet is probably devoted to growing food grains, and the climatic conditions there do not permit double-cropping. Second, although the double-cropping index in Shanghai and Peking may be high, a great portion of sown acreage in the two localities is probably used to grow vegetables to support the population of the two large municipalities. After the estimated grain-sown area in the three places is added to other provincial data, the totals, Column (3), are compared with *TGY* data, Column (4), in Table 8.6. The discrepancies in percentages are smaller than those in the comparison of official data on cultivated land shown in Table 8.4. Moreover, the discrepancies of sown area take on both negative and positive signs. Therefore, we may safely assume that they result mainly from estimation errors created in the process of filling in the missing official data.

Table 8.6 Comparison of Provincial Data and *TGY* Data on Grain-Sown Area, 1949–57 (million mou)

	Provincial data				
	Sum of provincial data, excluding Tibet, Shanghai, and Peking	Estimate of grain-sown area in Tibet, Shanghai, and Peking	Total	*TGY* data	(4)−(3)
Year	(1)	(2)	(3)	(4)	(5)
1949	1529.88	16.00	1545.88	1524.60	−21.28
1950	1562.65	16.00	1578.65	1572.05	− 6.60
1951	1604.18	16.00	1620.18	1604.52	−15.66
1952	1663.95	16.00	1679.95	1684.49	4.54
1953	1706.52	16.00	1722.52	1714.12	− 8.40
1954	1735.72	16.00	1751.72	1745.12	− 6.60
1955	1740.89	16.00	1756.89	1775.96	19.07
1956	1819.48	16.00	1835.48	1864.39	28.91
1957	1781.33	16.00	1797.33	1813.27	15.94

Sources:

Col. (1): From Appendix Table 10.
Col. (2): Estimated.
Col. (3): Col. (1)+Col. (2).
Col. (4): From *TGY*, p. 129.

Inasmuch as the statistics on cultivated acreage are biased, the data on the grain-sown area are bound to be inaccurate, since the latter were derived from the former. In addition, there are two other factors that would affect the reliability of these data. First, the degree of distortion in the sown acreage would depend on whether the concealed farmland was used primarily for growing grains or was distributed to all kinds of crops. Second, it would depend on the accuracy of the ratios of sown area to cultivated area in various localities. In other words, it is a problem of how close the ratios estimated by the hsien governments from their sample surveys, or through other methods, were to the true mean ratio in the hsien.

Since the unregistered farmland has never become the object of any special study or investigation, there is no information by which we can ascertain the general distribution of unregistered farmland among various crops in any year or period. All we can do is to speculate on the distribution on the basis of peasants' motives for underreporting their landholdings.

In prewar times, the motive was clearly tax evasion. The rate of Chinese land taxes in the 1930s was set mainly in accordance with estimated land incomes, though the precise classification of land and the rate structure varied from locality to locality.[66] One common feature, however, was the wide differential in statutory tax rates on good and poor land. For instance, in Yunnan the statutory rate on the best land was fifteen times that on the poorest land.[67] Therefore, if Chinese farmers wanted to conceal part of their landholdings to evade land taxes, it is only logical that they would conceal their good land, which usually had a relatively high yield or was used for the crops that commanded higher market prices.

The possibility of selective farmland concealment must have been strengthened after 1941 when the Chinese government began to collect land taxes in kind. According to the new regulations, farmers in seven provinces (Hunan, Chekiang, Kiangsi, Kwangtung, Kwangsi, Kiangsu, and Fukien) were required to pay rice only; in nine provinces (Szechwan, Hupeh, Shantung, Suiyuan, Shansi, Sikiang, Anhwei, Honan, and Shensi) peasants had the option of paying land taxes in either rice or wheat; and in only one province (Kansu) was wheat, corn, soybeans, or barley acceptable as payment for land taxes.[68]

This phenomenon of land concealment by Chinese peasants had apparently been carried over to the early years of the Communist period.

Reports reveal that peasants either underreported their land for main grain crops or purposely misreported grainland as land for soybeans or industrial crops.[69]

It is even more difficult to determine the general direction of distortion in the official ratios of sown area to cultivated area. If the ratios were obtained in production conferences or from model surveys, the results would very likely reflect the subjective biases of the investigators or the participants of the conferences. However, no fixed pattern of distortion can be discerned. For instance, a model sample drawn by the government investigators might be far from representative of the true local situation, but it is difficult to tell in what direction it was biased.[70] Consequently, there is no way for us to ascertain whether the underestimation was aggravated or partially offset after the cultivated acreage of a locality was converted into sown area.

It is difficult to derive a new set of grain-sown areas for each province on the basis of our adjusted data on cultivated land. Without further indicative information beyond that discussed above, we can make only two somewhat arbitrary assumptions for the purpose of adjusting the official grain-sown area data. First, it is assumed that all unregistered farmland prior to 1957 was exclusively grainland.[71] Second, the biases in the official data on cultivated land are assumed to have been carried over to the official data on grain-sown area. That is to say, the downward biases in the former which resulted from underreporting were not offset in any way by upward biases in the latter which stemmed from an overestimation of grain double-cropping indexes by the local governments. Therefore, the difference between our adjusted cultivated acreage and the official cultivated acreage represents unrecorded grainland, which had the same double-cropping index as the recorded grainland did. Using these procedures, we have obtained a set of adjusted sown areas for each province (see Appendix Table 11). The national totals of our estimates are presented in Table 8.7.

According to our new estimates, the sown area for grain in 1957 was about the same as in 1952; the only two substantial, but abrupt, increases in the period occurred in 1954 and 1956. One will recall that both 1954 and 1956 were years with relatively severe natural calamities. It is a common practice in China that when the principal crop in an area is apparently destroyed, farmers replant another crop which is better able to resist unfavorable crop conditions. Since the sown area measured by the Chinese Communists is not the harvested area, it would

Table 8.7 Estimates of Grain-Sown Area in Mainland China, 1949–57 (million mou)

Year	Sum of adjusted sown area for food grains, excluding Tibet, Shanghai, and Peking (1)	Sown area for food grains in Tibet, Shanghai, and Peking (2)	Sown area for food grains in the whole mainland (3)	Difference between adjusted and original sown area for food grains (4)
1949	1,741.10	16.00	1,757.10	211.22
1950	1,766.39	16.00	1,782.39	203.74
1951	1,773.06	16.00	1,789.06	168.88
1952	1,783.60	16.00	1,799.60	119.65
1953	1,792.24	16.00	1,808.24	85.72
1954	1,815.90	16.00	1,831.90	80.18
1955	1,794.75	16.00	1,810.75	53.86
1956	1,865.38	16.00	1,881.38	45.90
1957	1,781.33	16.00	1,797.33	0

Sources:
Col. (1): Appendix Table 11.
Col. (2): Assumed, See text, p. 209.
Col. (3): Col. (1)+Col. (2).
Col. (4): Col. (1) in this table, minus Col. (1) in Table 8.6.

show some increases in years of severe natural calamities. Furthermore, as was discussed in Chapter 7, it was in 1956 that the Chinese Communists extended the double-cropping system to a vast area in Central China. But the attempt was abandoned in 1957.

The fact that our estimates show about the same sown area for grains in 1952 and 1957 is in sharp contrast to the official claim of an increase of 128 million mou in the grain-sown area between those years.[72] The claimed increase is only statistical, coming from the recovery of unregistered grainland. However, this does not mean that there was no rise in the multiple-cropping index in the period 1952–57. There was some increase, though not so substantial as suggested by official data. But the increase in the index is not reflected in the sown areas for grain, mainly for the following two reasons.

First, the extension of grain double-cropping was largely offset by the use of grainland to grow nongrain crops whose sown acreage increased by about 112 million mou in the period.[73] Second, most provinces did show considerable increases in their indexes of multiple cropping over the period, but the provinces with relatively high indexes suffered reductions in farmland whereas the provinces with relatively low indexes gained in farmland. For instance, the land reclaimed during this period was concentrated in Heilungkiang and Sinkiang,[74] where only one crop could be raised in a year.

Table 8.8 Estimates of Total Sown Areas and Double-Cropping Indexes, 1952–57 (million mou)

Year	Official data of sown areas for non-grain crops (1)	Estimates of sown area for food grains (2)	Estimates of total sown areas (3)	Multiple-cropping indexes (4)
1952	434.35	1,799.60	2,233.95	134.28
1953	446.41	1,808.24	2,254.65	135.58
1954	473.76	1,831.90	2,305.66	138.71
1955	490.26	1,810.75	2,301.01	137.56
1956	523.20	1,881.38	2,404.58	142.57
1957	545.39	1,797.33	2,342.72	139.66

Sources:

Col. (1): The difference between the official total sown area and the official grain-sown area, taken from *TGY*, pp. 128, 129.

Col. (2): From Table 8.7.

Col. (3): Col. (1)+Col. (2).

Col. (4): Col. (3) divided by our estimated total cultivated area given in Table 8.5.

In view of the above discussion, we should recompute the multiple-cropping indexes for mainland China as a whole in various years during the period. The results are presented in Table 8.8.

Adjustment of Official Data on Unit Yield of Grains

The data for yield and for sown acreages were separately collected or derived by the Chinese Communist governments at the local level. The identifiable biases in the latter set may not necessarily have appeared in the former. In order to determine the reliability of the official statistics of grain yields, we must examine them independently. In the hope of detecting possible distortions, we have paid special attention to the information from the Chinese Communist press concerning crop yields of individual hsien, villages, or cooperatives. Unfortunately, available data of this type are insufficient to permit us to judge the reliability of provincial or national yield figures.

Another approach to this problem is to utilize prewar yield data as a comparison basis. We shall first compare the prewar (the 1930s) yield data and the Communist data for 1952–57. These two periods may be considered normal periods in a very general sense. Later on, a similar inquiry will be conducted into the yield data of 1949–51, the period immediately following the Sino-Japanese War and the Civil War, and in which agricultural production conditions more or less departed from a normal state. In order to facilitate such comparisons, we have converted, whenever possible, the prewar data according to the Communist classifications. Even so, the territories of several provinces in the interval between the two periods are not exactly comparable. However, since yield is a ratio, that is, output per unit of land for a given province, it may not be seriously affected by minor changes in territory. Our comparisons will be made both in terms of national averages and on the basis of provincial statistics.

Table 8.9 consists of comparisons of national average yields as estimated by the NARB, by Buck, and by the official claims of the Communist government. The 1952–57 average yields for the four crop categories fall short, by varying degrees, of the corresponding estimates for the prewar time. With this simple observation one might hurriedly conclude that the prewar yield estimates are upward biased because of sampling errors.[75] This conclusion is, however, too sweeping. Study will show that there are many factors responsible for the deviations:

Table 8.9 Comparison of Prewar and Communist Data on Grain Yield, by Crop (including tubers, catties per mou)

	Prewar		Communist		
Crop	NARB 1931–37 average (1)	Buck's most frequent yield 1929–33 (2)	1952 (3)	1957 (4)	1952–57 average (5)
Rice	338	447 433 (glutinous rice)	321	359	336
Wheat	144	141 (winter) 152 (spring)	98	114	106
Tubers	263 (sweet potatoes)	264 (sweet) 213 (Irish)	251	278	246
Coarse grains	158	151	136	139	134

Sources:

Col. (1): Shen, *Agricultural Resources*, pp. 374–77.

Col. (2): Buck, *Land Utilization*, 3:209.

Cols. (3), (4), and (5): *TGY*, p. 121.

some are real factors, such as the changed pattern of land utilization and cropping systems between the two periods, some are the differences in measuring crop yields, and others are purely statistical distortions.

As was mentioned in Chapter 7, although the input situation of Chinese agricultural production witnessed no significant improvement between the two periods compared, there were many changes in cropping systems and land utilization.

Specifically, important changes in land utilization during 1952–57 were: (1) converting some dry land into paddy fields, (2) expanding the area of rice double-cropping, (3) extending wheat production to poorer land, and (4) reclaiming marginal land for cultivation. All these developments have had certain effects on the yield per unit of sown area.

The rapid rise in the practice of multiple cropping was a result of governmental policy. It is obvious that a rapid expansion of the multiple-cropping system without a corresponding increase in the supply of fertilizer usually leads to some decline in the average yield per unit of sown area. This is one of the reasons that the Chinese statistical authorities, beginning in 1956, were anxious to use yield per unit of cultivated area to replace the yield indicator based on sown area. In extreme cases, even the yield per unit of cultivated area may fall when the multiple-cropping system has been improperly and excessively carried out. This phenomenon actually occurred in many localities in the 1950s and became quite common in 1956.

Attention should also be paid to two differences in measurement between prewar and Communist yield data. First, Buck's yield figures are "most frequent yields" which, according to him, are slightly higher than "average yields."[76] Second, what both the NARB and Buck have measured are the "harvest rates," namely, output per unit of harvested area. While the NARB *Crop Reports* explicitly state that the yields given are harvest rates obtained by the crop reporters of the bureau, Buck has not clearly defined his yield rates.[77] However, judging from the method he used to collect the yield information, it is quite obvious that what he measured was actually harvest rates. When his field workers asked farmers about crop yields, the answers they obtained were most likely to be the harvest rates. Yet, as we have mentioned earlier, the Communist SSB emphatically specified that it wanted to measure yields per unit of sown area, not harvest rates. Discrepancies that result from the second measurement difference are more serious for wheat than rice yields, because in China the rate of crop failure is higher in the wheat region than in the rice region, since climatic conditions are less favorable in the former. According to Buck, the ratio of harvested area to sown area in the 1930s was 99 percent in the rice region but only 96 percent in the wheat region.[78]

With this general understanding, let us compare yields of various crops in the two periods. As Table 8.9 shows, although the NARB estimate of the rice yield for the twenty-two provinces agrees closely with the 1952–57 average, Buck's figure is substantially higher. One important source of this discrepancy is the fact that Buck has used the arithmetic mean (unweighted). The median of his "most frequent yields" of rice is only 370 catties per mou,[79] which is not too far off the NARB estimate or the 1952–57 average. Even agricultural scientists in Communist China openly admitted that there was no increase in the rice yield between the 1930s and 1952–57.[80]

A comparison of provincial data on rice yields is more revealing. In Table 8.10 we have eliminated the provinces that had only an insignificant output of rice. For 1952–57, we have computed the average yields

Table 8.10 Comparison of Prewar and Communist Data on Rice Yield in Selected Provinces (catties per mou)

Province	Buck (1)	NARB (2)	Average of (1) and (2) (3)	1952–57 average (4)
Anhwei	325	282	304	343
Chekiang	294	336	315	
Fukien	407	372	390	
Honan	143	241	192	
Hopei	352	196	274	
Hunan	420	385	403	394
Hupeh	569	299	434	447
Kiangsi	359	329	344	271
Kiangsu	429	365	397	379
Kwangsi	349	309	329	235
Kwangtung	274	341	308	243
Kweichow	812	285	549	398
Szechwan	595	379	487	433
Yunnan	420	316	368	436

Sources:

Col. (1): T. C. Liu and K. C. Yeh, *The Economy of the Chinese Mainland* (Princeton, N.J., 1965), p. 287.

Col. (2): Shen, *Agricultural Resources*, pp. 374–77.

Col. (3): Averages of Col. (1) and Col. (2).

Col. (4): *PAS*.

whenever there are rice yield figures for three or more years in that time period. The three sets (Buck's, the NARB, and the 1952–57 averages) differ from each other substantially for most provinces. Buck's survey and the NARB reports were based on samples of localities, whereas the Communist data have a wider coverage. It is recognized that there must be sampling errors in Buck's and the NARB yield data for individual provinces, yet the exact nature of the possible biases in the two sets cannot be determined. Theoretically speaking, if the two estimates for each province are averaged, as Liu and Yeh did in their study, the combined sample is larger in size, hence the margin of error may be reduced.[81] The averages of the two prewar sets are presented in Column (3) of Table 8.10, and the results do show reduced discrepancies in most provinces. Kiangsi, Kwangsi, and Kwangtung are the only three cases where the prewar data are problematic.

The comparison of wheat yields is more complex. As given in Table 8.9, the NARB estimate of wheat yields and Buck's are almost identical, yet the difference between them and the 1952–57 average is the largest among the four categories of crops. We have conducted an operation similar to the one used in Table 8.10, but combining the provincial yields of the two prewar studies does not show any improvement. Apparently, this discrepancy is more than a matter of sampling errors, and answers have to be sought somewhere else. Thus far, the following responsible factors, some statistical and others real, are discernible.

1. Some statistical distortions can be spotted in Buck's computation of wheat yields. The spring wheat area, as defined in Buck's study, does not create any problem insofar as wheat yields are concerned. The unweighted average of wheat yields of Tsinghai, Kansu, and Shensi in 1952–57 is 161 catties per mou, which is reasonably higher than the average wheat yield of 151 catties per mou obtained by Buck for that area. Distortions must have come, therefore, from winter wheat yields. Among the seven agricultural areas producing winter wheat, two areas consisting of all the major wheat producing provinces in North China are combined and called by Buck the wheat region. The other five agricultural areas which produce rice as the major crop and wheat as one of the minor crops are included in the rice region. The average winter wheat yields in the two regions and for the twenty-two provinces as a whole are presented below, along with the unweighted averages of wheat yields in 1952–57 for the same two regions as computed from the Communist provincial data (all in catties per mou):[82]

	Buck	*1952–57 average*
The wheat region	127	117
The rice region	142	103
Twenty-two provinces	141	—

For the wheat region, Buck's estimate is not too different from the Communist figure for 1952–57. However, Buck's wheat yield for the rice region deviates substantially from the Communist figure. The cause of this sizable discrepancy in wheat yields in the rice region between the two periods will be discussed later. Here, attention is called to the distortion created by the weighting problem. Buck's average winter wheat yield for the twenty-two provinces is an arithmetic mean which gives an equal weight to each individual observation. From the above figures, one can derive that the implied weights in Buck's computation are 7 percent for the wheat region and 93 percent for the rice region.[83] These weights are diametrically different from the factual relative importance of the two regions in wheat production. If we use the 1955 sown area for winter wheat in the two regions as weights, they should be 74 percent for the wheat region and 26 percent for the rice region.[84] By applying the new weights to Buck's two yield figures, the weighted average for the twenty-two provinces is computed at 130.8 catties per mou.

2. It has been pointed out that Buck's yield data are the "most frequent" harvest rates. At least eight to ten catties of the discrepancy can be accounted for by these two measurement differences. In other words, if we put Buck's wheat yield on the same statistical basis as that used by the Communists, it would be further reduced from 130.8 to 120–122 catties per mou.

3. As we demonstrated in paragraph no. 1, the largest divergence in wheat yields between Buck's data and the 1952–57 averages occurs in the rice region; that is, in areas south of the Chinling Mountains and the Huai River, consisting of the provinces where wheat is not the main crop. A great portion of this discrepancy can be traced to a serious statistical distortion in Buck's computation of wheat yields. In compiling yield data, Buck recorded only the observations in the localities where a given crop was found on 20 percent or more of the farms surveyed. In the case of wheat yields, practically all the localities surveyed in the major wheat producing provinces (the wheat region) satisfied this selecting criterion. Consequently, the subsample for the wheat region had preserved its random nature so far as yield data are concerned, and the results are unbiased except the ordinary sampling errors associated with

any random sample. However, for the minor wheat producing provinces (the rice region), the subsample which was originally drawn at random had been converted into a seriously biased one because of the selecting criterion for recording yield data. This would be so because wheat was not the major crop in the rice region, and the percentage of farms growing wheat in any given locality in that region was closely correlated to the relative yield of wheat in that locality. More farms grew wheat because the wheat yield was relatively high, and vice versa. In effect, to set this criterion for recording wheat yields amounts to selecting special cases from a random sample. Therefore, the resulting average wheat yield in the rice region was bound to be biased upward. The distortion in Buck's study can be best illustrated by the situation of wheat yields in the double-cropping rice area. This area consisted of Fukien, Kwangtung, and Kwangsi, with eleven localities originally chosen for the survey. Yet in nine of the eleven localities, less than 20 percent of the farms grew wheat; only two localities met the selecting criterion, so that only their wheat yield data were recorded. It is highly probable that these two localities actually were special cases in the sense that the local soil and climatic conditions happened to be relatively favorable to wheat growth, hence the wheat yield was relatively high. However, the wheat yield of these two localities should not be taken to represent the average wheat yield for the whole double-cropping rice area. It is no wonder that Buck's wheat yield for this area (129 catties per mou) is more than double the 1952–57 average (60 catties per mou).

The upward bias in the wheat yield of the minor wheat-producing provinces would have been minimized if Buck had used a proper weighting system to arrive at the national average. After all, only a small proportion of total wheat output came from the rice region. Unfortunately, Buck used an arithmetic mean which amounts to assigning equal weights to all recorded yields. Consequently, the upward bias in the wheat yield of the rice region has been aggravated by the unduly high weight assigned to it.

4. There is another real factor that has lowered to some extent the wheat yield in the rice region in the 1950s from its prewar level. Some wheat land, usually better pieces, had been shifted to rice or oil-bearing crops in the early 1950s.[85] Since the percentage of total farmland sown for wheat was small in that region, even a moderate amount of withdrawal of better land from wheat cultivation could depress the average yield of wheat.

5. The decline in wheat yields in the major wheat-producing provinces such as Hopei, Honan, and Shantung is believed to be real. In the early 1950s, the widespread conversion from the old system of three crops every two years to a system of two crops a year (coarse grain and wheat) led to a reduction in yield of both crops. This phenomenon was especially pronounced in Hopei, where the total wheat sown area increased by 13.3 million mou, or 48 percent, between 1952 and 1956, yet the total output of grain in that province decreased by 19.2 percent in the same period.[86] Furthermore, the fertility of land in a vast part of Honan, Shantung, and Anhwei had deteriorated during World War II, because the Chinese government in 1938 blew up dikes along the Yellow River in Honan in an attempt to halt the advancing Japanese soldiers. The neighboring plains were immediately flooded. Since the river could not return to its banks, it finally created a new course which joined the Hwai River in Anhwei. It was nine years before the Yellow River was again confined to its original course. Although there is no way to assess the net result of this event, its impact on crop yields over a fairly large area was by no means negligible. In view of all these factors, the 8 percent reduction in wheat yield in the northern provinces from the prewar level does not sound unreasonable.

6. The inclusion of Manchuria in the Communist statistical coverage may have reduced somewhat the national average yield of wheat. The wheat yield in Liaoning varied from fifty to sixty catties per mou in 1952–56, and it fell as low as thirty-six catties per mou in 1956 in Kirin. Since the percentage of land devoted to wheat production in Manchuria was small, the impact of low wheat yields there on the national average should not be emphasized.

Considering all the relevant information, we have come to the conclusion that the Communist data on wheat yields for 1952–57 are generally acceptable.[87] Their deviations from prewar data can be explained, to a large extent, by certain statistical and real factors.

Yield data for tubers and coarse grains are so scanty that no detailed comparison can be made for them. It is not unreasonable, however, to apply our evaluation of rice and wheat yields to tubers and coarse grain yields. If no systematic biases can be detected in the former, the situation is likely to be true for the latter. Furthermore, yields of tubers and coarse grain between the two periods are reconcilable. The NARB and Buck's estimates for sweet potatoes are almost identical. The 1952–57 average is lower, probably because it includes white, or Irish, potatoes whose yield is lower than that of sweet potatoes.

One possible explanation for the lower yield of coarse grains in 1952–57 has already been mentioned—the rapid increase in the double-cropping system of coarse grains with one other crop. Since coarse grains generally have better resistance to unfavorable weather and soil conditions, and their prices are usually lower than those of rice and wheat, they are grown on inferior land. When the soil condition of the land used for coarse grains has improved, the land may be used to produce higher value crops. Furthermore, a considerable portion of newly reclaimed land in Inner Mongolia and the northwestern provinces during the early 1950s was inferior in quality and was used to grow only coarse grains with yields much below the national average.

It is true that underreporting of grain by agricultural cooperatives was occasionally discovered in 1952–57,[88] but, by and large, the underreporting was offset by the overreporting of enthusiastic cadres in the cooperatives, who were eager to show the superiority of collective farming. Furthermore, the improved statistical work in the rural sector and an increasing number of central government "business offices," which often conducted independent farm-production investigations, probably helped to reduce the degree of data falsification by farm households, cooperatives, and local governments.[89]

However, the conclusion that the 1952–57 official yield data are acceptable does not indicate that the 1949–51 yield data also can be accepted uncritically. It is also unjustified to assert that official agricultural statistics for 1949–51 are better in quality than prewar estimates. It is true that the Communist data for that period have a wider geographical coverage than the prewar agricultural surveys which were based on samples, but the quality of statistical returns from the Communist local governments may be poor. The NARB field reporters were hired workers who were personally indifferent or impartial toward the information they gathered, whereas the strong political interest of the local Communist officials in the information they were asked to compile and report may have introduced some subjective biases into the data.[90] The Communist cadres may have tended to depress the agricultural performance in the early years in order to exaggerate the difficult task of recovery and to boast of the progress during subsequent years.

The yield data for 1949–51 will be evaluated in two ways: (1) Using prewar estimates and allowing for possible errors, we may determine whether the 1949 reduction in crop yields from the prewar levels is justified or consistent with other relevant information. (2) Accepting the 1952 official yield data, we may attempt to determine whether the claimed increases from 1949 to 1952 are in reasonable ranges. The 1952 data are taken as reference points, because Peking declared that by 1952 agricultural production had been restored to its prewar normal conditions in most of China. Moreover, since 1952 was the base year for the First Five Year Plan, special efforts and greater care may have been exerted by the government to assess economic conditions in that year.[91] In Table 8.11 we compare the grain yields in 1949 in various provinces with the yields given in the NARB reports and with the figures for 1952.

Table 8.11 Comparison of Communist 1949 and 1952 and NARB Yields of Food Grains, by Province

	Quantity (in catties per mou)			Comparison (in percent)	
Province	NARB (1)	1949 (2)	1952 (3)	$(4) = \frac{(2)}{(1)}$	$(5) = \frac{(3)}{(2)}$
Anhwei	188	101	147	54	145
Chekiang	251	204	334	81	163
Fukien	300	204	263	68	129
Honan	150	103	114	69	111
Hopei	146	86	152	59	177
Hunan	306	272	324	89	119
Hupeh	206	171	244	83	143
Inner Mongolia	123	81	107	66	132
Kansu	131	101	115	77	114
Kiangsi	248	172	250	70	145
Kiangsu	230	144	223	63	155
Kwangsi	256	172	247	67	144
Kwangtung	314	191	213	61	112
Kweichow	226	230	257	102	112
Shansi	112	92	117	82	121
Shantung	175	116	154	66	133
Shensi	132	113	117	86	104
Szechwan	279	211	234	76	111
Tsinghai	149	131	150	88	115
Yunnan	215	218	239	101	110

Sources:
Col. (1): Shen, *Agricultural Resources*, pp. 374–77.
Cols. (2) and (3): From Appendix Table 12.

As can be seen from Column (4) of Table 8.11, the yield reduction in 1949 from the average level in 1931–37 is substantial in all provinces but two. The rate of reduction ranges from 11 percent in Hunan to 46 percent in Anhwei.

It is true that crop yields immediately after the war fell substantially below the prewar peak levels in many countries. But these reductions in yield resulted mainly from the greatly curtailed supply of chemical fertilizer on which agricultural production so heavily depends. In a subsistence agriculture like that of China in the 1930s and 1940s, modern inputs never played any important role in production.

There is no reason for us to believe that the farming techniques of Chinese peasants had regressed during that time interval. No factors inducing, or government policies forcing, farmers to change their crop systems are known to have occurred in that period. It is true that when such high-yield crops as rice and wheat are destroyed by natural calamities, Chinese farmers may attempt to replant coarse grains which have a relatively lower yield but a stronger ability to resist unfavorable weather conditions. However, this shift in grain mix is only temporary and represents farmers' effort to prevent the overall crop yield from falling to an otherwise extremely low level.

Unless there is substantiating evidence that the general quality of soil in China had deteriorated drastically during that period of time, as had happened in Honan, Shantung, and Anhwei when the Yellow River changed its course, one would expect Chinese grain yields to vary in relation to the weather conditions and the quantities of traditional agricultural inputs. But we have found no evidence suggesting that traditional agricultural inputs dropped greatly in 1949 from their prewar levels. Table 8.12 shows the numbers of various large animals in 1935, the

Table 8.12 Numbers of Large Animals in 1935 and 1949 (million head)

Animal	1935	1949	Percentage of decline, 1935–49
Oxen and water buffaloes	48.3	43.9	9
Horses	6.5	4.9	25
Donkeys	12.2	9.5	22
Mules	4.6	1.5	68
Total	71.6	59.8	16

Source: TCKT, 1957, no. 14, p. 9.

prewar peak year, and those in 1949, as computed by the SSB. One can see from this table that, although the total number of large animals in 1949 was 16 percent less than the prewar peak, the drop in the number of oxen and water buffaloes, the principal farming animals in China, was only 9 percent below the peak year 1935.[92]If we take the average number of oxen and water buffaloes in 1931–37 as the comparison basis, as the NARB grain yield data were based, the number of these animals in 1949 may not be smaller at all. According to the published reports of thirteen surveys conducted in eight provinces in 1950, eleven showed increases in the number of draft animals from their prewar levels by various percentages, and only two surveys indicated reductions. Among nine local surveys giving information about changes in the quantities of farming implements between some specified or unspecified prewar years to 1949–50, seven registered increases while only two showed reductions. As for the amount of traditional fertilizer applied, three cases reported increases and one reported reduction from their prewar levels.[93] But none of the reductions can be considered serious.

To consider the weather factor, 1949 is not known as an especially bad year with widespread natural disasters. In addition, the NARB yield esimates are averages over seven years (1931–37), some of which were good crop years whereas others were extremely bad.[94] According to Buck's survey for the early 1930s, the normal yield is about 27 percent higher than the average yield, and the best yield is about 45 percent higher than the average yield.[95]

The remaining explanatory factor would be combat activities between the Nationalist and Communist troops in 1949. Ordinarily, military actions seldom destroy land, but they may displace peasants or interrupt sowing activities, the timing of which may have an important impact on crop yields. However, by early 1949, the major campaigns of the civil war had already ended. Therefore, the effects of this factor should not be overemphasized either.

Having exhausted the possibly unfavorable factors to grain production in 1949, one still can argue that the sharp reductions in crop yieds may simply reflect an exaggeration in the NARB crop yields. To examine this possibility, we compare the 1949 and the 1952 official yield data. Numbers in Column (5) of Table 8.11 represent the recovery rates in grain yields, as officially claimed, in various provinces between the two years. In the case where the NARB's yield figure is an overstatement, the sharp reduction of the 1949 yield is expected to be accompanied by a slow recovery rate from 1949 to 1952. A good example is Kwangtung for which the NARB yield has been proven to be an upward biased estimate.[96] The 1949 yield for that province was only 61 percent of the NARB estimate, yet the yield grew only by 12 percent from 1949 to 1952.

Based on the same reasoning, for any province where a drastic yield reduction between the prewar time and 1949 is associated with an extraordinarily fast recovery rate between 1949 and 1952, the validity of the 1949 yield figure is subject to serious suspicion and some adjustment may be necessary. Thus seven provinces have been selected because of the unexplainably large fluctuations in their grain yields. For each of the seven provinces, the 1949 yield is assumed to be about 30 percent below the 1952 level and the 1950 and 1951 yields are raised accordingly, but by diminishing rates so that the change can be smoothed out in the interval of three years. The resulting estimates of yields are presented in Table 8.13.

Table 8.13 Adjustment of Food Grain Yields for Selected Provinces, 1949–52 (catties per mou)

	1949		1950		1951		1952
Province	Official	Adjusted	Official	Adjusted	Official	Adjusted	Official
Anhwei	101	119	88	135	155	155	147
Chekiang	204	257	228	278	295	304	334
Hopei	86	117	113	127	147	147	152
Hupeh	171	196	222	222	255	255	243
Kiangsi	172	192	191	208	187	227	250
Kiangsu	144	172	183	186	218	218	223
Kwangsi	172	190	219	219	245	245	247

Sources: All official yields are taken from Appendix Table 12. The adjusted yields are the author's own estimates.

Adjustment of Official Data on Total Grain Output

Table 8.14 gives a comparison of the sums of provincial grain output data and the *TGY* data. The results differ somewhat from the comparisons of cultivated areas (Table 8.4) and grain-sown areas (Table 8.6). Provincial data on grain output are practically complete for all provinces except Tibet, Shanghai, and Peking, hence no estimation errors are involved in this set. Yet for eight of the nine years covered, the sums of

Table 8.14 Comparison of Provincial Data and *TGY* Data on Grain Output, 1949–57 (million metric tons)

Year	Sums of provincial data, excluding Tibet, Shanghai, and Peking (1)	*TGY* data (2)	(2)−(1) (3)
1949	110.95	108.10	−2.85
1950	122.85	124.70	1.85
1951	139.67	135.05	−4.62
1952	154.96	154.40	−0.56
1953	158.16	156.90	−1.26
1954	167.40	160.45	−6.95
1955	176.06	174.80	−1.26
1956	183.74	182.50	−1.24
1957	186.54	185.00	−1.54

Sources:
Provincial data: From Appendix Table 13.
TGY data: From *TGY*, p. 119.

provincial data are larger than the *TGY* data, which include Tibet and the two municipalities. It may be true that grain yields in Tibet were so low that the inclusion or exclusion of Tibet makes almost no difference in the country's total grain output. It is also possible that some provincial output figures for the years before 1956 are still based on the old definition which includes soybeans, whereas the *TGY* data have been adjusted to exclude soybeans. However, this still leaves the discrepancies of 1956 and 1957 unexplained. It is suspected that the SSB may have revised downward the reports of grain output from provincial authorities in 1956 and 1957.

The need for further adjustments of official data on grain output in 1949–57 is clear. According to the method of computation in Communist China, the total output of grain in any year is the product of the total grain-sown area and the yield per unit of sown area. Since the last two sets of official statistics have proven to contain distortions, the same distortions must have been embodied in the output data.

For each province, the estimates of grain output have been derived from the adjusted grain-sown area data and the adjusted grain yields (see Appendix Table 14). The estimates for individual provinces have then been aggregated and the sums are taken to be national totals for various years in 1949–57. The omission of Tibet,, Shanghai, and Peking is assumed to have an effect of less than 1 percent on the total grain output in any year. Because of the less satisfactory methods used in adjusting the official data on grain-sown area and yields, our new estimates of grain output may be subject to larger margins of errors than the estimates of cultivated land.

In Table 8.15, the new estimates of grain output are compared with the sums of official provincial data, the *TGY* data, and two sets of estimates made by other Western scholars who used different estimation methods.

Table 8.15 Comparison of Grain Output in Communist China, by Source of Data, 1949–57 (million metric tons)

Year	Sums of original provincial data (1)	Sums of adjusted provincial data (2)	*TGY* data (3)	Liu-Yeh estimates (4)	Dawson estimates (5)
1949	110.95	134.19	108.10		150.00
1950	122.85	143.60	124.10		
1951	139.67	155.36	135.10		
1952	154.96	166.24	154.40	176.70	170.00
1953	158.16	169.91	156.90	180.40	166.00
1954	167.40	175.75	160.50	184.50	170.00
1955	176.06	181.79	174.80	186.40	185.00
1956	183.74	188.27	182.50	184.30	175.00–180.00
1957	186.54	186.54	185.00	185.00	185.00
		Average Annual Rate of Increase (in percent)			
1949–52	11.78	7.40	12.61		4.26
1952–57	3.78	2.33	3.68	0.92	1.70
1949–57	6.71	4.20	6.94		2.65

Sources:

Col. (1): Table 8.14.

Col. (2): Appendix Table 14.

Col. (3): *TGY*, p. 119.

Col. (4): Liu and Yeh, *The Economy of the China Mainland*, p. 132.

Col. (5): Joint Economic Committee, U.S. Congress, *An Economic Profile of Mainland China*, 2 vols. (Washington, D.C., 1967), 1:93.

Our estimates may throw some light on the prewar grain output. In a recent study, Buck has combined the grain output for the twenty-two provinces, as computed from the most frequent yields and sown areas in his *Land Utilization,* and the grain output for the regions outside these provinces.[97] The resulting amount is 181.9 million tons. He has also increased the NARB grain-sown area by his correction factor of 1.337

and multiplied them by the NARB yields. The resulting amount has then been added to the grain output outside the twenty-two provinces. Thus, another estimate of average grain output in prewar China has been obtained as 170.3 million tons. If we apply the NARB grain yields to our own estimates of grain-sown areas in various provinces in 1949, an amount of 174 million tons can be obtained. In other words, if the grain-sown areas in various provinces in 1949 were not too different from what they were in the 1930s and if the NARB yields are accepted, the average grain output in the 1930s is estimated to be around 174 million tons, which is between the two figures cited above.

Our estimation of grain output in 1949–57 agrees with Liu-Yeh's and Dawson's results in that they all indicate an understatement in the official data on grain output for the early years of the Communist regime. Liu and Yeh based their grain output estimates for 1952–55 on the assumptions that per capita grain consumption in those years was the same as in 1956–57 and that the percentage of total grains consumed as human food has gradually increased in this period.[98] How Mr. Dawson, a former United States agricutural attache in China, arrived at his estimates has not been made clear to the reader.

Dawson's 1949 figure is larger than our adjusted grain output; both his estimate and that of Liu-Yeh for 1952 are also higher than ours. Based on the computed growth rates, our series indicates a better performance in the Chinese agricultural sector during the whole period than Dawson and Liu-Yeh believed it to be. Liu-Yeh's average growth rate of 0.9 percent for 1952–57 is particularly suspected to contain some understatement.

Our estimate of grain output for 1949 is 134 million tons, or 21 percent larger than the original provincial sum and 24 percent larger than the *TGY* quantity. The degree of understatement in the official data declines year after year as the discrepancy becomes smaller and smaller. For the period as a whole, about two-thirds of the discrepancy comes from the sown area adjustment and one-third from the yield adjustment.

Inasmuch as the Communist data have understated grain output in the early years, the official growth rate of grain output must have an upward bias. Our adjustments have cut down the official growth rate by about 37 percent. In other words, more than one-third of the reported increases in grain production in this period could be just statistical. The relatively rapid increase in grain output in 1949–52 was caused by the recovery momentum. After agricultural production had more or less returned to its normal conditions by 1952, further development became rather sluggish. The estimated growth rate of 2.33 percent in 1952–57 was barely enough to match the growth rate of population in that period. In other words, the per capita grain output in China probably did not rise in 1952–57.

If the assumption that the unregistered land was exclusively grainland is replaced by the assumption that both grainland and nongrainland had been underreported by the same degree, the estimated grain output for 1949 would be reduced from 134.2 million tons to 131.5 million tons and the average growth rate for 1949–57 would be raised from 4.2 to 4.4 percent. Evidently our arbitrary assumption about the distribution of the unregistered farmland has only a negligibly small effect on our final estimates.

Chapter 9

Input-Output Relations in Grain Production, 1952–57

In this chapter we shall employ the data of 1952–57, as adjusted, to analyze input-output relations in grain production in that period. The central part of the task involves the construction of an aggregate input index for grain production. We follow very closely the methods developed by Professor Anthony M. Tang in his brilliant article on the performance of Chinese agriculture.[1] Since we deal with only a subsector of what Professor Tang's article has covered, and since our input series are measured in a different way, the numerical results of the two studies are not directly comparable. However, as will be pointed out later, many inferences derived from the numerical results in the two studies appear mutually reinforcing.

The input index for grain production may serve two important functions in our study. First, it may shed light on the efficiency of input utilization and the results of technological and institutional changes in grain production in Communist China during the period. In other words, with the help of the index we may measure productivity changes of the aggregate input. Second, the aggregate input index based on the 1952–57 data is instrumental to a projection of grain output during 1958–65. For the latter period, either no statistics of grain production have been directly reported by the Chinese government, or the reliability of official grain output data, though available, is questionable. However, discussion of the second issue will be left until the next chapter.

Selection of Input Series

The selection of the input series to be used in our input-output analysis for grain production in Communist China is dictated by two major considerations. First of all, since we are unable to produce complete statistical information for our intended study, only those agricultural inputs whose data are either readily available or can be reasonably estimated are included. Furthermore, the aggregate input index is to be used as a device for projecting outputs in 1958–65, hence the selection of inputs has to be tailored to the much-restricted data availability for the latter period. Fortunately, data on major inputs have been collected for both periods. Excluded are a few minor items whose data are accessible only for the first period, not for the second. However, because of their secondary importance, their exclusion should not be too damaging to our input-output analysis.

Second, the construction of an aggregate input index requires a procedure of weighting individual inputs, and an ideal weight system is difficult to obtain.[2] This is particularly so in a nonmarket economy where economic variables stated in value terms contain a certain degree of ambiguity. The ambiguity may be partially avoided by using the contributions in physical terms, whenever possible, of various inputs to current production as weights.[3] This is what we intend to do. Hence, input series are selected and grouped here in such a way that they will permit us to design a less ambiguous weighting system.

Inputs such as land and seed are absolutely indispensable in agricultural production. Because of the very nature of those inputs, it is difficult to measure directly their contributing shares in current production in physical terms. Moreover, for a country like China, where multiple cropping is extensively practiced and the multiple-cropping index varies from year to year, a special problem arises as to whether cultivated area or sown acreage should be used to measure the land input.

The case of fertilizer inputs is quite unlike that of the land input. Such inputs as fertilizer are not indispensable, in the sense that farm output would not fall to zero even when the combined quantity of them is reduced to zero. Thus it is possible to measure the yield responses of fertilizer application.

Between the two extreme categories are such agricultural inputs as labor, draft animals, and implements. Labor, on the one hand, is absolutely indispensable in farm production. But on the other hand, any extra amount of labor input, over and above the minimum requirement, may render a marginal contribution to output through better weeding, and so on.

Land appears to be the basic constraint in Chinese agriculture. The total cultivated acreage remained almost unchanged throughout 1952–57;

most efforts to promote agricultural output were in the form of applying more of other inputs to the given amount of land. In our input-output analysis we have removed the land factor from the input side. That is, the measured output of grain is the unit yield—the grain output per unit of sown area. In doing so, any other fundamental input, such as seed, that has a more or less fixed quantitative relation to sown area is also eliminated. What we are to analyze then is the relation between the remaining major inputs and the average unit yield of grain production over time.

Four major input series are left for the construction of an aggregate input index. They are (1) labor, (2) draft animals and tractor power, (3) irrigation facilities, and (4) fertilizer application. Tractors are not treated as an independent series, because the wide employment of farming tractors did not take place until some time after 1958. For the years before 1958, the contribution of tractors to grain production was nil. But to assign a zero weight to an input series amounts to excluding that series entirely, even though this input gained importance in later years. Therefore, we decided to combine draft animals and tractor power in view of the nearly perfect substitutability between the two. In fact, tractors were used in larger quantities after 1958 primarily to replace the draft animals lost during the Great Leap years.

Since we have decided to measure the unit yield of grain production on the output side, all input series should also be stated as quantities per unit of land. Among the four input series, labor, draft animals and tractor power, and irrigation facilities are in stock terms. They are divided by total cultivated acreage in each year rather than by sown acreage on the grounds that, in general, if these three inputs are available to the first crop, they will be automatically available to the second and third crops in that year. To divide the quantities of inputs in stock terms by sown acreage means to understate their true contributions to the unit yield. Fertilizers are a current input measured in flow terms, hence they have to be divided by sown acreage. In other words, only then can we determine the average application of fertilizers per unit of land for each crop in the year. Details of the four measured inputs are described below; their quantities and indexes for 1952–57 are presented in Table 9.1.

1. Labor input: The basic data are the number of persons in the agricultural labor force, namely the agricultural population falling in the age range of fourteen to sixty-four years in various years in this period.

Table 9.1 Four Major Inputs of Grain Production, 1952–57

	Labor		Draft animals and tractor power		Irrigation		Fertilizers	
Year	Quantity (men/mou)	Index	Quantity (hp/mou)	Index	Irrigated land as percentage of cultivated land	Index	Quantity of plant nutrients (kg/mou)	Index
1952	0.160	100.0	0.034	100.0	19.2	100.0	1.256	100.0
1953	0.162	101.3	0.036	105.9	19.8	103.1	1.389	110.6
1954	0.165	103.3	0.038	111.8	21.1	109.8	1.505	119.8
1955	0.168	105.0	0.039	114.7	22.1	115.1	1.615	128.6
1956	0.168	105.0	0.040	117.6	28.5	148.4	1.653	131.6
1957	0.174	108.7	0.038	111.8	31.0	161.5	1.943	154.7

Data sources and estimation procedures:

Labor: C. M. Hou's estimate II of agricultural population in the age group fourteen to sixty-four is used here (see A. Eckstein, W. Galenson, and T. C. Liu, *Economic Trends in Communist China* [Chicago, 1968], p. 345). Population figures are then divided by the adjusted cultivated areas given in Table 8.5.

Draft animals and tractor power: The numbers of oxen and buffaloes in each year (given in Chen, *Chinese Economic Statistics*, p. 340) are added to the number of horsepower of tractors in use (given in *TGY*, p. 135). The sum is then divided by the adjusted cultivated area (from Table 8.5).

Irrigation: Total irrigated areas are taken from *TGY*, p. 130. They are then divided by the adjusted cultivated areas in various years.

Fertilizers: Quantities of plant nutrient, per sown-area unit, from natural fertilizers are taken from Table 6.2. Quantities of plant nutrients from chemical fertilizers are computed from Table 6.5, then divided by the proportion of fertilizers distributed to grain land (Table 6.7). The resulting figures are then divided by the adjusted sown areas of grain (Table 8.7). The two types of fertilizers applied per unit of sown area are then added.

The labor force data have not been adjusted for changes in working hours, partly because this adjustment cannot be made without some relevant quantitative information. More important, however, is the fact that the increased intensity of labor mobilization in the countryside under the Communist regime took place primarily in the so-called idle seasons to construct water conservation projects, to collect natural fertilizers, and to undertake subsidiary production activities. Labor spent on subsidiary production in the farm sector is not contributive to the current output of grains, whereas that devoted to irrigation construction and fertilizer collection, though germane to grain output, would be fully reflected in the changes of those two inputs. Or to put it in another way, generally speaking, the total labor input in the crucial periods of planting and harvesting was a direct function of the number of able bodies on hand. The amount of agricultural labor force in each year is then divided by the total cultivated acreage existing in that year. The simplifying assumption involved here is that the labor input per unit of land is the same for both grain crops and nongrain crops.

2. Draft animals and tractor power: In order to combine them into one series, draft animals and tractors are measured by a common unit—horsepower. Chinese draft animals consist of oxen, buffaloes, horses, mules, and donkeys. However, the last three animals are employed mainly for local transportation and as power sources for food processing, milling for example, but rarely for plowing. Horses are used for plowing only in Manchuria. The chief types of farm animals are oxen and buffaloes, whose population figures are adopted in this input series. According to Professor Buck's rating,[4] the average Chinese ox has a draft power equivalent to that of a horse, but the water buffalo is slightly stronger. Unfortunately, the fact that the population data for oxen and buffaloes are not given as two distinct items for some years prevents us from applying two different power ratings to them, so we simply treat each as equivalent to one horsepower. To the number of horsepower of draft animals in each year we add the horsepower of tractors existing in that year. Although we are fully aware of the possible quality difference between animal plowing and tractor plowing and the possible difference in utilization rate between the two sources of farm power, the data situation does not permit us to make any further refinement. Again the total number of horsepower so derived for various years is then divided by the total cultivated acreage, with the same simplifying assumption that the sources of draft power in agriculture have been indiscriminately distributed to all types of crops.

3. Irrigation: There is no way to measure irrigation facilities as an input except by using the acreage of land actually irrigated in each year. The actual acreage of irrigated land is then divided by the total area of cultivated land in various years respectively. Consequently, the index numbers for this input series are nothing but the rates of changes in the proportion of irrigated land in total cultivated land.

4. Fertilizers: Data have been collected for the computation of total application, in terms of plant nutrients, of natural fertilizers and chemical fertilizers in each year. The total application of natural fertilizers in

a year is then divided by the total sown area in that year, because native fertilizers are, it is believed, collected and used locally with no discriminatory reallocation. However, chemical fertilizers have been supplied by the government to agricultural production units, and discriminatory distribution policies are known to be the rule. Therefore, it is considered appropriate to calculate the allotment of chemical fertilizers to grain production and divide this by the sown area of grain crops in the year. The two magnitudes—application of natural fertilizers per unit of area and application of chemical fertilizers per unit of area—are added for each year. Index numbers are derived therefrom.

Determination of Weights for Individual Inputs

Strictly speaking, if the underlying production function is believed to be the Cobb-Douglas type, the weights in the construction of an aggregate index should be the output elasticities of individual inputs contained in the production function. This kind of perfect weighting system is not always easy to derive, even in studies of individual industries in the West, let alone in Communist China. The best one can do here is to determine, as approximations, the average contributions in physical terms by the four major inputs to grain production in the base year of 1952. As was noted in the preceding section, it is relatively easy to determine the contribution shares of marginal inputs. Thus, we shall first calculate the contributions of fertilizer application and irrigation to the unit yield of grain on the basis of empirical data; the residual will then be distributed between labor and draft animals and tractor power, according to some relevant indications.

In an attempt to measure statistically the yield responses to fertilizer application in Communist China, Professor J. C. Liu has compiled numerous reports from Chinese agricultural journals on the results of applying chemical fertilizers to various crops.[5] He concludes that, so far as grain production is concerned, the yield responses to fertilizer application fall in the range of three to five kg of grains per kg of ammonium sulphate equivalent in gross weight, though the marginal yield diminishes, as one would normally expect.

This yield response ratio is thought too high by a number of Western scholars, on the grounds that the Chinese farmers may not have known how to use chemical fertilizers effectively or that there may not have been sufficient water on Chinese farms to assure the full effectiveness of fertilizer application.[6] These scholars suspect that the data of yield responses collected by Liu were the performances on a few experimental plots but nonrepresentative of the general application of chemical fertilizers in the whole country. These doubts are, however, not justified. In paddy fields, water usually is not a problem. In fact, the Chinese government's policy of distributing chemical fertilizers in concentrated doses to selected "strategic areas" has been designed to tackle the technical problems of applying them. The strategic areas were chosen because they were equipped with the complementary conditions to fertilizer application and showed good yield responses. The ratio of three to five kg of grain yield to every kg of chemical fertilizers has appeared not only in experiment reports but also in many documents where this ratio was used for planning purposes.[7] The lowest yield response ever reported is three kg of grain to one kg of ammonium sulphate equivalent (100 kg grain to 6.7 kg of plant nutrients).[8]

The strongest evidence supporting the claimed yield response is found in the relative prices of rice and chemical fertilizers. From the beginning of the Communist government, chemical fertilizers have been subject to centralized distribution with strict rationing quotas. Before mid-1956, the ratio between the rationing price per kg of ammonium sulphate and the rice price was set at 3 to 1.[9] Even then only occasionally were there reports that farmers considered it unprofitable to apply chemical fertilizers.[10] In most localities the sales agencies had no problem in selling fertilizers at the high official prices. After the adjustment of official fertilizer prices in 1957, the ratio became 2.5 to 1.[11] At the new prices, many farmers began to engage in black-market profiteering on chemical fertilizers by buying from the government supply agencies at the official prices and reselling at prices as high as twice the official prices.[12] These facts are definite proof that the yield response of rice to chemical fertilizers could not have fallen below 3 to 1, and very likely it was much above that ratio. Therefore, we have decided to use a yield response at 5.7 kg of nutrients to 100 kg of grain[13] (which is one kg of ammonium sulphate to 3.5 kg of grain). The consumption of plant nutrients was 1.26 kg per mou of grain-sown area in 1952. The computed contribution of fertilizers to the unit yield of grain in 1952 was 22.1 kg, or 23.9 percent. We do not use the lowest yield response reported by official sources to compute the weight for the fertilizer input, because we hope to use a slightly higher weight for this item so that it may also reflect the contribution of other modern inputs, such as insecticides, whose consumption has increased as rapidly as that of chemical fertilizers in the past years.

The contribution of irrigation to the unit yield of grains is more complicated. In his farm surveys Professor Buck found:

> Comparative yields on irrigated and nonirrigated land for wheat and millet show 60 to 70 percent increase in yields in favor of irrigation in the Wheat Region. The increase in the Rice Region is much less because of the greater rainfall. The profitableness of irrigation decreases from the north to the south as precipitation increases.[14]

In other words, in South China irrigation does not raise the yield per unit of sown area too much. Instead, irrigation makes it possible to extend double or multiple cropping into the dry season. The effect of irrigation is not shown in the rise in unit yield but is reflected in the expansion of sown acreage with a higher double-cropping index. In order to avoid double counting, the effect of irrigation on the expansion of sown acreage will not be considered here.

Computation of the contribution of irrigation on the unit yield of grain in 1952 is based on the following data and assumptions:

1. There were 320 million mou of irrigated land in 1952.[15]
2. About one-third of the irrigated land (107 million mou) was in the wheat region and two-thirds (213 million mou) in the rice region.[16]
3. The official figures of wheat-sown area and rice-sown area in 1952 were 371.7 million mou and 425.7 million mou respectively.[17]
4. The unit yields of wheat and rice in 1952 were 49 kg and 160.5 kg respectively.[18]
5. It is assumed that on the average irrigation raises wheat yield by 60 percent and rice yield by 20 percent.[19]

The grain output contributed by irrigation in 1952 is computed approximately as 8.85 million tons, or 5.3 percent of the 166.24 million tons of total grain output in that year.[20]

After subtracting the weights of fertilizers and irrigation from 100 percent, a residual of 70.8 percent is obtained. The residual will then be distributed between the labor input and draft animals and tractor power. As was pointed out in the preceding section, because of the very nature of these inputs it is impossible to identify their respective contributions in physical terms. Thus, we are compelled to resort to the cost proportions of these inputs in farming. From a number of samples of farming costs cited in Chinese publications, we have computed a mean ratio of 80 to 20 between the labor cost and the cost of draft animals and tractor power.[21] Thus, the weights for these two inputs are 56.6 and 14.2 percent respectively.

The Aggregate Input Index and Changes in Input Productivity

With the four major input series for grain production and their weights as determined above, an aggregate input index can be constructed for 1952–57. As is now well known, the aggregate input index so constructed is theoretically the output index (in our case the unit yield index) that would have been obtained in the absence of "changes in productivity" of inputs. Therefore, a productivity index is obtained by dividing the unit yield index by the aggregate input index. The results are tabulated below.[22]

	Index of observed unit yield	*Index of aggregate input*	*Index of input productivity*
1952	100.0	100.0	100.0
1953	101.7	104.5	97.4
1954	103.9	108.8	95.5
1955	108.7	112.6	96.5
1956	108.3	115.5	93.8
1957	112.4	122.8	91.5

The results show that, except for 1955, input productivity declined continuously, at an annual rate of 1.7 percent.[23] It should be noted that the term *productivity changes* as used here is rather ambiguous. It is the residual effect, lumping together all factors that were influential on grain production in China during that period but were not incorporated in our computation of the aggregate input index. To understand and evaluate the so-called productivity changes, one must examine the residual factors to see whether we can ascertain their behaviors in that period. From documented sources we know that both positive forces (those promoting productivity) and negative elements (those lowering productivity) were present; the measured change in productivity is merely the net effect of them. On the positive side the important factors probably were: (1) changes in cropping systems, especially shifts from low-yield to high-yield crops, on the same piece of land and without an increase in the double-cropping index; (2) selection of better seed; (3) some scale economies after the production units were enlarged from individual households to advanced cooperatives, namely better utilization of a given amount of inputs under the operation of larger farms;[24] and (4) better farming techniques without calling for additional inputs.

On the negative side the important factors influencing productivity were: (1) diminishing returns to increased doses of inputs applied per unit of land; (2) the possible disincentive effect of collective farming; (3) the effect of poor management on collective farms; (4) the disruption of production by frequent reorganizations in the rural sector during this period; and, finally, (5) the adverse weather conditions reported to have prevailed in some years in this period.

These factors, whether positive or negative in effect, may also be classified according to their sources: (1) those induced by technological changes; (2) those induced by institutional changes; and (3) weather variations. The three sources of productivity changes may display different behavior patterns.

Inasmuch as China's agriculture was in a backward state and yields could not be stabilized against the vicissitudinous weather conditions, weather is an important factor in grain production. However, the fluctuation of harvest conditions is rather random. The technological changes are usually gradual, possibly with some discernible trends, unless a technological policy has been introduced as a one-shot, crash program. On the contrary, the impacts of institutional changes may be manifested as discrete jumps or falls in farm productivity.

Theoretically speaking, if the impacts of crop conditions can be measured statistically and duly adjusted on the output side, the effects of institutional changes may be detected. For instance, Marxists contend that a socialist transformation of production organizations always has the merit of raising productivity, that is, an upward shift of the production function. If a rural reorganization or reform has been successful in the economic sense, one would expect to see a jerky jump in the farm productivity index, and vice versa.[25]

Unfortunately, it is by no means easy to measure the impact of weather conditions on grain output. Chinese sources have given both the acreages afflicted by natural calamities and losses of grain due to them in each year from 1952 to 1957.[26] Although we do not have full confidence in the accuracy of these official figures, they are the only quantitative information indicating the effects of weather conditions on grain crops in those years. The estimates of grain losses have been derived from the quantities of grain supplied by the government to the famine-stricken areas in various years. With the thin margins of grain surpluses in most of China even in good years, the degrees of food deficiency resulting from famine are reasonably good indicators of the importance of weather conditions. At least they are much more meaningful than are hydro-thermal indexes and cumulative temperature indexes, even if these indexes could be constructed for China, as a measurement of weather impact on a country with such a vast territory and such great climatic variations.

According to the Chinese Communist classification, 1952 was an abnormally good year, 1955 a good year, and 1953 an average year. Both 1954 and 1956 are called bad years. However, the grain loss reported for 1957 seems to be out of line with the other five years, although it was given by a person in authority, Liao Lu-yen, then the Minister of Agriculture. The year 1957 shows the heaviest grain loss in a six-year period, yet it has never been declared by any Chinese official as a year with bad harvest conditions. It is quite possible that Liao Lu-yen exaggerated the loss for that year to minimize the damages caused by erroneous policies. We shall come back to this point later.

	Total acreage affected by natural calamities (million mou)	*Losses of grain output (million tons)*
1952	—	0
1953	90	7.5
1954	160	8.9
1955	110	6.4
1956	230	12.3
1957	220	17.5

Based on the official evaluation, we may add the grain loss resulting from natural calamities in each year to the actual grain output of that year to obtain an adjusted index of the unit yield of grain. This new index, when used in conjunction with the same aggregate input index, leads to a new index of productivity, which is theoretically free of the impact of weather conditions. The new indexes are presented below.

	Index of observed unit yield, adjusted	*Index of aggregate input*	*Index of productivity, adjusted*
1952	100.0	100.0	100.0
1953	106.2	104.5	101.7
1954	109.1	108.8	100.3
1955	112.5	112.6	99.9
1956	115.3	115.5	99.8
1957	122.9	122.8	100.1

Although the statistical evidence is not strong enough to permit definite inferences, there appear to be some possibilities. First, the general trend of productivity for the whole period is neither rising nor falling. The publicized technological changes in this period, such as the increasingly widespread use of better varieties, were not as successful as claimed,[27] or their results were completely offset by equally strong negative forces. Second, judging from the 1953 productivity index, there might be some temporary favorable effects of land redistribution on the work incentives of peasants. Third, if the 1957 grain loss was an exaggerated figure, as noted earlier, there must be a rather sharp decline in productivity in that year. If we set the grain loss in 1957 at a level comparable to that of 1954, the productivity index of 1957 would show a drop of about 4 percent. This may imply a strong disincentive effect when associated with the advanced agricultural cooperatives which were formed on a nationwide scale in the latter part of 1956.

With the input series, an attempt may be made to analyze the sources of growth of the unit yield in grain production during the period. The unit yield of grains rose by 12.35 percent between 1952 and 1957. This increment may be distributed in percentages to the four inputs as follows: labor, 20.7; draft animals and tractor power, 7.3; irrigation, 14.6; and fertilizers, 57.4.[28] More than half of the increment resulted from the increased fertilizer application per unit of grainland. Especially important was the increase in natural fertilizers. About 20 percent of the growth in the unit yield was attributed to the increase in the labor input, and 15 percent, to the expansion of irrigation facilities. However, the contribution of irrigation construction to the total increment of grain output would be much higher than its contribution to the measure in unit yields, because the expansion of irrigation not only helped raise the sown area unit yield but also enlarged the sown acreage itself through the wider practice of double-cropping.

Chapter 10

Grain Output, 1958–65

As we discussed in detail and examined carefully in Chapter 8, Chinese Communist data on grain output for the years prior to 1957 are biased downward chiefly because of the diminishing underreporting of farmland in that period. The downward biases in farm output statistics can be corrected by adjusting the acreage of farmland in each year, so that the adjusted quantities of grain production depart from the official figures by a margin ranging from a few million tons to 26 million tons.[1] However, the nature of the official data on grain output since 1958 differs from that of the preceding period. Official grain production figures for 1958 and 1959 have been announced; but they, along with other production statistics for those two years, are suspected to contain great degrees of exaggeration. After 1959, during the period of economic crisis and the ensuing years of readjustment, no such statistics have appeared in Chinese publications. But some relevant information occasionally has been divulged by Chinese Communist leaders to foreign visitors. In this chapter, we shall utilize all possible means to ascertain the grain production in China in 1958–65.

Official Data on Grain Output, Reconstructed and Preliminarily Adjusted

One statistical question must be answered before there can be any meaningful discussion of official agricultural data for the post-1957 period. Has the Chinese government since 1959 really changed the measurement of crops from biological yields to barn yields, as some Western observers believe? According to some indications and to circumstantial evidence, our answer to this question is negative. No such revision took place in 1959 or thereafter.

It is true that in view of the statistical fiasco in 1958, the State Statistical Bureau (SSB) did propose in 1959 to improve the methods of gathering farm output statistics. The concrete proposal was reported in mid-1959 by Huang Chien-tuo, the chief of the SSB (the bureau reporting agricultural statistics), as follows:

Agricultural output statistics should be collected in three different ways at three different stages of production:

a. Estimation of biological yields before harvest.
b. Model-sample surveys on the basis of actual cutting during the harvest period.
c. Complete statistics of farm output that has been taken into barns or warehouses.

The third method of gathering statistics can be conducted by utilizing the original registrations or ledgers of actual barn intakes in communes.[2]

However, in the same report he remarked that, although all the three types of investigations should be carried out, the emphasis was placed on the methods a. and b., and especially on b. which would furnish by far the most useful information. The reason, as he saw it, was:

Since agricultural production in our country has not been mechanized and the whole series of work, from harvesting, transporting, threshing, drying, collecting clean grain, down to weighing and storing it in barns, is done manually with the help of animal power and simple instruments, a long time would lapse between harvesting and storing grains in barns. It would take still more time to collect the amount of actual barn intakes from all localities.[3]

In other words, Huang Chein-tuo was afraid that by the time the barn yield statistics became available, it would be too late to use them for planning. But they might serve as an accuracy check.

In a national conference, July 20–29, 1959, held for the purpose of examining the output of summer crop statistics, Huang Chien-tuo reiterated the stress on the model survey statistics based on actual cutting during the harvest, and he viewed this as the "central task" of acquiring reliable farm output statistics.[4] The vice-director of the SSB, Tao Jan, at the same conference said, "We should strengthen the preharvest estimation, do well in the actual cutting surveys, and gradually develop barn yield statistics."[5] During the fall harvest in 1959, a nationwide campaign was launched to check on the output of fall crops, with a total of 16 million investigators participating. Yet this campaign was focused also on sample surveys based on actual cutting. Some localities made attempts or experiments to collect barn yields, but many localities ignored this task.[6] In the same article in which Tao Jan summarized the achievements of agricultural statistical work in 1959, he mentioned an instruction from the central government that barn yields should be used as the bases of farm output statistics in the future.[7] However, there is no evidence that this instruction has actually been implemented. In view of the fact that after 1960 the communes were reorganized, their mess halls abolished, and their decision-making power and income distribution decentralized down to the brigade level, and later on to the production teams, it would be more difficult, circumstantially, to collect barn yield statistics. Therefore, unless some new evidence appears, we have no reason to believe that there was any definitional changes in the official data on grain output for 1958–65; distortions for this period came from other sources.

Now let us examine the official claim for grain output for each year from 1958 to 1965, year by year. Chinese official statistics for 1958 were utterly chaotic and unreliable because of the breakdown in the flow of statistical information, the Great Leap Forward Movement, and the decentralization of governmental administration in that year. It was first announced in April 1959 that grain output had soared from the 1957 level of 185 million tons to 350 million tons in 1958. However, the Chinese statistical authorities soon realized the tremendous exaggeration in this figure, and in August 1959 revised it drastically to 250 million tons. Even the revised figure is generally believed by Western observers to be too high, granted that 1958 was a year with favorable meteorological conditions prevailing in most of China. The Chinese Communist leaders must have the same feeling about the 250-million-ton grain output, for it has never been referred to again by official documents published after 1961. When a previous year's grain output was cited as a comparison basis, 1957 was often chosen. Apparently, the Great Leap claim of grain production in 1958 has been quietly dropped by the Chinese government as being no longer meaningful statistically.

Here it would probably make more sense to use some of the estimated increments of grain production made by Chinese planners or responsible officials in the early part of 1958. These estimates represent the still-objective assessments by the government of the farm production potential before the whole country began to embellish production statistics under the pressure of the Great Leap Forward Movement. One government source stated in June 1958 that, in view of the good crop conditions prevailing, the harvest of summer crops in that year was expected to exceed that of 1957 by about 10 million tons.[8] If this assessment is accepted as being close to the truth, and a increase of another 10 million tons is assumed for fall crops of that year, the total grain output of 1958 may be estimated approximately at 205 million tons.

The tendency to embellish statistics at the lower levels continued in 1959, despite the central government's embarrassment when it had to make a downward revision of the 1958 figure. The 1959 grain output was officially given as 270 million tons, or 8 percent over the revised amount for 1958. Yet 1959 was later declared by the Peking government to be the first of the three consecutive years of unprecedentedly severe natural catastrophes. Judging from the fact that state reserves of grains were used in 1959, the grain output in that year could hardly have exceeded 170 million tons. In other words, the psychology of falsifying statistics under the same Great Leap pressure was almost as strong in 1959 as in the preceding year.[9]

Since 1960 no official announcement of grain output has been made, but the leaders in Peking have on various occasions disclosed information to visiting dignitaries or foreign reporters about the current grain production in China.[10] Those reports are summarized below:

1. In 1960, 150 million tons of grains were produced.[11]
2. In 1962, the output was about 20 million tons larger than that of 1960.[12]
3. In 1964, the output was close to 200 million tons.[13]
4. In 1965, there was an output of about 200 million tons.[14]

Among the above reports, the figure for 1964 was only a preliminary estimate before final accounts were turned in; 200 million tons is probably a little too high. In another report Chou En-lai mentioned that the grain output in 1964 surpassed the 1957 level of 185 million tons.[15] Since this was the first time after 1960 that the Chinese government acknowledged that the 1957 grain output had been exceeded, we may reasonably assume that the 1963 output was still below 185 million tons. A grain output of 200 million tons for 1964 would be more than 8 percent above the 1957 level and about 10 percent higher than the 1963 level. The way in which Chou En-lai announced the achievement of 1964 was too light and too casual for such a substantial rise.[16] A better estimate for 1964 is probably 195 million tons.

The output for 1961 may be set at 160 million tons. One official publication said that the intensified application of chemical fertilizers was responsible for 60 percent of the increment of grain production between 1961 and 1965.[17] The total supply of chemical fertilizers to grainland was augmented by 7.1 million tons from 1961 to 1965. Based on the ratio of 3.5 tons of grain to one ton of chemical fertilizers, the ratio often used in the computations in official documents, a total of about 24 million tons of additional grain may be attributable to the increased fertilizer application. This in turn implies that grain output was raised by 40 million tons from 1961 to 1965. Thus 160 million tons were produced in 1961. In fact, when Viscount Montgomery talked to Mao Tse-tung in the fall of 1961, the Chinese government was expecting to have that much for the harvest.[18]

Thus the estimates of grain output for 1958–65, reconstructed from official information, are the following (in million tons):

1958	205	1962	170
1959	170	1963	182
1960	150	1964	195
1961	160	1965	200

While our estimates are very close to those of Mr. Edwin Jones, they differ considerably from the estimates made by a number of other Western observers for the same period.[19] Therefore, the criticisms received by Jones on his series have to be faced by us, too. The essence of the criticisms is that the estimates do not fit the information concerning grain consumption in China during that period. Specifically, 1959–61 grain outputs are suspected to be too low, whereas those for 1964 and 1965 seem to be high. For instance, in commenting on Mr. Dawson's estimate of grain output for 1965 (195 million tons), Professor Liu argues:

> The Dawson estimate would suggest that per capita grain consumption was somewhat better in 1965 than 1957. If this was actually the case, it would be very hard to explain why the Communist regime was willing to spend roughly 30 percent of its entire foreign exchange earning from exports on food imports during 1964–65. If a saving as large as 30 percent of the entire foreign exchange earnings could have been made merely by reducing per capita food consumption by less than 2 to 3 percent from the 1957 level, it is rather surprising that the Communist regime would not have done so.[20]

A possible reason for discrepancy is the inventory variation—a hedge between consumption and current output of grains. The inventory problem is often ignored in Western studies of China's agricultural production. There are two kinds of grain reserves in Communist China: those held by agricultural production units and those held by the state, or what is known as the "state reserve." In food balances constructed for various non-Communist countries, figures in the column "changes in stock" are usually either zero or negligibly small. It was probably equally true of the grain inventories held by Chinese farmers in normal years before the Communist era. The relatively affluent farmers in China might hold some small quantities of grain and maintain the level constant at normal time. This slim reserve could easily be exhausted in a famine year.

The same situation probably continued until the whole rural sector was collectivized. In 1956 and 1957, the government urged agricultural cooperatives to increase their grain stockpiles for emergencies. For instance, the National Program for Agricultural Development set the following as one of the targets:

> In the twelve years after 1956, all agricultural cooperatives, except those which engage mainly in mountain forestry or in growing industrial crops and are short of grain, should make concrete plans in accordance with their own conditions to build up a surplus of grain against times of urgent need that, in addition to that of the members' families, is sufficient for three, six, twelve, or eighteen months of consumption.[21]

It is possible that, although the government has announced such a target, the actual accumulation of grain reserves at the local level may not be as great as that expected by the National Program because of the low farm productivity and the small margin of farm surplus. One editorial in *JMJP* openly admitted that in spite of the urging of the government and the relatively rapid increase in grain inventories in farm households in recent years, only 20 to 30 percent of all farm households had a grain reserve in 1957.[22] It was reported that in Lushan Hsien, Honan Province, the total grain reserve held by agricultural cooperatives in 1957 was about 3 percent of the year's production.[23] But the amount rose sharply in 1958.

The state grain reserve was more significant. The Communist government was determined to build up a grain stock sufficient for one to two years' consumption. And the actual quantities of grain stockpiles are known for some years. At the end of June 1950, there was a 1.18 million ton grain reserve, excluding that in Manchuria.[24] The total state grain reserve became 12.69 million tons at the beginning of the 1953–54 food year (June 1953) and reached 20.84 million tons at the end of the 1956–57 food year (June 1957).[25] It should be remembered that China suffered substantial crop losses due to poor weather in 1954 and 1956.[26] Thus the state reserve of grains must have increased faster in the 1957–58 and 1958–59 food years. As a conservative calculation, the amount may have surpassed 30 million tons by June 1959. It is necessary to point out that grain procurement and state reserves in Communist China are stated in terms of husked grains, versus the statistics of annual grain output measured in terms of unhusked grain.[27] The official conversion ratio between the two is 85 to 100. Therefore, 30 million tons in the state reserve are equivalent to about 35 million tons of unhusked grain.

However, according to the report of Viscount Montgomery, during his visit to Peking he was informed by Mao Tse-tung that all the "state reserves" of grain had been virtually exhausted by mid-1961.[28] Even if grain inventories held by communes prior to the agricultural crisis are assumed to be quantitatively negligible, the above fact still implies that the combined amount of grain outputs in 1959 and 1960 fell short of the minimum level of consumption by at least 30 million tons. In a sense, the food supply situation in China was probably the worst in the 1961–62 food year. The increase in grain output in 1961 was not substantial, and the food deficiency could no longer be met by drawing from inventories which had been exhausted.

Heavy purchases of grain from abroad began in 1961 and continued at the same high level through 1965. The Chinese Communist leadership obviously realized the great danger of operating a planned economy without any food reserves on hand. The need to replenish grain inventories was reinforced by the international atmosphere that turned increasingly against Communist China. Yet mediocre crops in 1962 and 1963, plus current imports of grain, were barely sufficient to meet the country's minimum consumption requirement. The earliest opportunity for Peking to replenish grain reserves was the period 1964–65. Perhaps the Chinese planners were anxious to restore grain stocks to a minimum safety margin before the inauguration of the third Five Year Plan in 1966. This could be done only through the continued imports of grains in 1964–65.

After combining all relevant information concerning output claims, population, consumption levels, and inventory changes, a coherent picture would look like Table 10.1. Note that even in 1964 and 1965, our computation shows a per capita level of grain consumption considerably lower than that prevailing in the 1953–57 period.[29] Therefore, to postulate even lower figures of grain consumption for 1964 and 1965 would be implausible.

Supplies of Inputs

The above estimates, which are essentially reconstructed official figures, have to be checked further against the input situation in that time period (see Table 10.2). No matter how consistent they appear to be with the information about consumption, population, and inventory variations, output estimates would still be implausible if they are proven impossible to obtain from the quantities of inputs available in that period. Although officially released statistics of farm inputs in that period are also incomplete, the gaps can be filled with estimates involving a fairly narrow margin of possible error. Various inputs for grain production will be discussed below.

1. Grain-sown area: Variations in the grain-sown area in this period have been affected by a number of factors. First, the total cultivated acreage changed. The cultivated area in 1958 and 1959 was officially given as having dropped from 1,677 million mou in 1957 to 1,617 million mou in 1958,[30] and as dropping further to 1,600 million mou in 1959.[31] While there was extensive reclamation during the two years, the farmland added was overbalanced by the tremendous amount of land lost to irrigation and other construction projects. Because of the high cost, the reclamation of virgin land has always been undertaken by the government; especially important has been the reclamation carried out by demobilized soldiers in the form of state farms. Large-scale reclamation was discontinued in 1960–64, probably because of the financial difficulty confronted by the regime. It was resumed in 1965 when the economy had fully recovered.[32] However, the large amount of land reclaimed in 1965 did not help agricultural production in that year; it could not be used to grow crops until the following year. Consequently, no new farmland was added during 1960–65.

Nor was the cultivated acreage reduced by any significant amount through construction during the period. Some effort was made to improve existing irrigation systems, but no new water conservation projects were initiated. It is also true that industrial construction was kept to a minimum until 1964–65. In fact, some of the land confiscated by the government in previous years, for construction that had not actually been done, was returned to the farmers for cultivation.[33]

Yet it is reported that the total cultivated acreage in 1965 was 1,533

Table 10.1 Supply and Consumption of Grain, 1958–66

	Supply of grain			Consumption of grain			Inventory changes
Food year	Domestic output (million tons) (1)	Net imports (million tons) (2)	Total supply (million tons) (3)	Population (thousands) (4)	Per capita consumption (kg) (5)	Total consumption (million tons) (6)	(million tons) (7)
1958–59	205	−1.4	203.6	661,610	290	191.9	+11.7
1959–60	170	−1.8	168.2	671,500	270	181.3	−13.1
1960–61	150	−1.2	148.8	678,220	250	169.6	−20.8
1961–62	160	4.9	164.9	685,000	245	167.8	−2.9
1962–63	170	4.6	174.6	693,920	255	176.9	−2.3
1963–64	182	5.0	187.0	706,410	265	187.2	−0.2
1964–65	195	4.5	199.5	720,540	275	198.1	+1.4
1965–66	200	5.5	205.5	734,950	275	202.1	+3.4

Sources of data and estimation procedures:

1. Domestic grain output estimates are given in the text. However, what is used here is the food year rather than calendar year. All grain crops, say, of 1958, are assumed to be available for the food year 1958–59, namely from July 1958 to June 1959.

2. Net grain imports: Again, a half-year time lag is assumed. Therefore, 1958 imports, say, would be available for consumption in the food year 1958–59. Net grain imports are converted into equivalents of crude grain by using the ratio of 85:100. 1958–60: data taken from U.S. Department of Agriculture, *Trends and Developments in Communist China's World Trade in Farm Products, 1955–60* (Washington, D.C., 1962), pp. 20, 32, 33. Data of grain exports from China are incomplete for 1960. Only the statistics of rice exports are available for that year. However, since rice usually accounted for nearly 90 percent of grain exports from China, we use the ratio of rice exports in 1959 to estimate the total grain exports in 1960. Imports of grains in these three years were negligible.

1961–65: Data are given in Joint Economic Committee, U.S. Congress, *Economic Profile of Mainland China*, 1:601.

3. Total supply: The sum of Col. (1) and Col. (2).

4. Population: The year-end population is taken as the average population for the food-year population. Thus the population at the end of 1958 becomes the average population of 1958–59. Population figures are derived in the following steps:

a. The total population in mainland China on June 30, 1964, has been officially given as 713.4 million, in *China Monthly*, no. 56 (Nov. 1968), p. 15.

b. The official figures of population at the end of 1956 and 1957 are:
1956: 627.8 million (*TCKT*, 1957, no. 11, p. 24).
1957: 656.63 million (*TGY*, p. 8).

c. The population on June 30, 1957, is then interpolated as 642,215,000.

d. Based on the population growth rate prior to 1957 and the nonquantitative information concerning the general health of the Chinese people during the crisis years, a set of yearly population growth rates are postulated for interim years between 1957 and 1964. The 1964 growth rate is carried over to 1965.

Sources of data and estimation procedures for Table 10.1, continued

e. The year-end population figures are derived by interpolating the midyear population data.

The resulting population estimates are tabulated below.

Year	*Midyear population (thousands)*	*Growth rate (percent)*	*Year-end population (thousands)*
1957	642,215	2.0	656,630
1958	655,060	2.0	661,610
1959	668,160	2.0	671,500
1960	674,840	1.0	678,220
1961	681,590	1.0	685,000
1962	688,410	1.0	693,920
1963	699,420	1.6	706,410
1964	713,400	2.0	720,540
1965	727,670	2.0	734,950

5. Per capita consumption of grains: Figures are assumed on the basis of circumstantial evidence and refugee reports on changes in rationing quotas in Communist China. However, figures here represent total consumption inclusive of human consumption and nonhuman consumption stated in per capita terms; 1959–60's consumption level did not fall too much from the previous level because of a number of reasons. First, the chaotic farm statistics in that year prevented the authorities from making any realistic assessment of the current food situation. Second, there were plenty of grain reserves on hand. Third, even if the government later on became aware of the drop in grain output in 1959, it did not anticipate the severe famines to last for three years. Consequently, no effort was made to curtail food rations in that year. In 1960–61, 1961–62, and 1962–63, the government had lowered food rations in accordance with the total availability of grains. That low level of food consumption could not be maintained over a prolonged period without jeopardizing people's health or causing depopulation, hence, the consumption level had been raised since 1963 in accordance to the improved crop situation.

6. Total consumption: Col. (4)×Col. (5).

7. Inventory changes: Col. (3)−Col. (6).

million mou, a reduction of about 77 million mou from the acreage of 1959.[34] It is believed that salinization caused some land to be retired from cultivation and thus accounted for the reduction in cultivated acreage—another damaging result of the magnitude of water conservation projects in 1958.

At the present stage, and with given farming techniques, further extension of the multiple-cropping system in China must depend on the expansion of irrigation facilities. Since there was no such expansion between 1959 and 1965, the multiple-cropping index very likely remained more or less unchanged during that period. Thus the total sown acreage would vary only in accordance with changes in the amount of cultivated land.

There is, however, a complicating factor in deriving the grain-sown

Table 10.2 Four Major Inputs of Grain Production, 1958–65

	Labor		Draft animals and tractor power		Irrigation		Fertilizers	
Year	Quantity (men/mou)	Index	Quantity (hp/mou)	Index	Irrigated land as percent of cultivated land	Index	Quantity of plant nutrients (kg/mou)	Index
1952	0.160	100.0	0.034	100.0	0.192	100.0	1.26	100.0
1958	0.180	112.5	0.041	120.6	0.377	196.4	2.07	165.1
1959	0.183	114.4	0.041	120.6	0.381	198.4	2.27	180.1
1960	0.185	115.6	0.029	85.3	0.385	200.5	2.04	162.3
1961	0.197	123.1	0.019	55.9	0.385	200.5	1.74	138.3
1962	0.207	129.4	0.020	58.8	0.355	184.9	1.93	154.0
1963	0.215	134.4	0.021	61.8	0.359	187.0	2.29	182.3
1964	0.221	138.1	0.024	70.6	0.313	163.0	2.47	196.4
1965	0.227	141.9	0.026	76.5	0.326	169.8	2.99	237.7

Sources of data and estimation procedures:

1. Labor: The labor input per mou of cultivated land is derived in the following steps:

a. Total agricultural labor force in 1958–60 is given in Hou's article, Eckstein et al., *Economic Trends in Communist China*, p. 345.

b. It is assumed that the change in the farm labor force in a given year is mainly determined by the birth rate of fourteen years ago, adjusted for some deaths and current outflow of population of the rural sector to other sectors.

c. There was no substantial outflow of rural population after 1960. But about twenty million urban dwellers were reportedly sent by the government to the rural areas in the crisis years. It is assumed that 80 percent of them fell in the age group of fourteen to sixty-four (i.e., 16 million), and that 8 million joined the farm labor force in 1961 and the other 8 million joined in the next year.

d. The acreages of cultivated land for 1958–65 are taken from Appendix Table 15. The basic data from which the labor inputs per mou of land are derived are tabulated below.

Year	*Total agricultural labor force (million)*	*Cultivated acreage (million mou)*
1958	291.5	1617
1959	293.0	1600
1960	293.4	1585
1961	307.3	1560
1962	321.3	1550
1963	329.9	1533
1964	338.3	1533
1965	348.3	1533

2. Draft animals and tractor power: The number of tractors in use is taken from Table 4.3. The numbers of oxen and buffaloes are estimated in the following ways:

Sources of data and estimation procedures for Table 10.2, continued

a. For 1958–59: Using the basic data given in Chen, *Chinese Economic Statistics*, p. 340, we compute the proportion of oxen and buffaloes in the total number of large draft animals in 1957 and then apply this ratio to the total number of large animals in 1958 and 1959 respectively.

b. For 1960–65: Estimated from the information furnished by Edwin Jones in *Economic Profile of Mainland China*, p. 82.

The estimated numbers of oxen and buffaloes in various years are shown below (1,000 head):

1958	64,820	1962	28,866
1959	65,010	1963	31,130
1960	45,280	1964	34,526
1961	27,734	1965	38,488

c. The total hp of draft animals and tractors in each year is then divided by the cultivated acreage.

3. Irrigation: As used here, the "effectively irrigated land." A considerable portion of irrigation facilities built in 1958 did not function effectively. In the following years, some of the facilities that had been effective were not in use, because they had caused salinization of the land irrigated. The areas effectively irrigated in various years are as follows (million mou):

1958	610	(*JMJP*, April 7, 1960)
1959	610	(Interpolated)
1960	610	(Interpolated)
1961	600	(Interpolated)
1962	550	(Taken from Table 5.1)
1963	550	(Taken from Table 5.1)
1964	480	(Taken from Table 5.1)
1965	500	(Taken from Table 5.1)

The effectively irrigated areas are then divided by the cultivated acreages.

4. Fertilizers: Quantities of plant nutrient per sown-area unit from natural fertilizers are taken from Table 6.2. Quantities of plant nutrient from chemical fertilizers are taken rom Table 6.5, divided by the proportions of fertilizers distributed to grainland (given in Table 7.7), and then divided by the sown areas of grains (Appendix Table 15). Plant nutrients from the two sources per unit of sown area are then totaled.

acreage from total sown acreage in each year, and that is the land shifted from growing nongrain crops to growing grain. In China, such industrial crops as cotton and oil-bearing seeds are marginal crops in the sense that they are grown only when the country is more or less self-sufficient in food crops, and they are the first to be sacrificed if the country is faced with a major agricultural crisis. Therefore, industrial crops suffered the sharpest decline in 1961–62. Prior to that time, some districts had become areas producing industrial crops exclusively. Farmers there sold their produce to the government and in turn bought grain from government grain distribution organizations. However, since there was a general shortage of grain during the crisis years, farmers in these districts found it very difficult to acquire grain from government organizations. As a result, they utilized a large portion of their land to grow grain for subsistence. In fact, the government encouraged them to make this change.[35] Since recovery was under way after 1962, some of these regions gradually returned to the production of industrial crops. But even by 1964, the sown acreage of cotton in China had not yet been restored its 1957 level.[36]

By assembling such scattered pieces of relevant information as those mentioned above, we can construct a series of sown acreages for grain in 1958–65. The estimates are then checked against some provincial data concerning sown acreages for individual crops in the period. We have collected data of this sort for several provinces. These data become samples which, when compared with their counterparts in 1957, may show the direction and degree of change in sown area for the country as a whole. Computational details and the data sources for estimating them are presented in Appendix Table 15.

2. The agricultural labor force: There are several factors underlying the variations in the agricultural labor force. The population is one of them. However, no demographical information was published by the Chinese Communist government between 1958 and 1967. In September 1968 two Communist newspapers in Hong Kong disclosed a new set of population data for the twenty-nine provinces, special districts, and municipalities in mainland China.[37] Except for two provinces, the new population data are believed to result from the 1964 census, but the data had not been disclosed by the Chinese government until 1968. The annual growth rate, as indicated by the 1957 population and by the new counts in 1964, is 1.4 percent. This growth rate, if accurate, is much lower than the 2.0–2.2 percent growth rate in 1953–57. Apparently the food shortage during the crisis years had a significant impact on population growth in China, although there is no evidence of mass starvation. However, the primary impact of a food shortage would be on the birth rate and on the death rate of the old and the very young, not so much the population of working ages.[38] Therefore, the agricultural labor force is believed to have been determined more by the previous age structure and growth rate than by the current growth rate. Aside from the natural increase in the rural labor force, there has been some sectoral migration. Reports show that the Chinese government moved large numbers of urban dwellers to villages in 1960–61 to alleviate the food crisis in cities. No doubt these people participate in agricultural production after being

sent to the rural sector. Based on the information concerning the above-mentioned factors, the size of the labor force in the agricultural sector is estimated for each year of the period.

3. Draft animals and tractor power: As was shown in Chapter 4, the available data on tractors in use in various years during this period are quite good. Missing is concrete information about the number of farm draft animals. The Great Leap caused serious losses among large animals which had died of overwork or malnutrition. We use samples of provincial data to derive rough estimates of the total number of draft animals for the country as a whole.

4. Irrigation and fertilizer application: Data are taken from Chapters 5 and 6. The production of chemical fertilizers has received high priority in recent years, and its performance has been relatively impressive. Therefore, the Peking government is least restrictive in releasing these statistics. As a matter of fact, the Chinese Communists have used the statistics of fertilizer production as showpieces to reveal a relatively bright spot in a generally dark picture.

By assembling all the input data and using the weights given in the preceding chapter, one can construct an aggregate input index for grain production in 1958–65. The results are shown in Table 10.3. Again, our input series refers to the quantity applied per unit of grain-sown area, and the resulting aggregate input index should be interpreted as the index

Table 10.3 Projected Grain Output, 1958–65

Year	Aggregate input index (1952=100) (1)	Projected yield (kg/mou) (2)	Grain-sown area (million mou) (3)	Projected grain output (million tons) (4)
1958	130.68	120.7	1,819	219.6
1959	135.45	125.1	1,669	208.8
1960	126.96	117.3	1,721	201.9
1961	121.29	112.1	1,725	193.4
1962	128.20	118.4	1,723	204.0
1963	138.33	127.8	1,687	215.6
1964	143.77	132.8	1,685	223.8
1965	157.00	145.0	1,661	240.8

Sources:
Col. (1): Derived from Table 10.2.
Col. (2): The aggregate input index multipled by the 1952 unit yield (92.38 kg).
Col. (3): Taken from Appendix Table 15.
Col. (4): Col. (2)×Col. (3).

of unit yield of grain in the absence of changes in productivity. The aggregate input index, combined with the data of grain-sown area, will furnish a set of projected grain outputs for this period, if input productivity were constant. These results also are presented in Table 10.3.

The fact that our projected outputs of grain are uniformly much higher than the reconstructed official figures implies that the latter are not impossible to achieve, given the quantities of inputs in that period. The sizable discrepancies between the two sets represent, theoretically, productivity changes. In view of the extremely abnormal conditions in the period, productivity changes are expected to be large. Important factors that may have had negative effects on productivity in the period include: (1) diminishing returns on certain inputs, (2) adverse weather conditions, (3) weakened work incentives of farmers as a result of the commune movement, and (4) weakened physical strength of farmers because of malnutrition. Unfortunately, the impacts of these factors are inextricably mingled and difficult to quantify. Nevertheless, we shall attempt to make some crude estimates.

In the period, there was no expansion in either cultivated acreage or sown acreage, but there was a remarkable rise in the aggregate index of other inputs applied per unit of land, so that a diminishing return seems inevitable. However, the increase in the aggregate input index came exclusively from two items: labor and fertilizers. Total irrigation facilities and draft animals and tractor power actually declined as compared with the 1958 levels. Furthermore, there seems to be no appreciable fall in the yield response to the application of fertilizers, as evidenced by the fact that the average amount of fertilizers per unit of farmland was still small in China, and by the fact that the government had to continue the rationing of chemical fertilizers at high prices in spite of the increased supply. By way of elimination, the labor input is left as the only suspect item sustaining diminishing returns in the period. This should not be surprising at all. It is often thought that the labor input in China's agriculture has already approached the maximum point, and any further increase would render no contribution to farm output.[39]

To take care of the diminishing return on the labor input, we may adjust crudely the labor input series by assuming that there was no increase in effective labor input since 1957. The economic interpretation of the assumption is that all the increments in the agricultural labor force beyond the 1957 level were actually redundant and the amount of labor that had been effectively absorbed in production remained constant; that is, it was the maximum quantity that could be fruitfully used on a given acreage of farmland. The projected grain outputs for various years from 1958 to 1965 become as follows (in million tons):

1958	216.0	1962	185.4
1959	203.9	1963	192.9
1960	195.6	1964	197.9
1961	180.3	1965	212.0

Now let us consider the impact of harvest conditions in various years. According to Chinese official reports, 1958 and 1964 are regarded as having good weather in most of China. The years 1963 and 1965 may be considered as having average harvest conditions in the sense that floods and droughts of moderate degree occurred in some areas of the country. However, 1959 through 1961 are labeled as the "three consecutive years of unprecedentedly severe natural calamities." It was declared that 650 million mou, or 40 percent of the total cultivated acreage in the country, were affected by natural calamities of various degrees in 1959. Of this amount, 320 million mou suffered from droughts. From the 1953–56 data, the average loss rate was 59,000 tons of grain per million mou of land affected by natural calamities.[40] If the same loss rate is applied to 1959, the total loss from natural calamities in that year would be 38 million tons.

A total acreage of 900 million mou, or about 56 percent of the total cultivated acreage, are said to have been affected by calamities of all sorts in 1960.[41] If the same loss rate is applied, the 1960 total loss of grains would be as high as 53 million tons, or about 40 percent higher than that in the preceding year. However, many Western observers tend to think not only that the seriousness of the calamities in the two years may have been exaggerated by the Peking government but also that Peking may have attributed everything to uncontrollable natural factors to cover up human errors that were also responsible for crop failures. In other words, the reported damages from natural calamities are believed actually to have included the disincentive effects of the commune movement.

Communes were organized on a nationwide scale beginning in August 1958, hence the impact was not felt on the summer crops, but on the fall crops. An unusually large quantity of grain was abandoned in the fields during the autumn harvesting time in that year; so the government had to launch a campaign in late fall to glean the fields.

In the following two years, although the structure of communes and their income distribution system had been modified, the disincentive effects nevertheless remained. Now the impacts permeated all types of farming activities. However, as was pointed out earlier, to a very large extent the losses in grain output caused by this factor have already been reflected in the calamity damage. On the one hand, the Chinese Communist government tended to exaggerate the scope of natural calamities. On the other hand, some of the "natural calamities" were not really natural but stemmed from the peasants' lack of incentive. This was especially clear in 1960 when the government declared that a vast area of the country was plagued by "weed calamities," as exemplified by the following local reports:

1. Shansi Province: 82 percent of the sown area in the province was affected by weed calamities, and 50 percent of the rural labor force was thrown into the battle of weeding.[42]
2. Heilungkiang Province: On 30 percent of the farmland, weeds overgrew crop plants; 230,000 cadres were sent to the countryside to fight weeds.[43]
3. Liaoning Province: 10 percent of the farmland in the province suffered weed calamities; more than 2 million people, including employees of industrial enterprises, government offices, schools, and garrisons, were mobilized to participate in the weeding.[44]
4. Shantung Province: Weed calamities occurred in 48 million mou, or one-third of the total cultivated area of that province. Weeds were so high that men could hardly enter the field to weed. In August 7.3 million participated in the weeding work, and an additional 800,000 government employees were later sent to help weed. The number of people engaged in this task finally reached 12 million.[45]
5. In five districts in Hopei Province, the weed calamity spread to 11 million mou of farmland; 6 million people were mobilized for weeding.[46]
6. Honan Province: 16 million mou, or 12 percent of total cultivated land, were plagued by weeds.[47]

It is well known that weeds had never before been a "natural calamity" in China, because farmers used to weed from time to time during the entire growing season.

By 1961, during which the harvest conditions were officially described as "no better than the preceding year,"[48] Chinese farmers probably had realized that, no matter how bad the system under which they lived and worked, they must manage to survive. Refusing to work because of a lack of incentive amounts to suicide. In other words, the desire for survival now began to set a floor for the disincentive effects. Farmers had to make an effort if they were to achieve subsistence. Besides, by 1961 communes had been completely restructured, and such measures as the reinstating of private plots and the reopening of limited free markets in rural areas had been undertaken by the government in an effort to save the country from complete collapse. Therefore, it should not be surprising that the grain output in 1961 would be better than that of 1960, even if harvest conditions were actually "no better" in 1961.

While 1962 was not described by the Chinese Communists as another year of severe natural catastrophes, no detailed reports are available about the actual harvest conditions in that year. The reconstructed official estimate of grain output for 1962 fell short of the level projected on the basis of input quantities. A variety of explanations may be found for the discrepancy. First of all, farmers' incentives were not yet fully restored in spite of the new agricultural policies adopted by the regime. The wounds were too deep and too enduring to be healed quickly. Besides, institutional changes in the past were so frequent that farmers now had grave doubts as to whether the new policy would be more than temporary. Moreover, some responsible officials in Peking have admitted that bad crops for three years in a row, plus the poor farming practices introduced in the Great Leap years, had reduced the quality of the land as well as of the seed.[49] Consequently, even if weather conditions in 1962 were fairly favorable, productivity would be much below the normal level. In fact, these conditions lasted through 1965, or even later, and diminished only slowly over time.

For 1963 and 1965, the two "average" years, we may put the grain loss at about 10 million tons per year. This is comparable to the loss in 1954 but less than that in 1956. The year 1964 was reported to be a "good" one with a minimal loss of grains from natural calamities.

All the resulting adjustments in this section are summarized in Table 10.4. So far, the cross-checks against the independent input series as modified by productivity changes have not revealed any inconsistency with the reconstructed official figures on grain output. This fact, in conjunction with the discussion in the preceding section, supports the as-

Table 10.4 Reconciliation of the Projected Grain Output and the Reconstructed Official Data, 1958–65 (million tons)

Year	Projected grain output (1)	Adjustment for redundant labor input (2)	Adjustment for other factors of productivity changes and harvest conditions (3)	Reconstructed official data (4)
1958	219.6	3.6	11.0	205
1959	208.8	4.9	33.9	170
1960	201.9	6.3	45.6	150
1961	193.4	13.1	20.3	160
1962	204.0	18.6	15.4	170
1963	215.6	22.7	10.9	182
1964	223.8	25.9	2.9	195
1965	240.8	28.8	12.0	200

Sources:
Col. (1): From Table 10.3.
Col. (2): See text, p. 257.
Col. (3): See text, pp. 257–59.
Col. (4): From Table 10.1.

sumption that the reconstructed official data are good approximations for grain output in China in this period.

Chapter 11

Production of Nongrain Crops

According to the Chinese Communist classification, one major nongrain crop is soybeans.[1] China has been for many years the leading seller of soybeans in the world market. Aside from exportation, soybeans have a number of domestic uses. A large portion of the soybean output is consumed as food; the Chinese make a wide variety of food products from soybeans. Since they have a high oil content, ranging from 11 to 25 percent, they are also crushed for oil. After the oil is extracted, the residue may be used as a livestock feed, or, more profitably, pressed into cakes which are an important natural fertilizer.

Another major category of nongrain crops consists of the so-called technical crops, sometimes referred to as industrial crops, consisting of textile fibers (cotton, ramie, jute, hemp, and so on), oil-bearing seeds (peanuts, rapeseed, sesame, and others),[2] tobacco, and sugar-making materials (sugarcane and beets). These crops are the raw material for industrial production and are subject to the government procurement regulations. Another category is composed of all miscellaneous supplementary foods such as vegetables, tea, fruits, and so on.

Virtually all technical crops in China once were marginal in the sense that, in competition with grain for the limited land, their production would be the first to be sacrificed whenever there was a serious food shortage resulting from famine or war. In prewar times, very few farmers in China specialized in the production of technical crops. Their main aversion to these crops was a lack of security. Because of the poor marketing and high transportation costs of farm products, it would be both insecure and uneconomical for farmers to produce technical crops exclusively for sale and then to buy food grains from other sources. The same concern also applied to the need for animal feed. Most grain crops supply fodder as a by-product, whereas most technical crops do not. A

Table 11.1 Sown Area and Output of Nongrain Crops, 1949–58 (area, 1,000 mou; output, 1,000 tons)

Crop	1949 Sown area	1949 Output	1950 Sown area	1950 Output	1951 Sown area	1951 Output	1952 Sown area	1952 Output	1953 Sown area	1953 Output
Soybeans	124,782	5,086					175,191	9,519	185,430	9,931
Cotton	41,550	444.5	56,790	692.5	82,270	1,303.5	83,636	1,303.5	77,700	1,174.5
Jute	342	32					1,244	191	902	120
Flax							427	33	565	50
Tobacco							6,405	435	5,905	407
Peanuts	18,816	1,268					27,064	2,316	26,628	2,127
Rapeseed	22,725	734					27,946	932	25,007	879
Sesame	12,402	325.5					15,848	480.5	16,334	521
Sugarcane	1,623	2,642					2,737	7,116	2,885	7,209
Sugar beets	239	191					526	479	730	505

district which grew technical crops exclusively would have to buy fodder from an outside source. The transportation cost per unit of value was even higher for shipping fodder than for grain. Farmers considered technical crops to be risky also because these crops required a much longer time to mature than grain crops. Therefore, farmers specializing in these crops might find it too late to replant if the technical crops showed signs of failure for some reason.

After the Chinese Communists came to power, the government had tried to persuade some farmers to specialize in the production of important technical crops in the places most suited to them. The attempt was fairly successful. For cotton, sugarcane, and sugar beets, concentrated and specialized production gradually developed in many localities. The program of unified purchases and unified sales is believed to be conducive to this development. In the districts growing technical crops exclusively, farmers sold their produce to the government and in turn bought grain and animal feed from the government's distribution agencies. The government tried to guarantee stable supplies of grain and feed to these areas, regardless of the general situation of grain production in the country.

However, the situation changed in the early 1960s. Because of severe crop failures in three consecutive years, the government could no longer maintain the guaranteed supply of food to the districts specializing in technical crops. Consequently, in 1961 farm units there began to switch large amounts of their land to the production of grain in order to achieve

Table 11.1, *continued*

1954		1955		1956		1957		1958	
Sown area	Output	Sown area	Output	Sown area	Output	Sown area	Output	Sown area	Output
189,806	9,080	171,626	9,121	180,699	10,234	191,223	10,045		10,500
81,930	1,065	86,591	1518.5	93,834	1,445	86,629	1,640	85,840	2,100
976	128	1,663	250	1,959	249	2,049	295		
736	75	875	88	599	72	522	58		
6,090	400	6,840	485	8,690	570	8,130	418		
31,449	2,767	34,025	2,926	38,725	3,336	38,124	2,571		2,800
25,596	878	35,070	969	32,477	920	34,619	888		1,100
15,661	229	17,199	463.5	14,269	339	14,130	312		
3,281	8,592	3,063	8,110	3,316	8,678	3,999	10,393		13,525
1,095	989	1,723	1,596	2,241	1,654	2,390	1,501		2,900

Source: Chen, *Economic Statistics*, pp. 286–87, 338–39.

self-sufficiency. In fact, the Chinese government encouraged this alteration, because it could alleviate the problem of food shortage confronted by the whole country. It was only after 1963, when the food situation had considerably improved, that the government again shifted attention to the production of technical crops.

No prewar statistics were systematically collected concerning the output and acreage of nongrain crops in China, because of their secondary importance, scattered production, and wide fluctuation. The rough estimates available admittedly lack reliability.[3] The data on these crops (Table 11.1) compiled by the Chinese Communist government in the mid-1950s are believed to be significantly improved in quality. This is particularly true for the major technical crops which are subject to the government procurement. For example, more than 90 percent of all cotton produced has to be surrendered by farm units to the government.[4] In addition to the regular reports submitted by local authorities, many of the government agencies responsible for procurement have conducted their own independent surveys, thus providing a double check of the agricultural statistics collected through regular channels.[5] The quality of statistics for 1949–51 may be poorer, but there is no basis on which we can make any adjustment, one way or another. The data for 1958, as in practically all other cases, must contain exaggerations and should be discounted.

For items included in the table, the total sown area rose from 341.1 million mou in 1952 to 381.8 million mou in 1957, an increase of 11.2

percent. The only item that suffered a decrease in sown acreage in this period was sesame. During 1952–57, the output of sugar-producing material saw the most rapid growth, especially sugar beets whose output more than tripled. This increase resulted from the rapid development of new beet fields in Manchuria, North China, and Inner Mongolia. The output of sugarcane rose by 46 percent during the period, although its production was still confined to the southern regions: Kwangtung, Kwangsi, Fuchien, Szechwan, Yunnan, and Chekiang. Increases in the output of fiber plants were also quite impressive, ranging from 25.8 percent for cotton to 75.8 percent for flax. Soybeans increased moderately, whereas tobacco decreased moderately during this period. The production of oil-bearing seeds as a group suffered a considerable decline.

The government openly admitted that the production of oilseeds fell short of the target set in the First Five Year Plan. The important responsible factor was the unreasonably low price set by the government in procuring oil-bearing materials from farmers.[6] The procurement prices were even lower than the prices of the cakes produced from the residue of oilseeds after extraction processes, which were sold by the government to farmers as fertilizers. Among all technical crops, this is the only clear case where the procurement system adversely affected production. In 1958 the Chinese government raised the priority of oilseeds in agricultural production planning and adjusted upward the procurement prices.[7]

Although the exaggerated output figures for 1958 should be discounted, it is most likely that major technical crops reached their peak level in that year. It is difficult, however, to ascertain exact production figures except for a few items. In 1959 and 1960, the first two of the three consecutive years of agricultural crisis, while there was no announced policy to curtail the sown acreage of technical crops, the output of these crops probably dropped precipitously because of the lower unit yields. The growers of technical crops shifted a large amount of farmland to the production of grain in 1961–62, partly because of the government's advice and partly because of their own desire to become self-sufficient. A review of current agricultural policy was made in the Eighth Session of the Tenth Central Committee, which was convened in the later part of 1962, led to a new resolution that, because of the improved situation in agriculture, greater emphasis gradually should be given to the production of technical crops. Thus farmers were encouraged to enlarge their sown acreages for technical crops, and the distribution quotas of chemical fertilizers for these crops were raised.

There were signs of rapid recovery in the production of technical crops after 1963. It was claimed that the harvest of sugarcane and sugar beets in the 1963–64 crop year exceeded the all-time high, and that the harvest of 1964–65 was even higher. As a result, during these two crop years the sugar-manufacturing industry had to prolong the extraction period one month longer than the normal period.[8] One official source gave the following percentage increases in 1964, as compared with 1963: vegetable oilseeds, 72; peanuts, 26; tobacco, 28; sugarcane, 47; and sugar beets, 170.[9] The rapid rate of recovery in cotton production during 1963 and 1964 was also impressive. By 1965, it would seem that most of the above items had regained or surpassed their 1957 output level.

Among nongrain crops in China, cotton undoubtedly commands the paramount importance and, therefore, deserves our special attention here. Before the Sino-Japanese war, China produced about 10 percent of the world's total cotton output.[10] There were two major cotton belts in China—the Yellow River and the Yangtze River valleys—each of which contributed an almost equal share. New cotton-producing areas have been developed during the Communist period, notably Sinkiang and Liaoning.

Except for 1949–51, the official data on cotton output and acreage, as given in Table 11.1, appear fairly reliable. According to the estimates of the Nationalist government, the average sown acreage for cotton in 1931–37 in the twenty-two provinces of China proper was 57 million mou, and it rose to 60 million mou by 1947. The average output for 1931–37 was 809,500 tons, and it increased to 844,000 tons in 1947.[11] However, the Communist figures for both output and acreage in 1949 are substantially lower than those for 1947. It is difficult to ascertain the real causes for these discrepancies.

As we did in our study of grain production, we have compiled provincial data on cotton output during 1949–57 and have compared them with the national statistics published in *Ten Great Years*. The results are shown in Table 11.2. Although only seventeen provinces are included in the provincial statistics presented in this table, they include nearly all of the cotton-producing areas in China. The two sets are fairly consistent with each other for 1952–57. In each year of the period, the national total output is larger than the sum of provincial data by a few thousand tons; the difference represents the marginal output in the area outside the seventeen provinces. The discrepancies, though small in quantity,

Table 11.2 Comparison of Provincial Data and *TGY* Data on Cotton Output, 1949–57 (million catties of ginned cotton)

Year	*TGY* data for the whole country	Sum of data for seventeen provinces	Difference
1949	889	961	−72
1950	1,385	1,403	−18
1951	2,061	2,076	−15
1952	2,607	2,547	60
1953	2,349	2,301	48
1954	2,130	2,102	28
1955	3,037	2,966	71
1956	2,890	2,815	75
1957	3,280	3,223	57

Sources:
TGY data: From *TGY*, p. 119.
Provincial data: From Appendix Table 18.

show wider year-to-year fluctuations, because cotton production in those places was so insignificant that farmers did not bother to maintain a stable output for it. However, the national total falls short of the sum of provincial data in the three years from 1949 to 1951 by varying degrees. This fact suggests that the State Statistical Bureau probably had adjusted downward the provincial data on cotton output for those three years.

Because of the close relation between cotton and industrial production, the Peking government assigned a high priority to cotton production as early as 1950. The bulk of the increase in cotton output resulted from the great expansion of cotton land in the early 1950s. However, by 1952 the planners recognized the acute conflict between cotton and grain for the use of the land, and they could not decide whether to reduce or further enlarge the sown acreage of cotton. Because of this policy uncertainty, the total acreage of cotton land fluctuated from year to year. Between 1953 and 1957, the instability of sown acreage, plus the variation in crop conditions, resulted in a fluctuating cotton output which rose in two years (1955 and 1957) and fell in the other three (1953, 1954, and 1956).

So far as the pricing policy is concerned, the procurement price of cotton has been the most favorable as compared with the prices set for other technical crops. Furthermore, unlike the producers of other technical crops, cotton-growers were entitled to procurement prepayments.

The government was also more generous in extending farm credits to cotton-growers.

Attempts were made during the First Five Year Plan period to rearrange the scattered cotton fields into a relatively concentrated pattern. This measure was especially effective in raising cotton output in 1957. After the whole rural sector was organized into advanced cooperatives (collectives), each cooperative in the cotton areas was urged to select the most suitable land for cotton and to form a specialized production team to till the cotton land.[12] Another important advantage resulting from the consolidation of cotton fields was the higher effectiveness of insecticide application. Cotton production was a clear case where collectivization did have some beneficial influence.

One established policy of the Chinese Communist government was to give preferential treatment in the distribution of chemical fertilizers and insecticides to the high-yield, consolidated cotton fields. This discriminatory policy was to some extent responsible for the wide differential in the unit yield of cotton fields, as indicated by the following statistics for 1957.[13]

Yield (Catties of ginned cotton)	*Sown acreage (1,000 mou)*
Over 100	4,180
60 to 100	9,440
20 to 60	52,900
Below 20	20,000
Total	86,520

In the 1958 production plan, approximately 15 million mou of high-yield cotton land was to receive 150,000 tons of chemical fertilizers, whereas a total of only 50,000 tons of fertilizers was allotted to the remaining 70 million mou of cotton land.[14]

An improvement in the quality of Chinese cotton was reported during the First Five Year Plan period. A total of twenty improved varieties of cotton had been bred.[15] Among them Taitze cotton became the most popular. In 1957, improved seeds were planted on 82 million of the total 86.5 million mou of cotton land.[16] The average staple length for Chinese cotton increased from 23 mm in 1952 to 27 mm in 1957 and to 27.5 mm in 1958.[17]

As was noted earlier, the decision of the Chinese government to stimulate cotton production was closely related to its desire to expand the textile industry during the First Five Year Plan period. On the one hand, the imports of raw cotton gradually had been reduced from the high level of 134,000 tons in 1950.[18] On the other hand, efforts were made to increase the production capacity of the cotton textile industry, as Table 11.3 indicates. However, the planners apparently had overesti-

Table 11.3 Number of Spindles Installed in the Cotton Textile Industry, 1949–57 (1,000 spindles)

Year	Spindles
1949	4,996
1950	5,128
1951	5,284
1952	5,610
1953	5,891
1954	6,306
1955	6,671
1956	6,820
1957	7,604

Sources:
1949–51: *CH*, p. 154.
1952–56: *CH*, p. 162.
1957: Estimated by adding the number of spindles produced in 1956 to the number of installed spindles in 1956. The former is obtained from *CH*, p. 161.

mated the growth potential of cotton production in China, and there was an overexpansion of the cotton textile industry by 1957. It is officially estimated that the utilization rate of equipment for producing cotton yarns was only 74 percent in 1957; all cotton spinning mills in the country had to suspend work for an average of forty-nine days during that year.[19]

However, in spite of the increase in the output of raw cotton and in the domestic production of cotton textiles, there had been no substantial increase in the per capita consumption level of cotton textiles up to 1957. In fact, the Chinese government had maintained a nearly constant yearly ration of less than eight yards of cotton cloth per person during the whole period of 1953–57.[20] This was caused by (1) the rapid population growth, (2) the substitution of domestically produced yarns for imported yarns, and (3) the rising exports of cotton textiles in this period.

The last factor deserves some special attention. It was a determined policy of the Chinese Communist government to develop the textile industry to earn foreign exchange. China's exports of cotton yarns and fabrics grew about eightfold during 1953–57. In 1958, cotton fabric exports reached a total of 450 million yards,[21] or about 9 percent of the preceding year's total output.[22] The Soviet Union became a big customer who bought three-fourths of its total textile imports from China in 1959, the year of peak Sino-Soviet trade.[23] Southeast Asia has been another major target of China's export drive.

It is in the competitive market of Southeast Asia that Chinese Communists have demonstrated their energetic and aggressive selling techniques. They have taken advantage of the large Chinese population in that area to promote sales. Occasionally, long-term credits with unusually low interest rates were extended to the importing country to finance the purchase of Chinese goods. The most important weapon in China's export drive, however, has been the pricing policy. It is reported that Chinese trading companies in Southeast Asia usually quoted cotton textile prices that were about 10 percent cheaper than the prices of comparable goods exported by other countries. Some Western observers are convinced that the prices quoted for Chinese cotton goods in world markets were actually below their production costs.[24]

It is difficult to assess in concrete terms cotton production in China since 1958. Summarized in Table 11.4 are our estimates made on the basis of scattered official information. Except for 1960 and 1961, the cotton-sown acreages are estimated independently of the estimates of output and unit yields, yet the three series appear quite consistent with each other. This fact gives us confidence in the validity of our estimates.

The cotton output figure for 1958 has been revised twice by the Peking government. It was first given as 3.5 million tons, more than double the 1957 level, and was subsequently scaled down to 3.3 million tons.[25] The final figure, which appeared in *TGY*, was 2.1 million tons, or 28 percent higher than the 1957 output.[26] The fact that this was the only round figure in the whole series of cotton output statistics given in *TGY* implies that the Peking government was still not absolutely sure about the accuracy of the final figure for 1958. However, judging from the sown acreage, from the crop conditions prevailing in China in that year, and from the fact that cotton-growers had to deliver more than 90 percent of their current output to the government, the final output figure may contain only a slight upward bias, if any. The 1959 output was given as 2.4 million tons.[27] Apparently this was the sum of the

Table 11.4 Cotton Production, 1957–65

Year	Output (million tons)	Sown area (million mou)	Unit yield (catties per mou)
1957	1.64	87	38
1958	2.00	86	47
1959	1.80	84	43
1960	1.02	73	28
1961	0.88	55	32
1962	1.03	53	39
1963	1.24	61	40
1964	1.70	69	49
1965	2.10	71	59

Sources:

Sown area: From Appendix Table 15.

Output and unit yield:

1957: Official data given in *TGY*, pp. 119, 121.

1958: The finalized output of 2.1 million tons, as given in *TGY*, p. 119, is suspected to be biased slightly upward and is scaled down here by 5 percent.

1959: According to the information given in *JMJP*, Dec. 31, 1964, and *HKWHP*, Mar. 4, 1965, cotton output in 1959 should be below the 1958 level but higher than that in 1957.

1964: Output of 1964 is said to have exceeded the 1957 level (*JMJP* Dec. 31, 1964), but it is still below the 1959 output (*HKWHP*, March 4, 1965). The unit yield is, however, a record high (*JMJP*, Dec. 31, 1964).

1963: Cotton output increased by 37 percent and unit yield by 23 percent in 1964 (*JMJP*, Dec. 31, 1964).

1962: Cotton output increased by about 20 percent in 1963 (*PR*, Oct. 4, 1963).

1960 and 1961: The unit yield for 1960 is assumed to be 28 catties whereas that for 1961 is assumed to be 32 catties. The former is slightly lower, and the latter slightly higher, than the unit yield (30 catties) for 1956, a year with a poor cotton crop. Although there was bad weather in the country in 1960 and 1961, the unit yield of cotton in 1961 is believed to be better than in 1960, because a considerable amount of cotton land was switched to grain production in 1961. The remaining cotton land had relatively high yields.

1965: Both the unit yield and output were claimed to be a record high (*CKHW*, Feb. 9, 1966).

production reports submitted by individual communes before double-checking with the procurement results, and it must contain a great deal of overstatement, like the first report of cotton output for 1958 compiled in the same way. No doubt, the State Statistical Bureau in Peking had checked and adjusted the initial output figure at a later time in accordance with procurement results. Unfortunately, the final figure for cotton output for 1959 has not been released.

As the situation of grain supply further deteriorated in 1960 and

1961, more and more cotton land was shifted to grain production. The cotton fields that remained unaltered in 1961–62 are believed to be the land having absolute advantages for growing cotton. While the sown acreage remained at a low level in 1962, the unit yield rose considerably as a result of doubling the quota of chemical fertilizers distributed to cotton land.[28]

In the latter part of 1962 the Party leadership decided to resume the high priority for cotton production. A national conference was held in December of that year,[29] and the government urged representatives from the cotton-producing areas to enlarge the cotton-sown acreage. The following three years witnessed a rapid recovery of cotton as a result of the gradual restoration of sown acreage and the continued increase in fertilizer application. By 1965, the total output of cotton had surpassed the previous peak achieved in 1958, although the sown area was still short of the 1958 acreage.[30]

The recovery of cotton production led to an upsurge in cotton textile production and a new investment drive in the textile industry in the ensuing years. A remarkable increase has been claimed for textile production in 1964.[31] In 1965 and in the first eight months of 1966, the output of the textile industry is said to have been the highest in the entire history of the Communist regime.[32] There were 1.5 million production workers in the textile industry in 1965,[33] as compared with the peak level of 0.94 million in the pre-Leap period.[34]

An accelerated program of investment in the textile industry was launched in 1965, apparently because the production capacity of 1964 had reached full utilization, or nearly so, and a further rapid increase in cotton output was anticipated in the near future. There were forty-six major projects under construction in that year, including thirty-seven cotton textile mills, six printing and dyeing plants, and three silk mills.[35] Some of the projects were new, while others were carried over from previous years. Compared with the corresponding period in 1964, the output of textile machinery and equipment in the first half of 1965 almost doubled.[36] During that time period (January–June 1965) approximately 0.7–0.8 million spindles had been installed.[37] By December 1965, the total number of new spindles installed in that year reached 1.4 million,[38] which is equal to the number of new spindles installed in 1959 but exceeds the investment level in any other year.

In fact, textile production played an especially significant role in the Chinese economy during and immediately after the crisis years. First, the textile industry was, and is still, the largest employer in the whole industrial sector. The Peking government tried hard to keep textile mills operating on reduced work schedules to mitigate the unemployment problem in the urban areas. Secondly, Chinese textile products, which had a well-established world market by the 1960s, were among the few items that China could depend on for acquiring the badly needed foreign exchange to purchase imported grain during the famine years. The desperate need to export textiles can be clearly seen from China's trade statistics presented in Table 11.5. Except for 1962, China's imports of

Table 11.5 Imports and Exports of Textile Fibers and Products, 1957–63

	Fiber import		Textile products exports	
Year	Value (million U.S. dollars)	Percentage of total imports	Value (million U.S. dollars)	Percentage of total exports
1957	101.9	9.5	180.4	13.2
1958	106.9	7.6	200.2	12.2
1959	91.7	5.6	269.2	15.0
1960	134.9	9.1	305.7	18.9
1961	101.6	10.0	272.9	22.8
1962	78.7	9.5	263.0	21.8
1963	136.9	15.1	252.2	20.4

Source: Alexander Eckstein, *Communist China's Economic Growth and Foreign Trade* (New York, 1966), pp. 106, 107, 113, 114.

textile fibers were not curtailed during the crisis years, as compared with the levels in 1957–59. The exports of textile goods in 1960–63 were considerably higher than in 1957–58. Textile fabrics became the leading item in China's export basket during those four years and furnished about one-fifth of the total foreign exchange earned in that period. It should be pointed out, however, that the step-up of textile exports had further depressed the domestic per capita consumption of textile goods during the crisis years.

Chapter 12

Summary and Conclusions

From the analyses in the previous chapters, one can hardly escape the conclusion that the Chinese Communist experience in developing agriculture has been far from successful. The agricultural policy of the regime consisted of two main components—socialist transformation and technological transformation. However, since there was a lack of general consensus among the Communist leaders, both transformations were characterized by uneven development, with abrupt escalations and sharp reversals.

In reviewing the variations of agricultural policy after the early economic recovery, three periods are distinguishable: 1952 to mid-1955, mid-1955 to 1960, and 1960 to 1965. The fundamental strategy for economic development was formulated in the first period. The country was to marshall all possible resources for industrialization, while agriculture was to be relegated to a supporting role. However, both transformations in this period were carried out slowly and cautiously. More important, collectivization was not viewed as an effective developmental policy for agriculture. There existed, in fact, a fear among some Communist leaders that a rush to collectivize agriculture might influence agricultural production adversely. As for technological transformation, although its positive effects on farm production were not in doubt, it was not implemented at a high speed because the planners were unwilling to divert a substantial portion of investable funds from industry to agriculture and because there was a shortage of technical manpower to carry out such a transformation on a large scale.

A new phase began in mid-1955, and both transformations were greatly accelerated in this second period. Among various factors underlying the policy changes in the period, an important one was the constraint on industrialization created by an agriculture which had stagnated. As an instrument to accommodate planned industrialization, agriculture must be made to move forward, and preferably this should be done without draining investment funds from industry. Thus, socialist transformation came to be used as a developmental policy, and it was rapidly escalated. Yet, much to the despair of the designer of this policy, its eventual result was catastrophic.

In retrospect, it seems that the existence of two groups in the party hierarchy, who had divergent views about the potential merits and demerits of agricultural collectivization, did not function as a restraining force but actually precipitated the tragedy. Although the conservative group managed to apply some braking power from time to time, their actions aroused overreactions of the radical group in the form of further escalations whenever the latter group gained control. Therefore, the overall tempo of collectivization was by no means slowed down. Moreover, the escalation of collectivization was accompanied by repeated purges and thought-reform campaigns which caused local authorities and cadres to respond erratically to collectivization drives. As a result, a barrier was erected which prevented the men in power from assessing objectively the true situation at the lowest level until the whole economy was pushed to the brink of collapse. One may wonder whether there would have been a commune movement if Communist China had launched a vigorous collectivization drive and had encountered strong resistance in the beginning, that is, in 1953–54. To pose the question in a different way, if some painful lesson had to be learned by Chinese Communists sooner or later, would it not have been less painful to learn it sooner?

Technologically, a new strategy was mapped out in the second period to meet the dilemma caused by the necessity to promote farm production at quicker steps and the reluctance to sacrifice industrial investment, along with the shortage of technical manpower. Thus the technological policies adopted in the second period were generally characterized by the following two features: (1) They were usually carried out in the form of crash programs to be enforced uniformly and mandatorily in the whole country, or a large part of it, in a short period of time. (2) The so-called mass line was emphasized, as reflected in the mobilization of traditional inputs and the production of modern inputs with native resources and indigenous methods. The two features became especially pronounced in 1958 and 1959.

It is true that the promotion of technological innovations through the process of natural dissemination entails a longer time and a tremendous number of technical personnel. Uniform technological policies, enforced by government fiat, have proven to be an effective way of alleviating those serious constraints ordinarily faced by underdeveloped countries. However, there is a great danger in employing such a shortcut, especially in agriculture which is more suited to decentralized decision-making. The experience of Communist China clearly testifies to this. The introduction of wrong crop systems, the misuse of new plows in 1956, and the fiasco of water conservation construction in 1958 are the outstanding examples at hand. Especially disastrous was the last program which was in a large measure responsible for the severe agricultural crisis in 1959–61 and the slowness in the subsequent recovery.

The attempt to intensify the utilization of traditional inputs in order to save investment had only a limited success. Traditional inputs are neither inexhaustible nor truly costless. For instance, traditional sources of fertilizers had been almost fully utilized under the intensive farming in China. The Communist drive to mobilize the last drops of them incurred heavy costs to farmers, though not to the state. Even labor in the rural sector was sometimes used by the government as something with no opportunity cost so that ordinary farming activities were impeded. More important, as has been pointed out by the agricultural experts familiar with the situation in China, even before Communist rule, Chinese agriculture had already been pushed close to the limit along the traditional production function; the pay-off for further intensification of cultivation was already in a state of diminishing returns.

The first decade under the Communist regime did see a rising trend in the use of modern farm inputs, but the application was not sufficiently widespread to make an appreciable effect on the total agricultural output. Furthermore, there was an apparent confusion among Chinese decision-makers as to whether new methods and inputs should be selected to raise labor productivity or land productivity.

The period 1961–65 may be called one of normalization insofar as agricultural policies are concerned. Most biases seen in the previous periods were now being corrected. Beginning in 1961, a reversal in the economic policy accorded the highest priority to agricultural production, above all the other economic sectors. An appropriate approach for technological progress had been formed through earlier trial and error, and a large share of investment was now being channelled to agriculture.

The socialistic nature of farm organizations was also reduced, step by step. While it is still not too clear whether these new measures represented only short-run, compensatory adjustments, or were meant to be a permanent reorientation, the policy reversal nevertheless has saved China from complete collapse and has brought about economic recovery.

The above analyses are borne out by the statistics of Chinese agricultural production. After an adjustment for the underreporting in the early years of the Communist period, the statistics of grain output show an annual growth rate of 7.4 percent for 1949–52, due mainly to the recovery momentum. But the average annual rate of increase for 1952–57 was as low as 2.3 percent. This was barely enough to match the population growth rate and represented a stagnant level of per capita output in that period.

The productivity index for grain, which has been derived from the index of unit yield and the aggregate input index, manifests no increase for the 1952–57 period. Either the publicized technological progress was actually fruitless, or its positive effects on productivity were offset by the negative effects of collectivization. In fact, there is some indication of a sharp decline in productivity per unit of resources in 1957, the year immediately after the whole farm sector was organized into advanced cooperatives.

We are less certain about the statistics for grain production in Communist China since 1958 because of the relatively meager information available to us. However, except for 1958 and 1959, for which the exaggeration in official statistics is obvious and adjustments must be made, the reconstructed official claims of grain output for 1960–65 seem to be consistent with the consumption situation and with supplies of major farm inputs. Grain output reached a peak of 205 million tons in 1958 but dropped to a low point of 150 million tons in 1960. The subsequent recovery brought it back to about 200 million tons in 1965. It naturally follows that the per capita grain output must have declined yearly over this time interval by about 1.5 percent, which was also the average population annual growth rate during the same period.

Because of their closer relationship with industrial production, technical crops have received relatively more support from the state. Consequently, major technical crops increased in output more rapidly than grain in 1949–57. However, since technical crops are more sensitive to procurement prices and compete with grains for land, there were wider fluctuations in their sown acreages and outputs even in normal years.

During the crisis years, these technical crops were the first to be sacrificed under the pressure of food shortages. But as soon as the crisis was over, their production rapidly regained priority in the government's agricultural policy. There are indications that the output of cotton and sugar-making materials had surpassed the previous peaks by 1964–65.

The outside world knows very little about the agricultural situation in Communist China since 1965. Only a few speculations can be advanced here. Western observers generally agree that the disruptive impacts of the Great Proletarian Cultural Revolution which lasted from mid-1966 to the end of 1968 were less damaging to the rural areas than to the urban sector. To the extent that agriculture was impeded, the effects were felt mainly in the later stage of the Cultural Revolution. Unlike industrial enterprises, many of which were engulfed in the vehement struggle between anti-Mao and pro-Mao advocates or between different pro-Mao groups throughout the entire Cultural Revolution, the villages remained fairly calm and peaceful in the early part of this troubled period.

In view of the disturbances in industry, the production of chemical fertilizers, on which Chinese agriculture has become increasingly dependent, may have fallen short of its potential level during 1966–68. It is unclear, however, whether there was an absolute reduction in chemical fertilizer output, as compared with the level of 1965. It is probably true that disruptions in the transportation system during the Cultural Revolution may have prevented timely deliveries of fertilizers to farmers in some localities. Again there is no way for us to ascertain the degree of this interference. Other than chemical fertilizers, there is no reason to believe that any major farm input has been curtailed as a result of the internal strife.

As to the prospects in the near future, the direction of technological improvement seems to be well established. Even Mao Tse-tung and his followers must have realized by now the limitations in developing China's agriculture along traditional lines of production possibilities. They must also have obtained an answer from experience as to the modern inputs and methods that are most suitable to Chinese conditions.

It is uncertain, however, whether the new group of leaders in Peking will follow the old pattern of implementing agricultural innovations through a uniform and mandatory policy. The temptation to use such a policy in order to shorten the dissemination time and to reduce the number of technicians required still exists. What is more uncertain is the attitude of the new Communist government toward farm institutions in the near future. There already are strong indications that Mao Tse-tung still prefers a socialized and regimented structure for the rural areas. Whether this indicates a restoration of the commune system in its original form or some compromised form of agricultural organization remains to be seen. The disincentive effect of socialized farming has been definitely confirmed by both the Chinese experience and historical records in the Soviet Union and in eastern European countries. The general trend in European Communist countries is to move gradually away from the collective farm system. But Mao Tse-tung seems to have envisioned another possible way out, that is, to indoctrinate Chinese farmers thoroughly with the selfless communistic spirit. Thus ideological indoctrination becomes a special type of investment in human capital. Mao tried this approach in the past, but without success; it is still doubtful whether it will work in the future. If self-interest is really a basic drive of human nature, it can hardly be reformed once and for all by artificial means. Therefore, if the commune system is to be reinstated in China without hindering agricultural production, the Chinese Communist Party must repeat these special investment activities periodically. This is, of course, a costly thing to do.

Appendix Tables

Notes

Bibliography

Index

Appendix Table 1 Provincial Data on Cultivated Area, 1949–57 (10,000 mou)

Province	1949	1950	1951	1952
Anhwei	7,700	8,030	8,330	8,730
Chekiang	(3,380)	(3,380)	(3,380)	(3,380)
Fukien	2,100	(2,160)	(2,220)	(2,280)
Heilungkiang	8,546	(8,926)	(9,316)	9,716
Honan	13,100	13,100	13,100	13,100
Hopei	(10,960)	(11,670)	(11,960)	(12,450)
Hunan	(5,021)	(5,121)	(5,271)	5,483
Hupeh	(6,450)	(6,410)	(6,380)	(6,340)
Inner Mongolia	6,360	(6,710)	(7,100)	7,530
Kansu	(5,400)	(5,400)	(5,400)	5,468
Kiangsi	3,542	3,540	(3,680)	(3,825)
Kiangsu	5,100	(5,900)	(6,750)	7,725
Kirin	6,860	(6,910)	(6,960)	7,020
Kwangsi	3,306	(3,306)	(3,370)	(3,430)
Kwangtung	5,192	5,192	5,354	5,200
Kweichow	2,697	(2,697)	(2,760)	2,827
Liaoning	6,730	(6,800)	(6,880)	6,998
Shansi	(6,400)	(6,400)	(6,400)	7,000
Shantung	13,797	13,500	13,386	13,500
Shensi	5,348	(5,348)	(5,404)	(5,700)
Sinkiang	1,810	1,879	2,008	2,382
Szechwan	11,340	10,537	(10,840)	11,202
Tsinghai	766	(790)	821	829
Yunnan	3,380	(3,380)	(3,580)	(3,820)

Sources of data and estimation procedures:

All figures without parentheses are taken from *PAS*. The figures in parentheses are estimates. Except those indicated below, they are interpolated.

Chekiang, 1949–56: With no relevant information, we have assumed that, in the official records, the cultivated area in this province remained approximately constant.

Hopei, 1949–53: Estimated by using the grain-sown areas in these years and the ratio of cultivated area to grain-sown area in 1954.

Appendix Table 1, *continued*

1953	1954	1955	1956	1957
9,230	9,215	9,200	9,070	8,800
(3,380)	(3,380)	(3,380)	(3,380)	3,378
2,240	(2,170)	2,100	(2,170)	2,233
9,726	9,750	9,750	10,440	10,930
13,262	13,378	13,600	13,950	13,460
(12,600)	12,720	(13,220)	13,846	13,503
(5,600)	(5,730)	(5,860)	6,000	5,741
(6,310)	(6,270)	6,230	6,300	6,430
(7,730)	(7,940)	(8,150)	8,376	8,315
(5,588)	(5,720)	(5,860)	6,000	5,939
(3,970)	4,121	4,140	4,200	4,220
7,728	(8,080)	(8,440)	(8,840)	9,300
(6,985)	6,941	6,955	7,196	7,078
3,507	3,400	3,700	3,700	3,796
5,109	5,500	5,700	5,400	5,740
(2,900)	2,969	3,100	(3,075)	3,050
(7,020)	(7,045)	(7,070)	(7,100)	7,126
(7,065)	(7,250)	7,550	7,600	6,812
13,900	13,900	13,900	13,944	14,000
(6,020)	(6,470)	6,830	6,830	6,700
2,340	2,310	2,552	2,787	3,022
10,000	(10,500)	11,000	11,000	11,530
(800)	(770)	731	743	750
4,110	(4,100)	4,100	4,165	4,262

Sources of data and estimation procedures for Appendix Table 1, continued

Hunan, 1949–51 and 1953–55: Buck's prewar figure is used for 1949; amounts for the other years are interpolated.

Hupeh, 1949–54: Buck's prewar figure is used for 1949; amounts for the other years are interpolated.

Kansu, 1949–51: Assumed to be the same as in 1952.

Shansi, 1949–51 and 1954: Since there was very little double-cropping, the total sown area in these years is used for this estimation.

Appendix Table 2 Land Reclaimed by State Farms, by Province (10,000 mou)

Province	1949	1950	1951	1952	1953	1954	1955	1956	1957
Anhwei	0	0.3	0.7	2.5	1.2	1.2	2.6	5.0	4.6
Chekiang	0	0.2	0.5	1.9	0.9	0.9	2.0	3.8	3.5
Fukien	0	0.2	0.5	1.9	0.9	0.9	2.0	3.8	3.5
Heilungkiang	14	19.0	22.0	62.0	64.0	76.0	86.0	360.0	224.0
Honan	0	0.5	1.5	5.4	2.5	2.6	5.7	10.8	9.8
Hopei	0	0.6	1.6	5.9	2.8	2.8	6.2	11.8	10.7
Hunan	0	0.6	1.5	5.5	2.6	2.7	5.8	11.0	10.0
Hupeh	0	0.3	0.9	3.2	1.5	1.6	3.4	6.4	5.8
Inner Mongolia	0	0.3	0.8	2.8	1.3	1.4	2.9	5.6	5.1
Kansu	0	0	0	0	0	0	0.3	2.9	18.3
Kiangsi	0	0.4	1.0	3.8	1.8	1.8	4.0	7.6	6.9
Kiangsu	0	1.1	2.9	10.6	5.0	5.1	11.1	21.2	19.3
Kirin	0	1.9	5.2	19.3	9.0	9.3	20.1	38.4	35.0
Kwangsi	0	1.0	2.8	10.3	4.8	5.0	10.8	20.6	18.8
Kwangtung	0	2.5	6.6	24.7	11.5	11.9	25.8	49.2	44.8
Kweichow	0	0.1	0.2	0.8	0.4	0.4	0.8	1.6	1.5
Liaoning	0	0.7	2.0	7.3	3.4	3.5	7.7	14.6	13.3
Shansi	0	0.2	0.4	1.5	0.7	0.7	1.6	3.0	2.7
Shantung	0	0.7	1.8	6.8	3.2	3.3	7.1	13.6	12.4
Shensi	0	0.1	0.2	0.8	0.4	0.4	0.8	1.6	1.5
Sinkiang	0	7.1	19.1	71.3	33.3	34.3	74.6	142.1	129.5
Szechwan	0	0.2	0.4	1.5	0.7	0.7	1.6	3.0	2.7
Tsinghai	0	0	1	0.5	2.5	4.0	5.3	8.0	12.5
Yunnan	0	1.1	2.9	10.7	5.0	5.2	11.2	21.4	19.5

Sources of data and estimation procedures:

The statistics for state farms appear fairly consistent. State farms include both arable farms and livestock farms; the latter have also reclaimed some land for agricultural cultivation.

Administratively, state farms in China belonged to two systems: those under the Ministry of State Farms and Reclamation in the central government and those under various provincial or local governments.

Our computation is made with the following information and procedures:

1. Land reclaimed by all state farms, central and local, in 1953–57 was 20.86 million mou (*CHCC*, 1958, no. 2, p. 21).

2. Altogether, 710 central state farms existed in 1957 (*TGY*, p. 134). The distribution of them by province and municipality in 1957 is also known (*JMJP*, Mar. 18, 1958).

Sources of data and estimation procedures for Appendix Table 2, continued

3. The annual amounts of reclamation by central state farms are known for 1952–57 (*TGY*, p. 134; and *CKNK*, 1957, no. 4, pp. 24–25). They add up to 15.21 million mou.

4. The total cultivated land owned by state farms at the end of 1951 was said to be 863,000 mou (*CCTP*, Feb. 5, 1952). Although this source did not specify, the amount is believed to refer to the central state farms only. In fact, there were very few local state farms prior to 1953. Using this figure and the information in par. 3, the central state farms had reclaimed a total of 12.11 million mou by July 1, 1956, which is consistent with the reported total of 13.62 million mou by the end of 1956 (*TKP*, Mar. 14, 1957).

5. Based on the above pieces of information, total reclamation by both central and local state farms in 1949–57 can be computed as follows, in thousands of mou: 1949–51, 963; 1952, 2,236; 1953–57, 20,860; for a total of 24,059. Now, the question is how to distribute the total to individual provinces in various years.

6. For the following three provinces, the annual amounts of reclamation by state farms are known or can be computed.

Heilungkiang: from *HLKJP*, Sept. 30, 1959; and *JPRS*, no. 15388 (Sept. 1962). The total for 1949–57 is 9.27 million mou.

Kansu: from *CKNK*, 1959, no. 20, p. 17; and no. 19, p. 10. The total for the whole period is 215 thousand mou.

Tsinghai: from *CKNK*, 1959, no. 20, p. 6. The total for the whole period is 329 thousand mou.

7. For each of the following eleven provinces we know the total reclamation but not the breakdown for individual years. None of the provinces had state farms in 1949.

Province	*Total reclamation in 1950–57 (1,000 mou)*	*Source of information*
Anhwei	182	*AHJP*, Oct. 1, 1959
Honan	388	*CKNK*, 1959, no. 20, p. 19
Hopei	425	*CKNK*, 1958, no. 1, p. 6; 1959, no. 19, p. 12
Hunan	394	*CKNK*, 1958, no. 6, p. 6
Hupeh	232	*CKNK*, 1958, no. 1, p. 6
Inner Mongolia	200	*NMKTC*, p. 158
Kiangsu	760	*CKNK*, 1957, no. 4, p. 1; 1959, no. 20, p. 19
Kirin	1,380	*KRJP*, July 17, 1958
Kwangtung	1,770	*CKNK*, 1959, no. 20, p. 11
Shantung	486	*TCJP*, Aug. 19, 1957
Sinkiang	5,118	*CKNP*, 1959, no. 19, p. 22

Continued on following page

Sources of data and estimation procedures for Appendix Table 2, continued

8. For the remaining ten provinces, we know only the numbers of state farms existing in 1957 (*JMJP*, Mar. 18, 1958). We have utilized these numbers to estimate the average size of state farms in the ten provinces, as existing in 1957. In doing so we have assumed that: (a) the numbers of arable farms are better indicators and the numbers of livestock farms should be ignored, and (b) the six state farms in Peking and Tientsing had obtained their land through means other than reclamation. There were altogether 106 state farms (arable) in the ten provinces in 1957, with an estimated total area of cultivated land of 2,910 thousand mou (24,059 thousand mou minus 21,149 thousand mou; see pars. 5, 6, and 7. Therefore, the average size of those farms was 27,453 mou. Using this average size we can approximately estimate the total cultivated land owned by state farms in each of the ten provinces in 1957.

Province	*Number of state farms*	*Reclamation in 1949–57 (1,000 mou)*
Chekiang	5	137
Fukien	5	137
Kiangsi	10	275
Kwangsi	27	741
Kweichow	2	55
Liaoning	19	522
Shansi	4	110
Shensi	2	55
Szechwan	4	110
Yunnan	28	769

9. The next step is to distribute the total reclamation by state farms in each province to individual years, except in the three cases mentioned in par. 6. This is done by utilizing the indexes of annual reclamation by all central state farms. Since all provinces but Heilungkiang did not have state farms in 1949, the indexes are computed with 1950 = 100.

Year	*Reclamation in the year (1,000 mou)*	*Index*
1949	140	
1950	223	100
1951	600	269
1952	2,236	1,003
1953	1,044	468
1954	1,076	483
1955	2,340	1,049
1956	4,455	1,998
1957	4,060	1,821

Appendix Table 3 Land Reclamation in Heilungkiang, 1953–57 (10,000 mou)

	Total reclamation (1)	Reclamation by state farms (2)	Reclamation by new settlers (3)	Other types of reclamation (4)
1953	209	64	113	32
1954	248	76	135	37
1955	280	86	153	41
1956	456	360	76	20
1957	494	224	213	57
Total	1,687	810	690	187

Sources of data and estimation procedures:

Quantities in Col. (1) are derived from the information provided in *HLKJP*, Sept. 30, 1959, and *JPRS*, no. 15388 (Sept. 1962), whereas the numbers in Col. (2) are taken from Appendix Table 2. The difference between the totals of these two columns is 8,770 thousand mou. Of this amount, 6,900 thousand mou is attributable to reclamation by new settlers in Heilungkiang in the whole period 1953–57 (for a detailed explanation see text p. 205). The residual 1,870 thousand mou (8,770 thousand mou minus 6,900 thousand mou), listed as "other types of reclamation," represents the total amount of two components: (1) increases in land of existing agricultural cooperatives and farmers, and (2) the discovered land concealment. To derive the figures for Col. (3) and Col. (4), we divide the difference between Col. (1) and Col. (2) in each year according to the ratio 6,900 to 1,870.

Appendix Table 4 Increase in Cultivated Area Resulting from Collectivization, by Province, 1955–57

Province	Total increase in cultivated area, unadjusted (1,000 mou) (1)	Rural population (10,000 persons) (2)	Density of rural population (persons per 10,000 mou) (3)	Correction factor (4)
Anhwei	1,117	2,977	3,236	1.07
Chekiang	434	2,163	6,055	2.00
Fukien	255	1,216	5,790	1.91
Heilungkiang	1,184	883	905	0.30
Honan	1,651	4,293	3,157	1.04
Hopei	1,604	3,416	2,584	0.85
Hunan	711	3,213	5,483	1.81
Hupeh	756	2,632	4,224	1.39
Inner Mongolia	968	689	864	0.29
Kansu	711	1,212	2,068	0.68
Kiangsi	503	1,621	3,915	1.29
Kiangsu	1,024	3,507	4,155	1.37
Kirin	843	838	1,204	0.40
Kwangsi	449	1,750	4,729	1.56
Kwangtung	691	3,258	5,715	1.89
Kweichow	376	1,508	4,865	1.61
Liaoning	857	1,277	1,806	0.60
Shansi	917	1,302	1,724	0.57
Shantung	1,687	4,718	3,394	1.12
Shensi	830	1,494	2,187	0.72
Sinkiang	309	458	1,795	0.59
Szechwan	1,335	6,201	5,637	1.86
Tibet		111		
Tsinghai	89	170	2,326	0.77
Yunnan	497	1,670	4,073	1.34

Sources of data and estimation procedures:

Col. (1): The total increase in cultivated area resulting from the removal of boundary lines, graves, etc., is officially given as 19.8 million mou (*CHCC*, 1958, no. 2, p. 21). We initially distributed this total among the provinces in proportion to the ratio of cultivated land in each province to the total cultivated area for the country in 1955 as listed in Appendix Table 1.

Col. (2): Rural population figures for 1953 and 1958 are given by province in Ernest Ni, *Distribution of the Urban and Rural Population of Mainland China: 1953 and 1958*, (Washington, D.C., 1960), p. 11. An annual growth rate was estimated for each province and applied to the figure for 1953 to obtain the estimate for 1955.

Appendix Table 4, *continued*

Total increase in cultivated area, corrected (1,000 mou) (5)	Total increase in cultivated area, adjusted (1,000 mou) (6)	Increase in cultivated area, by year (1,000 mou)		
		1955 (7)	1956 (8)	1957 (9)
1,195	1,106	940	166	0
868	804	643	161	0
487	451	180	158	113
355	329	276	33	20
1,717	1,590	1,272	318	0
1,363	1,262	1,010	252	0
1,287	1,191	774	357	60
1,051	973	730	195	48
658	609	243	305	61
483	447	224	179	44
649	601	541	30	30
1,403	1,299	1,039	260	0
337	312	109	203	0
700	648	421	227	0
1,306	1,209	60	1,028	121
605	560	280	224	56
514	476	238	238	0
523	484	242	242	0
1,889	1,749	962	700	87
598	554	416	83	55
182	168	67	59	42
2,483	2,299	345	1,494	460
		0	0	0
69	64	6	32	26
666	617	247	308	62

Sources of data and estimation procedures for Appendix Table 4, continued

Col. (3): For each province the density is obtained by dividing the number of rural population given in Col. (2) by the amount of cultivated area in 1955 in that province, as shown in Appendix Table 1.

Col. (4): The correction factor is the provincial density divided by the national density of rural population per unit of cultivated land. The latter is calculated as 3,031 persons per 10,000 mou.

Col. (5): Col. (1) times Col. (4).

Col. (6): Col. (5) is decreased by .926, the ratio of 19.8 million to the total of Col. (5), so that the total will equal 19.8 million mou.

Cols. (7), (8), and (9): For each province the amount in Col. (5) is distributed to the three years by using the percentage of rural population brought into cooperatives in these years respectively. The latter data are taken from *PAS*.

Appendix Table 5 Official Data on Irrigated Acreage, by Province, 1949–57 (10,000 mou)

Province	1949	1950	1951	1952
Anhwei	1,700	1,737	1,743	1,764
Chekiang	1,950	2,025	2,110	2,206
Fukien	860	940	1,027	1,050
Heilungkiang	81	90	100	115
Honan	720	720	840	1,275
Hopei	1,230.5	1,291	1,358	1,597
Hunan	1,300	1,300	2,000	3,008
Hupeh	2,253	2,300	2,350	2,400
Inner Mongolia	427	447	526	630
Kansu	482	503	579	649
Kiangsi	1,671	1,780	1,890	2,000
Kiangsu	2,730	2,730	2,980	3,097
Kirin	130	140	152	165
Kwangsi	708	708	860	1,230
Kwangtung	1,290	1,290	1,260	1,260
Kweichow	284.7	335	385	435
Liaoning	91	112	118	124
Shansi	368	443	491	584
Shantung	353	357	540	660
Shensi	353	378	451	489
Sinkiang	1,612	1,681	1,810	1,955
Szechwan	1,100	1,100	1,250	1,450
Tsinghai	74.8	75	80.5	86
Yunnan	443	443	450	468
Total	22,212	22,925	25,350.5	28,697

Sources of data and estimation procedures:

Except for the following items, the data are taken from *PAS:*

1. Anhwei, 1950–54: Extrapolated by using the acreage of water conservation projects in the province in those years. See *AHJP*, Dec. 25, 1957.
2. Chekiang, 1951 and 1953–56: Interpolated.
3. Hunan, 1950–53: For each of these four years, the difference between the total rice-sown area and the late rice-sown area is taken as the sown area for early rice.

Appendix Table 5, *continued*

1953	1954	1955	1956	1957
1,774	1,790	2,113	2,840	3,400
2,260	2,320	2,380	2,440	2,500
1,250	1,500	1,500	1,490	1,480
130	151	164	270	450
1,320	1,400	1,451	1,850	4,300
1,611	1,619	1,679	2,577	2,700
3,589	3,630	4,100	4,167	4,277
2,500	2,600	2,700	2,750	2,800
697	770	878	1,094	1,206
686	740	810	1,300	1,800
2,140	2,520	2,600	2,726	2,900
3,167	3,247	3,320	3,400	3,830
170	180	198	396	486
1,475	1,558	1,681	2,185	2,496
1,380	1,513	1,585	1,740	2,090
443	455	470	782	793
130	138	190	630	730
639	712	723	838	1,130
670	720	800	2,400	3,700
570	545	596	824	973
2,042	2,099	2,150	2,332	2,577
1,650	1,700	2,135	3,050	5,535
100	112	102	157	166
518	620	768	1,140	1,230
30,913	32,639	35,093	43,378	53,499

Sources of data and estimation procedures for Appendix Table 5, continued

The amount of new irrigated area in each year is assumed to be the increase in the sown area of early rice in that year. All data used in this computation are taken from *PAS*.

4. Hupeh, 1950–54 and 1956: Before 1955 there was a negligible acreage of paddy fields for double-cropping. Therefore, the total rice-sown area, instead of the sown area of early rice, is taken as the size of irrigated fields. The 1956 figure is estimated by interpolation. The data on the rice-sown area are taken from *PAS*.

Appendix Table 6 Farmland Consumed by Construction of Irrigation Systems, by Province, (10,000 mou)

Province	1950	1951	1952
Anhwei	1.332	0.216	0.756
Chekiang	2.700	3.060	3.456
Fukien	2.880	3.132	0.828
Heilungkiang	0.324	0.360	0.540
Honan	0	4.320	15.660
Hopei	2.178	2.412	8.604
Hunan	0	25.200	36.288
Hupeh	1.692	1.800	1.800
Inner Mongolia	0.720	2.844	3.744
Kansu	0.756	2.736	2.520
Kiangsi	3.924	3.960	3.960
Kiangsu	0	9.000	4.212
Kirin	0.360	0.432	0.468
Kwangsi	0	5.472	13.320
Kwangtung	0	0	0
Kweichow	1.811	1.800	1.800
Liaoning	0.756	0.216	0.216
Shansi	2.700	1.728	3.348
Shantung	0.144	6.588	4.320
Shensi	0.900	2.628	1.368
Sinkiang	2.484	4.644	5.220
Szechwan	0	5.400	7.200
Tsinghai	0.007	0.198	0.198
Yunnan	0	0.252	0.648
Total	25.668	88.398	120.474

Sources of data and estimation procedures:

According to *CCYC*, 1965, no. 3, p. 40, an average of 3.6 mou of land had been used by water distribution courses to irrigate 100 mou. Figures in this table are obtained by applying this ratio to annual increments of irrigated fields, derived from Appendix Table 5. The five decrements were considered to be zero.

Appendix Table 6, *continued*

1953	1954	1955	1956	1957
0.360	0.576	11.628	26.172	20.160
1.944	2.160	2.160	2.160	2.160
7.200	9.000	0	0	0
0.540	0.756	0.468	3.816	6.480
1.620	2.880	1.836	14.364	88.200
0.504	0.288	2.160	32.328	4.428
20.916	1.476	16.920	2.412	2.160
3.600	3.600	3.600	1.800	1.800
2.412	2.628	3.888	7.776	4.032
1.332	1.944	2.520	17.640	18.000
5.040	13.680	2.880	4.536	6.264
2.520	2.880	2.628	2.880	15.480
0.180	0.360	0.648	7.128	3.240
8.820	2.988	4.428	18.144	11.196
4.320	4.788	2.592	5.580	12.600
0.360	0.360	0.540	11.232	0.396
0.216	0.288	1.872	15.840	3.600
1.980	2.628	0.396	4.140	10.512
0.360	1.800	2.880	57.600	46.800
2.916	0	1.836	8.208	5.364
3.132	2.052	1.836	6.552	8.820
7.200	1.800	15.660	32.940	89.460
0.504	0.432	0	1.980	0.324
1.800	3.672	5.328	13.392	3.240
79.776	63.036	88.704	298.620	364.716

Appendix Table 7 Basic Construction Investment in Industry, by Province, (100 million yuan)

Province	1950	1951	1952	1953	1954	1955	1956	1957
Anhwei	0.07	0.15	0.28	3.20	3.70	3.70	1.40	1.30
Chekiang	0.18	0.23	0.14	0.25	0.28	0.29	0.46	0.43
Fukien	0.02	0.03	0.08	0.17	0.19	0.19	0.31	0.78
Heilungkiang	0.51	1.06	1.97	3.61	4.09	4.20	6.71	14.30
Honan	0.21	0.44	0.82	1.50	1.70	1.75	2.80	2.60
Hopei	0.38	0.79	1.47	2.70	3.06	3.14	5.02	4.67
Hunan	0.11	0.22	0.41	0.75	0.85	0.87	1.39	1.29
Hupeh	0.30	0.62	1.14	2.10	2.38	2.44	3.90	3.64
Inner Mongolia	0	0	0	0.45	0.50	1.00	2.00	2.00
Kansu	0.35	0.72	1.34	2.47	2.80	2.87	4.59	5.00
Kiangsi	0.06	0.13	0.25	0.45	0.51	0.53	0.84	0.78
Kiangsu	0.15	0.20	0.22	1.17	1.33	1.36	2.18	1.46
Kirin	0.51	1.06	1.97	3.61	4.09	4.20	6.71	14.30
Kwangsi	0	0.03	0.10	0.19	0.21	0.22	0.35	0.58
Kwangtung	0	0	0	2.98	3.37	3.46	5.53	5.35
Kweichow	0	0.09	0.16	0.29	0.33	0.26	0.54	0.50
Liaoning	1.46	3.02	5.61	10.31	11.67	11.97	19.13	17.81
Shansi	0.08	0.18	0.33	0.63	0.71	0.73	1.16	1.08
Shantung	0.17	0.35	0.65	1.20	1.36	1.39	2.23	2.07
Shensi	0.23	0.48	0.89	1.65	1.87	1.92	3.07	2.85
Sinkiang	0	0.29	0.53	0.98	1.11	1.14	1.82	1.70
Szechwan	0.30	0.61	1.14	2.10	2.37	2.44	3.89	3.62
Tsinghai	0	0.09	0.16	0.30	0.34	0.35	0.56	0.52
Yunnan	0	0.11	0.20	0.37	0.42	0.43	0.69	0.64
Total	5.09	10.90	19.86	43.43	49.24	50.85	77.28	89.27

Sources of data and estimation procedures:

The provincial investment figures are either gleaned from a great many issues of provincial newspapers or estimated by using a variety of methods, depending on the relevant information available to us. The accuracy of these estimated figures is admittedly very low. When the provincial investment figures for each year are added, the sums are, on the average, about 25 percent higher than the amounts of industrial investment shown in *TGY*, p. 57. However, the growth rates indicated by the sums are very close to the rates shown in *TGY*, p. 57.

Appendix Table 8 Farmland Occupied by Nonagricultural Construction Projects, by Province (10,000 mou)

Province	1950	1951	1952	1953	1954	1955	1956	1957
Anhwei	0.40	0.87	1.62	18.50	21.39	21.39	8.09	7.52
Chekiang	1.04	1.33	0.81	1.45	1.62	1.68	2.66	2.49
Fukien	0.12	0.17	0.46	0.98	1.10	1.10	1.79	4.51
Heilungkiang	2.95	6.13	11.39	20.87	23.65	24.28	38.80	82.68
Honan	1.21	2.54	4.74	8.67	9.83	10.12	16.19	15.03
Hopei	2.20	4.57	8.50	15.61	17.69	18.15	29.02	27.00
Hunan	0.64	1.27	2.37	4.34	4.91	5.03	8.04	7.46
Hupeh	1.73	3.58	6.59	12.14	13.76	14.11	22.55	21.05
Inner Mongolia	0	0	0	2.60	2.89	5.78	11.56	11.56
Kansu	2.02	4.16	7.75	14.28	16.19	16.59	26.54	28.91
Kiangsi	0.35	0.75	1.45	2.60	2.95	3.06	4.86	4.51
Kiangsu	0.87	1.16	1.27	6.76	7.69	7.86	12.60	8.44
Kirin	2.95	6.13	11.39	20.87	23.65	24.28	38.80	82.68
Kwangsi	0	0.17	0.58	1.10	1.21	1.27	2.02	3.35
Kwangtung	0	0	0	17.23	19.48	20.00	31.97	30.93
Kweichow	0	0.52	0.93	1.68	1.91	1.50	3.12	2.09
Liaoning	8.44	17.46	32.44	59.61	67.47	69.21	110.60	102.97
Shansi	0.46	1.04	1.91	3.64	4.11	4.22	6.71	6.24
Shantung	0.98	2.02	3.76	6.94	7.86	8.04	12.89	11.97
Shensi	1.33	2.78	5.15	9.54	10.81	11.10	17.75	16.48
Sinkiang	0	1.68	3.06	5.67	6.42	6.59	10.52	9.83
Szechwan	1.73	3.53	6.59	12.14	13.70	14.11	22.49	20.93
Tsinghai	0	0.52	0.93	1.73	1.97	2.02	3.24	3.01
Yunnan	0	0.64	1.16	2.14	2.43	2.49	3.99	3.70
Total	29.42	63.02	114.85	251.09	284.69	293.98	446.80	516.14

Sources of data and estimation procedures:

One official source indicates that 20 million mou of land were requisitioned by the state in the period 1949 to 1957 for construction projects (*JMJP*, Jan. 7, 1958). We divide this amount by the total investment of all provinces in this whole period, as shown in Appendix Table 7, and find that, on the average, 57,817 mou of land were used for each 100 million yuan of investment. We then use this ratio to convert all provincial figures in Appendix Table 7 to land areas in Appendix Table 8.

Appendix Table 9 Estimates of Cultivated Area, by Province, 1949–57 (10,000 mou)

Province	1949	1950	1951	1952
Anhwei	8,816	8,815	8,814	8,812
Chekiang	3,320	3,317	3,312	3,309
Fukien	2,211	2,208	2,205	2,204
Heilungkiang	9,940	9,951	9,963	9,974
Honan	13,469	13,468	13,462	13,443
Hopei	13,521	13,516	13,510	13,494
Hunan	5,732	5,731	5,705	5,668
Hupeh	6,431	6,427	6,422	6,415
Inner Mongolia	8,301	8,301	8,298	8,295
Kansu	6,055	6,052	6,045	6,035
Kiangsi	4,204	4,200	4,196	4,191
Kiangsu	9,199	9,198	9,198	9,187
Kirin	7,167	7,164	7,159	7,153
Kwangsi	3,750	3,750	3,745	3,734
Kwangtung	5,636	5,636	5,639	5,645
Kweichow	3,021	3,019	3,017	3,014
Liaoning	7,530	7,521	7,504	7,474
Shansi	6,811	6,808	6,806	6,801
Shantung	13,964	13,962	13,955	13,948
Shensi	6,738	6,736	6,731	6,725
Sinkiang	2,794	2,791	2,752	2,761
Szechwan	11,547	11,545	11,536	11,523
Tsinghai	739	739	739	739
Yunnan	4,188	4,188	4,188	4,189
Total	165,084	165,043	164,892	164,733

Sources of data and estimation procedures:

Estimates are derived from the data in Appendix Tables 1, 2, 3, 4, 6, and 8. For each province, we begin with the cultivated area in 1957 as officially given and compute retroactively by subtracting all the land that has been added and adding all the land that has been used for other purposes. For land reclamation, we assume that there was a one-year lag. That is, any year's reclamation will increase the cultivated acreage for the next year. For example, for any province the estimated area of cultivated land in 1956 is: the official cultivated area in 1957, minus 1956 reclamation, minus 1957 increase of land resulting from collectivization, plus land used for irrigation systems in 1957, and plus land used for other construction in 1957.

Appendix Table 9, *continued*

1953	1954	1955	1956	1957
8,796	8,775	8,837	8,822	8,800
3,307	3,304	3,366	3,379	3,378
2,198	2,189	2,206	2,222	2,233
10,015	10,168	10,381	10,581	10,930
13,438	13,428	13,545	13,552	13,460
13,484	13,469	13,553	13,523	13,503
5,648	5,644	5,703	5,734	5,741
6,402	6,386	6,443	6,442	6,430
8,293	8,289	8,305	8,319	8,315
6,019	6,001	6,005	6,979	5,939
4,187	4,173	4,223	4,220	4,220
9,188	9,183	9,281	9,303	9,300
7,151	7,136	7,131	7,126	7,078
3,735	3,735	3,777	3,790	3,796
5,649	5,636	5,631	5,722	5,740
3,013	3,011	3,037	3,046	3,050
7,421	7,357	7,313	7,218	7,126
6,797	6,791	6,811	6,826	6,812
13,948	13,941	14,030	14,036	14,000
6,713	6,703	6,732	6,715	6,700
2,824	2,848	2,881	2,894	3,022
11,505	11,490	11,496	11,591	11,530
737	737	739	743	750
4,196	4,195	4,217	4,241	4,262
164,664	164,589	165,643	167,024	166,115

Appendix Table 10 Official Data on Sown Area for Food Grains, by Province, 1949–57 (10,000 mou)

Province	1949	1950	1951	1952
Anhwei	9,200	(9,900)	(10,600)	11,400
Chekiang	4,115	4,196	(4,209)	(4,222)
Fukien	2,728	2,730	2,750	2,790
Heilungkiang	6,293	(6,530)	(6,770)	7,022
Honan	14,880	15,073	15,310	16,226
Hopei	10,535	11,218	(11,500)	11,971
Hunan	(4,690)	(5,120)	(5,425)	6,325
Hupeh	6,100	(6,300)	(6,510)	(6,730)
Inner Mongolia	4,930	5,513	5,895	6,134
Kansu	4,554	(4,850)	(5,150)	5,539
Kiangsi	(4,496)	(4,496)	(4,496)	(4,608)
Kiangsu	9,236	(9,200)	(9,140)	9,088
Kirin	5,000	(5,030)	(5,070)	5,118
Kwangsi	4,325	4,325	(4,445)	4,570
Kwangtung	8,377	8,500	8,500	8,862
Kweichow	(2,520)	2,710	(2,680)	(2,640)
Liaoning	5,838	5,567	5,500	5,385
Shansi	5,628	5,087	5,800	6,227
Shantung	13,617	13,710	13,905	14,225
Shensi	(6,370)	(6,370)	(6,440)	6,795
Sinkiang	1,400	1,500	1,724	1,720
Szechwan	14,170	14,200	14,300	14,340
Tsinghai	450	455	465	475
Yunnan	(3,536)	(3,685)	(3,834)	(3,983)
Total	152,988	156,265	160,418	166,395

Sources of data and estimation procedures:

Except those indicated below, all estimates are interpolated. When other estimation methods are used, the data involved are taken from *PAS*.

1. Anhwei, 1953–56: Increases in the sown area for double-cropping rice in these years are taken as the increases in the sown area for food grains as a whole.

2. Kiangsi, 1949–54 and 1956: Since more than 80 percent of the total sown area for food grains was for rice, we compute the exact ratio of the sown area for all food grains and that for rice in 1955 and 1957. The 1955 ratio and the official sown acreage for rice in various years in 1949–54 are used to estimate the total sown acreage for all food grains in 1949–54. The same estimation method is used for 1956 except that the ratio used is that of 1957.

3. Kweichow, 1949: The difference between the total sown area for all crops and the sown area for technical crops.

Appendix Table 10, *continued*

1953	1954	1955	1956	1957
(11,500)	(11,660)	(11,838)	(12.468)	11,938
(4,235)	(4,248)	4,260	4,680	4,089
2,790	2,890	2,982	3,149	3,095
7,030	7,051	7,085	7,516	7,390
16,752	17,048	16,754	16,531	16,300
12,254	12,221	11,804	11,970	10,000
(6,865)	(6,970)	(7,460)	(8,433)	8,121
(6,960)	(7,200)	(7,450)	(8,100)	8,031
5,930	6,057	5,952	6,423	6,344
(5,620)	5,699	(5,730)	5,760	5,658
(4,608)	(4,608)	4,615	(5,850)	5,484
(10,060)	(9,820)	(10,300)	(12,200)	11,874
4,843	4,962	5,186	5,273	5,081
5,553	6,086	5,815	5,820	5,615
8,972	9,100	9,400	9,800	10,040
(2,700)	(2,770)	2,650	(3,100)	3,691
5,780	5,637	5,445	5,580	5,395
5,910	6,083	6,016	5,800	5,912
14,292	14,714	14,643	14,415	14,488
6,859	(6,858)	(6,550)	(6,250)	5,747
1,754	2,099	1,913	1,900	2,027
(14,700)	(15,000)	(15,300)	15,800	16,278
553	(510)	612	551	580
(4,132)	(4,281)	(4,430)	4,579	4,955
170,652	173,572	174,190	181,948	178,133

Sources of data and estimation procedures for Appendix Table 10, continued

4. Shensi, 1949–51: The ratio of cultivated area to sown area for food grains in 1952 and the official sown acreages of cultivated land in 1949–51 are used for estimation.

5. Tsinghai, 1954: The ratio of the area sown to food grains and the wheat-sown area in 1955 and the sown area of wheat in 1954 are used for estimation.

6. Yunnan, 1949–55: Increases in sown area for food grains are assumed to have come from two sources: (a) increase in cultivated land and (b) increase in double-cropping resulting from the expansion of irrigation facilities. According to official data, cultivated land increased by 7.2 million mou and the irrigated area increased by 3.25 million mou in Yunnan between 1949 and 1955. The sum of these two figures is equally distributed to the seven years as the estimated increase in sown area for food grains in those years.

Appendix Table 11 Estimates of Sown Area for Food Grains, by Province, 1949–57 (10,000 mou)

Province	1949	1950	1951	1952
Anhwei	11,229	11,289	11,512	11,565
Chekiang	4,115	4,196	4,209	4,222
Fukien	2,900	2,803	2,750	2,790
Heilungkiang	7,687	7,555	7,417	7,280
Honan	15,418	15,615	15,850	16,760
Hopei	13,096	13,064	13,050	13,015
Hunan	5,605	5,945	6,025	6,584
Hupeh	6,100	6,325	6,572	6,844
Inner Mongolia	6,871	7,104	7,093	6,899
Kansu	5,209	5,502	5,795	6,106
Kiangsi	5,753	5,750	5,449	5,277
Kiangsu	11,480	11,480	11,480	11,483
Kirin	5,307	5,284	5,269	5,251
Kwangsi	4,928	4,928	4,958	4,990
Kwangtung	9,153	9,287	8,996	9,703
Kweichow	2,999	3,208	3,069	2,916
Liaoning	6,638	6,288	6,124	5,861
Shansi	6,071	5,523	6,234	6,227
Shantung	13,852	14,373	14,734	14,884
Shensi	7,867	7,854	7,873	7,885
Sinkiang	2,384	2,412	2,468	2,099
Szechwan	14,460	15,712	15,325	14,802
Tsinghai	450	455	465	475
Yunnan	4,538	4,687	4,589	4,442
Total	174,110	176,639	177,306	178,360

Sources of data and estimation procedures:

1. For each province in each year, the difference between the figure in Appendix Table 9 and Appendix Table 1 is taken as the area of unreported farmland existing in that year.

Appendix Table 11, *continued*

1953	1954	1955	1956	1957
11,500	11,660	11,838	12,468	11,938
4,235	4,248	4,260	4,680	4,089
2,790	2,920	3,159	3,238	3,095
7,317	7,469	7,716	7,657	7,390
17,031	17,128	16,754	16,531	16,300
13,138	12,970	12,134	11,970	10,000
6,940	6,970	7,460	8,433	8,121
7,104	7,386	7,803	8,348	8,031
6,493	6,406	6,107	6,423	6,344
6,051	5,980	5,875	6,739	5,658
4,994	4,698	4,758	5,888	5,484
11,594	11,670	11,715	13,052	11,874
5,009	5,157	5,362	5,273	5,081
5,925	6,702	5,954	5,983	5,615
10,032	9,372	9,400	10,456	10,040
2,866	2,832	2,650	3,100	3,691
6,181	5,949	5,688	5,698	5,395
5,910	6,083	6,016	5,800	5,912
14,361	14,775	14,770	14,548	14,488
7,580	7,101	6,550	6,250	5,747
2,238	2,637	2,242	2,007	2,027
15,143	16,566	16,072	16,767	16,278
553	510	612	551	580
4,239	4,401	4,580	4,678	4,955
179,224	181,590	179,475	186,538	178,133

Sources of data and estimation procedures for Appendix Table 11, continued

2. The unreported farmland is multiplied by the official or estimated grain double-cropping index for that province in that year (data are taken from *PAS*) to obtain the unreported sown area for food grains.

3. The unreported sown area is then added to the official sown area given in Appendix Table 10.

Appendix Table 12 Official Data on Yields of Food Grains per Unit of Sown Area, by Province, 1949–57 (catties per mou)

Province	1949	1950	1951	1952
Anhwei	101	(87.9)	(154.7)	146.5
Chekiang	204	228	(294.6)	(333.5)
Fukien	204	224	247	263
Heilungkiang	160.5	152.2	155.4	183.9
Honan	102.6	(104.2)	(118.2)	113.6
Hopei	86	(113.4)	(147)	152
Hunan	(272)	(291)	(304.1)	324
Hupeh	(170.5)	(222.2)	(255)	(243.7)
Inner Mongolia	81	76	57	107
Kansu	101	(101)	(112.6)	115
Kiangsi	(172.4)	(191.3)	(186.8)	(249.6)
Kiangsu	144	(182.6)	(217.5)	223
Kirin	178	(157.5)	(167.7)	193
Kwangsi	172	(219)	(245.4)	(247.3)
Kwangtung	191	165	176	213
Kweichow	(230.2)	236	(234.7)	(257.2)
Liaoning	122	164	(170)	182
Shansi	92	102	100	117
Shantung	116	128	137	154
Shensi	(113)	(116.2)	(131.5)	117
Sinkiang	142.1	143	167	191.3
Szechwan	211	(218.3)	(225.9)	234
Tsinghai	131	140	146	150
Yunnan	(217.8)	(217.1)	(221.7)	(238.5)

Sources of data and estimation procedures:

Figures without parentheses are taken from *PAS*. Figures in parentheses are derived from the figures in Appendix Tables 10 and 13 in the corresponding years.

Appendix Table 12, *continued*

1953	1954	1955	1956	1957
(126.1)	(132.9)	(179.1)	(162)	192.2
(337.7)	(322.5)	337	312	381
275	270	258	278	283
162	157	191	166	178.9
118.9	127.5	139.5	144.5	150
125	123	146	130	196
(303)	(298.4)	(300.3)	(244.3)	277
(281.6)	(277.8)	(252.3)	(249)	273
114	122	104	134	89
(106.8)	133	(137)	188	178.3
(249.6)	(249.6)	266	(222.2)	249
(233.6)	(234.2)	(250)	(196.7)	198.8
181.7	172.5	186	187	168.2
218	230	223	(180.4)	192.7
216	242	232	245	243
(271.1)	(289.9)	321	(306.5)	285
173	189	206	238	220
137	130	124	138	120.6
135	157	164	178	179
135.7	(147.1)	(137.6)	(173.8)	157
200.8	173	200	221	203
(247.1)	(263.3)	(264.7)	282	277
127.5	(205.7)	230	221	220.5
(246.9)	(261.6)	(242.1)	259	252

Appendix Table 13 Official Data on Output of Food Grains, by Province, 1949–57 (100 million catties)

Province	1949	1950	1951	1952
Anhwei	91	87	164	167
Chekiang	84	103.4	124	140.8
Fukien	55.66	61.2	68	73.26
Heilungkiang	101	(99.4)	(105.2)	129
Honan	130	(157)	(181)	184.3
Hopei	91	127.2	169	181.7
Hunan	127.59	149	165	204.96
Hupeh	104	(140)	166	164
Inner Mongolia	39.9	41.9	33.6	65.9
Kansu	46	49	58	63.7
Kiangsi	77.5	86	84	115
Kiangsu	133	168	198.8	201
Kirin	89	79.2	85	99
Kwangsi	74.4	94.6	109.1	113
Kwangtung	160	140	150	189
Kweichow	58	64	62.9	67.9
Liaoning	71.4	91.3	(93.5)	98.1
Shansi	51.9	52	(58)	73.2
Shantung	158	175	190	219
Shensi	72	74	84.7	79.5
Sinkiang	19.9	21.4	28.72	32.1
Szechwan	298.94	(310)	(323)	335.7
Tsinghai	5.9	6.36	6.8	7.13
Yunnan	77	80	85	95
Total	2,219.09	2,456.96	2,793.32	3,099.25

Sources of data and estimation procedures:

Figures without parentheses are taken from *PAS*. Figures in parentheses are extrapolated by using the rate of change in the major grain crop in that province.

Appendix Table 13, *continued*

1953	1954	1955	1956	1957
145	155	212	202	230
143	137	151.8	153	156
76.7	78	76.8	87.4	87.54
114	111	133	125	123
199.1	217.4	233.8	238.8	245
153.2	150.2	172	155.6	195
208	208	224	206	224
196	200	188	210	219.3
67.6	73.9	61.9	87.5	56.2
60	75.8	78.5	108.6	103
115	115	123	130	136.6
235	230	257.4	240	236
86	85.6	96.5	98.72	85.5
121.4	139.5	129.5	105	107.5
194	220	218	240	244
74	80.3	86	95	105
100.1	106.3	112.2	133.2	118.7
81	79.2	74.5	79.9	71.3
193	231	240	256	259
94.8	100.9	90.1	108.6	90
34.4	36.39	38.25	38.68	40.7
363.3	395	405	445.2	459.6
6.62	10.49	11.78	12.2	12.8
102	112	107.24	118.4	125
3,163.22	3,347.98	3,521.27	3,674.80	3,730.74

Appendix Table 14 Estimate of Output of Food Grains, by Province, 1949–57 (100 million catties)

Province	1949	1950	1951	1952
Anhwei	133.6	152.4	178.4	169.4
Chekiang	105.8	116.6	128.0	140.8
Fukien	59.2	62.8	67.9	73.4
Heilungkiang	123.4	115.0	115.3	133.9
Honan	158.2	162.7	187.3	190.4
Hopei	153.2	165.9	191.8	197.8
Hunan	152.5	173.0	183.2	213.3
Hupeh	119.6	140.4	167.6	166.8
Inner Mongolia	55.7	54.0	40.4	73.8
Kansu	52.6	55.6	65.3	70.2
Kiangsi	110.5	119.6	123.7	131.7
Kiangsu	197.5	213.5	250.3	256.1
Kirin	94.5	83.2	88.4	101.3
Kwangsi	93.6	107.9	121.5	123.4
Kwangtung	174.8	153.2	158.3	206.7
Kweichow	69.0	75.7	72.0	75.0
Liaoning	81.0	103.1	104.1	106.7
Shansi	55.9	56.3	62.3	72.9
Shantung	160.7	184.0	202.0	229.2
Shensi	88.9	91.3	103.5	92.3
Sinkiang	33.9	34.5	41.2	40.2
Szechwan	305.1	343.0	346.2	346.4
Tsinghai	5.9	6.4	6.8	7.1
Yunnan	98.8	101.8	101.7	105.9
Total	2,683.9	2,871.9	3,107.2	3,324.7

Sources of data and estimation procedures:

Estimates are derived by multiplying the sown area for food grains in Appendix Table 11 by yields per unit of sown area. The official yields (Appendix Table 12) are used, except for Anhwei, Chekiang, Hopei, Hupeh, Kiangsi, Kiangsu, and Kwangsi, for which the adjusted yields for 1949–51, as given in Appendix Tables 9–13, are used.

Appendix Table 14, *continued*

1953	1954	1955	1956	1957
145.0	155.0	212.0	202.0	229.4
143.0	137.0	143.6	146.0	155.8
76.7	78.8	81.5	90.0	87.6
118.5	117.3	147.4	127.1	132.2
202.5	218.4	233.7	238.9	244.5
164.2	159.5	177.2	155.6	196.0
210.3	208.0	224.0	206.0	225.0
200.0	205.2	196.9	207.9	219.2
74.0	78.2	63.5	86.1	56.5
64.6	79.5	80.5	126.7	101.0
124.7	117.3	126.6	130.8	136.6
294.2	273.3	293.0	256.7	236.1
91.0	89.0	99.7	98.6	85.5
129.2	154.1	132.8	107.9	108.2
216.7	226.8	218.1	256.2	244.0
78.6	82.1	85.9	95.0	105.2
106.9	112.4	117.2	135.6	118.7
81.0	79.1	74.6	80.0	71.3
193.9	232.0	242.2	259.0	259.3
102.9	104.5	90.1	108.6	90.2
44.9	45.6	44.8	44.4	41.1
423.6	436.2	425.4	472.8	451.0
7.1	10.5	14.1	12.2	12.8
104.7	115.1	110.9	121.2	124.9
3,398.2	3,514.9	3,635.7	3,765.3	3,732.1

Appendix Table 15 Computation of Cultivated and Sown Areas, 1957–65 (million mou)

Year	Culti-vated area	Multiple-cropping index	Sown area: Total all crops	Soybeans	Cotton	Other tech-nical crops	Green manure	Other non-grain crops	Grain
1957	1,678	139.7	2,343	191	87	107	51	109	1,798
1958	1,617	145.0	2,344	147	86	119	63	110	1,819
1959	1,600	138.9	2,222	142	84	151	66	110	1,669
1960	1,585	139.0	2,203	140	73	90	69	110	1,721
1961	1,560	139.0	2,168	137	55	69	72	110	1,725
1962	1,550	139.0	2,155	129	53	65	75	110	1,723
1963	1,533	139.0	2,131	120	61	75	78	110	1,687
1964	1,533	140.0	2,146	115	69	85	82	110	1,685
1965	1,533	140.0	2,146	115	71	87	102	110	1,661

Sources of data and estimation procedures:

1. Cultivated area:
   1957–1958: *TGY*, p. 128.
   1959: *China Pictorial*, Feb. 1961, p. 2.
   1965: *CKCN*, 1966, no. 9, p. 16.
   Other years: Interpolated.
2. Multiple-cropping Index:
   1957: Table 8.8.
   1958: *TGY*, p. 128.
   1959: An official figure quoted in a U.S. government publication.
   1960–65: Estimated. The multiple-cropping index is primarily affected by the extent of irrigation. Since the ratio of effectively irrigated land to total cultivated land in these years was comparable to that of 1957, the multiple-cropping indexes in these years should be around the 1957 level, too.
3. Total sown area:
   1957–58: *TGY*, p. 128.
   1959–65: Cultivated area multiplied by the multiple-cropping index.
4. Sown area for soybeans.
   1957: Table 11.1.
   1958, 1959, and 1963: Official figures quoted in a U.S. government publication.
   1960–62 and 1964–65: Estimates.

Sources of data and estimation procedures for Appendix Table 15, continued

5. Sown area for cotton:

Data on cotton-sown areas have been collected from Chinese Communist sources for various years in 1959–65. Each reported figure may be compared with its counterpart in 1957 to see the direction and magnitude of change. Therefore, for each year we have a sample of provinces, which can be used to estimate the change in the cotton-sown area for the whole country. Presented below are the relevant statistics (sown areas in million mou):

	1959	*1960*	*1961*	*1962*	*1963*	*1964*	*1965*
a. Number of provinces reporting for the year	14	13	4	8	13	13	12
b. Total cotton sown area reported for the year	79.7	64.5	15.0	28.2	49.4	56.0	55.0
c. Total cotton sown area existing in 1957 for the reporting provinces	82.0	72.1	23.7	46.2	70.3	70.3	67.3
d. Coverage of the reporting provinces as a sample (%)	94.7	83.2	27.4	53.3	81.1	81.1	77.7
e. Rate of change as shown by the reporting provinces, with 1957 as 100%, (*b*) ÷ (*c*)	97.2	83.8	63.2	61.0	70.3	79.6	81.7

The so-called coverage in line *d* is simply the amount in line *c* divided by the national total cotton-sown area in 1957, which is 86.6 million mou. In other words, it is the total cotton-sown area of all reporting provinces existing in 1957, as a percentage of the national total of cotton-sown area in 1957. The sample coverage is high for all years but 1961. In every year in the period, the reporting provinces show some reduction in cotton land, as compared with the 1957 level, see line *e*. In view of the high coverage, it would be credible to estimate the national totals of cotton land in various years from the reduction rates shown by the samples. The procedure is simply to multiply the figures in line *e* by the national total of cotton land in 1957 (86.6 million mou).

6. Sown area for other technical crops:

1957 and 1959: Chinese official figures quoted in a U.S. government publication.

1958: A residual of subtracting all other items of sown areas from the total sown area for that year.

1960–65: Assumed to have suffered the same rates of reduction as cotton land in various years.

7. Sown area for green manure:

1957–58 and 1964–65: Officially given; see the sources of data for Appendix Table 16.

Other years: Interpolated.

Continued on following page

Sources of data and estimation procedures for Appendix Table 15, continued

8. Sown area for other nongrain crops:

   This category consists of mainly vegetables and fruits. The sown acreage of vegetables, as supplementary foods, probably did not decrease during the period of food shortages. Fruit trees are perennials and the land for them could not be converted for short run considerations. Therefore, the sown area for this category is assumed to have remained the same as it was in 1957.

9. Sown area for grains:

   The figures used in this table are residuals of subtracting all other items from the total sown acreages in various years.

However, another set of grain-sown acreages has been estimated. Data on sown areas for individual grain crops in various provinces have been collected for the years in this period. An estimation procedure similar to that used in the case of cotton land has been tried. The relevant statistics are presented below (sown areas in million mou):

	1959	*1960*	*1961*	*1962*	*1963*	*1964*	*1965*
a. Number of items reported for the year	46	36	11	15	26	33	27
b. Total grain sown area reported for the year	1,170	831	220	414	548	737	705
c. Total sown area in 1957 for reported items	1,323	841	250	483	628	834	815
d. Coverage of the sample (%)	73.6	46.8	13.9	26.9	34.9	46.4	45.4
e. Rate of change as shown by the sample, with 1957 as 100%, (*b*)÷(*c*)	88.4	98.8	88.1	85.6	87.2	88.4	86.4
f. Estimated total sown area for grains for the country as a whole	1,590	1,776	1,584	1,625	1,568	1,589	1,554

The validity of this set of estimates is questionable, however. The sample coverage is generally small, below 50 percent except for 1959. Furthermore, an inspection of the reported items will show that virtually all of them are fine grains, namely rice and wheat. It is well known that the Chinese farmers have a tendency to shift some land from fine grains to coarse grains in poor harvest years, because the latter have much better ability to endure unfavorable weather and soil conditions. Therefore, this set of estimates of grain-sown acreages are suspected to contain some degree of downward bias. This suspicion would become more evident if we add the estimated grain-sown areas and all other types of sown areas to arrive at total sown areas in various years. The total sown areas so derived suggest that the multiple-

Sources of data and estimation procedures for Appendix Table 15, continued

cropping index varies from 131 to 135 in the period 1959–65. It is too low to be believed. Salinization in this period might lead to the retirement of some farmland from cultivation, but it would not force farmers to convert double-cropping land to single-cropping land. Given the total area effectively served by irrigation facilities in that period, the multiple-cropping index could not be so much lower than the 1956–57 level. For the above reasons, we have rejected this set of estimates of grain-sown area.

Appendix Table 16 Application of Natural Fertilizers, 1952–66 (1,000 tons)

	Night soil		Pig manure		Large animal manure		Compost plant residues	
	Gross weight	Nutri-ents	Gross weight	Nutri-ents	Gross weight	Nutri-ents	Gross weight	Nutri-ents
1952	176,500	874	125,200	351	267,500	910	70,600	233
1953	188,800	935	142,300	398	297,700	1,012	74,600	246
1954	202,900	1,004	158,700	444	331,400	1,127	75,800	250
1955	218,000	1,078	144,200	404	358,300	1,218	81,000	267
1956	231,600	1,146	144,500	405	375,700	1,277	81,000	267
1957	245,500	1,215	262,600	735	375,600	1,277	77,400	255
1958	245,500	1,215	288,000	806	382,900	1,302	78,900	260
1959	245,500	1,215	324,000	907	384,300	1,307	79,100	261
1960	254,500	1,260	226,200	633	274,200	932	56,500	186
1961	269,800	1,385	129,300	362	168,000	571	34,600	114
1962	275,200	1,362	161,600	452	174,800	594	36,000	119
1963	280,700	1,389	193,900	543	188,500	641	38,800	128
1964	286,300	1,417	226,200	633	209,100	711	43,100	142
1965	292,000	1,445	258,600	724	233,100	793	48,000	158
1966	297,800	1,474	274,700	769	257,100	874	53,000	175

Sources of data and estimation procedures:

Seven types of natural fertilizers are included in this table. Mud from rivers and ponds is lumped together with "others" as a catch-all item. Estimation procedures of the seven items in gross weights are explained below according to their computational order.

1. Compost plant residues: This item includes barn compost and outdoor compost of litter material and plant residues. A total of 81 million tons was estimated by O. L. Dawson as the total available compost to farmers in 1956 (J. L. Buck, O. D. Dawson and Y. L. Wu, *Food and Agriculture in Communist China* [New York, 1966], p. 138). By using this amount for 1956 and the numbers of large animals as indicators, we compute the amounts of this item for all other years. Numbers of large animals in 1952–59 are given in N. R. Chen, *Chinese Economic Statistics: A Handbook for Mainland China* (Chicago, 1967), p. 340. For numbers of large animals in 1960–66, we have computed the following indexes on the basis of the information given by E. Jones (in Joint Economic Committee, U.S. Congress, *An Economic Profile of Mainland China*, 2 vols. [Washington, D.C., 1967], 1:82.)

1952 = 100.0	1961 = 49.0	1964 = 61.0
1957 = 109.6	1962 = 51.0	1965 = 68.0
1960 = 80.0	1963 = 55.0	1966 = 75.0

Appendix Table 16, *continued*

Oilseed cakes		Green manure		River, pond mud, and others		Total		Nutrients per mou	
Gross weight	Nutri-ents	Gross weight	Nutri-ents	Gross weight	Nutri-ents	Gross weight	Nutri-ents	Culti-vated area (kg)	Sown area (kg)
4,590	310	11,200	66	73,000	15	728,590	2,759	1.66	1.24
4,730	320	15,000	88	73,000	15	796,130	3,014	1.81	1.34
4,910	332	20,000	117	73,000	15	866,710	3,289	1.98	1.43
4,500	304	25,000	146	73,000	15	904,000	3,432	2.05	1.49
4,550	308	30,000	176	73,000	15	940,350	3,594	2.13	1.50
5,090	344	38,500	225	73,000	15	1,077,690	4,066	2.42	1.74
5,000	338	47,300	276	73,000	15	1,120,600	4,212	2.61	1.80
5,220	353	54,000	316	73,000	15	1,165,120	4,374	2.73	1.97
5,720	387	60,000	351	73,000	15	950,120	3,764	2.38	1.71
4,500	304	66,000	386	73,000	15	745,200	3,267	2.01	1.45
4,500	304	72,000	421	73,000	15	797,100	3,267	2.11	1.51
4,730	320	78,000	456	73,000	15	857,630	3,692	2.41	1.73
5,090	344	81,700	478	73,000	15	924,490	3,740	2.44	1.74
5,090	344	82,000	480	73,000	15	991,790	3,959	2.58	1.85
5,090	344	102,000	597	73,000	15	1,062,690	4,248		

Sources of data and estimation procedures for Appendix Table 16, continued

2. Oilseed cakes: According to the Ministry of Food and Agriculture of India, *Report of the Indian Delegation to China on Agricultural Planning and Techniques* (1956), p. 146, a total of 4.5 million tons of oilseed cakes were used in 1955 as agriculture fertilizers. Two-thirds of this amount consisted of soybean cakes. Therefore, we use official and estimated figures of the soybean crop in various years as indicators to extrapolate this item of fertilizer. Official data on soybean output are available for 1952–59 (see Chen, *Chinese Economic Statistics*, pp. 338–39). For 1960–66 the indexes of soybean output are estimated as follows:

1955 = 100	1961 = 100	1964 = 113
1957 = 113	1962 = 100	1965 = 113
1960 = 127	1963 = 105	1966 = 113

Continued on following page

Sources of data and estimation procedures for Appendix Table 16, continued

3. Green manure: The following data are officially released concerning green manure:

	Crop area of green manure (million mou)	*Yield per mou (kg)*	*Source*
1952	34.46	325	*CKNP*, 1959, no. 17, p. 35
1957	51.30	750	Ibid.
1958	63.00	1,250	Ibid.
1964	81.67		*JMJP*, June 5, 1965
1965	101.67		*TK*, 1966, no. 3, p. 23

Like all yield statistics in 1958, the unit yield of green manure is suspected to contain serious exaggeration. It is hardly conceivable for the unit yield to jump at such a high rate in a single year. Thus, we apply the 1957 unit yield to 1958 and assume 1,000 kg as the unit yield in 1964 and 1965. Total quantities of green manure can then be computed for these four years. Quantities for all other years are interpolated on the basis of the five figures.

4. River and pond mud and others: This item is meant to contain all the unimportant types of natural fertilizer that have only marginal contributions. According to a Chinese Communist source (*CKNP*, 1958, no. 17, p. 35), in 1952, about 60 percent of cultivated land received fertilizers (natural) with an average amount of 750 kg per mou. Using the official figure of total cultivated land existing in 1952 (*TGY*, p. 128), we can compute the total amount of natural fertilizers applied in that year as 728.45 million tons. It is assumed that 10 percent of this amount represents river and pond mud and other minor types of natural fertilizers, because, when the pressure of the government on farmers for fertilizer accumulation was not too strong, farmers tended naturally to concentrate their efforts only on the major and more effective types of fertilizers. The same amount is assumed for all other years. The amounts of these fertilizers actually collected in later years could be several times larger than we have assumed here, but the extra amount was really useless. For example, river mud is so heavy in gross weight per unit of nutritive element that only those farms situated quite close to rivers and canals can use it conveniently. Even on those farms there is a limitation for the amount to be applied per unit of land surface. The absorption rate of the nutrient content in river mud, when applied in moderate quantity per unit of land surface, is already very low. When it is applied in an excessive quantity, for example, piling up one hundred kg on a surface area of one square meter, the absorption rate is reduced almost to zero simply because plant roots can never reach all the nutritive elements to absorb them.

5. Night soil: From the total amount of 728.45 million tons of natural fertilizers applied in 1952, we subtract the amounts of the above four items as computed for 1952. The residual is 569.22 million tons. This amount is believed to consist of night soil, pig manure, and draft animal manure. Excreta of sheep and goats are ignored because these animals are raised in the pastoral regions. We adopt from *JMJP*, Nov. 18, 1957, the following average annual yields of night soil and manure per head:

Night soil	500 kg
Pig excreta	2,000 kg
Large animal excreta	5,000 kg

Sources of data and estimation procedures for Appendix Table 16, continued

The data are generally confirmed by *KSNTH*, 1958, no. 6, pp. 19–22; *HTNYKHTP*, 1958, no. 4, pp. 202–8; and the Japanese data cited by Dawson (Buck et al., *Food and Agriculture*, p. 139). Using the figure of rural population in 1952 (in J. S. Aird, *The Size, Composition, and Growth of the Population of Mainland China* [Washington, D.C., 1961], p. 36) and the number of pigs and large animals in 1952 (Chen, *Economic Statistics*, p. 340), we compute the theoretical availabilities of the three types of natural fertilizers in 1952, in millions of tons, as follows:

	Amount	*Percentage distribution*
Night soil	251.60	31
Pig manure	179.53	22
Manure of large animals	380.87	47
Total	812.00	100

However, the actual amount of these three types of fertilizers used in 1952 has been computed as 569.22 million tons. This means that only 70 percent of the amount theoretically available was actually utilized. This utilization rate is in conformity with what other experts on Chinese agriculture have thought (Dawson, in Buck et al., *Food and Agriculture*, p. 139). Now, we assume a uniform utilization rate of 70 percent for all the three types of fertilizers in 1952. We further assume that as the government's pressure on farmers in connection with fertilizer collection rose, the utilization rate rose accordingly until it reached 90 percent in 1957. The assumed utilization rates, in percentage, are then:

1953	74	1956	86
1954	78	1957	90
1955	82		

The utilization rate is assumed to have remained at the high level of 90 percent since 1957. Amounts of night soil utilized in agriculture in various years can then be derived from the above information and the following data on the rural population.

1952–57: Given in Aird, *Population of Mainland China*, p. 36.

1958–59: Same as in 1957. See C. M. Hou, "Sources of Agricultural Growth in Communist China," *Journal of Asian Studies* 27 (August 1968):732.

1960: Increased by 20 million. See *HC*, 1961, no. 5, p. 12.

1961–66: See Table 10.1.

6. Pig manure: Quantities are derived from the annual yield of excreta per head of pig and the utilization rates in various years, as shown above, and numbers of pigs in various years. The following data on pig population have been used:

1952–1959. From Chen, *Economic Statistics*, p. 340.

For other years, indexes have been estimated.

1952 = 100	1961 = 80	1964 = 140
1957 = 162.5	1962 = 100	1965 = 160
1960 = 140	1963 = 120	1966 = 170

Continued on following page

Sources of data and estimation procedures for Appendix Table 16, continued
The hog population declined drastically after the commune movement and during the crisis years of 1960–62. However, since the cycle in hog breeding is relatively short, the hog population is believed to have been restored to its 1957 level by 1965.

7. Manure of large animals: The estimation procedures are similar to those for pig manure. We use in our derivation the annual per animal yield of excreta, the utilization rates, and the number of large animals in various years.

8. All the gross weights are then converted to plant nutrients according to the following conversion rates, which are computed from Table 6.1, namely the percentage of total nutrients multiplied by the absorption rate in each case.

Type of fertilizer	*Conversion rate (kg per 100,000 kg of gross weight)*
Night soil	495
Pig manure	280
Manure of large animals	340
Compost plant residues	330
Oilseed cakes	6,760
Green manure	585
River and pond mud and others	20

9. To derive the nutrients per unit of land we use the total cultivated acreages given in Table 8.5 and Appendix Table 15 and the total sown acreages given in Table 8.8 and Appendix Table 15. No figure is obtained for 1966 because no acreage data are available for that year.

Appendix Table 17 Supply of Chemical Fertilizers, 1949–66 (thousand tons)

	Domestic production					
	Ammonium sulfate	Ammonium nitrate	Phosphorous fertilizers	Total	Imports	Total supply
1949	27	0	0	27		
1950	70	0	0	70		
1951	129	5	0	134		
1952	181	7	0	188	130	318
1953	226	23	0	249	343	592
1954	298	27	1	326	476	802
1955	332	50	21	403	852	1,255
1956	523	80	100	703	905	1,608
1957	631	120	120	871	1,073	1,944
1958	811	307	344	1,462	1,246	2,708
1959	1,333	444	450	2,227	1,078	3,305
1960		2,000	550	2,550	865	3,415
1961		1,430	570	2,000	882	2,882
1962				3,000	991	3,991
1963				4,200	1,789	5,989
1964		4,100	1,800	5,900	1,134	7,034
1965		6,900	2,000	8,900	1,989	10,889
1966				11,600	2,305	13,905

Sources of data and estimation procedures:

1. 1949–58:

a. With two exceptions, the data on domestic production of various types are taken from Kang Chao, *The Rate and Pattern of Industrial Growth in Communist China*, (Ann Arbor, Mich., 1965), pp. 123, 129. The two exceptions are the outputs of ammonium nitrate in 1955 and 1956, for which no official data are available. The two quantities are results of interpolation.

b. Data on the total supply of chemical fertilizers are taken from *TGY*, p. 171.

c. The yearly import is the difference between the total supply and the total quantity of domestic production. Strictly speaking it is not precisely the total imports in that year. A part of current production and current imports may not become available as "current" supply because of the time lag involved in transporting and distributing fertilizers. Moreover, there may be inventory changes.

Continued on following page

Sources of data and estimation procedures for Appendix Table 17, continued

2. Domestic production in 1959–66:

a. 1959: It is claimed in *SSB Communique, 1959* that chemical fertilizer output in 1959 was 1,333,000 tons, an increase of 64 percent from the 1958 quantity. Judging from the percentage increase, the 1959 output obviously refers to ammonium sulfate only. The 1959 outputs of ammonium nitrate and phosphorous fertilizers are estimated on the basis of the preceding year's production.

b. 1960: The planned target for total production of all types of chemical fertilizers for 1960 was 2.8 million tons. In the first half of that year, production of chemical fertilizers advanced even faster than was required by the planned schedule (see *PR*, Oct. 25, 1960, p. 13). However, production sharply dropped in the second half of the year. The actual output for 1960 is given by *NCNA* (May 14, 1961) as 2.55 million tons, falling short of the target by 250,000 tons. This output figure is confirmed by another Communist source (*HKTKP*, Oct. 1, 1962) which states that the total output of chemical fertilizers increased at an average annual rate of 41.7 percent in 1957–60. The total amount of 2.55 million tons is then broken down into nitrogen and phosphorous fertilizers on the basis of the 1961 distribution.

c. 1964: The production of chemical fertilizers in other years can be computed by starting with the information for 1964. According to Chou En-lai, the total supply of chemical fertilizers in 1964 was more than three times that of 1957 (*JMJP*, Dec. 31, 1964). The total supply in 1957 is officially given as 1,944,000 tons (*TGY*, p. 171). The absolute quantity for 1964 is given by Wu Chen, Deputy Minister of Agriculture in Communist China, to a Japanese reporter as 7 million tons (*Asaki shimbun* (Tokyo), Mar. 7, 1965), which is 360 percent of the 1957 amount. We accept this figure and subtract from it the total imports in 1964 to obtain domestic production. The estimated output of 5.9 million tons is consistent with the following progress reports:

(1) A total of 2.27 million tons was produced in January–April 1964. (See *CKHW*, May 27, 1964.)

(2) The fertilizer output in January–August 1964 is said to be 53 percent higher than the output in the corresponding period in 1963 (*JMJP*, Sept. 26, 1964). Output in the first eight months in 1963 is given as 2.8 million tons (*CKHW*, Sept. 26, 1963). Therefore, the output in January–August 1964, should be 4.28 million tons.

It is disclosed that the production capacity of phosphorous fertilizers reached 2 million tons in 1964 (*CKHW*, Aug. 4, 1964). We assume that 90 percent of the production capacity was utilized in that year; namely an output of 1.8 million tons of phosphorous fertilizers. Thus, 4.1 million tons would be nitrogen fertilizers and small amounts of potassium fertilizer whose production began in 1959 (*PR*, Oct. 25, 1960, p. 13). One Communist source (*EB*, Mar. 15, 1965) reports that in 1964 there were more than 40 small factories producing nitrogen fertilizers and nearly 100 small plants manufacturing phosphorous fertilizers. The combined output of these small plants accounted for about 30 percent of the total chemical fertilizer production in that year. According to another report (*TKP*, June 15, 1966), output of small nitrogen fertilizer plants in 1965 was 12.4 percent of the total output. This means that about 20 percent of total output of chemical fertilizers in 1964 was phosphorous fertilizers produced by small factories alone. Of course, there must be some production from the large and medium phosphorous fertilizers plants.

Sources of data and estimation procedures for Appendix Table 17, continued

d. 1962: Output in the first half of 1964 is said to equal the total amount produced during the year 1962 (*CKHW*, Sept. 2, 1964). From the information given in par. c., the 1962 output is estimated to be 3 million tons. According to *CKHW* (Sept. 26, 1963), 2.8 million tons of fertilizer were produced in January-August 1963, representing a 43.8 percent increase over the corresponding period of 1962 (*PR*, Oct. 4, 1963, p. 18). Thus, the output in the first eight months in 1962 was 1.95 million tons, which is perfectly consistent with our estimated annual output for the year.

e. 1961: The 1962 output is said to be 50 percent higher than that of 1961 (*CKHW*, Jan. 4, 1963). Of the 2 million tons, 1.43 million tons was nitrogen fertilizer (*HKTKP*, Oct. 1, 1962).

f. 1963: This year's output is 39 percent higher than the 1962 level (*JMJP*, Jan. 1, 1964; *CKHW*, Aug. 14, 1964).

g. 1965: The output increased by 3 million tons (*NCNA*, June 6, 1966). The 2 million tons production capacity of phosphorous fertilizers in 1964 is assumed to have been fully utilized now.

h. 1966: Output increased by at least 30 percent (*NCNA*, Jan. 3, 1967).

3. Imports in 1959–66: Data are taken from Liu, *Study of the Chemical Fertilizer Industry*, Chap. 4, Table 4.2.

4. Total supply: Sums of imports and domestic production.

Appendix Table 18 Official Data on Cotton Output, by Province, 1949–57 (million catties of ginned cotton)

Province	1949	1950	1951	1952	1953	1954	1955	1956	1957
Anhwei	25.5	(34)	45	72.5	62.5	(60)	74.9	77	98
Chekiang	13.5	27.6	36	43	47	49	85	33	88.5
Honan	166.8	261.8	334.6	271	238	273	328	330	360
Hopei	175	336	483	588	462	537	680	469	627.5
Hunan	14	27	67.5	62	44	10	39	46	44
Hupeh	78	118	193	296	269	81	322	422	454
Kansu	5.3	5.8	8.5	7.3	5.3	5.6	10.3	18.9	16.8
Kiangsi	3.2	5	(10)	30	18.6	11.3	20	41	51.6
Kiangsu	92	108	189	260	361	219	474	253	381
Kweichow	3.1	(3.6)	4.5	6.6	6.7	5.4	6.2	6.2	6.2
Liaoning	69	(95)	133	148	105	58	54	109	80.6
Shansi	40.4	52	110	182	154	187	165	181	197
Shantung	146	154	(225)	312	234	283	371	391	362
Shensi	88	(119)	160	147	173	180	152	192	207
Sinkiang	9.8	15.6	19.1	31.9	32.8	33.1	55.6	115	102
Szechwan	30.5	38	(54)	86	83	106	125	125	140
Yunnan	1	(2.3)	(3.4)	4.1	4.7	3.6	4	6.8	6.8
Total	961.1	1402.7	2075.6	2547.4	2300.6	2102	2966	2815.9	3223

Sources of data and estimation procedures:

1. All figures in parentheses are estimates.
2. For other data:
   a. 1949–51 and 1957: Taken from *PAS*.
   b. 1952–56 for all provinces except for Anhwei and Shensi: Computed from the 1957 output data and the annual rates of increases given in *NTKTTH*, 1958, no. 4, p. 8.
   c. 1952–56 for Anhwei and Shensi: For each of the two provinces the annual rates of increases given in *NTKTTH* are drastically inconsistent with the cumulated growth over the whole period of 1952–57 given in the same source. There must be serious errors. Since it is impossible to identify the errors, we decided to use the data in *PAS* for the two provinces in 1952–56.

Notes

For the titles of Communist Chinese publications, see the bibliographical listing on pages 349–54. In the notes, abbreviated titles, dates, issue number, and page numbers of publications are given.

Introduction

1 This was the figure for 1957, as computed from the official data given in *Ten Great Years: Statistics of the Economic and Cultural Achievements of the People's Republic of China* (Peking, 1960), pp. 8, 128.

2 Professor Anthony Tang has convincingly demonstrated that bottlenecks in industrial production were created by stagnant agriculture in the early years of the regime. See his "Policy and Performance in Agriculture," in *Economic Trends in Communist China,* eds. A. Eckstein, W. Galenson, and T. C. Liu (Chicago, 1968), pp. 459–507.

3 Mao Tse-tung, *Selected Works,* 4 vols. (London, 1955), 1: 32.

4 *TGY,* pp. 118, 120.

5 For example, see D. H. Perkins, *Market Control and Planning in Communist China* (Cambridge, 1966), Chapters 3 and 4; K. R. Walker, *Planning in Chinese Agriculture* (Chicago, 1965); K. R. Walker, "Organization for Agricultural Production," in Eckstein et al., *Economic Trends in Communist China,* pp. 397–458; and K. R. Walker, "Collectivization in Retrospect: The Socialist High Tide of Autumn 1955–Spring 1956," *China Quarterly,* no. 26 (Apr.–June 1966), pp. 1–43; and C. Y. Cheng, *Communist China's Economy 1949–1962* (South Orange, N.J., 1963), chap. 4.

Chapter 1

1 *JMJP,* Nov. 13, 1955.

2 Ibid., Nov. 25, 1968.

3 Ibid. In fact, Mao's theory can be traced back to the days of the Kiangsi Soviet.

4 Liu Shao-chi, "On the Problem of Land Reform," published in an internal document, June 14, 1950, and quoted in *HC,* 1967, no. 16, p. 20.

5 Liu Shao-chi, "An Instruction to Mr. An Tzu-wen and Others," published in an internal document, Jan. 23, 1950, and quoted in *HC,* 1967, no. 16, pp. 19–20.

6 *HC,* 1967, no. 16, p. 22.
7 *CCYC,* 1965, no. 9, p. 16.
8 This statement is quoted in *KMJP,* July 22, 1967.
9 Teng Tzu-hui's speech in the Eighth Congress of the Chinese Communist Party held on September 22, 1956. See *JMST,* 1957, p. 89.
10 Li Shien-nien later noted that "in the past . . . about the principle of agricultural cooperativization laid down by the leadership of the Party, we had no doubts. . . . But in considering the speed of developing agricultural cooperatives, there often existed some empiricism." See *TKP,* Nov. 8, 1955. The fact that Li called those people "empiricists" rather than "men with rightist biases," as used by other critics, seems to imply that he himself was one of them.
11 *JMST,* 1953, pp. 314–15; *JMST,* 1956, p. 92.
12 See *JMST,* 1956, pp. 80–86. Teng Tzu-hui has been identified as the man responsible for this action, because he was then actually in charge of agrarian affairs in the Party and had the authority to make such a decision.
13 The meeting was held in October 1953. See *JMST,* 1956, p. 93.
14 *CCYC,* 1965, no. 8, pp. 1–13.
15 *NYKHTH,* 1959, no. 19, p. 653.
16 *Cooperative Farming in China* (Peking, 1963).
17 *HHYP,* 1955, no. 8, pp. 1–22.
18 *JMST,* 1957, p. 147.
19 This point was later elaborated by Chen Po-ta. See *JMST,* 1957, p. 213. Chen held that the majority of Chinese farmers, instead of being conservative, as was ordinarily assumed, were highly revolutionary, because they were actually the proletarians in the rural sector.
20 *KMJP,* July 22, 1967; Dec. 19, 1968; and *HC,* 1967, no. 16, p. 22. According to Liu Shao-chi's "Confession," the proposal to dissolve 200,000 cooperatives was made by Teng Tzu-hui in a "Central Conference" with Liu Shao-chi presiding. "The fact that I did not refute his proposal," Liu confesses, "means that in effect I approved his plan." See *China Monthly,* Sept. 1969, p. 35.
21 *HC,* 1967, no. 16, p. 22; and *JMST,* 1957, p. 147.
22 *JMST,* 1956, p. 82.
23 Ibid, p. 84.
24 As will be shown in Chapter 5, most Chinese Communist leaders had for many years a great confusion as to which "productivity" was to be raised in order to increase farm output.
25 *HHYP,* 1955, no. 8, p. 52. Chen Yun has described a situation where the consumption of grain is highly income elastic. There might also be a slight Pigou effect.
26 *TKP,* Nov. 8, 1955.
27 *Compilation of Materials of the Chinese Communist Great Cultural Revolution,* 4 vols. to date (Hongkong, 1967), 1: 612; *HHYP,* 1955, no. 8, p. 53.

28 *HHPYK*, 1956, no. 5, p. 89.
29 *JMST*, 1956, p. 87.
30 *HHYP*, 1955, no. 11, p. 9.
31 *JMJP*, Oct. 22, 1955.
32 Published in 1955. See *HHPYK*, 1956, no. 3, p. 1.
33 *JMJP*, Jan. 26, 1956.
34 *HHPYK*, 1956, no. 4, p. 1.
35 *JMJP*, Dec. 13, 1955.
36 Ibid., Mar. 4, 1956.
37 Ibid., May 8, 1956.
38 *HHPYK*, 1956, no. 12, pp. 54–59; no. 13, pp. 50, 51; no. 14, pp. 57–61; and no. 18, p. 67.
39 *JMST*, 1957, pp. 44, 61.
40 *HHPYK*, 1958, no. 5, p. 127.
41 Ibid., 1957, no. 22, p. 128.
42 Ibid., 1958, no. 5, p. 13; no. 11, p. 5.
43 For instance, *JMJP*, July 8, 1958.
44 *HHPYK*, 1958, no. 17, p. 69; no. 18, p. 66.
45 Ibid., 1958, no. 18, pp. 1–2.
46 Ibid.
47 *JMJP*, Oct. 1, 1958; and Dec. 19, 1958.
48 *China Monthly*, 1968, no. 3, pp. 42–44. Part of the letter was revealed in *KMJP*, Aug. 18, 1967.
49 This is a term referring to Mao's three major economic policies: the general line of constructing a socialist economy, the Great Leap Forward, and the commune movement.
50 *Compilation of Materials*, 1: 674.
51 There was no discussion of military affairs in Peng's letter delivered during the Lushan Conference. But his objection to Mao's military line was divulged in considerable detail late in 1967 (*KMJP*, Aug. 18, 1967). A connection between his ouster and his military viewpoint can also be drawn from the fact that he and Huang Ke-cheng, Chief of Staff of the Chinese Red Army, were fired at the same time.
52 Mao has stated that he was treated by Liu and others during that period "as if I were their dead parent," meaning that, although he was still respected, his instructions concerning policy matters were not heeded or that he was not even consulted on those matters.
53 Teng Hsiao-ping was the person mainly responsible for the drafting. See Teng's "Confession," *China Monthly*, Sept. 1969, p. 37; and *Compilation of Materials*, 1: 486, 491.
54 *JMJP*, Nov. 23, 1967.
55 The destination of Liu Shao-chi was Hunan Province where he stayed for 44 days (from April 2 to May 16) and visited three communes in three different hsien (see *Compilation of Materials*, 1:313–15). In one commune, he and his wife stayed for eighteen days, and there he introduced the responsibility land system for experimentation (*KMJP*, Nov.

24, 1967). To the people of another commune visited, he admitted that the commune system was carried out against the will of the masses and that it had resulted in "broken families and deaths of people." He was also reported to have said, "What really happened was a man-made disaster; to call it a natural calamity will never convince people." In summarizing the facts he had collected in his journey, he made the castigating remark: "In some places the economic foundation was damaged so deeply and so many people died [that] for those places the result is indeed a devastation, and the recovery will require a long time. . . ." Teng Hsiao-ping, Peng Chen, and Chu Teh made trips to other regions in the same period. See *KMJP,* Aug. 9, 1967, and *Compilation of Materials,* 1:593, 615. They all concluded that the agricultural crisis was attributable mainly to the lack of incentives of farmers.

56 *KMJP,* Aug. 9, 1967.

57 Ibid.; and *Compilation of Materials,* 1:256. Seventy-eight persons participated in this top-level meeting.

58 *Compilation of Materials.* 1:613, 619–20. This was probably the meeting held Feb. 21–26, with Liu Shao-chi presiding. One of the items discussed was the final accounting of the 1960 state budget. The fact that the final accounts of the 1960 budget were not closed and examined until 1962 clearly indicated the chaotic conditions existing in 1960–61. It is also reported that the participants of the meeting were shocked when they "discovered" serious budgetary deficits in the 1960 accounts. This fact led them to reach an "extremely pessimistic evaluation" of the economic situation. Chen Yun later presented to the State Council an address based on the conclusions reached in that meeting. A similar report was also distributed to all provincial committees. As a result, the "wind" of private farming was spread to various provinces (see Liu's "Confession," *China Monthly,* Sept. 1969, p. 35). Extremely severe criticisms of the Great Leap Forward and the communes had been expressed by many Party leaders on other occasions during this period. Tao Chu was quoted as saying that "the hardship during the Long March is dwarfed by that of the Great Leap Forward" (*Compilation of Materials,* 1:531). Yang Shang-kun said, "The Great Leap Forward has set back our national economy by several years and has delayed a Five Year Plan" (*Compilation of Materials,* 1:586). Chen Yun proposed an outright restoration of private farming (*Compilation of Materials,* 1:616). Teng Hsiao-ping supported this idea by saying, "We do not care whether it is a black or white cat [referring to socialism and capitalism]; as long it catches mice, it is a good cat" (*Compilation of Materials,* 1:482, 487).

59 In the May meeting, Teng Tzu-hui reported on the merits of the responsibility land system as shown in the experiment in Anhwei Province. He further proposed the adoption of a nationwide system to set "guaranteed production quotas" for individual farm households instead of

production teams. Another comrade proposed the distribution of farmland to households, that is, an outright restoration of private farming (see Liu's "Confession," *China Monthly,* Sept. 1969, p. 35). These proposals were then brought to the Tenth Session of the Eighth Central Committee, held in September that year, for resolution (see *Compilation of Materials,* 1:256). It should be noted that the series of important meetings in the first six months or so of 1962 were held when Mao Tse-tung was not in Peking.

60 *Compilation of Materials,* 1:24, 257. This document is often referred to as the "Ten Articles" because it consisted of ten points. According to Liu's "Confession," the document was issued on April 1, 1964. While April 1 is a correct date, 1964 is probably a misquotation.

61 Ibid.; *JMJP,* Nov. 23, 1967. Liu's version also contained ten points aimed at "Four-Clearance." The Maoists, however, make a distinction between the two documents by referring to Mao's original draft as the "former Ten-Article" or the "true Four-Clearance" and calling Liu's version the "latter Ten-Article" or the "faked Four-Clearance." The latter Ten-Article was drafted in September and openly announced on November 14. Apparently, it was drafted by Peng Chen but was approved by Liu. See Liu's "Confession."

62 *JMJP,* Nov. 23, 1967, and *Compilation of Materials,* 1:24. The new document is referred to as the "23-Article."

63 *HHPYK,* 1958, no. 11, pp. 5–6.

Chapter 2

1 T. H. Shen, *Agricultural Resources of China* (Ithaca, 1951), p. 96.

2 J. L. Buck, *Land Utilization in China* (Shanghai, 1937), pp. 194–96. These figures are the results of his Farm Survey (b), p. 196, and are also the statistics that Professor Buck chose to use in his text.

3 Ibid., p. 198.

4 J. L. Buck, *Chinese Farm Economy* (Chicago, 1930), p. 424.

5 Ibid., pp. 159–66.

6 The moderation of land policy was a concession to the United Front agreement in 1937.

7 N. Georgescu-Roegen, "Economic Theory and Agrarian Economics," *Oxford Economic Papers* 12 (Feb. 1960):1–40; and V. M. Dandekar, "Economic Theory and Agrarian Reform," *Oxford Economic Papers* 14 (Feb. 1962):69–79.

8 Buck, *Land Utilization,* p. 197.

9 Buck, *Farm Economy,* p. 150.

10 Ibid., p. 156. Buck says, "It is significant that tenant farms have larger net profits per crop mou and this must be due to better management."

11 Ibid., p. 155.

12 Ibid., p. 147; and Shen, *Agricultural Resources,* p. 96.

13 Buck, *Farm Economy,* p. 156.

14 Chiao Chi-ming, *Economics of the Chinese Agricultural Society* (Shanghai, 1946), p. 265.
15 Shen, *Agricultural Resources,* pp. 99–106.
16 *TCKT,* 1957, no. 4, p. 12.
17 Article 20 of the Land Reform Act, promulgated June 30, 1950, stipulated that once land reform was concluded the government would recognize the rights of all landowners to manage, purchase, sell, or rent land freely. There was no limit to the landholding a family could own in the future.
18 *CCYC,* 1965, no. 8, p. 7.
19 See Table 9.1.
20 Actually, the compensation payments to landlords in land reform may serve two important economic functions. On the one hand, the compensation requirement prevents the rate of marketed grain from falling. On the other hand, it is instrumental to the channelling of farm surplus into industrial investment. Barred from making investment in agriculture, landlords would be inclined to use the proceeds of the compensation payments to embark on new industrial undertakings, if a viable industrial sector existed. In the Chinese Communist land reform, both functions were missing.
21 *Cooperative Farming in China,* p. 2.
22 *JMJP,* August 3, 1954.
23 The intention of the Chinese Communist government was to let the proportion of income distributed as land dividends gradually decline until it completely vanished at the conversion of the cooperative into a collective.
24 See B. Ward, "The Firm in Illyria: Market Syndicalism," *American Economic Review* 48 (Sept. 1958):566–89; and E. D. Domar, "The Soviet Collective Farm as A Producer Cooperative," *American Economic Review* 56 (Sept. 1966):734–57. Since the manager in the Ward-Domar "pure model" cooperative tends to maximize the value of work points, he behaves much like his "capitalist twin."
25 According to *Model Regulations for An Agricultural Producers' Cooperative,* all working peasants, men and women who had reached the age of sixteen, or other working people able to take part in the work of the cooperative, may apply to join. Every member enjoys the right to take part in the work of the cooperative and to receive the payment which is due him. A member who commits a serious crime and is deprived of political rights must be expelled from the cooperative. A member who gravely violates cooperative regulations or commits many serious mistakes and refuses to repent and correct them, after being repeatedly admonished and penalized, may be expelled from the cooperative by the decision of a general meeting of members following discussion of his case. The same regulations were maintained in advanced cooperatives.

26 For instance, Joan Robinson, "The Organization of Agriculture," *Bulletin of the Atomic Scientists* (June 1966), pp. 28–32.
27 The situation of water conservation construction during the Communist period will be surveyed in Chapter 5.
28 Cooperative accountants received one month of training in programs conducted by the government. See *HHYP*, 1955, no. 2, p. 114.
29 The indirect pressures were exerted in the form of refusing to extend farm credits to individual farmers or in the form of setting higher procurement quotas for them.
30 J. F. Karcz, "Thoughts on the Grain Problem," *Soviet Studies* 18 (Apr. 1967):426.
31 T. P. Bernstein, "Leadership and Mass Mobilization in the Soviet and Chinese Collectivization Campaigns of 1929–30 and 1955–56: A Comparison," *China Quarterly* 31 (July-Sept. 1967):11, 29.
32 *JMST*, 1957, p. 143.
33 *JMJP*, Mar. 8, 1955.
34 *JMST*, 1957, p. 33.
35 The percentage of peasant households collectivized reached 89.6 percent by 1936. See *Sotsialisticheskoe stroitel'stvo SSSR (1936)* [Socialistic construction, USSR], p. 278.
36 *HHPYK*, 1956, no. 23, p. 61.
37 *HHYP*, 1955, no. 3, p. 134; no. 10, p. 189; and no. 12, pp. 185–88.
38 *HHPYK*, 1956, no. 5, pp. 108–9.
39 Ibid., no. 12, p. 59.
40 *CKNP*, 1957, no. 4, pp. 16–18.
41 Ibid., 1956, no. 12, p. 4.
42 *HHPYK*, 1957, no. 8, p. 86.
43 Ibid., 1958, no. 5, p. 129.
44 *JMST*, 1957, p. 198.
45 *HHPYK*, 1957, no. 8, p. 85.
46 *JMST*, 1957, pp. 197–200.
47 *HHPYK*, 1956, no. 12, p. 55; and no. 18, p. 67.
48 *JMST*, 1957, pp. 198–200.
49 *TCYC*, 1958, no. 8, p. 12.
50 The seven guarantees include meals, clothing, housing, education, maternity expenses, medical cares, and wedding and funeral expenses; the ten guarantees added haircuts and baths, entertainment, and heating costs to the above seven.
51 Actually, the "wage" distribution had variations also. Some communes fixed the value of each work point—wage in the strict sense—others were still using a work-point system with a variable value for each point.
52 *HHPYK*, 1958, no. 17, pp. 75–81.
53 *JMJP*, July 8, 1958; and *HHPYK*, 1958, no. 16, pp. 90–92.
54 *JMJP*, Aug. 29, 1959.

55 *PR,* Nov. 1, 1963, p. 9.
56 *HHPYK,* 1958, no. 24, p. 9.
57 *KMJP,* Jan. 11, 1969.
58 Tao Chu, *The People's Communes Forge Ahead* (Peking, 1964), p. 26.
59 *KMJP,* June 11, 1968; Aug. 22, 1968.
60 Ibid., Aug. 22, 1968.
61 Ibid., July 17, 1968, June 11, 1968, and Nov. 17, 1968.
62 Ibid., Nov. 23, 1967.
63 Ibid., June 18, 1969.
64 *TKP,* Feb. 1965.
65 Robinson, "The Organization of Agriculture," p. 29.
66 *KMJP,* July 17, 1968; and Nov. 17, 1968.
67 *JMJP,* July 19, 1957; Nov. 18, 1957; June 11, 1968; and June 18, 1968.
68 The degree of differential in 1964 was described as more serious than that in 1953–54. See *TKP,* Feb. 17, 1965.
69 See *JMJP,* Feb. 7, 1965; and Feb. 25, 1965.
70 As can be computed from Table 2.2, even the average grain yield per unit of cultivated area is lower than the national average yield per sown area in all the years.
71 *HHPYK,* 1957, no. 12, p. 122.
72 *TCYC,* 1958, no. 8, p. 9.
73 *HHPYK,* 1957, no. 7, p. 80.
74 Ibid., no. 12, p. 119.

Chapter 3

1 *CKNP,* 1958, no. 3, p. 7.
2 Theodore W. Schultz, *Transforming Traditional Agriculture* (New Haven, Conn., 1964), pp. 118–19.
3 See *CCYC,* 1963, no. 9, p. 12; 1964, no. 3, p. 10; 1965, no. 2, p. 20; and *JMJP,* Mar. 22, 1965.
4 *JMJP,* June 2, 1963.
5 *TGY,* pp. 57, 59.
6 Kang Chao, *Capital Formation in Communist China* (forthcoming monograph).
7 A. Eckstein, W. Galenson, and T. C. Liu, eds., *Economic Trends in Communist China* (Chicago, 1968), pp. 170–71. The amount includes the value of rural residential housing.
8 The average rural population in 1952–57 was 525 million.
9 This type of investment was negligible in 1952–54 but became heavier in 1955–56 when agricultural cooperativization was accelerated.
10 Eckstein et al., *Economic Trends,* pp. 170–71.
11 *TCKT,* 1957, no. 10, p. 32.
12 *TCYC,* 1958, no. 8, p. 11.
13 "Loan sharks" were still active in the rural areas in 1953–54. See *CCYC,* 1965, no. 8, p. 5.

14 See *NTCY,* 1957, no. 12, p. 14. The following data indicate the rapid expansion of activities of rural credit cooperatives (in million yuan):

	Deposits at the year end	*Amount of loans outstanding*
1954	190	120
1955	590	470
1956	780	1,210

15 *HHPYK,* 1958, no. 9, p. 81.
16 Ibid.
17 *NTCY,* 1957, no. 19, p. 10.
18 *CHCC,* 1958, no. 2, p. 18; and *CKNP,* 1959, no. 19, p. 32.
19 *CKNP,* 1959, no. 19, p. 32.
20 *NYKHTH,* 1959, no. 19, p. 660.
21 *CKHW,* Feb. 12, 1965.
22 *NYKHTH,* 1959, no. 19, p. 659.
23 Ibid.
24 Ibid., p. 662.
25 See *HHYP,* 1955, no. 4, p. 132; no. 5, p. 158; *CKNP,* 1959, no. 19, p. 32; and *CHCC,* 1958, no. 2, p. 18.
26 *CKHW,* Feb. 12, 1965.
27 Chu-yuan Cheng, *Scientific and Engineering Manpower in Communist China, 1949–1963* (Washington, D.C., 1965), p. 78.
28 *CHCC,* 1958, no. 2, p. 18.
29 Ibid.
30 *HHYP,* 1955, no. 4, p. 132.
31 *CHCC,* 1958, no. 2, p. 19.
32 Ibid.
33 *CKHW,* Mar. 28, 1965.

Chapter 4

1 Early Chinese Communist publications did not mention the names of those who participated in the debate. Identities of holders of the different views were revealed later during the Great Cultural Revolution. See *HC,* 1967, no. 16, pp. 18–29.
2 *CCYC,* 1956, no. 1, p. 16.
3 Mao Tse-tung, "The Question of Agricultural Cooperation," *JMST,* 1956, p. 84.
4 Marx stated, "In industry the victory of large-scale production is obvious at once, but in agriculture too we see the same phenomenon. The superiority of big Capitalistic agriculture increases; there is growing application of machines; the peasant economy falls into the noose of money capital, declines and collapses under the weight of a backward technique." This passage is quoted in David Mitrany, *Marx Against the Peasant: A Study in Social Dogmatism* (London, 1951), p. 241.

5 Ibid., p. 30.
6 Ibid., p. 35.
7 *CCYC,* 1956, no. 1, pp. 9–11.
8 *JMST,* 1956, p. 84.
9 This information is given in an article in *Nung-yeh chi-hsieh chi-shu* (Agricultural Machinery Technology), 1967, no. 5, and is cited in *China Monthly,* 1968, no. 2, p. 42.
10 *CKNP,* 1957, no. 21, p. 40; and 1958, no. 3, p. 3.
11 Ibid., 1957, no. 21, pp. 40–44.
12 Ibid., 1958, no. 3, p. 10.
13 *JMJP,* Jan. 6, 1955.
14 *HHPYK,* 1958, no. 9, p. 82; and *CCYC,* 1956, no. 1, p. 14. The actual achievements of tractor stations in 1957 fell short of the planned targets. The expectation was that, by the end of 1957, there would be a total of 427 tractor stations with 20,970 standard tractor units to cultivate 32.6 million mou of land (*CKNP,* 1956, no. 8, p. 10). In actuality, there were 383 tractor stations equipped with 12,036 standard tractor units and a total tractor-cultivated area of 26.2 million mou (*JMJP,* Jan. 18, 1958).
15 *CKNP,* 1957, no. 21, pp. 42–44.
16 Ibid., 1958, no. 3, p. 7.
17 *JMJP,* July 3, 1958, stated, "During the Great Leap Forward, in industry and agriculture over the whole country, there has arisen the problem of labor shortages. This problem is particularly severe in the country. . . . Farmers in many areas have been compelled to neglect some routine work and delay many important farming processes. . . . Farmers in many areas have to use nights as days." Another official source (*HHPYK,* 1958, no. 16, p. 121) reported, "There are three common problems we face daily at the present time—shortage of labor, raw materials, and investment funds. Among the three problems, the labor shortage is the most acute one." Teng Tzu-hui, a cabinet member responsible for agricultural production, described the labor shortage as the "most spectacular phenomenon in this year's high tide of agricultural production." *HHPYK,* 1958, no. 17, p. 92.
18 *JMJP,* Nov. 4, 1958.
19 *CCYC,* 1959, no. 3, p. 39.
20 *NYCH,* 1959, no. 11, inside cover.
21 *HC,* 1960, no. 4, p. 6.
22 Po I-po was criticized during the Great Cultural Revolution period for his "truncation of Chairman Mao's ten-year program of agricultural mechanization." The draft of the Third Five Year Plan for 1966–70, formulated under his direction, was said to deliberately omit farm mechanization as one of the major technical policies. The scheduled annual investment in the industry producing agricultural machinery in the five year period was only 39 percent of the figure for 1960. The

of the few items
d in 1960.
s about ten years.
and actually used
y occur. One may
cause of the rela-
more, inadequate
ng the Great Leap
rage life-span of

ina to other Asian

tput of tractors in

no. 24, pp. 26–27;

s 20,000 yuan, and
on of each tractor
8, no. 4, p. 45.

st degree of mecha-
ultivated by tractors

ung-yeh chi-hsieh chi-shu, 1967,
, no. 2, p. 43.

ws were first borrowed by the
P, 1960, no. 1, p. 2.
more efficient than old Chinese
it of land by 10 to 20 percent.

YK, 1956, no. 14, p. 2.
, 1956, no. 4, p. 4. This state-
subsequently revised versions
the two-wheeled share plows

cing the figure of actual sales
6, 1958.

. 17, p. 92; and *CCYC,* 1959,

r irrigation, and many other
ise, manual as well as animal-
chanized implements so long
earings. The term was later
toothed wheels, wind power,
such as cable-carriers). See

4, p. 19.

and Oct. 18, 1966.
p. 82; and *JMJP,* Oct. 15,

and sizes are measured in

ral machine-building enter-
gross value of that industry

standard units. See *JMJP,*

Mar. 31, 1960. Tractor production was probably on where the planned targets were fulfilled or overfulfill

48 The average life-span of tractors in other countries However, since most Chinese tractors were designed for multiple functions, a higher depreciation rate ma also expect poorer durability of Chinese tractors be tively low level of production technique. Furthe maintenance and lack of spare parts, especially duri period, must have shortened considerably the av Chinese tractors.

49 A symbolic number of tractors was exported by Ch countries every year.

50 *KMJP,* Oct. 18, 1966, anticipated a record high ou 1966.

51 *EB,* no. 887 (1964), p. 12.

52 *JMJP,* May 19, 1965.

53 *CKHW,* Sept. 27, 1965.

54 *KMJP,* Oct. 18, 1966.

55 *HHYP,* 1954, no. 4, p. 155.

56 *CKNP,* 1956, no. 8, p. 10.

57 *JMJP,* Apr. 13, 1966.

58 *CHCC,* 1958, no. 7, p. 38.

59 *CKNP,* 1957, no. 14, p. 9.

60 Ibid., no. 10, pp. 13–15; no. 14, pp. 10–11; 1958, and *CHCC,* 1958, no. 4, pp. 44–45.

61 *CKNP,* 1958, no. 3, p. 12.

62 Ibid., no. 24, p. 27.

63 *JMJP,* Nov. 23, 1961.

64 *CKNP,* 1963, no. 11, p. 7.

65 Ibid., 1958, no. 3, p. 13.

66 *NYCH,* 1959, no. 1, p. 5.

67 The average total fixed investment per tractor wa the working capital required for normal operati ranged from 4,000 to 5,000 yuan. See *CHCC,* 19

68 *KMJP,* Oct. 10, 1966.

69 Even in Heilungkiang, the province with the high nized farming, only 10 percent of farmland was in 1957. See *JMJP,* Mar. 13, 1958.

70 *SCMM,* 1964, no. 451.

71 *HHYP,* 1954, no. 11, p. 6.

72 *CKNP,* 1957, no. 14, p. 9.

73 *EB,* no. 751 (1962), p. 51.

74 *NCNA,* Jan. 2, 1963.

75 Ibid., Aug. 26, 1962.

76 *EB,* no. 751 (1962), p. 51.

77 *NCNA,* Sept. 29, 1965.

78 Ibid., Oct. 22, 1963.

79 In 1955, 72 of the 138 AMS were located in the cotton areas (*CKNP,* 1956, no. 8, p. 10); by 1965, 20 percent of cotton land was cultivated by tractors (*CKHW,* July 14, 1965). In Hopei, 40 percent of the wheatland was plowed by tractors in 1961 (*EB,* no. 751 (1962), p. 51).

80 *CKNP,* 1957, no. 14, p. 10; 1958, no. 3, p. 11; and *CHCC,* 1958, no. 4, p. 44.

81 In 1956 the average cost of using tractors for plowing was slightly below 1.50 yuan per mou in most AMS (*CKNP,* 1957, no. 14, p. 10), yet in 1963, 90 percent of the AMS still had an average cost above 1.30 yuan per mou (*NCNA,* Jan. 5, 1964).

82 *CCYC,* 1964, no. 2, p. 10.

83 See *HPNYKH,* 1958, no. 5, p. 295.

84 See *CKNP,* 1957, no. 14, p. 11. This means that the total fuel cost for cultivating one mou of land could come to 1.30 yuan.

85 According to *CKNP,* 1956, no. 3, p. 10, there were 1470 tractor units (equivalent to 2,353 standard units) and 6,459 employees, including 2,659 operators, in all AMS at the end of 1955.

86 *CKNP,* 1968, no. 3, p. 11.

87 *JMJP,* Feb. 28, 1961.

88 *CHCC,* 1958, no. 9, p. 41.

89 The time needed for major repairs ranges from 650 to 1,000 hours per unit of tractors. See *KJJP,* Mar. 31, 1963.

90 *CKNP,* 1963, no. 11, p. 7.

91 *CKHW,* Feb. 23, 1965.

92 *CKNP,* 1963, no. 11, p. 4.

93 *NCNA,* Oct. 19, 1964.

94 *JMJP,* Jan. 4, 1966.

Chapter 5

1 *JMJP,* Dec. 22, 1957.

2 Ibid., Dec. 12, 1955; and *SLYTL,* 1958, no. 4, p. 20.

3 *SLYTL,* 1958, no. 4, p. 20.

4 Buck, *Land Utilization,* p. 186.

5 If we use the percentages of cultivated land in both regions, 51 percent for the wheat region and 49 percent for the rice region (Buck, *Land Utilization,* p. 33), as weights, the weighted ratio for the two regions combined would be 41.5 percent instead of Buck's 46 percent. If we use the percentages of cultivated land in the eight areas to weight the ratios of irrigated land in the individual areas, the weighted average would be further reduced.

6 Buck rejected this estimate because 37 percent of the crop area in China was rice land which was almost all irrigated. See Buck, *Land Utilization,* p. 186.

7 *HHPYK,* 1957, no. 23, p. 169.

8 Ibid., no. 9, p. 104.

9 *CHCC,* 1958, no. 1, p. 15.
10 In 1953–57, 60 percent of the state investment in water conservation went to large projects. See *JMJP,* July 24, 1957.
11 Ibid.
12 Some of them are the People's Victory Canal in Honan, the Yeh-Yuan Canal in Shantung, the Ching-Hui Canal and the Wei-Hui Canal in Shensi, the Kuan-Sung-Peng-Nien Canal in Szechwan, and the Yung-Chen Canal in Hopei. See *HHPYK,* 1958, no. 2, p. 109.
13 *EB,* no. 895 (1964), p. 20.
14 Buck, *Land Utilization,* pp. 230–31.
15 The new policies were resolved in the Third Plenary Session of the Eighth Central Committee of the Chinese Communist Party in 1957. See *HHPYK,* 1957, no. 22, p. 160; and 1958, no. 11, p. 16.
16 This was the point stressed by Krylov, a Soviet expert. He states, "The solution of the irrigation problem in China depends to a considerable extent on the artificial control of the subsoil waters by a complex system of ameliorative measures." See *JPRS* 8015, Mar. 31, 1951, p. 4.
17 *HHPYK,* 1957, no. 23, p. 169.
18 Ibid., 1958, no. 5, p. 65.
19 *JMJP,* Oct. 14, 1958; and *HHPYK,* 1958, no. 10, p. 116.
20 *JMJP,* Mar. 11, 1958.
21 Ibid. In one case the leading water channel was connected to more than 7,000 small reservoirs and ponds. See *EB,* no. 895 (1964), p. 21.
22 *HHPYK,* 1958, no. 13, p. 89.
23 *JMJP,* July 30, 1958.
24 *HHPYK,* 1958, no. 8, p. 121; and *CKNP,* 1959, no. 11, p. 15.
25 *JMJP,* May 3, 1958.
26 *CKNP,* 1959, no. 11, p. 15.
27 *HHPYK,* 1958, no. 7, p. 114.
28 Ibid. The Peking government proudly took this as proof of the superiority of collectivization.
29 For instance, Anthony M. Tang, "Input-Output Relations in the Agriculture of Communit China," an unpublished paper presented at the Conference on the Agrarian Questions in the Light of Communist and Non-Communist Experience, August 23–26, 1967, Seattle, Washington.
30 *JMJP,* Jan. 23, 1960; and Dec. 29, 1960.
31 *PR,* Aug. 23, 1963.
32 For instance, A. M. Tang, "Input-Output Relations in the Agriculture of Communist China."
33 *JMJP,* May 24, 1956.
34 J. L. Buck, O. L. Dawson, and Y. L. Wu, *Food and Agriculture in Communist China* (New York, 1966), p. 160.
35 Ibid., p. 161.
36 For example, the network in Anhwei was designed to discharge only 2 percent of its water during flood period (400 mm rainfall in ten days). See *HHPYK,* 1958, no. 13, p. 93.

37 *HHPYK,* 1958, no. 3, p. 99; and *JMJP,* Oct. 20, 1958.
38 *CKSL,* 1958, no. 4, pp. 36–38.
39 Victor P. Petrov, *China: Emerging World Power* (Princeton, N.J., 1967), p. 48.
40 *JMJP,* Dec. 29, 1960.
41 *CHCC,* 1957, no. 9, p. 8.
42 *JMJP,* June 13, 1956.
43 *HHPYK,* 1958, no. 7, p. 117; and *JMJP,* Oct. 20, 1958.
44 *HHPYK,* 1958, no. 5, p. 66.
45 *JMJP,* May 24, 1958.
46 Ibid., Apr. 10, 1960.
47 *JPRS* 30123, May 18, 1965.
48 For instance, 116 of the 286 small projects built in Ningteh, Fukien, either collapsed or became useless by 1963. See *TKP,* June 8, 1965. In a single month, June 1959, 28,000 large and small water conservation structures in Kwangtung were destroyed by floods. See *HKWHP,* June 24, 1959.
49 The planned target was 1.5 billion mou. See *JMJP,* Oct. 14, 1958.
50 See *JMJP,* Nov. 25, 1958. Of 40 million mou of land, 4 million mou were used for water conservation construction.
51 *HHPYK,* 1958, no. 13, p. 93.
52 Ibid., 1957, no. 9, p. 106.
53 *JMJP,* Mar. 11, 1958.
54 *JPRS* 922-D, Sept. 18, 1959.
55 *TGY,* pp. 128, 134.
56 *JMJP,* June 26, 1962.
57 Ibid., Mar. 2, 1958; and *CCYC,* 1964, no. 4, p. 49.
58 *JMJP,* May 24, 1956.
59 *CKNP,* 1961, no. 10, p. 17.
60 *SLHP,* 1960, no. 1, p. 13.
61 *JMJP,* Dec. 18, 1962.
62 *TLHP,* 1964, no. 1, p. 9.
63 *CKNYKH,* 1962, no. 12, p. 20.
64 On October 24, 1959, the Central Committee and the State Council jointly issued the "Directive on the Continuing Development of the Large-Scale Movement for Water Conservation Construction and for Fertilizer Accumulation in Various Places During This Winter and the Next Spring." See *JMJP,* Oct. 25, 1959.
65 *CCYC,* 1965, no. 6, p. 20.
66 *EB,* no. 6 (1965), p. 20.
67 Kang Chao, *The Construction Industry in Communist China* (Chicago, 1968), p. 66.
68 Ibid. The two main targets of the water conservation programs, announced by the Peking government for 1964, were (1) to improve management and (2) to add the missing constituent parts of existing irrigation structures (see *JMJP,* Nov. 30, 1963). The construction work

done in 1965 has also been described as being of the same nature (see *CKHW,* Dec. 18, 1965).

69 *EB,* no. 938 (1965), p. 12.
70 *CCYC,* 1965, no. 3, p. 40; and *EB,* no. 895 (1964), pp. 20–21.
71 *PC,* 1957, no. 20, pp. 22, 27; and *JPRS* 8015, (1961), p. 5.
72 *PC,* 1957, no. 20, p. 22; and *HHPYK,* 1956, no. 14, p. 110.
73 *TKP,* June 29, 1956.
74 *LNJP,* Feb. 16, 1957.
75 *HKTKP,* Oct. 1, 1963.
76 It was planned in 1957 to expand the area irrigated with mechanical and electric power to 80 million mou by 1962. See *CHCC,* 1958, no. 1, p. 20.
77 *CKNP,* 1959, no. 11, p. 14.
78 *HHPYK,* 1958, no. 17, p. 97.
79 Ibid., 1957, no. 8, p. 97.
80 *NYKHTH,* 1959, no. 19, p. 690.
81 *SLFT,* 1958, no. 17, p. 1.
82 *HC,* 1960, no. 13, p. 8.
83 Kang Chao, *The Electric Power Industry in Communist China,* Institute for Defense Analyses, Research paper no. 348 (June 1967), p. 5.
84 *SLFT,* 1958, no. 19, p. 9.
85 It is found that in practically all underdeveloped countries, the small-scale power units for village development are not operating efficiently. The load factor is generally below 30 percent.
86 Chao, *Electric Power Industry in Communist China,* p. 15.
87 *HKTKP,* Oct. 23, 1963.
88 Chao, *Electric Power Industry in Communist China,* p. 17.
89 *EB,* no. 895 (1964), p. 21.
90 *JMJP,* Sept. 25, 1964.
91 *EB,* no. 895 (1964), p. 21.

Chapter 6

1 Farmland in North China generally contains only 1 percent organic matter. See *NYKHTH,* 1954, no. 9, p. 455.
2 See Buck et al., *Food and Agriculture,* pp. 139–41.
3 *CKNP,* 1959, no. 17, p. 35.
4 *HTNYKHTP,* 1958, no. 2, pp. 72, 68.
5 Buck, *Land Utilization,* p. 265.
6 Ibid., p. 258.
7 Some Chinese Communist studies use a flat conversion rate of 50 kg of animal manure and night soil to one kg of ammonium nitrate (with 20 percent N). See *JMJP,* Aug. 26, 1960. If this rate is used, Buck's figure of prewar fertilizer application can be converted to 2.6 kg of plant nutrient per mou.
8 Buck, *Land Utilization,* p. 259.

9 For instance, see *HHPYK,* 1958, no. 9, p. 81; and *CKNP,* 1959, no. 17, p. 35.

10 *CKNP,* 1959, no. 17, p. 35.

11 *HTNYKHTP,* 1958, no. 4, pp. 202, 205.

12 *AHJP,* Aug. 1 to Aug. 10, 1958.

13 Ibid., Jan. 17, 1959.

14 *CKNP,* 1959, no. 17, p. 35. However, this bulletin implies in one place that the amount of plant nutrient received by each mou of land was about 13 kg in 1958. Even this figure must be regarded as containing a serious overstatement.

15 This practice began in 1956 when the movement of collecting fertilizers was accelerated. Some cadres in the agricultural cooperatives forced farmers to tear down their houses, and then the dirt of walls was used as fertilizers. Consequently, the farmers lost their houses and had to squeeze into other households. See *JMJP,* July 9, 1956; and *NFJP,* Oct. 12, 1956.

16 *NFJP,* Mar. 30, 1957.

17 *JMJP,* July 19, 1957.

18 See, for instance, *JMJP,* Aug. 17, 1960; and Dec. 11, 1960.

19 *CKNYKH,* 1965, no. 8, pp. 22–25.

20 Ibid., pp. 22, 24.

21 *HHKY,* 1959, no. 15, pp. 35–36.

22 Ibid., no. 5, pp. 28–30.

23 For instance, all of the twenty-seven small chemical fertilizer plants erected in 1958 in the city of Wushih had been closed by 1961. See *HHKY,* 1961, no. 23, p. 1.

24 *TKP,* June 15, 1966.

25 *JMJP,* Sept. 26, 1964; and *CKHW,* Sept. 26, 1964.

26 *JMJP,* Dec. 7, 1956.

27 *Shin chugoku nenkan* [Yearbook of New China] (Tokyo, 1965), p. 211.

28 *JMJP,* Mar. 1, 1964.

29 *TKP,* June 15, 1966.

30 *EB,* Mar. 15, 1965; and *CKHW,* Feb. 7, 1965.

31 *EB,* Mar. 15, 1965.

32 See J. C. Liu, *A Study of the Chemical Fertilizer Industry in Communist China* (forthcoming) chap. 4, table 4.5.

33 This comparison should not be construed to indicate a higher unit yield on Chinese farms than in the U.S.A. Because of the poorer basic fertility of the soil, the higher multiple-cropping index, the inferior seeds used, and a number of other technical factors, the unit yield in China is actually lower than in the U.S.A.

34 Japan and Taiwan are known to have been using native fertilizers very heavily. While the population density of these countries is higher, the number of farm animals is lower than in Communist China; therefore, the total availability of night soil and animal manure may not be lower in Communist China. What is more important is that neither of the

two countries is under such a high pressure to make use of natural fertilizers as Communist China was.

35 See *JMJP,* July 17, July 19, and Nov. 18, 1957.

36 *CFJP,* Jan. 21, 1952.

37 Using 1957 as an example, the ratio of chemical fertilizers applied to cotton and grain was 7 to 100, whereas the ratio of sown areas of the two crops was only 4.8 to 100.

38 This policy has been frequently reiterated. See *JMJP,* Mar. 15, 1955; and *HHPYK,* 1958, no. 11, p. 106.

39 *CHCC,* 1958, no. 4, p. 12.

40 The specific strategic areas are not identified. It was disclosed that 267 hsien were classified as strategic cotton areas. See *KJJP,* Mar. 4, 1965.

41 Computed from the information given in *CKHW,* Sept. 26, 1964.

42 *JMJP,* June, 6, 1964.

Chapter 7

1 Buck, *Land Utilization,* pp. 23–91. For details of the physiographical conditions in the eight agricultural regions, the reader may consult Buck's study and Shen's *Agricultural Resources,* pp. 132–40.

2 Shen, *Agricultural Resources,* pp. 138–40.

3 Buck, *Land Utilization,* p. 216. A double-cropping index is the ratio of total sown (crop) acreage to total cultivated acreage.

4 Computed from *TGY,* p. 128. The validity of official indexes of double-cropping will be examined in Chapter 8.

5 *CKNP,* 1957, no. 10, p. 8; 1956, no. 23, p. 3; 1957, no. 24, p. 4; and 1959, no. 9, p. 17.

6 *HTNYKHTP,* 1957, no. 11, p. 575.

7 *CKNP,* 1957, no. 10, pp. 8, 9.

8 Ibid., 1956, no. 23, p. 7.

9 For details, see the three articles appearing in *CKNP,* 1957, no. 6, pp. 19–20; no. 11, pp. 9–12; and no. 12, pp. 24–25.

10 *HTNYKHTP,* 1958, no. 3, pp. 113–15; *KSNYTH,* 1956, no. 19, pp. 663–66; and 1957, no. 20, pp. 570–71.

11 *KSNYTH,* 1956, no. 19, p. 663.

12 *CKNP,* 1957, no. 12, pp. 16–19; and no. 15, p. 13.

13 *CKNP,* 1957, no. 15, pp. 12–15; no. 18, p. 32.

14 *NYKHTH,* 1958, no. 4, p. 183; and *CKNYKH,* 1962, no. 12, p. 18.

15 *HHPYK,* 1958, no. 11, p. 97; and *JMJP,* May 24, 1958.

16 *NYKHTH,* 1958, no. 4, p. 183.

17 *CKNYKH,* 1962, no. 12, p. 21.

18 *HHPYK,* 1958, no. 11, p. 99.

19 *CKNYKH,* 1962, no. 12, p. 20.

20 *JMJP,* Oct. 31, 1959.

21 *TGY,* p. 129.

22 *JMJP,* Feb. 6, 1965.

23 *Acta Agriculturae Sinica* 8 (1957):157.

24 *HHPYK*, 1958, no. 9, p. 82. The percentage of 56.5 is slightly higher than that given in *TGY* and reproduced in Table 7.5.

25 *NYKHTH*, 1959, no. 19, p. 659.

26 *CKNYKH*, 1961, no. 8, p. 2.

27 D. Gale Johnson, "The Environment for Technological Change in Soviet Agriculture," *American Economic Review* 56 (May 1966): 148.

28 *CKNYKH*, 1961, no. 8, pp. 1–6.

29 Shen, *Agricultural Resources*, p. 189.

30 For example, wheat that yields more flour or contains a higher percentage of protein, oilseeds that bear more oil, and cotton that has longer fibers.

31 For example, the introduction of a rice with low but stiff straw into the coastal provinces in southeast China to reduce crop losses resulting from typhoons. See *CKNYKH*, 1964, no. 10, p. 10.

32 The data in Table 7.5 are taken from *TGY*. They occasionally differ quite substantially from similar data revealed in other official sources, for example, the data for 1957 as given in *HHPYK*, 1958, no. 9, p. 82. This clearly reflects the difficulty in defining "improved seeds."

33 *HHPYK*, 1958, no. 9, p. 82.

34 *NYKHTH*, 1954, no. 9, p. 456. The 7.5 million mou were in 41 hsien of Shensi Province.

35 *NYKHTH*, 1956, no. 7, p. 406.

36 *HPNYKH*, 1958, no. 3, p. 149.

37 Ibid., p. 151.

38 *CKNYKH*, 1961, no. 8, p. 6.

39 *HPNYKH*, 1958, no. 3, p. 151.

40 Ibid.; *CKNYKH*, 1961, no. 8, p. 6.

41 *CKNP*, 1956, no. 22, p. 17.

42 *JMJP*, Oct. 12, 1956.

43 *CKNP*, 1957, no. 1, p. 23.

44 Ibid., p. 25.

45 Ibid., 1956, no. 22, pp. 17–21.

46 Ibid.

47 *HTNYKHTP*, 1957, no. 3, p. 133; *CKNP*, 1957, no. 13, p. 12. This variety was planted on more than 1 million mou in Kiangsu and over the whole province of Szechwan.

48 *CKNP*, 1956, no. 22, p. 17; and 1957, no. 13, pp. 12–13.

49 *CKNYKH*, 1961, no. 8, p. 7.

50 *JMJP*, June 12, 1962.

51 *CKNP*, 1965, no. 3, p. 13.

52 *KMJP*, Mar. 12, 1968; *JMJP*, June 12, 1962.

53 *KMJP*, Mar. 12, 1968.

Chapter 8

1 *CKNP*, 1958, no. 8, p. 25.

2 *HHPKY*, 1956, no. 20, p. 37.

3 *TCKT,* 1957, no. 21, p. 16.

4 *TCKTTH,* 1956, no. 6, p. 16; and 1956, no. 12, p. 30.

5 The details for defining sown area are given in *HASW,* pp. 9, 10.

6 Toward the end of this period an alternative indicator defined as yield per unit of cultivated area was introduced and used; but no agreement had been reached until 1958 as to how it should be measured. See *TCYC,* 1958, no. 5, pp. 33–38; *TCKT,* 1957, no. 9, pp. 13–16; and *KTNYTH,* 1958, no. 3, pp. 45–46.

7 *TCKTTH,* 1956, no. 6, p. 16.

8 Ibid. (for a detailed discussion); *TCKT,* 1955, no. 5, pp. 20–23; no. 3, pp. 15–16; *TCKTTH,* 1956, no. 10, pp. 16–17; and *HASW,* p. 9.

9 This discussion is based primarily on *TCKTTH,* 1955, no. 2, pp. 20–23, an article in which the Agricultural Statistics Section of the SSB explains the evolution and current technique of measuring sown area.

10 *TCKTTH,* 1955, no. 6, pp. 26–27.

11 Ibid., 1956, no. 8, pp. 6–7. Actually this system begun much earlier in Manchuria and on state farms elsewhere. See *TCKTTH,* 1954, no. 7, p. 23; and 1954, no. 4, p. 34.

12 *TCKTTH,* 1956, no. 8, pp. 6–7.

13 The whole rural sector had been converted into 700,000 cooperatives. See *TCKT,* 1957, no. 8, p. 6; no. 22, p. 7; no. 27, p 9.

14 *TCKT,* 1958, no. 4, p. 2; 1957, no. 22, p. 8–9. Only Anhwei province practiced random sample surveys in 1957. See *TCYC,* 1958, no. 4, pp. 27–31.

15 *TCKT,* 1957, no. 27, p. 10; and 1958, no. 3, p. 13.

16 In addition, there are a few more sets of estimates made by individual Chinese economists: (1) Chen's estimates (see Chen Chang-heng, "A Preliminary Comparison of China's Land and Population and Discussion on Policies Concerning the National Economic Reconstruction," *TLHP,* 1935, no. 4, p. 1–44); (2) Chiao's estimates (see *Chung-kuo jen-kou yu shih-liang wen-ti* [China's population and food problems] [Shenghsi, 1939], pp. 27–28); and (3) Lieu's estimates (see his article "Statistics of Farm Land in China," *Chinese Economic Journal,* 1928, no. 3, pp. 181–213).

17 National Agricultural Research Bureau, *Crop Reports* (Nanking, 1933–37). Some of the information has been quoted by Shen in *Agricultural Resources of China.*

18 Published in Nanking by the Directorate of Statistics of the National Government. The combined issue for January and February 1932 supplied the data used.

19 Buck, *Land Utilization,* p. 163. One survey in the Yangtze delta area had revealed that nearly one–fourth of the land was unregistered. In Kwan Hsien, Szechwan, an independent study indicated that one-half of the cultivated land was unregistered. See Buck et al., *Food and Agriculture,* p. 9.

20 Buck, *Land Utilization,* p. 165.

21 Ibid., pp. 21–29.

22 They are quoted in Shen, *Agricultural Resources,* p. 142. According to the footnote on p. 141, the data were given by the Directorate of Statistics of the National Government, *Statistical Abstract of the Republic of China, 1947* (Nanking, June 1948).

23 Without recognizing them as one set of his own estimates, Buck calls the DS-1946 data new official estimates. See Buck et al., *Food and Agriculture,* p. 12. See also Shen, *Agricultural Resources,* p. 132, *n*3.

24 Buck, *Land Utilization* (statistical volume), p. 29, note c, states, "in Szechwan, parts of the hsein included are outside the area. The total used is that of the Szechwan Rice Area only. No figures were given for Tsingshi, but an estimate of cultivated percentage was made for the comparatively small area (9,300 square miles) falling within the Spring Wheat Area."

25 The Directorate could not adopt Buck's other estimates because they, unlike his estimate IV, were not broken down by province.

26 Ma Yen-chu, *Tsai-Chen-hsueh yu Chung-kuo tsai-Cheng* [Public Finance in China] (Shanghai, 1948), pp. 37, 243, 245.

27 Ma Li-yuan, "Another Estimate of China's Farmland," *Ching-chi chien-she chi-kan* [Economic Construction Quarterly], 1944, no. 2, pp. 157–64.

28 Ibid.; Ma Yen-chu, *Public Finance in China,* pp. 243, 246. For instance, in Shan Hsien, Honan, the new acreage exceeded the old land record by 680,000 mou; in Tangtu, Anhwei, by 280,000 mou; and for Chekiang province as a whole, by 17 million mou.

29 Ma Li-yuan, *Estimate of China's Farmland,* pp. 157–64.

30 Ma Yen-chu, *Public Finance in China,* pp. 243–45.

31 Shen, *Agricultural Resources,* p. 142.

32 *TCKT,* 1957, no. 18, p. 6. Similar statements are also found in *TCKTTH,* 1954, no. 2, p. 20; and *TCYC,* 1958, no. 4, p. 31.

33 *TCHP,* p. 274.

34 Ibid.

35 Ibid. The hsien government also estimated the rate of overreporting population. The rate varied from 3.49 to 29.59 percent.

36 See various survey reports in *TCHP.*

37 *TCYC,* 1958, no. 4, p. 31; and *TCKT,* 1957, no. 18, p. 6.

38 *TCKT,* 1957, no. 14, p. 12.

39 *SSB Communique, 1953, revised.*

40 *FFYP.*

41 *HHYP,* 1955, no. 11, pp. 181–89.

42 Ibid.

43 *TGY,* p. 128.

44 *CKNP,* 1958, no. 8, p. 25.

45 Moreover, the *TGY* data include the cultivated land in Tibet whereas the prewar data do not.

46 For instance, see *CHCC,* 1958, no. 2, p. 22.

47 *TCKT,* 1957, no. 21, p. 23.
48 Ibid., no. 27, p. 10.
49 *TCKTTH,* 1956, no. 8, p. 6.
50 *TCKT,* 1957, no. 10, pp. 22–23.
51 In the early stage of collectivization in 1955–56, a major source of underreporting in the collectivized sector was the private plots of member peasants of cooperatives. See *TCKT,* 1957, no. 10, pp. 22–23. However, private plots became subject to more strict control in the "advanced" type of cooperatives formed in 1957.
52 It should be noted that the official figure for 1958 was based on reports submitted by farming units to the government shortly after July 1 of that year. Unlike other economic statistics compiled at the end of 1958 or early in 1959, it is relatively free of exaggerated boasting of the achievements of the Great Leap Forward policy.
53 See *JPRS* 15388, Sept. 1962; and *CHCC,* 1958, no. 2, p. 21.
54 *CHCC,* 1958, no. 2, p. 21.
55 Land reclaimed by state-owned livestock farms for agricultural cultivation is included.
56 *CHCC,* 1958, no. 2, p. 23.
57 *TTJP,* Mar. 18, 1956; and *CFJP,* Mar. 17, 1956.
58 See *CKNPS,* 1957, no. 12, p. 3; *HHPYK,* 1956, no. 23, p. 62; and *CHCC,* 1958, no. 2, p. 23.
59 The percentage of total rural population brought into the collective farming system in the year is used to measure the progress of collectivization.
60 All the densities refer to farm population per unit of cultivated land.
61 *CCYC,* 1965, no. 3, p. 40. The ratio may have varied from locality to locality and from year to year. Generally it was much higher in 1958 than in previous years. For instance, it was reported that irrigation canals and ditches under construction in 1958 in the plains of Hunan province had reduced cultivated land by one-fifth to one-third (*JPRS* 922-D, Sept. 18, 1959, p. 16). Official statistics showed a total reduction of 61 million mou of cultivated area for the whole country from 1957 to 1958 (*TGY,* p. 128). The bulk of the reduction is believed to result from the extensive construction of water conservation projects all over China in that year.
62 *JMJP,* Jan. 7, 1958.
63 The total amount of wasteland reclaimed was officially given as 6.8 million mou in 1941 and 0.8 million mou in the first nine months of 1942. See *China Handbook, 1937–1943,* p. 592ff.
64 *TGY,* p. 128.
65 For water conservation projects alone, the total volume of earth work done in 1958 was given 58 million cubic meters. See *SLSTCS,* 1959, no. 22, p. 8.
66 Ma Yen-chu, *Public Finance in China,* pp. 230, 246

67 Ibid., p. 368. However, Buck's study shows rather narrow differentials among the "average rates of tax payments per unit of land" for three classes of land in various regions. See Buck, *Land Utilization,* pp. 323–24. This may be attributable to the fact that Buck measured the average actual tax payment per unit of area for each class of land. The tax payment included both land taxes and surtaxes. Rates for the latter did not vary too much according to land quality. However, since surtaxes on landowners were supposedly temporary and changed from year to year in most localities, it may be reasonable to assume that Chinese farmers would select land for concealment primarily according to the rate structure of land taxes per se. Moreover, the results obtained by Buck are suspected as already reflecting the selective nature of land concealment by farmers. If farmers generally tended to underreport their high-grade land to the tax authorities, the computed average tax payment on good land would be much lower than the statutory rates.

68 Ma Yen-chu, *Public Finance in China,* pp. 246, 366.

69 See *TCKTTH,* 1954, no. 7, p. 25; and no. 3, p. 17.

70 Both upward and downward biases have been reported. *TCKTTH,* 1956, no. 2, pp. 21–22; 1955, no. 6, p. 26; and 1956, no. 7, p. 22.

71 It may be desirable to make an alternative assumption that both grainland and nongrainland had been underreported by the same degree and to see what difference the alternative assumption would make in the output estimates. This has been done and will be discussed later.

72 *TGY,* p. 129.

73 Ibid., pp. 128–29.

74 According to our computation, the total increase in cultivated land between 1952 and 1957 was 13.8 million mou; of this amount 12.2 million mou were in Heilungkiang and Sinkiang.

75 Strictly speaking, the NARB *Crop Reports* were not sample surveys: there was no sampling in the choice of hsien, but rather an attempt to reach as many hsien as possible. Nevertheless, errors may have occurred because of the incomplete coverage.

76 Buck, *Land Utilization,* p. 223. For the country as a whole, the average yield was 98 percent of the most frequent yield.

77 On another occasion Buck points out the different usages of "yields" between the prewar surveys and the Communist data. See Buck et al., *Food and Agriculture,* pp. 5, 20, 21.

78 Buck, *Land Utilization,* p. 179.

79 Buck et al., *Food and Agriculture,* p. 21.

80 For instance, Chu Ke-chen, a leading Chinese geographer, admitted that the average rice yield in 1934–38 was 340 catties and that it had increased only to 342.6 catties in 1953–57. See *TLHP,* 1964, no. 1, p. 3.

81 J. C. Liu and K. C. Yeh, *The Economy of the Chinese Mainland* (Princeton, N.J., 1965), p. 287.

82 Buck, *Land Utilization* (statistical volume), p. 209.

83 That is, let x be the weight for the wheat region, hence the weight for the rice region is $(1 - x)$. And we obtain:

$$127x + 142(1 - x) = 141$$

So, $x = 7\%$ and $1 - x = 93\%$

84 See *CKNP,* 1957, no. 12, pp. 16–19. The original distribution of wheat sown area in 1955 was: 65.8 percent, winter wheat region; 22.8 percent, rice region; and 11.4 percent, spring wheat region. Since we are here dealing with winter wheat only, the third item is excluded.

85 *CKNP,* 1957, no. 12, p. 17.

86 Ibid., no. 15, pp. 13–14.

87 To accept the 1952–57 official wheat yields does not indicate that we have full confidence in their reliability. There is still some information that casts doubt on them. For example, one source (*HHPYK,* 1956, no. 24, p. 68) states that in 1955, twenty-two of the seventy hsien in Kiangsu had average wheat yields in the range of 150 to 240 catties per mou. Yet, the official wheat yield for the whole province in 1955 was given at 115 catties per mou. This would imply extraordinarily low yields of wheat in the other forty-eight hsien. More puzzling is a set of average wheat yields for Honan in 1950–56, as cited by a Chinese article (*CKNP,* 1957, no. 12, p. 17); they are much higher than those officially given. Following is a comparison of the two sets of wheat yields for Honan (catties per mou):

	1950	*1951*	*1952*	*1953*	*1954*	*1955*	*1956*
CKNP data	118.4	134.7	112.1	147.7	175.2	151.7	147.1
Official data	81.6	102.0	86.5	80.7	109.4	94.7	117.4

The reason for the differences is not clear to us.

88 *TCKT,* 1957, no. 22, p. 9; 1958, no. 4, p. 2; and *TCYC,* 1958, no. 4, p. 27.

89 The following offices had conducted their own surveys: local offices of the Ministry of Agriculture, branches of the Oil Trading Company, branches of the Textiles Trading Company, and Agricultural Credit Cooperatives. See *TCKTTH,* 1955, no. 5, p. 27; *TCKT,* 1957, no. 22, p. 9; and 1958, no. 4, p. 8.

90 *TCKT,* 1958, no. 13, pp. 7–13.

91 One official source states, "When the First Five Year Plan was being drafted, the 1952 annual statistical returns were incomplete in coverage and with many omissions, and it took two full years of repeated checking with local sources and frequent revisions before the base year figures for the plan were arrived at." See *TCKT,* 1958, no. 2, p. 9.

92 Horses, donkeys, and mules were used by Chinese farmers mainly for local transportation. The losses in the number of these large animals probably resulted from confiscation by troops during the war.

93 See *TCHP* for summaries of various survey reports.

94 For instance, 1931 was the year of a great Yangtze River flood.

95 Buck et al., *Food and Agriculture,* p. 24.
96 Ibid., p. 22.
97 Ibid., p. 58.
98 Liu and Yeh, *Economy of the Chinese Mainland,* p. 52.

Chapter 9

1 Anthony M. Tang, "Policy and Performance in Agriculture," in *Economic Trends in Communist China,* eds. A. Eckstein, W. Galenson, and T. C. Liu (Chicago, 1968), pp. 459–508.
2 If the underlying production function is assumed to be the Cobb-Douglas type, the weights should be the output elasticities of individual inputs respectively. Income shares of these inputs often are used as approximations.
3 Another alternative is to borrow the factor shares from another economy which closely resembles the one in question yet has a more meaningful structure of prices and factor earnings.
4 Buck, *Land Utilization,* p. 473.
5 Jung-chao Liu, "Fertilizer Application in Communist China," *China Quarterly* 24 (Oct.-Dec. 1965):44–45.
6 See, for instance, R. M. Field, "How Much Grain Does Communist China Produce?" *China Quarterly* 33 (Jan.-Mar. 1968):104–5; and W. Klatt's comment, *China Quarterly* 33 (July-Sept. 1968): 156.
7 Such a ratio has been quoted in numerous planning documents. See, for instance, *CCYC,* 1959, no. 3, p. 32; *CKNP,* 1959, no. 7, p. 36; and *JMJP,* Nov. 18, 1957.
8 *JMJP,* Nov. 18, 1957.
9 J. C. Liu, *A Study of the Chemical Fertilizer Industry in Communist China* (forthcoming monograph).
10 *JMJP,* July 19, 1957; and *CCYC* 1958, no. 2, p. 8. Only the rationing prices of phosphorous fertilizers were considered too high by farmers in some localities.
11 See *CCYC,* 1958, no. 2, p. 8; and 1959, no. 3, p. 32.
12 At a price twice as high as the official price, 1,900 tons of fertilizers went into the blackmarket in Shantung. *TKP,* March 8, 1957.
13 This is the unweighted average yield response for rice, wheat, corn, and potatoes, as given in *CKNP,* 1959, no. 3, p. 36.
14 Buck, *Land Utilization,* pp. 230–31.
15 *TGY,* p. 130.
16 *JMJP,* Oct. 16, 1965.
17 *TGY,* p. 129.
18 Ibid., p. 121.
19 These increases in yield due to irrigation are based on Buck's findings but are much lower than the Communist claims shown in Table 5.2. The latter refer to the combined results of irrigation and "other complementary measures."

20 The computational procedures are the following:

a. Let x be the additional yield due to irrigation in the North, and y be the yield of nonirrigated land in the North $x/y = 0.6$, and

$$[(x + y) \times 107{,}000{,}000 + y\ (371{,}700{,}000 - 107{,}000{,}000)] \div 371{,}700{,}000 = 49 \text{ kg.}$$

Solve to obtain:

$$x = 25 \text{ kg and } y = 42 \text{ kg.}$$

So, the contribution of irrigation in the North is:

$$25 \times 107{,}000{,}000 = 2{,}675{,}000 \text{ tons of grain.}$$

b. Let x be the additional yield due to irrigation in the South, and y be the yield of nonirrigated land in the South.

$$x/y = 0.6 \text{ and}$$
$$[(x + y) \times 213{,}000{,}000 + y\ (425{,}730{,}000 - 213{,}000{,}000)] \div 425{,}730{,}000 = 321 \text{ kg.}$$

Solve to obtain:

$$x = 29 \text{ kg and } y = 145 \text{ kg.}$$

So, the contribution of irrigation in the South is $29 \times 213{,}000{,}000 = 6{,}177{,}000$ tons.

The total contribution of irrigation is then $2{,}675{,}000 + 6{,}177{,}000 = 8{,}852{,}000$ tons.

The share of contribution is $8{,}825/166{,}240 = 5.3$ percent.

21 Data are taken from *HHPYK,* 1958, no. 23, p. 77; *TCKTTH,* 1955, no. 8, p. 42; and *CCYC,* 1959, no. 12, p. 25.

22 The index of observed unit yield is derived from the data in Col. (3) of Table 8.7 and Col. (2) of Table 8.15.

23 Both the arithmetic mean of five yearly changes and the geometric mean (negative growth rate) for the whole period give the same rate of 1.7 percent.

24 Increases in land resulting from the removal of boundary lines and intensified labor mobilization under the collective farming system do not belong to this category. They represent a better mobilization of inputs but not a better utilization of given amounts of inputs.

25 By the same token, one may use productivity indexes to make a cross section comparison of different agricultural organizations in the country. For example, one may compare state farms and collective farms to see which organization is generally superior in terms of efficiency in utilizing farm inputs.

26 *JMJP,* Dec. 22, 1957; *HHPYK,* 1958, no. 5, p. 129; and *CHCC,* 1958, no. 1, p. 15.

27 The Chinese government claimed that the use of bettter seed had raised

grain output by 11.6 million tons between 1952 and 1957. See *HHPYK,* 1958, no. 9, p. 82.

28 The distribution is derived from the percentage increase of inputs, as given in Table 9.1, and the weights of the four inputs.

Chapter 10

1 See Table 8.14.

2 *CHYTC,* 1959, no. 8, pp. 19–20.

3 Ibid.

4 Ibid., 1959, no. 11, p. 8.

5 Ibid.

6 Ibid., 1960, no. 1, p. 19.

7 Ibid, p. 21.

8 *TCYC,* 1958, no. 6, p. 19.

9 Based on our estimates, the total exaggeration of the grain output amounted to about 145 million tons in 1958, and it was reduced only to 100 million tons in 1959.

10 It is recognized that there is no way to check the authenticity of those reports.

11 A statement of Mao Tse-tung to Viscount Montgomery, *Times* (London), October 15, 1961. However, *KTTH* (April 19, 1961, no. 16, p. 20) gave the "total farm production" in 1960 at a level comparable to that of 1957. It is not clear what was included in total farm production other than grain.

12 Given by Chou En-lai to a Pakistani reporter see *Dawn* (Karachi), April 11, 1963.

13 Given by Chou En-lai to Edgar Snow. See *Asahi* (Tokyo), February 27, 1965.

14 *Chinese News Summary,* Apr. 28, 1966.

15 *JMJP,* Dec. 1964.

16 In fact, only one important grain-growing region (Kiangsu) had reported a 10 percent rise in grain production in 1964. See *JMJP,* Jan. 31, 1965.

17 *JMJP,* Jan. 16, 1966.

18 *Times* (London), October 15, 1961.

19 See Field, "How Much Grain Does Communist China Produce?" p. 100; and the Joint Economic Committee of the U.S. Congress, *An Economic Profile of Mainland China,* 2 vols. (Washington, D.C., 1957), 1:93.

20 Ping-ti Ho and Tan Tsou, eds., *China in Crisis,* 2 vols. (Chicago, 1967), 1:68.

21 *HHPYK,* 1957, no. 22, p. 130, Article 25 of the Program.

22 *JMJP,* Nov. 26, 1957.

23 *HHPYK,* 1958, no. 19, p. 117.

24 Ibid., 1957, no. 22, p. 130; no. 10, p. 108.

25 See *HHPYK*, 1957, no. 22, pp. 171–72. The amount of the state grain reserve is derived in the following way:

In the period from July 1953 to June 1957, a total of 171.35 million tons of grain had been procured or collected by the state. Of this quantity, 9.4 percent, or 16.1 million tons, was used for stockpiling and exportation. Total exports of grain in the four-year period are given as 7.95 million tons. Thus, the total increase in inventories in the period is derivable at 8.15 million tons. The same article also states that the total availability of grain in the 1956–57 crop year, that is, inventories in July 1956, plus total production in the crop year, was 20.3 percent higher than that for the 1953–54 crop year. Production figures are given as 142.53 million tons for 1953–54 and 165.89 million tons for 1956–57. Now, let x be the amount of state grain reserve existing in July 1953, then:

$$[165.89 + (x + 8.15)] \div (142.53 + x) = 1.203$$

Therefore, $x = 12.69$ million tons.

And the state reserve in June 1957 was 20.84 million tons. Note that all the figures mentioned here are the specifically designated state reserve in the official grain accounts, not just temporary stocks of grain after harvest.

26 So far as yearly inventory changes are concerned, we know only that more than 3.5 million tons of grains were added in the 1953–54 food year. See *HHPYK*, 1957, no. 10, p. 106.

27 See *HHYP*, 1955, no. 8, p. 51. Husked grain is called commercial grain, whereas unhusked grain is called crude grain.

28 *Times* (London), October 15, 1961. Although Montgomery used the term "reserve," not "state reserve," Mao Tse-tung must have meant the latter.

29 The average per capita consumption of grain for the four food years from 1953–54 to 1956–57 may be computed as follows. We know:

Total grain output in that period: 715.72 million tons.

Total exports and increases in stocks, measured as unhusked grain, in that period: 18.94 million tons.

Imports of grains in that period: nearly zero.

Cumulated population in the four years: 2,432,130.

Therefore, the average per capita consumption of grain was 287 kilograms.

30 *TGY*, p. 128.

31 *China Pictorial*, Feb. 1961, p. 2.

32 *Mir sotsializma v tsifrakh i faktakh 1965 god* [The world of Socialism in figures and facts, 1965] (Moscow, 1967), p. 76.

33 *Compilation of Laws, 1962–63* (Peking, 1964), p. 69.

34 *CKCN*, 1966, no. 9, p. 16.

35 *JMJP*, Mar. 12, 1965.

36 Ibid., Dec. 31, 1964.

37 The data appeared in *Wen Hui Pao* (Hong Kong), Sept. 7, 1968, and *Hsin Wen Pao,* Sept. 13, 1968, and later were cited in *China Monthly,* 1968, no. 56, p. 13–16. The quality of the new population data remains to be examined.

38 To the extent that the working-age population became physically weaker from malnutrition, this change would be reflected in lower labor productivity, which will be discussed later.

39 For instance, see Chi-ming Hou, "Sources of Agricultural Growth in Communist China," *The Journal of Asian Studies* 27 (Aug. 1968):721–37. It should be noted, however, that a serious labor shortage did occur in the rural sector in 1958. But this resulted from the large-scale construction of irrigation projects.

40 *JMJP,* Jan. 23, 1960; Aug. 26, 1959; Dec. 22, 1957; and *HHPYK,* 1958, no. 5, p. 129.

41 *JMJP,* Dec. 29, 1960.

42 Ibid., July 23, 1960.

43 Ibid.

44 Ibid., July 27, 1960.

45 Ibid., Aug. 14, 1960.

46 Ibid., Aug. 7, 1960.

47 Ibid., July 27, 1960.

48 *PR,* Aug. 23, 1963.

49 It is reported that Chen Yun said that the Great Leap had caused the regression of seeds and deterioration of several hundred million mou of good land. See *Compilation of Materials,* 1:619.

Chapter 11

1 Soybeans were included statistically in food grains before 1956.

2 Cottonseed also can be crushed for oil. Among the various oil-bearing seeds, peanuts are the most important, and they accounted for 60 percent of all oil-bearing seeds (excluding soybeans) produced in China in 1957. See *HHPYK,* 1958, no. 16, p. 80.

3 Shen, *Agricultural Resources,* pp. 217, 237, 244–45, 248–49, 309, 374–77. For his comments on the quality of those statistics, see pp. 242 and 309.

4 *JMJP,* Jan. 15, 1965.

5 See *TCKTTH,* 1955, no. 5, p. 27; and *TCKT,* 1957, no. 22, p. 9; 1958, no. 4, p. 8.

6 *HHPYK,* 1958, no. 5, p. 129.

7 Ibid., No. 16, p. 82.

8 *CKHW,* Jan. 21, 1965; and *JMJP,* Mar. 11, 1965.

9 *CKNP,* 1965, no. 2, p. 1.

10 Shen, *Agricultural Resources,* p. 308.

11 Ibid., p. 309. Cotton production outside the twenty-two provinces was negligible.

12 *HHPYK,* 1958, no. 1, p. 109.

13 Computed from the data given in *CHCC,* 1958, no. 4, pp. 11–12.
14 Ibid.
15 *CKNYKH,* 1961, no. 8, p. 2.
16 *CHCC,* 1958, no. 4, p. 12.
17 *NYKHTH,* 1959, no. 19, p. 690.
18 *CH,* p. 182.
19 Ibid., p. 186.
20 U.S. Department of Agriculture, *Communist China's Cotton Textile Exports* (Washington, D.C., 1959), pp. 1, 8. The ration of cotton cloth was above 8 yards in 1956 but was cut to 5.8 yards in the following year.
21 Ibid.
22 *TGY,* p. 99.
23 Joint Economics Committee, U.S. Congress, *An Economic Profile,* 2 vols. (Washington, D.C., 1967), 2:593.
24 *China's Cotton Textile Exports,* p. 12.
25 *JMJP,* Nov. 5, 1958; May 8, 1959.
26 *TGY,* p. 119.
27 *CKHW,* Mar. 23, 1960.
28 *TKP,* July 27, 1962.
29 *China Monthly,* 1965, no. 7, p. 22.
30 *CKHW,* Feb. 9, 1966.
31 *JMJP,* Sept. 26, 1964.
32 *CKHW,* Feb. 19, 1966; and *JMJP,* Sept. 21, 1966.
33 *JMJP,* Sept. 21, 1966.
34 That was the number in 1956. See *CH,* p. 174.
35 *PH,* 1965, p. 559.
36 *PR,* Sept. 24, 1965.
37 *PH,* 1965, p. 559; and *CKHW,* Sept. 15, 1965.
38 *JMJP,* Dec. 25, 1965.

Bibliography

Chinese Communist Publications

AHJP	*Anhwei jih-pao* (Anhwei Daily)
CCHJP	*Ch'ang-chun jih-pao* (Chang chun Daily)
CCJP	*Ch'ang-chiang jih-pao* (Chang chiang Daily)
CCKJP	*Chang-chou kung-jen pao* (Chang chou Workers' Daily)
CCTP	*Ching-chi tao-pao* (Economic Bulletin)
CCYC	*Ching-chi yen-chiu* (Economic Research)
CFJP	*Chieh-fang jih-pao* (Liberation Daily)
CH	*Wo-kuo kang-tieh tien-li mei-tan chi-hsieh fang-chih tsao-chih kung-yeh ti chin-hsi* (The Present and Past of Our Iron and Steel, Power, Coal, Machinery, Textile, and Paper Manufacturing Industries), Peking, 1958
CHCC	*Chi-hua ching-chi* (Planned Economy)
CHCJP	*Ch'un-chung jih-pao* (Popular Daily)
CHHNY	*Chi-hsieh-hua Nung-yeh* (Mechanized Agriculture)
CHKJP	*Chungking jih-pao* (Chungking Daily)
CHYTC	*Chi-hua yu tung chi* (Planning and Statistics)
CKCN	*Chung-kuo ching-nien* (Chinese Youth)
CKCNP	*Chung-kuo Ch'ing-nien pao* (Chinese Youth Daily)
CKHW	*Chung-kuo Hsin-wen* (China News)
CKJP	*Chekiang Jih-pao* (Chekiang Daily)
CKKJP	*Chekiang Kung-jen-pao* (Chekiang Workers' Daily)
CKLY	*Chung-kuo Lin-yeh* (China's Forestry)
CKNK	*Chung-kuo nung-ken* (China's Agricultural Reclamation)
CKNP	*Chung-kuo nung-pao* (Chinese Agricultural Journal)
CKNYKH	*Chung-kuo nung-yeh ko-hsueh* (Chinese Agricultural Science)
CKSL	*Chung-kuo shui-li* (China's Water Conservation)
CNAJP	*Chi-nan jih-pao* (Chinan Daily)
CR	*China Reconstructs* (An English language publication)
CSJP	*Chang-sha Jih-pao* (Changsha Daily)
CTKP	*Chungking Ta-Kung-pao* (Chungking Ta kung Daily)
EB	*Economic Bulletin*, Hong Kong
FFYP	*The First Five Year Plan*
FKJP	*Fukien jih-pao* (Fukien Daily)

HASW *Handbook of Agricultural Statistical Work,* translated in *Current Background,* no. 434, January 15, 1957
HC *Hung-chi* (Red Flag)
HCJP *Hang-chou jih-pao* (Hangchou Daily)
HCS *Hsin-chien-she* (New Construction)
HH *Hsueh-Hsi* (Study)
HHJP *Hsin-hua jih-pao* (New China Daily)
HHKY *Hua-hsueh kung-yeh* (Chemical Industry)
HHNP *Hsin hu-nan-pao* (New Human Daily)
HHPYK *Hsin-hua pan-yueh kan* (New China Semi-Monthly)
HHYP *Hsin-hua yueh-pao* (New China Monthly)
HKTKP *Hong Kong ta-kung-pao* (Impartial Daily)
HKWHP *Hong Kong wen-hui pao* (Wen hui Daily)
HLKJP *Heilungkiang Jih-pao* (Heilungkiang Daily)
HLKNM *Heilungkiang Nung-min* (Heilungkiang's Farmer)
HMNJP *Hsia-men jih-pao* (Hsia men Daily)
HNJP *Honan jih-pao* (Honan Daily)
HNNMP *Hu-nan Nung-min-pao* (Hunan Farmers' Daily)
HPCCTL *Hua-pei Ching-chi Ti-li* (Economic Geography of North China), Peking, 1957
HPJP *Hopei Jih-pao* (Hopei Daily)
HPNYKH *Hsi-pei nung-yeh ko-hsueh* (Northwestern Agricultural Science)
HTNYKHTP *Hua-tung nung-yeh ko-hsueh tung-pao* (Bulletin of Eastern China Agricultural Science)
HUPJP *Hupeh Jih-pao* (Hupeh Daily)
HWCK *Hsin-wen-chou-k'an* (News Weekly)
JMJP *Jen-min Jih-pao* (People's Daily)
JMST *Jen-min shou-tse* (People's Handbook)
KCJP *Kuang-chou Jih-pao* (Kuangchou Daily)
KGSJP *Kiangsi Jih-pao* (Kiangsi Daily)
KJJP *Kung-jen Jih-pao* (Workers' Daily)
KLNMP *Kuei-lin nung-min pao* (Kueilin Farmers' Daily)
KMJP *Kuang-ming Jih-pao* (Kuangming Daily)
KRJP *Kirin Jih-pao* (Kirm Daily)
KSJP *Kansu Jih-pao* (Kansu Daily)
KSNMP *Kiang-su nung-min pao* (Kiangsu Farmers' Daily)
KSNYTH *Kuang-si nung-yeh tung-hsin* (Kuangsi Agricultural Bulletin)
KTCCTL *Kuang-tung ching-chi ti-li* (Economic Geography of Kuangtung), Peking, 1956
KTCNP *Kuang-tung ching-nien pao* (Kuangtung Youth Daily)
KTNYTH *Kuang-tung nung-yeh tung-hsin* (Kuangtung Agricultural Bulletin)
KTTH *Kung-tsao tung-hsin* (Bulletin of Activities)
KUCJP *Kuei-chou Jih-pao* (Kuei chou Daily)

KUCNM *Kuei-chou nung-min* (Kuei chou Farmers)
KWSJP *Kwangsi Jih-pao* (Kuangsi Daily)
LCJP *Liu-chou Jih-pao* (Liu chou Daily)
LNJP *Liaoning Jih-pao* (Liaoning Daily)
LS *Liang-shih* (Food)
LSKT *Liang-shih Kung-tso* (Food Management)
NCJP *Nan-ching Jih-pao* (Nanching Daily)
NCNA *New China News Agency Broadcasts*
NFJP *Nan-fang Jih-pao* (Southern Daily)
NHJP *Ning-hsai Jih-pao* (Ninghsai Daily)
NMKJP *Nei-meng-ku Jih-pao* (Inner Mongolia Daily)
NMKTC *Nei-meng-ku tzu-chih-chu ching-chi ho wen-hua chien-she cheng-chiu ti tung-chi* (Statistics on Achievements of the Inner Mongolian Autonomous Region in Economic and Cultural Construction), Peking, 1960
NNJP *Nan-ning jih-pao* (Nanning Daily)
NTCY *Nung-tsun ching-yung* (Finance of Rural Areas)
NTKTTH *Nung-tsun kung-tsao tung-hsin* (Bulletin of Activities in Rural Areas)
NYCH *Nung-yeh chi-hsieh* (Agricultural Machinery)
NYCS *Nung-yeh chih-shieh* (Agricultural Knowledge)
NYKHTH *Nung-yeh Ko-hsueh tung-hsin* (Bulletin of Agricultural Science)
PC *People's China* (An English language publication)
PJP *Pe-king jih-pao* (Peking Daily)
PR *Peking Review* (An English language publication)
SAJP *Sian Jih-pao* (Sian Daily)
SCCJP *Shih-chia-chuang Jih-pao* (Shih chia chung Daily)
SCFJP *Shanghai Chieh-fang Jih-pao* (Liberation Daily)
SCJP *Szechwan Jih-pao* (Szechwan Daily)
SHSJP *Shensi Jih-pao* (Shensi Daily)
SHSNM *Shensi Nung-min* (Shensi Farmers)
SITT *Shen-si tu-ti li-yung wen-ti* (Problems of Land Utilization in Shensi), Shanghai, 1956
SKJP *Si-kang jih-pao* (Sikang Daily)
SLFT *Shui-li fa-tien* (Hydroelectric Generation)
SLSP *Shui-li hsueh-pao* (Journal of Hydrology)
SLSTCS *Shui-li shui-tien chien-she* (Water Conservation and Hydroelectric Construction)
SLYTL *Shui-li yu tien-li* (Water Conservation and Electric Power)
SNKJ *Sin-kiang jih-pao* (Sinkiang Daily)
SNKNM *Sin-kiang nung-min* (Sinkiang Farmers)
SSB *State Statistical Bureau* Communique
SSJP *Shan-si jih-pao* (Shansi Daily)
SSNM *Shan-si nung-min* (Shansi Farmers)
SYJP *Shen-yang jih-pao* (Shen yang Daily)

TC *Tsai-cheng* (Public Finance)
TCHP *Liang-nien-lai ti chung-kuo nung-tsun ching-chi tiao-cha hui-pien* (Compilation of Surveys of Rural Economy in China in the Past Two Years), Shanghai, 1952
TCJP *Ta-chung jih-pao* (Popular Daily)
TCKT *Tung-chi kung-tsao* (Statistical Work)
TCKTTH *Tung-chi-kung-tsao tung-hsin* (Bulletin of Statistical Work)
TCYC *Tung-chi yen-chiu* (Statistical Research)
TGY *Ten Great Years: Statistics of the Economic and Cultural Achievements of the People's Republic of China,* Peking, 1960
TKP *Ta-kung Pao* (Impartial Daily)
TLCS *Ti-li Chih-shih* (Geographical Knowledge)
TLHP *Ti-li hsueh-pao* (Journal of Geography)
TPJP *Tung-pei Jih-pao* (Northeastern Daily)
TSHJP *Tsinghai Jih-pao* (Tsinghai Daily)
TSJP *Tientsin Jih-pao* (Tientsing Daily)
TTJP *Tsingtao Jih-pao* (Tsingtao Daily)
WHP *Wen-hui-pao* (Wenhui Daily)
WL *Kiangsu, The Waterland,* Shanghai, 1956
YNJP *Yun-nan Jih-pao* (Yunnan Daily)

Non-Communist Publications in Chinese

Chiao, Chi-ming. *Chung-kuo jen-kou yu shih-liang wen-ti* (China's Population and Food Problems). Shanghai, 1939.

———. *Chung-kuo nung-tsun she-hui ching-chi* (Economics of the Chinese Agricultural Society). Shanghai, 1946.

China Handbook, 1937–1943. New York, 1943.

China Monthly. Hong Kong.

Chinese Economic Journal.

Ching-chi chien-she chi-kan (Economic Construction Quarterly).

Compilations of Materials of the Chinese Communist Great Cultural Revolution. 4 vols. to date. Hong Kong, 1967.

FCYC. Fei-ching yen-chiu (Study of Communist China).

Ma, Yen-chu. *Tsai-cheng-hsueh yu chung-kuo tsai-cheng* (Public Finance in China). Shanghai, 1948.

Statistical Abstract of the Republic of China, 1947. Nanking, 1948.

Statistical Monthly. Nanking.

TK. Tsu-kuo Weekly. Hong Kong.

Non-Communist Publications in English

Aird, J. S. *The Size, Composition, and Growth of the Population of Mainland China.* Washington, D.C., 1961.

Bernstein, T. P. "Leadership and Mass Mobilization in the Soviet and Chinese Collectivization Campaigns of 1929–30 and 1956–57: A Comparison." *China Quarterly* 31 (July-September 1967): 1–47.
Buck, J. L. *Chinese Farm Economy*. Chicago, 1930.
———. *Land Utilization in China*. 3 vols. Shanghai, 1937.
———; Dawson, O. L.; and Wu, Y. L. *Food and Agriculture in Communist China*. New York, 1966.
Chao, Kang. *The Rate and Pattern of Industrial Growth in Communist China*. Ann Arbor, Mich., 1965.
———. *The Construction Industry in Communist China*. Chicago, 1968.
———. *Capital Formation in Communist China*. Ann Arbor, Mich., forthcoming.
———. *The Electric Power Industry in Communist China*, Research Paper P–348. June 1967.
Chen, Nai-Ruenn. *Chinese Economic Statistics: A Handbook for Mainland China*. Chicago, 1967.
Cheng, Chu-yuan. *Scientific and Engineering Manpower in Communist China, 1949–1963*. Washington, D.C., 1965.
———. *A Study of the Machine Building Industry in Communist China*. Forthcoming.
Dandekar, V. M. "Economic Theory of Agrarian Reform." *Oxford Economic Papers* 14 (February 1962): 69–79.
Domar, E. D. "The Soviet Collective Farm as a Producer Cooperative." *American Economic Review* 56 (September 1966): 734–57.
Eckstein, A. *Communist China's Economic Growth and Foreign Trade*. New York, 1966.
———; Galenson, W.; and Liu, T. C., eds. *Economic Trends in Communist China*. Chicago, 1968.
Field, R. M. "How Much Grain Does Communist China Produce?" *China Quarterly* 33 (January-March 1968): 98–101.
Georgescu-Roegen. "Economic Theory and Agrarian Economics." *Oxford Economic Papers* 12 (February 1960): 1–40.
Ho, Ping-ti, and Tang, Tsou, eds. *China in Crisis*. Chicago, 1968.
Hou, Chi-ming. "Sources of Agricultural Growth in Communist China." *Journal of Asian Studies* 27 (August 1968): 721–37.
Johnson, D. G. "The Environment for Technological Changes in Soviet Agriculture." *American Economic Review* 56 (May 1966): 145–53.
Joint Economic Committee, U.S. Congress. *An Economic Profile of Mainland China*. 2 vols. Washington, D.C., 1967.
JPRS. *Joint Publications and Research Service*. Translation series.
Karcz, J. F. "Thoughts on the Grain Problem." *Soviet Studies* 18 (April 1967): 426.
Liu, Jung-chao. "Fertilizer Application in Communist China." *China Quarterly* 24 (October–December 1965): 44–45.
———. *A Study of the Fertilizer Industry in Communist China*. Forthcoming.

Liu, Ta-chung, and Yeh, K. C. *The Economy of the Chinese Mainland.* Princeton, N.J., 1965.

Mitrany, D. *Marx Against the Peasant—A Study in Social Dogmatism.* London, 1951.

Ni, Ernest. *Distribution of the Urban and Rural Population of Mainland China, 1953 and 1958.* Washington, D.C., 1960.

PAS. *Provincial Agricultural Statistics for Communist China.* Washington, D.C., 1969.

Perkins, D. H. *Market Control and Planning in Communist China,* Cambridge, Mass., 1966.

Petrov, V. P. *China: Emerging World Power.* Princeton, N.J., 1967.

Robinson, J. "The Organization of Agriculture." *Bulletin of the Atomic Scientists.* June, 1960, pp. 28–32.

Schultz, T. W. *Transforming Traditional Agriculture.* New Haven, Conn., 1964.

SCMM, *Survey of China Mainland Magazines.* A Translation Series. U.S. Consulate General, Hong Kong.

Shen, T. H. *Agricultural Resources of China.* Ithaca, N.Y., 1951.

Sunday Times, London.

U.S. Department of Agriculture. *Trends and Development in Communist China's World Trade in Farm Products, 1955–60.* Washington, D.C., 1962.

———. *Communist China's Cotton Textile Exports.* Washington, D.C., 1959.

Walker, K. R. *Planning in Chinese Agriculture.* Chicago, 1965.

———. "Collectivization in Retrospect: The Socialist High Tide of Autumn 1955–Spring 1956." *China Quarterly* 26 (April-June 1966): 1–43.

Ward, B. "The Firm in Illyria: Market Syndicalism." *American Economic Review* 56 (September 1958): 566–89.

Index